THE FORMATION OF NATIONAL ELITES

The European Science Foundation is an association of its 56 member research councils and academies in 20 countries. The ESF brings European scientists together to work on topics of common concern, to co-ordinate the use of expensive facilities, and to discover and define new endeavours that will benefit from a co-operative approach.

The scientific work sponsored by ESF includes basic research in the natural sciences, the medical and biosciences, the humanities and the social sciences.

The ESF links scholarship and research supported by its members and adds value by co-operation across national frontiers. Through its function as co-ordinator, and also by holding workshops and conferences and by enabling researchers to visit and study in laboratories throughout Europe, the ESF works for the advancement of European science.

THE FORMATION
OF
NATIONAL ELITES

COMPARATIVE STUDIES ON GOVERNMENTS
AND NON-DOMINANT ETHNIC GROUPS IN
EUROPE, 1850–1940

Volume VI

Edited by
ANDREAS KAPPELER
in collaboration with
FIKRET ADANIR and ALAN O'DAY

European Science Foundation
NEW YORK UNIVERSITY PRESS
DARTMOUTH

Published by
Dartmouth Publishing Company Limited
Gower House
Croft Road
Aldershot
Hants GU11 3HR
England

Published in the U.S.A. by
New York University Press
Washington Square
New York, NY 10003

British Library Cataloguing in Publication Data
The formation of national elites.
   1. Europe. International relations. Role of ethnic
      groups, history
   I. Kappeler, Andreas   II. Adanır, Fikret   III.O'Day, Alan
      IV.   Series

Library of Congress Cataloging-in-Publication Data
The Formation of national elites / edited by Andreas Kappeler, in
   collaboration with Fikret Adanır and Alan O'Day.
      p.   cm. – (Comparative studies on governments and non-
   dominant ethnic groups in Europe, 1850–1940; v. 6)
      "Published for the European Science Foundation."
      ISBN 0–8147–4608–X
      1. Nationalism–Europe–History.   2. Nationalists-Europe–
   History.   3. Minorities–Europe–Political activity–History.
   I. Kappeler, Andreas.   II. Adanır, Fikret.   III. O'Day, Alan.
   IV. Series.
   D350.7.F67   1991
   323.1'4'09034–dc20   90–40034
                                                                   CIP

ISBN 1 85521 114 9

Printed and bound in Great Britain by
Billing and Sons Ltd, Worcester

Contents

SELECTED PROBLEMS IN COMPARATIVE PERSPECTIVE

List of Tables

List of Figures and Maps

Figure

Maps

Notes on Contributors

FIKRET ADANIR, born 1941 in Foça, Turkey; studied at the Universities of Istanbul and Frankfurt am Main; Magister Artium 1971; Dr. phil. 1977; Research Assistant at the University of Giessen and Free University of Berlin; since 1986 Professor for Southeast European and Ottoman-Turkish History at the Ruhr University, Bochum; his publications include: *Die Makedonische Frage. Ihre Entstehung und Entwicklung bis 1908* (Wiesbaden 1979); 'Heiduckentum und osmanische Herrschaft', *Südost-Forschungen* 41 (1982).

GERHARD BRUNN, born 1939 in Reinhausen, Germany; studied at Göttingen, Rio de Janeiro and Cologne; received his Dr. Phil. degree in 1967; and habilitation in 1977; since 1980 Professor at the University of Cologne; since 1979 active in the Research Department of the Institute of History at the University of Cologne; currently Jean Monnet Professor at the University-GH Siegen; his publications include: *Deutschland und Brasilien 1890–1914* (Cologne 1971); 'Die Organisation der katalanischen Nationalbewegung 1859–1923' in Theodor Schieder and Otto Dann (eds), *Nationale Bewegung und soziale Organisation I* (Munich/Vienna 1978); *Hauptstadt. Zentren, Residenzen, Metropolen in der deutschen Geschichte* (ed. with Bodo Baumunk) (Cologne 1989).

ERICH HOFFMANN, born 1926 in Flensburg, Germany; studied at the University of Kiel; received his Dr. phil. in 1951 and Staatsexamen, 1953; Grammar School teaching, 1953–69; received his habilitation in 1972, Apl. Professor, 1976; since 1978 Full Professor for the History of Schleswig-Holstein at the University of Kiel; his publications include: *Königserhebung und Thronfolgeordnung in Dänemark bis zum Ausgang des Mittelalters* (Berlin/New York 1976); *Die heiligen Könige bei den Angelsachsen und den Skandinavischen Völkern* (Neumünster 1975).

MIROSLAV HROCH, born 1932 in Prague, Czechoslovakia; studied history and literature at Charles University, Prague, 1951–6; Assistant Professor in the Department of General History, 1956; received his Ph.D. in 1962 and habilitation in 1968 in General History; presently Professor of General History, Charles University, Prague;

his publications include: *Handel und Politik im Ostseeraum während des Dreissigjährigen Krieges* (Prague 1976); *Social Preconditions of National Revival in Europe. A Comparative Analysis of the Social Composition of Patriotic Groups among the Smaller Nations* (Cambridge 1985); *Ecclesia militans. The Inquisition in the Times of Counter-Reformation* (with A. Skýbová) (New York 1990).

ANDREAS KAPPELER, born 1943 in Winterthur, Switzerland; Dr. phil. 1969; habilitation University of Zürich in 1979; since 1982 Professor of East European History at the University of Cologne; his publications include: *Russlands erste Nationalitäten. Das Zarenreich und die Völker der Mittleren Wolga vom 16.–19. Jahrhundert* (Cologne/Vienna 1982); 'Historische Voraussetzungen des Nationalitätenproblems im russischen Vielvölkerreich' in *Geschichte und Gesellschaft* 8 (1982); *Die Muslime in der Sowjetunion und in Jugoslawien* (co-ed) (Cologne 1989); *Die Russen. Ihr Nationalbewusstsein in Geschichte und Gegenwart* (ed.) (Cologne 1990); *Russland als Vielvölkerreich* (Munich 1992).

JIŘÍ KOŘALKA, born 1931 in Šternberk, Czechoslovakia; studied at Charles University, Prague, 1950–5; Ph.D. degree in 1958; associate of the Historical Institute of the Czechoslovak Academy of Sciences, 1955–74; fellow of the Alexander von Humboldt-Stiftung, Cologne, Germany, 1965–6; visiting professor at The University of Kent, Canterbury, England, 1969, and at the University of Bielefeld, Germany, 1987–8; leading historian at the Hussite Museum, Tabor, 1975–91; his publications include: *Všeněmecký svaz a česká otázka koncem 19. století* (The Pan-German League and the Czech Question at the End of the 19th Century) (Prague 1963); *Co je národ?* (What is a Nation?) (Prague 1969); *Die tschechische Bürgertumsforschung* (Bielefeld 1989); *Tschechen im Habsburgerreich und in Europa 1815–1914. Sozialgeschichtliche Zusammenhänge der neuzeitlichen Nationsbildung und der Nationalitätenfrage in den böhmischen Ländern* (Vienna and Munich 1991).

WITOLD MOLIK, born 1949 in Kórnik, Poland; studied history at Adam Mickiewicz University of Poznań, 1967–72; Assistant in the Department of History 1972–7 and Lecturer since 1977; received his Ph.D. in 1977 and post-doctorate degree in 1988; his publications include: *Jan Działyński jako mecenas nauki i sztuki* (Jan Działyński as a patron of science and arts) (Warszawa-Poznań 1974); *Kształtowanie sie inteligencji polskiej w Wielkim Ksiestwie Poznańskim 1841–1870* (The formation of Polish intelligentsia in the Grand Duchy of Poznań 1841–1870) (Warszawa-Poznań 1979); *Polskie peregrynacje uniwersyteckie do Niemiec 1871–1914* (Polish travels to the universities in Germany 1871–1914) (Poznań 1989).

ALAN O'DAY, born in Detroit, Michigan, USA; received his B.A. from the University of Michigan; M.A.s at Roosevelt and Northwestern Universities and Ph.D. from the University of London; Lecturer in Economic History at the University of East Anglia; Lektor in Area Studies Universität Giessen; presently, Senior Lecturer in History at the Polytechnic of North London and for 1991–92, Visiting Professor in History, Concordia University, Montréal; Fellow National Endowment for the Humanities, 1980–81; sometime Visiting Fellow, St John's College and Wolfson College, Oxford; Visiting Fellow, St Aidan's College, Durham and Institute for Advanced Studies in the Humanities, Edinburgh; his publications include: *The English Face of Irish Nationalism* (Dublin 1977), *Parnell and the First Home Rule Episode* (Dublin 1986); (co. ed.) *Parnell in Perspective* (London 1991); (co. ed.), *Britain Since 1945* (London 1991).

LORENZ RERUP, born 1928 in Flensburg, Germany; received his M.A. in 1963 at the University of Copenhagen; 1963–6 head of the research section of the Danish Central Library for South Schleswig, in Flensburg; 1966–72 Lecturer in History at the Institute of History, University of Aarhus; since 1972 Professor (full) of Modern History at the Institute of History and Social Research, Roskilde University; his publications include: *Marcus Rubins brevveksling 1870–1922* 4 vols (The Letters of the Historian and Statistician Marcus Rubin) (Copenhagen 1963); *Slesvig og Holstens historie efter 1830* (the History of Schleswig and Holstein after 1830) (Copenhagen 1982); *Danmarks historie, tiden 1864–1914* (Denmark's history, the years between 1864 and 1914) (Copenhagen 1989).

Comparative Studies on Governments and Non-dominant Ethnic Groups in Europe, 1850–1940

Titles in the Series

Schooling, Educational Policy and Ethnic Identity
Edited by *J.J. Tomiak* in collaboration with *K.E. Eriksen, A. Kazamias* and *R. Okey*

Religion, State and Ethnic Groups
Edited by *D. Kerr* in collaboration with *M. Breuer, S. Gilley* and *E. Suttner*

Ethnic Groups and Language Rights
Edited by *S. Vilfan* in collaboration with *G. Sandvik* and *L. Wils*

Governments, Ethnic Groups and Political Representation
Edited by *G. Alderman* in collaboration with *J. Leslie* and *K. Pollmann*

Ethnic Groups in International Relations
Edited by *P. Smith* in collaboration with *K.K. Koufa* and *A. Suppan*

The Formation of National Elites
Edited by *A. Kappeler* in collaboration with *F. Adanır* and *A. O'Day*

Roots of Rural Ethnic Mobilisation
Edited by *G. von Pistohlkors* in collaboration with *D. Howell* and *E. Wiegandt*

Ethnic Identity in Urban Europe
Edited by *M. Engman* in collaboration with *F.W. Carter, A.C. Hepburn* and *C.G. Pooley*

Series Preface

This series of eight volumes represents the results of the first major project in historical research to be undertaken by the European Science Foundation. The project's title, adopted also for the series, was carefully constructed to convey with precision the subject matter, and approach, of the enquiry; for the specialist, the lawyer, the diplomat, or the politician there are crucial differences between 'ethnic groups' and 'nationalities' and between 'non-dominant ethnic groups' (which may well be majorities) and 'ethnic minorities'. In plain language, however, and ignoring a multitude of qualifications, this is a study of some of the characteristic historic (as distinct from twentieth-century extra-European immigrant) non-dominant ethnic groups of Europe (usually minorities) and the ways in which their lives, their survival, and their development were affected by governments and the institutions of the state. The aim is strictly historical, to study what has happened in the past and try to understand and explain it. But the existence of ethnic minorities, their aspirations and their problems, is never far below the consciousness of every country in Europe, and they have contributed to many of the most dramatic and significant events in the remaking of the European scene in 1989 and 1990. The strength of deeply-rooted distinctions of religion, language, and culture in determining current political actions has been repeatedly demonstrated; and the apparently unsuspected existence of minorities within minorities, like so many Russian dolls, has continually startled Western press and television reporters. The past definitely does not predict the future: but it does give rise to the present. These volumes are, therefore, essential to the understanding of one of the most fundamental as well as most complex dimensions of contemporary Europe.

The problem addressed in these volumes can be defined as the problem created by imposing the concept of the nation–state on a mosaic of frequently intermingled peoples of differing religion, language, and culture, whose geographical distribution and pattern of settlement simply did not conform to the abstract specifications assumed by the concept. The idea of the nation as a large, supra-local, community of people with certain characteristics and purposes in common, and of the state as the legitimate embodiment of judicial, coercive, and military power, were far from new in the nineteenth century. The fusion of the two ideas, however, owed much to the French Revolution and the Napoleonic Wars; and multiple aspirations for forming new nation–states were the main driving force of the 1848 Revolutions. In spite, and often because, of the reality on the ground, the ideal of one nation, one state commanded increasingly general acceptance, outside some dynastic and aristocratic circles; it was widely believed that no nation could achieve full expression of its distinctive identity unless it was embodied in a state, and that no state could have legitimate authority over its people unless those formed a single nation.

These principles were patently and glaringly contradicted by the great multi-national empires of the nineteenth century, the Habsburg, the Russian, the German, and the Ottoman. It was less noticed that the United Kingdom also belonged to this group, perhaps because it was more liberal, and more unified in language although not in religion, perhaps because the dominance of the English was of such long standing that the existence of the other three nations had become all but invisible to the rest of the world. While most of the other European sovereign states could plausibly claim, for external purposes, to fit the nation–state model, there was scarcely one whose territories did not contain minorities with aspirations for recognition, autonomy, independence, or union with a mother country. France, Spain, Italy, Belgium or Sweden, for example, fit such a description; while the Swiss, uniquely in Europe a nation which was multi-lingual and federal, did not escape minority issues.

The First World War was a power struggle, a struggle for mastery, not a war of nationalities, but as the fighting went on it became increasingly like that as governments sought to sustain popular commitment to the war, or to undermine the unity of their enemies. Its conclusion, for a mixture of practical and idealistic reasons, saw the not too blatantly partisan application of the principle of self-determination to the map of Europe in the treaties of Versailles and Trianon. The multi-national empires, apart from the United Kingdom, fell apart or were dismembered. A new multi-national state, Yugoslavia, was created; and Europe came as close as it has ever been to appearing as a collection of independent sovereign nation–states.

Some of the successor states, such as Poland or Lithuania, were revived after years or centuries of oblivion, while others, such as Czechoslovakia, were new creations. In all of them the previously non-dominant groups gained control, and promptly found themselves faced with minorities within the new borders, consisting chiefly of the former masters. In western and Mediterranean Europe there was no similar *bouleversement*, aside from the withdrawal of southern Ireland from the United Kingdom, and the identity of non-dominant groups remained unchanged throughout the whole study period. Minorities certainly did not cease to exist or to be important in 1940; the Second World War, however, started a markedly different phase in their history, which has lasted for fifty years. During the war several minorities were treated with unsurpassable and previously unthinkable savagery and inhumanity; grievously depleted, they survived. Then, through the years of the Cold War, in some countries minorities were driven underground, marginalised, and virtually deprived of any official, public, existence; minority questions, along with nationalist issues, largely disappeared from the agenda of European international relations; and several western European countries became for the first time countries of large-scale immigration, hosts to new, non-historic, minorities. Europe seemed to have changed irrevocably, to have left history behind, to have jettisoned old minority problems and acquired new ones. Then in 1989 and 1990 the Europe of 1939, or something with a passing resemblance to it, came rushing back to life, and there was more than a hint that elements of the pre–1914 world were re-awakening. All of a sudden it became clear that historians dealing with the events of 1850 to 1940 were, in effect, also throwing light on current affairs.

In the long, and open-ended, continuum of the history of minorities in European countries the period between roughly 1850 and 1940 thus has a distinct unity; the sharp discontinuity of 1914 was, in this perspective, the hinge around which aspirations for national independence were converted into reality. Such was the general context for the proposal by the Norwegian historian John Herstad that the European Science Foundation should mount a major collaborative study of minorities, or more specifically of governments and non-dominant ethnic groups. This proposal was developed into a research programme by a planning committee chaired by Gerald Stourzh, of Vienna, consisting of members from ten different countries, including the late Professor Benjamin Akzin (Jerusalem) and the late Professor Hugh Seton-Watson (London). This programme then ran for the five years 1984-8, with an overall steering committee chaired by myself. The aim of the project was not to produce a narrative or descriptive history of each and every minority or non-dominant ethnic group in Europe, nor to produce an exhaustive, and exhausting, history of the policies and actions of each government towards its minority groups. The aim was at once simpler, more limited, and more demanding: to undertake a number of case studies on a selection of well-defined themes providing different angles of approach to the central topic, and lending themselves to comparative evaluation. From a much larger number of possibilities, eight themes were chosen, and these furnish the eight volumes of the series: Schooling; Religion; Language Rights;

Political Representation; International Relations; Formation of National Elites; Rural Settlements; Urban Settlements.

John Herstad's original idea was that studies in depth of minority groups in particular, sometimes quite small, localities could reveal much about group survival strategies, the most significant and tenacious characteristics of ethnic identities, the most important influences on assimilation, the actual impact and effect of legislation and administrative practices, and many other features which tend to get lost or obscured in the generalisations and rhetoric of national histories. This call to employ local history as a methodology has been followed where the nature of the material permits, especially in the rural and urban volumes. The claim is not that the particular villages and towns chosen for study necessarily merit intense international attention for their own sakes, but that they are microcosms of the larger world in which more general features of ethnicity, culture, custom, and law can be observed in action in the lives of individuals and families. In other chapters and other volumes the emphasis is necessarily on larger regions, and states, whose educational systems, laws and institutions, judiciaries and bureaucracies, ecclesiastical organisations and economic and social structures, set the framework within which direct interaction between non-dominant ethnic groups and the long arm of government took place. In both types of case study the selection of localities, regions, and countries is representative of the variety of different situations, different levels of economic and social development, and different forms of government which were to be found in Europe; but it does not set out to be comprehensive in its coverage, and that is not necessary to the achievement of the objective of writing a thematic, comparative, history.

That objective was pursued by assembling eight teams of experts drawn from 18 countries and a wide range of disciplines: history, law, theology, education, sociology, anthropology, and geography. More than 90 scholars took part in the project, and although all of them had extensive previous research involvement in the field, they developed, deepened, and extended their personal research in order to tackle the specific formulation of issues in the project and in order to put their own material into thematically comparable form. More preparation and research went into this task than can appear in these volumes, whose chapters in many cases are distillations and summaries of larger pieces of work. Several of the individuals who have taken part hope to publish separately longer and more complete versions of their work, especially when it was originally written in a language other than English. The decision to have a single language publication, in English, was made after much discussion and heart-searching. It goes against many long-held traditions of European scholarship in the humanities, but for a science foundation it is clearly the right decision and the one best calculated to make the results of the project most widely accessible. Hence many of the contributions are translations, and while the sense has not been altered the loss of some of the finer points of argument and subtleties of style is regrettably unavoidable.

The working programme of each group was arranged by a co-ordinator, assisted by the collective efforts of his team; and the co-ordinators, assisted by small editorial teams drawn from their colleagues, have been the editors of their individual volumes. Each group has been fully European, multi-national, multi-cultural, and multi-lingual; the coordinator–editors have performed difficult feats of academic organisation and intellectual discipline with much tact, and with a success which can be judged in these volumes. Each group, and hence each volume, has a different structure, and the significance of the separate contributions and the conclusions to be drawn are excellently handled by the volume editors; it is not the province of this general preface either to anticipate or to summarise them. One general feature of the enterprise, so obvious that it can easily be overlooked, does however deserve emphasis. The humanities work within national cultures and languages in a way that is not true of the natural or experimental sciences. In this project researchers brought up in many very different scholarly traditions have learned each other's ways, and while continuing to speak in many tongues have adopted a common 'language' for identifying the problems for intellectual enquiry and the methods for investigating them. This is the key to successful international cooperation in the humanities, and to have come so far towards achieving it in this project is a major innovation in the methodology of European scholarship. Without sacrificing any of the particularity and individuality of specific circumstances and situations in different places at different times, which are fundamental to the historical method, the varieties of experience of non-dominant ethnic groups have been approached and analysed in a common way which for the first time has made wide-ranging comparative assessment based on firm empirical evidence possible and meaningful.

In an enterprise of this size and complexity many friendships have been formed and many individuals and institutions have given their help. Above all, everyone who has participated in the project would wish to have recorded their appreciation of the incomparable contribution made by Christoph Mühlberg, Secretary of the Humanities Committee of the European Science Foundation throughout the major part of the programme, whose skill in administrative organisation has been matched only by his grasp of the intellectual challenges of the theme and the soundness of his suggestions for meeting them.

F.M.L. Thompson
Institute of Historical Research,
University of London

1 Introduction

GERHARD BRUNN, MIROSLAV HROCH and ANDREAS KAPPELER

The term 'non-dominant ethnic group' has proved to be an inspiring and productive neologism. It designates the colourful and hetero-geneous majority of European ethnic groups otherwise called national (or ethnic) minorities, small nations, nationalities or sub-nationalities. Their common attribute is that they either have no share in the political power of the state in which they live or that this role is, at least, subordinate to that of the dominant nation or people. An important advantage of this term is that its use eliminates those misunderstandings which are hidden in the semantic differences between the terms 'nation, national, etc' in the English and French usage and their meaning in the German and, analogously, the Slav languages.

However, the term 'non-dominant ethnic group' comprises such a large spectrum of phenomena that new misunderstandings might result from indiscriminate use. For this reason it is advisable to respect the intrinsic differentiations of the groups designated by the term. Three fundamental situations can be distinguished, each of which merits further categorisation.

Firstly the term designates the nations in the process of formation during the nineteenth century. These were communities which had not yet attained all attributes necessary for a full national existence. The 'deficits', conditions lacking for a full national existence, were political sovereignty, linguistic–cultural integrity and development of a complete social structure. The deficits were of varying import-ance between the many groups in European societies.

For the middle of the nineteenth century further differentiation into types can be made:

- national communities lacking only political sovereignty (or unity) for the formation of a complete nation as, for instance, the Germans before the 1848 revolution, the Poles, the Italians or the Greeks.
- communities having two deficits such as political sovereignty and absence of full linguistic–cultural development (the Magyars in the

beginning of the nineteenth century, for instance) or an in-complete social structure. The Irish represent an example of this second type.

- ethnic groups having all the three deficits which they had to overcome on the way towards modern nationhood. This type corresponds to the groups designated by M. Hroch as 'small nations'.[1] Special cases belonging to this situation are small ethnic groups which, for the time covered by the study, did not have the first essentials for forming a nation such as the Sorbs, the Kashubians, the Lapps (Sami) or the West Frisians.

The second situation is that of ethnic groups which, though forming a non-dominant ethnic group within the state on whose territory they live, linguistically, culturally and consciously belong to another extant nation and who therefore did not form themselves into an autonomous nation. This was the case for instance with the Danes and Germans in Schleswig, the Greeks in Romania and the Germans in Hungary. Such groups constituted 'national minorities' or, if they settled near a frontier, 'borderland minorities'. Sometimes these minorities had a rather shifting identity such as the Alsatians. Special cases among the category of 'national minorities' are ethnic groups not occupying a compact territory such as the Poles in the Ruhr region or the Irish in Britain.

The third fundamental situation are diaspora groups who did not have compact territories of their own at all. A classic instance is the Jews.

Another way of sub-dividing and typologising the emerging nations is by state tradition. This is the much quoted and rightly criticised distinction between so-called historical and unhistorical peoples made by Hegel and Engels. The latter has given rise to the well-known denunciation of the so-called 'unhistorical peoples' as 'ruins' or 'rubbish' by Engels. Therefore the distinction coined by H. Seton-Watson of 'old continuous nations' and 'new nations' is more suitable.[2] Instances of ethnic groups who had lost their state existence are the Poles, Irish, Czechs and Catalans among others. Slovaks, Estonians and Finns represent cases of ethnic groups which lacked a history of a former state.

The three categories with their subdivisions constitute ideal types. In historical reality mixed forms are frequent. Moreover between 1850 and 1940 different groups changed their situations making reclassification essential. The fundamental situations must be borne in mind in assessing non-dominant ethnic groups, not least because of distinctions of their social positions and relations with the dominant nation. A significant difference also existed in national consciousness. Leaders of the emerging small nations, or of those peoples striving for national unity, saw their quest as having unique value. Each believed the disappearance (assimilation) of their people was a fate comparable to the death of the individual. In the national minority situation, for example, leaders attempted to secure frontier adjustments or sought the active cultural leadership of the mother country.

Existence of all these groups took on particular significance when they, or rather their representatives on the political stage, formulated ethnic group based goals. With the rise of national movements non-dominant ethnic groups became a subject of political activity. A national movement can be defined as a purposeful striving to attain all missing attributes of a complete national existence, that is the elimination of the existing 'deficits'. To achieve its objective leaders had to stimulate and mobilise the sentiments of the masses. National movements were not metaphysical phenomenons. They were fostered, directed and organised on the ground by real people. The success of these leaders was dependent on developing a group consciousness which could be moulded into national activism. The stronger this consciousness became, the more authoritative – and also more differentiated – the leading groups of the movement appeared.

This leads to the main focus of the study – those personalities who took a decisive part in the national movement – as organisers, patrons, speakers, ideologues, propagandists and also as patriotically minded cultural figures, artists or scientists. For the most part these leaders did not belong to the ruling class of the state or society, and it is therefore problematical to call them 'elites'. Protagonists of the national move-ment were not always linked to the ruling class of their state. On the contrary they struggled against the dominant nation and consequently against the ruling elites. Moreover many non-dominant ethnic groups did not have a complete class structure, and their leadership therefore did not belong to the elites of society as a whole.

The term 'national elites' is used for the politically conscious and active persons of the non-dominant ethnic groups who took the lead in the patriotic movement. It is vital to place them as precisely as possible in the social strata of the sub-society of the non-dominant ethnic group. In order not to confuse them with those groups designated by the comprehensive term 'elite' (of the entire state and society) and with the social elite of the non-dominant group which was not necessarily politically active, the terms 'leaders' or 'activists' are most appropriate for those members of the ethnic groups who were at the forefront of the national movement. The term 'leaders' is appropriate for those key personalities who formulated pro-grammes, ideologies and strategies. 'Activist' cuts deeper, com-prising a broader and more numerous stratum of nationally minded members of the movement.

Every activist appears as a personality with different qualities and opinions, with a specific social and intellectual background. Each had a separate career. Individuals are important for the comparative study when a pattern with recurring and socially relevant features emerges. Common features include shared convictions, modes of organisation, types of communication, political demands, cultural endeavours and similar characteristics. At this level activists appear as a more or less organised cadre which, though increasingly differentiated internally, was indispensable as the vanguard of the non-dominant ethnic group's march to nationhood. Activists were not a limited or self-contained group but on the contrary groups whose social function was transformed by the influx of a growing number of followers leading ultimately to full mass organisation.

What linked all these activists was their patriotic convictions. United by these they represented the interests of their non-dominant ethnic group – or what they thought these to be – to the external world and most particularly to the governments which were in the hands of the dominant nation. Political manifestations of these externally directed activities are treated elsewhere. In this volume the focus is on how the 'national elites' differed from general social 'elites' and from the ruling class of the dominant nation, and on what they had in common with these other elites.

The effectiveness of activists hinged on the policy of governments. Three types of government response can be distinguished: assimilation, segregation and integration. An assimilation approach did not imply force necessarily, it often was realised through conferment of benefits, the so-called natural absorption. Segregation can be seen distinctly in the case of the Jews. Integration – endeavours to foster cultural pluralism – have been of secondary importance. The assimilation process was not a one way road. Members of the non-dominant ethnic group could just as well become conscious activists of the emerging small nation as assimilated into the dominant society. Part of the external efforts of the activists was directed at curtailing assimilation, even towards the winning back of members of their group already integrated into the dominant culture, at least superficially. The other road, that of attempts at isolation, was not always successful either.

Forms of government were also important particularly in view of the broad spectrum of different political systems in nineteenth century Europe, from the British parliamentary regime to Tsarist autocracy. Unfortunately too little is known about the changes brought about for the members and activists of the non-dominant ethnic group when the late feudal absolutism was replaced by constitutionalism. 'Governments' has been taken to mean both those taking part in political power and the allied administrative bodies. A vital problem concerns the opportunities afforded by different forms of government to activists.

General analysis has to be derived from concrete representative cases. Not every type or region has been included and the omission of studies on the Estonians, Basques, Alsatians, Finns and Jews, though initially represented in the working group, are notable. But the final representation is not arbitrary; most essential types of national movements (or of the activists of the non-dominant ethnic groups) have been treated. Representative cases by type are of particular importance for the comparative approach. As this is a volume organised around a methodology of 'types', not geography, the case studies appear in the order of their representational function.

The Polish national movement in the Grand Duchy of Poznań exemplifies the former ruling, but now politically subjugated, nation. Ireland illustrates the situation where political and social deficits had to be eliminated. Other cases consider national movements belonging to different variants of 'small nations'. Three types have been distinguished.[3] The integrated type which rose early is represented by the Czechs. Norwegian and Croatian experiences were of the same variety. Ukrainians in Russia represent the belated type, a national movement which began at a late date in a socio-economically backward European territory and was not fully successful. Lithuanian and White Russian national movements followed a similar pattern. Catalans represent the disintegrated type, a national movement taking place in the west European context with success attained at a very late date. A fourth variation, the insurrectional type, is to be found in the Macedonian case. There the movement started late, relied on violent methods and was in the ambiguous position of being forged between Bulgarian and Macedonian identity. An important special type which can be placed between the integrated and the belated type is not among the cases treated – it was initially represented by the Estonian movement. However in the comparative chapters which follow it will be partly taken into account. Finnish, Slovak and Slovene national movements also belong to this intermediate type. Yet it must be stressed that many national movements had attributes of more than a single category.

Two case studies illustrate the problem of national minorities and their movements. They were active in the same region, but from rival positions: the German minority (under Danish rule) and Danish minority (under German rule). This complementary situation illuminating the national conflicts in a territory with shifting frontiers has a fascination and importance of its own. The classic diaspora group – initially represented by the case of the Jews in eastern Europe – has not been treated in this volume.

A majority of cases are of formerly existing states. The importance of this factor – the traditions of a political nation – as a mobilising force was, however, unequal. It was crucial for the Poles, Czechs, Irish and Catalans; less so for the Ukrainians. Macedonians and Estonians lacked this inspiration. Different types of political systems – multi-national empires, one language national states, parliamentary regimes, autocracy without a constitution – are all represented.

The course of national movements was clearly asynchronous. The beginnings of the Czech national movement date from the second half of the eighteenth century whereas the Catalan movement did not start before the late 1860s. The Macedonians' movement began even later. Consequently asynchronousness also appears when pinpoint-ing the moment of success of the separate national movements. The Polish, Irish and Czech activists had won over broad strata of their community as early as the middle of the nineteenth century; the Catalan activists only succeeded in doing so around 1900. By then neither the Macedonians nor the Ukrainians in Russia had reached that stage. The underlying ideas, mentality, demands and dreams of the activists of different national movements were however very similar, in spite of the time and geographical gaps between them.

It may be stated that any comparative study of European national movements based on synchronousness of events can at best come to the commonplace conclusion that the course of these movements was so disparate that a synchronously conceived study would hardly make sense. Comparative analysis requires alternative methodology. However it is essential to enquire into the reasons and conditions underlying this asynchronism. A hypothesis is that the asyn-chronous development of national movements is a consequence of great disparities in economic and social development, and may even be caused by these differences. Does this supposition correspond to historical reality?

Modern nations – even when emerging from non-dominant ethnic groups – form part of the social transformation from late feudal to capitalist society. It was – in non-Marxist terms – a component of social modernisation. Modernisation, or capitalist conditions, were realised unevenly throughout Europe. Whereas in England and Belgium capitalist mechanisms of exchange had been reached as early as the first half of the nineteenth century, it was only after 1850 that it and industrialisation triumphed in central Europe. In eastern and south eastern Europe the first steps towards capitalism were only taken during the second half of the nineteenth century, about 100 years later than in the advanced regions of western Europe. The time lag in social and economic development influenced the spread of ideas only in those cases where retardation was also accompanied by political repression. Delay and development though was much more important for the spreading of national activities to the broader strata of the population. In several instances patriotic ideas were imitated but success in spreading these notions was not equally rapid everywhere.

There can be no doubt that a comparative study of the role of the activists would not make sense synchronously for certain short periods or, generally, over even the entire 100 year span of the project. Other methods of comparison are essential. Development from non-dominant ethnic group into modern nation, though asynchronous, was characterised by an analogous series of events. The beginnings of the national movement were as a rule connected with the activities of a small group of educated people, above all scholars. The peak of the movement was reached when the nationally minded masses became involved. Progression to a mass movement was the fruit of the labours of activists.

In each national movement three phases can be distinguished which are characterised by the part played by the activists and by the extent and strength of national consciousness developed among the masses. During the first phase the activists above all showed a scholarly interest in the cultural, linguistic, social and sometimes historical characteristics of the non-dominant ethnic group, termed Phase A. Most of them however did not take the further step of presenting specifically ethnic demands to the rulers of the existing state. Subsequently a new type of activist emerged. They regarded national or ethnic individuality as valuable and set themselves the goal of winning over as many members of the non-dominant group as possible to their ideal of national autonomy. Their agitation aimed at spreading national consciousness generally throughout the non-dominant ethnic community. The rate and timing of success, when it happened at all, differed between groups. This period of patriotic agitation has been termed Phase B.

This phase was successful when a mass support was aroused which regarded their national identity as having special value. From this moment it is appropriate to speak of a national mass movement – Phase C. It was only during this phase that differentiation between democrats and liberals or between conservatives and clericals respectively, which had been present though often latent during earlier development, deepened and became apparent. Differentiated political programmes were typical of Phase C. This does not mean however that the modern nation had already been fully formed within the non-dominant ethnic group, for that was a process which required an extended time span.

Although not every agitation ended in a successful mass movement the periodisation outlined provides a starting point for analysis of activists in a comparative format. Each of the asynchronously developing national movements reached Phase B at some juncture and most achieved the transition to a mass movement afterwards. National agitation played a crucial part in the movements and its consequence determined whether the non-dominant ethnic group would develop into a nation. Research therefore concentrates on Phase B and – in the case of those national movements which developed early – on the beginnings of Phase C. It has tested also the Hroch phase model. Hroch's periodisation is important for two reasons:

- It permits comparative analysis over time, investigating the analogous situations of a range of national developments; and
- It affords a reminder that activists have to be assessed in a differentiated manner – the social profile and mentality were not identical between the three phases. These factors affected their role in society and their relations with governments. It should also be borne in mind that the role of the activists was transformed when the national movement reached the stage of the fully formed nation enjoying statehood. In the movements analysed below, however, this was the case only with the Irish, Poles and Czechs. With the attainment of sovereignty the activists themselves naturally become a dominant ethnic group, a ruling elite.

The arrangement of the volume and way in which the contents of the different chapters have been structured have been determined by a common set of guidelines, by an intention to examine the role of the activists in the national movements and their interaction with the governments on a comparative basis. In this way both unique and common local and ethnic features can be assessed. Every national movement arose within a specific environment. Authors have coordinated case studies and organised their work to fit the comparative approach. Each case study addressed a set of common issues. Not all questions were relevant to each study but the various articles have been shaped by an agreed agenda.

Case studies treated the following points:

- General conditions
  - geographic, demographic, confessional, linguistic, economic, social, occupational pre-conditions, literacy, schools and communication networks;
  - political structures, administration, legal aspects and nationalities policy

- The national movement and its activists
  - phases of the movement
  - social and territorial origin and structure of the activists

- the formation of the national 'elites', social mobility, the role of educational institutions
- the assimilation pressure of the dominant nation and opposing strategies of the national 'elites'
- national activities (cultural and political): organisation and communication with broader parts of the ethnic group
- the development of national consciousness, the activists as myth makers.

- The government and the formation of national activists
  - government policy and administrative measures
  - reactions of the activists
  - significance of the factor 'government' for the formation of national 'elites'.

The opportunities to evaluate the separate national movements in a comparative manner, with special attention given to the activists, are limited by the restricted number of cases. For that reason stress has been placed on certain central sets of problems which also are examined systematically in comparative chapters. Five problems have been investigated:

- Who were the activists? To which social classes and groups did they belong? What were their social origins? Where did they live and function?
- Where and how did the activists obtain their education? What part did the institutions of secondary and higher education take in the formation of the activists?
- How were the activists organised during their national struggle? What forms did their organisations take? What goals did they pursue?
- How did they communicate with each other? How was communication with the members of their ethnic group arranged?
- How were arguments derived from their own conception of history? To what extent did they create historical myths?

The volume is arranged in three parts: case studies, comparative chapters and a short conclusion.

Notes

1 Hroch, M. (1968), *Die Vorkämpfer der nationalen Bewegung bei den kleinen Völkern Europas. Eine vergleichende Analyse zur gesellschaftlichen Schichtung der patriotischen Gruppen*, Praha (Acta Universitatis Carolinae Philosophie et Historiae, Mono-

graphia XXIV); *ibid:* (1985), *Social Preconditions of National Revival in Europe. A Comparative Analysis of the Social Composition of Patriotic Groups among the smaller European Nations*, Cambridge. Compare the similar typology of Józef Chlebowczyk (1980), *On Small and Young Nations in Europe*, Wrocław, Warszawa, Kraków, Gdańsk, p. 19.
2 Hugh Seton-Watson (1977), *Nations and States. An Enquiry into the Origins of Nations and the Politics of Nationalism*, London, pp. 6–9.
3 Hroch (1985), pp. 25–30.

CASE STUDIES

2 The Poles in the Grand Duchy of Poznań, 1850–1914

WITOLD MOLIK

Introduction

The dynamic development of the Polish national movement in the Duchy of Poznań already had inspired a keen interest in historians, economists and journalists by the turn of the twentieth century. The successes of the Poles in their struggle with the Prussian government and the economically much stronger Germans were written and spoken of as the Greater Poland phenomenon and served as an example for other national minorities in Europe. The German economist Ludwig Bernhard wrote in his introduction to the third edition of the widely read *Die Polenfrage* that the fate of the Poles in the Grand Duchy of Poznań (*Grossherzogtum Posen*) had assumed an important place in world history. They provided a universal and historical example of 'how a national minority may retain an independent existence, and even strengthen it, despite contrary efforts on the part of a much stronger state power'.[1]

In Poland, the struggle of Polish society with the Prussian authorities and the German population in the Grand Duchy of Poznań in the nineteenth century recently has come to be called 'one of the longest wars in Europe'. Apart from numerous books and articles, a multi-instalment, semi-documentary film *The Longest War in Modern Europe* became a great success and was shown twice on Polish television. In the course of a wide discussion which followed in various journals the war came to be acknowledged as one of the finest chapters in Polish history.

General Conditions

The Grand Duchy of Poznań was created in 1815 out of the Polish territories comprising 28 940 sq km that had been granted to Prussia at the Congress of Vienna. A large portion of Greater Poland, the most westerly province of the former Polish state, found itself within the Grand Duchy's borders. The Grand Duchy performed an important strategic function in the Hohenzollern monarchy, providing a convenient link between the monarchy's southern and north eastern provinces. In the event of a Prussian–Russian war the Grand Duchy would have been the most threatened of all the monarchy's territories. The fall of Poznań would have opened the shortest route to Berlin to a Russian army.

Due to the absence of certain basic sources it is impossible to recreate precisely the national composition of the Grand Duchy's population. Prussian authorities regularly conducted a census; however, they did not classify the population by nationality. They merely recorded individual religious affiliation and native language. Many historians believe that the officials responsible for conducting the census often interpreted the information provided by the bilingual Poles to the advantage of Germans. Data in the table below are based on official German sources and thus offer only approximate information about the province's ethnic composition. The Polish population is underestimated.[2]

Table 2.1: Absolute and relative changes in the population of the Poznańian nationalities 1825–1910

	Poles (absolute number)	%	Germans (absolute number)	%	Jews (absolute number)	%	Total provincial population
1825	648 000	62.9	318 500	30.8	65 000	6.3	1 032 000
1849	809 000	60.7	448 000	33.6	76 800	5.7	1 334 000
1871	966 000	61.0	556 000	35.1	62 000	3.9	1 584 000
1890	1 112 650	63.6	594 650	33.9	44 300	2.5	1 752 000
1910	1 352 650	64.7	720 650	34.0	26 500	1.3	2 100 000

The Grand Duchy of Poznań possessed the largest Polish population in the Prussian state's provinces. Of roughly 2 200 000 Polish Prussian subjects in 1867, 39 per cent lived in the Grand Duchy, 34 per cent in the Opole regency of Silesia, 20 per cent in Western Prussia, and seven per cent in Eastern Prussia.[3] Poles were the most numerous non-dominant ethnic group in the Prussian state. Between 1867 and 1910 they represented about ten per cent of the Prussian population. Germans constituted a large majority in only four northern and four western districts of the Grand Duchy of Poznań. Poles enjoyed a clear numerical advantage in the 18 remaining districts. Relatively few Germans resided in the eastern and southern districts bordering on the Kingdom of Poland. Jews migrated in increasing numbers to the central and western Prussian provinces and were quickly germanised. Simultaneously the percentage of Jews in the Duchy's total population steadily declined. By 1850 only 25 per cent of the Duchy's population lived in the cities. Only two out of 144 cities had more than 10000 inhabitants: Poznań with 44000, and Bydgoszcz with 13000. As many as 110 cities had fewer than 3000 residents. In the second half of the nineteenth century the percentage of urban dwellers as a proportion of population grew slowly: in 1890 they constituted 29 per cent of the Duchy's population and in 1910 around 34 per cent.[4]

As a fundamental component of the eighteenth century Polish kingdom, Greater Poland was the most economically developed region of Poland.[5] The transition to Prussian rule had important repercussions for the region's economy. The highly developed cloth industry declined when markets in the east were incorporated into the Russian state. Numerous cloth manufacturers in Greater Poland were unable to resist the influx of cheaper industrial goods from other provinces of the Hohenzollern monarchy. In this situation agriculture became the leading branch of the economy and the Grand Duchy of Poznań acquired the status of a 'granary' for the industrial provinces of Germany.

The Prussian state implemented land reforms – an essential step for the transformation from a feudal to a capitalist agricultural structure – while offering full protection for large landowners. An edict issued in 1823 (and introduced gradually up to 1865) gave only those peasants who exploited more than 25 hectares of land rights to purchase their holdings and then at a high price. Thousands of peasants who were either landless or who farmed only small amounts of land were excluded from this reform. Cities were also restructured along capitalist lines. In 1833, 1853 and 1869, laws were issued abolishing the remaining feudal institutions in the cities (land rents, obligatory guild membership etc). Moreover the principles governing the election of urban authorities were defined.

These economic and governmental reforms 'conducted from above' heralded significant social transformations. Polish society in the Grand Duchy of Poznań evolved from an estate based to capitalist community. The Polish *szlachta* (aristocracy) occupied the top of this new society's social hierarchy. This aristocracy however was not as numerous in the Prussian partition as in the Polish territories occupied by Russia and Austria. In 1831 1022 (78.2 per cent) of 1307 landed estates belonged to Poles while 285 (21.8 per cent) were in German hands. As a result of the Prussian authorities' germanisation policies, their own spendthrift lifestyle, and a general inability to adapt to new farming conditions, increasing numbers of Polish landowners lost their estates to German immigrants. In 1886 only 649 (39 per cent) of 1659 large land holdings belonged to Poles whereas Germans had by then acquired 1010.[6]

Between 1841–70 the intelligentsia developed into a separate social group occupying the middle position in the social hierarchy. Prussian authorities effectively prevented the Polish intelligentsia from developing numerically by, for example, limiting Polish access to positions in the administration, courts and schools. The size of the Polish intelligentsia in 1870 had been estimated at 1000–1200. If primary school teachers are included (many historians do not consider them to be members of the intelligentsia) this number rises to approximately 2500.[7] At this time the Polish intelligentsia consisted mainly of Catholic priests, physicians, journalists and secondary school teachers. Unfortunately no studies quantify the numerical growth of the intelligentsia for 1871–1918, however its increase must have been slow.

Trade for many years remained the domain of Germans and germanised Jews. They were also the owners of a majority of large and specialised workshops. Among Poles small traders dominated. During the 1880s however a fundamental change occurred. The Polish lower middle class began to grow dynamically. In 1882, 27.6 per cent of all people in trade were Poles. By 1907 this proportion had risen to 49.2 per cent. Advance was evident in the crafts sector as well: by 1907 the Poles owned 46.8 per cent of all small urban workshops.[8] In terms of wealth, however, the Polish lower middle class remained markedly behind its German counterpart. As late as 1910 German city dwellers paid almost 72 per cent of income taxes while urban Poles contributed only 28 per cent.[9]

The demand for workers in the small food and agricultural machine factories that were dominant in the Grand Duchy grew only slowly. Thus in 1882 only 118 000, and in 1907 approximately 187 000, workers were employed outside agriculture. The majority of these workers were Polish. They also dominated among landed peasants. This social category expanded numerically and grew stronger economically. In 1907 62 803 land holdings containing from 5–100 hectares existed. The agricultural proletariat, which represented the most numerous social group, consisted almost exclusively of Poles. In 1843 57 500 village workers lived in the Grand Duchy of Poznań and by 1907 this number had grown to about 230 000.[10] Polish society within the Grand Duchy of Poznań was primarily agrarian and possessed neither a grand bourgeoisie nor a working class employed in large industry. With Poles constituting the poorer part of the population they possessed, despite their numerical advantage, the position of an ethnic minority and incurred the limitations and consequence of this status.[11]

In the so-called 'occupation document' of 15 May 1815 and in the final act of the Congress of Vienna, the Prussian king, Friedrick Wilhelm III, guaranteed the Polish population in the Grand Duchy of Poznań a 'political existence'. It quickly became clear however that these promises were a fiction whose implementation depended solely on circumstances. Guided by its own *raison d'état* Prussia never intended to retreat from its policy of closely integrating the seized Polish lands with its own provinces and germanising the local population. Of course the Prussians did not always base their internal policies in the eastern provinces on clearly and distinctly defined principles. In other words they did not devise a well thought out strategy in their *Polenpolitik* (Polish policy). During the years 1815–70 they alternately decreased and increased the intensity of germanisation. During this period the Prussians satisfied themselves with the loyalty of the 'Polish speaking Prussians'. Above all they sought to integrate the Grand Duchy of Poznań economically, legally and politically into the Hohenzollern monarchy. With this goal in mind they introduced the same administrative structure that existed in the other Prussian provinces in 1815: the Prussian *Landrecht* (Land right law) in 1817; and a law on obligatory school attendance in 1825. Prussian authorities also issued a series of decrees designed to hinder the growth of a Polish national movement. Although Prussia did support the development of a primary school system it refused the establishment of a Polish university in Poznań. In the primary schools in which Poles comprised a majority Polish was the language of instruction and some space was also allotted to Polish in the secondary schools. Until 1830 Polish enjoyed equal status with German in the courts and administration. After 1830 it was reduced to the same status as other foreign languages.[12]

After 1870 the Polish population in the Grand Duchy of Poznań became the object of relentless germanisation conducted in all areas of national and social existence and characterised by the application of rigorous measures. Despite Polish protests the Grand Duchy was incorporated into the North German Federation in 1867 and into the German *Reich* in 1871. The primary and secondary schools were subjected to complete germanisation. Polish was banned from the secondary schools completely (in 1900 study of Polish, even as a supplementary subject, was discontinued). In primary schools, on the other hand, Polish continued as a second language until 1887, after which it was used only in religious education. During this period the Prussian authorities recognised that the methods pre-viously applied no longer sufficed to strengthen the Germans and to restrain the 'pressure' of the Polish population. Thus they resorted to

new means. As their main goal they sought not merely to denational-
ise Poles but also to remove them from strategic positions. Under a
decree issued by the Minister of Internal Affairs on 26 May 1885,
30 000 people (mainly Poles) were expelled from the country because
they were not Prussian citizens. Moreover in order to strengthen the
Germans numerically and economically the Prussian authorities
established the so-called Colonisation Commission in 1886. During
the period 1886–1913 its total cost amounted to the huge sum of 955
million marks, clearly an enormously expensive policy. Yet the
Commission succeeded in purchasing only a small number of land
holdings from the Polish *szlachta* and settled only 21 000 German
peasant families in the east. In effect this result represented nothing
more than compensation for the losses incurred as the result of
Ostflucht (the migration of the German population from the eastern
provinces to the industrialised provinces of the Second *Reich*).[13]

At this time nationalist slogans gained increasing numbers of
adherents among the Germans, particularly in the eastern provinces.
They gave much more support to the authorities' policies of
germanisation. Local *junkers* (landowning gentry) led the nationalist
groups in the Grand Duchy of Poznań. Under their initiative, the
German *Ostmarkenverein* (Eastern Marches Association), referred to
by the Poles as *Hakata*, was founded in 1894. This organisation
contributed to the acceleration of certain germanisation measures
and played a substantial role in fanning anti-Polish sentiments.[14] At
the end of the nineteenth century the Prussian authorities developed
a new course of action in the eastern provinces known as *Hebungs-
politik* (Development Policy). As a part of this programme they
allotted significant sums of money for the architectural alteration of
the cities in these provinces to make them look more like municipalities in the *Reich*. Local Germans also received financial support from
the authorities. A series of further exceptional laws applicable to the
Polish population were pushed through parliament. The 'expro-
priation law' of 1908 provided for the forced eviction of Poles, though
with financial compensation, from their land holdings, while the
'muzzle' law of 1908 prohibited them from organising public meetings in cities in which their numbers were less than 60 per cent of the
total population.

In the second half of the nineteenth century an increasingly
peculiar legal situation existed in the Grand Duchy of Poznań. The
Polish population was relegated to the status of second class citizens
subject to numerous special decrees that were often in violation of the
Prussian constitution.[15] A series of liberal laws passed in Prussia, and
later in the Second *Reich*, were not applied to this province. However
Poles who obeyed the laws that were frequently directed against
them were legally able to create their own economic and social

organisations as well as to circulate their own publications, even though they were often critical of the Prussian government's policies. The Prussian tradition of the rule of law did not always work to the Poles' disadvantage. Prussian courts frequently anulled illegal decisions made by the Prussian administration. In gradually liquidating Polish illiteracy Prussian authorities were concerned above all with germanisation. Paradoxically they created the conditions for the development of a Polish mass press. The activities of Polish delegates to the Prussian *Landtag* (local assembly) in 1848 and the German *Reichstag* (national parliament) from 1871 were also important. But these were only small factions in both legislative bodies and they did not play a decisive role. They did however protest against the authorities' policies of germanisation and thereby informed German public opinion about the restrictions imposed on the Polish minority in Prussia.

The Polish National Movement and its Activists

Development of the national movement among the Polish population of the Grand Duchy of Poznań initially took a different course from that of similar movements among the small nations of Europe examined by M. Hroch.[16] For these nations the birth of a group of intellectuals was characteristic of the initial phase. These intellectuals studied native history and language but they avoided agitation among the masses of the people. Intellectuals who studied Polish language and history were also active. However representatives of the *szlachta* played the leading role in the Polish movement and among these individuals the traditions of independent statehood were still very much alive. The Polish kingdom had only ceased to exist at the close of the eighteenth century. Many Polish patriots had acquired their education or had even begun their public careers during the lifetime of this state. As a result the Polish movement was politicised from its initial phase and not designed solely to promote culture and science.

During the first phase, which lasted until the end of the 1820s, the Poles of Poznań enjoyed significant civil liberties. This advantageous period began between 1807 and 1814 while the area belonged to the Duchy of Warsaw, a satellite state established by Napoleon. With the return of Prussian rule in 1815 the prospects for public activity markedly declined. Among the *szlachta*, which was at the time the dominant social group, the majority advocated a legal struggle for Polish rights. Only a portion of the poorer *szlachta* united itself in the secret 'Scythemen's Union' which sought to initiate a national uprising. Gentry activists concentrated their defence of 'national rights' mainly in the provincial parliament which was convened for the first time in 1827 but possessed only very limited powers. In 1828 they attempted to establish a legal society designed to press their views in various areas of public life. Prussian authorities however refused to sanction this organisation's existence. The November uprising of 1830–1 in the Polish kingdom led to a change in the attitudes of the Polish elite in the Grand Duchy of Poznań. Leaders from the *szlachta* who had previously advocated legal forms of national activity joined the armed uprising in the Russian partition. About 3000 volunteers from the Grand Duchy including many townspeople, peasants and craftsmen participated in the revolt.[17]

A second phase of the national movement extended through the 1830s to the 1840s – more specifically, between 1831 and 1848. During this period a generation of activists who had been born after Poland's loss of independence began to participate in the national movement. A significant number of these activists came from the urban middle class. Intensification of the policies of germanisation at this time brought about a reaction in Polish society and led to a search for new defensive measures. Two currents within the Polish national movement arose. The first was centred on landowners and members of the still small intelligentsia, all of whom were opposed to an armed uprising and to broad social reforms. They contended that organised legal activity designed to encourage the nation's economic and cultural development would be most advantageous to Poles. These activists formulated the programme of so-called 'organic work' within which they urged modernisation of agriculture, the development of Polish crafts and trade, the expansion of education and the support of science. A second group consisted of those representatives of the *szlachta*, intelligentsia and urban middle class who strove to initiate an armed uprising. These activists were opposed to 'negotiating' with the conquering powers and postulated more radical solutions to social problems.

Initially the adherents of 'organised work' acquired a stronger influence than their more radical opponents and were responsible for numerous economic and educational initiatives. Construction of a central building for Polish public life – the hotel 'Bazar' in Poznań (1838–41) – and the founding of the Society for Scientific Help in 1841, an institution which provided talented but poor students from secondary schools and universities with material support, proved to be their greatest successes. The conspiratorial movement initially had an elitist character. In 1839 the Poznanian Committee, which worked closely with the Polish Democratic Society in France, was established. The members of the committee intended to initiate an armed national uprising. Towards the end of 1843 and the beginning of 1844 more radical conspirators founded the Plebeian Union and formulated its programme which called for the restoration of Poland within its pre–1772 borders, abolition of estate privileges, implementation of a universal right to work and equal wages for all. Plebeian Union radicalism forced the Poznanian Committee to accelerate its own plans for an uprising, which was then scheduled for 21 February 1846. However wealthy members of the *szlachta* betrayed the entire plan to the Prussian police. Virtually all of the leaders of the conspiracy found themselves imprisoned. They were tried in Berlin in 1847 and received long sentences.

In 1848 it became evident that the struggle to regain independence had developed into an issue that interested a wide range of social groups. This was the year that marked the onset of the third phase of the Polish national movement. On 20 March 1848, after learning of the outbreak of revolution in Berlin, the Polish population in the Grand Duchy of Poznań armed itself and established a National Committee. Masses of Polish peasants and townspeople joined in the uprising, providing the bulk of the 9000 member insurgent army. However despite several victorious battles between April and May 1848 this force was dispersed by a 30 000 strong Prussian army.[18]

Following suppression of the uprising proponents of the moderate 'organic work' approach once again occupied a prominent position. In June 1848 they founded the Polish League which was intended 'to promote the national cause and the Polish cause in general' through all available legal means. In the ensuing months the advocates of 'organic work' established approximately 300 local branches in the Grand Duchy of Poznań and Western Prussia. Around 37 000 individuals joined the Polish League which engaged in educational propaganda among the peasantry and lower middle class in harmony with the interests of the *szlachta*, in the spirit of national solidarity in other words. The Prussian authorities quickly realised that the main purpose of the Polish League was to provide hierarchic and central-ised guidance to the cultural, social and political life of Poles in the provinces where they were most densely settled. Thus they ordered its abolition in April 1850.

As a result of repressive measures applied by the Prussian authorities at the beginning of the second half of the nineteenth century the Polish national movement regressed significantly. It experienced a new vitality before the outbreak of the January uprising of 1863. Approximately 6000 to 7000 volunteers from the Grand Duchy of Poznań supported this Polish insurgency. In addition Poles from the Grand Duchy provided their countrymen in the Kingdom of Poland with quantities of weapons, ammunition and medical supplies. In July 1864 the Prussian authorities in Berlin tried 149 of the most active members of the insurgent organisations in the

Grand Duchy of Poznań on charges of high treason. The court imposed severe sentences on 38 of those convicted.[19]

The defeat of the January uprising brought about a sharp discontinuity in the outlook of Polish society. Poles lost hope of regaining independence by armed struggle and recognised that only strenuous and unspectacular day-to-day work would lead to success. The concept of 'organic work' once again triumphed. Between 1864 and 1914 Poles gradually constructed a system of specialised organisations which encompassed virtually all aspects of peoples lives. Separate organisations arose for peasants (agricultural clubs in 1866), the lower middle class (industrial societies in 1849), and lower middle class and working class youth (gymnastic groups belonging to the organisation *Sokół* (Hawk) in 1884). These organisations combined a specific instruction with supplementary study of Polish history. They also encouraged members to inculcate their children in a national and Catholic spirit. National organisations extended to the following areas of social life at the turn of the twentieth century:

- agricultural education and self-help: the Central Farming Society (1861); numerous agricultural clubs; the Union of Landowners (1900)
- education and self-help in industry and trade: the Union of Industrial Societies (1895); the Union of Commercial Societies (1905); the Federation of Commercial Youth (1907)
- workers' education and self-help; the Union of Catholic Workers' Societies and the Polish Professional Association (1902)
- cooperatives: the Union of Business and Farming Partnerships (1871); the Bank of the Union of Business Partnerships (1886)
- folk culture and physical education: the Society of Popular Reading Rooms (1880); the Union of Singing Societies (1892)
- scientific research: the Society of the Friends of Science (1857)
- training and education of young people: the Society of Scientific Help (1841); secret student organisations in secondary schools; student organisations in German university centres; the *Sokół* Union (1893).[20]

After 1890 increasing differentiation characterised the Polish national movement. For instance separate political parties were created. The National Democratic Society, which already had many adherents several years before its official founding in 1909, enjoyed the greatest support. The society was a cadre based party that mainly attracted members of the intelligentsia and the lower middle class. Landowners grouped themselves together in conservative organisations: the National Union of 1910 and the Citizen's Centre of 1912.

The Polish Socialist Party in the Prussian partition did not secure many adherents though the German Social Democratic party supported its Polish counterpart financially. The largest mass based political organisation was the 'Watch', founded in 1905, which sought to defend Polish economic and civil rights. By 1907 it numbered 22 000 members.

Estimates by W. Jakóbczyk indicate that Polish organisations in 1890 embraced almost 50 000 men, meaning that very large numbers of Polish families in the Grand Duchy of Poznań were continuously exposed to the cultural and educational influence of the national spirit.[21] Thus in Phase C the Polish national movement had an ever expanding mass based character. Most ethnic economic, cultural and educational organisations formed a dense network in precisely those areas inhabited by a Polish majority. They operated effectively and pursued a programme that was attractive to the masses. Polish credit and savings unions in the lands under Prussian rule were among the best in Europe at the beginning of the twentieth century. By 1913, at the height of the development of the organised defence of national interests, the movement had achieved a high degree of mobilisation of the masses. Marian Seyda, the editor of the widely read *Poznanian Currier*, estimated at the time that approximately 140 000 people actively participated in the movement.[22] Assuming that these people were the heads of four to five member families, approximately half a million or about 40 per cent of the Grand Duchy's Poles found themselves under the direct influence of this movement.

Prior to examining the group of activists in the national movement it is essential to resolve questions of terminology. Activists are defined as individuals who performed different functions in the national movement extending from its lowest to highest ranks. This categorisation includes leaders of different types of national societies and institutions and also people such as newspaper distributors and organisers of protest actions, patriotic celebrations and collectors of money. Because of source deficiencies the expansion of patriotic participation can only be reconstructed approximately. Towards the end of Phase A in 1828 around 50 representatives of the landowners and wealthier *szlachta* guided the Polish national movement. The generation which became active in the second phase was a much larger group which grew gradually. Lists drawn up by the Prussian authorities during the Poznanian uprising of 1848 include names of about 600 Polish activists.[23] This information is incomplete however. Around 1890 according to W. Jakóbczyk, the 'guiding element' of the Polish national movement 'could have amounted to' no more than 2000 individuals and by 1914, 3–4000.[24] An American historian, W.W. Hagen, estimated the size of the Polish elite in 1914 at about 3000.[25] However these figures are somewhat too high. Hagen mistakenly includes over 100 German Catholic priests as well as all landowners even though a significant proportion of them did not play any part in the Polish national movement. Thus the Polish activists in the Grand Duchy of Poznań would have consisted of approximately 1500 individuals in 1890 and around 2500 in 1914.

It is very difficult to reconstruct the occupational profile of the activists because the source material is not illuminating on this topic. In the first column in Table 2.2 below[26] a small group of Polish leaders has been omitted due to the lack of source material. In the second column, derived from an incomplete list drawn up by Prussian officials, only the most influential activists in the third phase have been included.

Table 2.2: The professional and social profile of activists in the Polish national movement in the Grand Duchy of Poznań

Profession	1841–44		1905–6	
	#	%	#	%
Landowners	82	64.1	79	20.8
Intelligentsia	35	27.3	218	57.4
priests	5		63	
physicians	6		38	
lawyers	2		13	
journalists	1		17	
white collar workers	8		56	
booksellers	4		5	
others	9		26	
Lower middle class	10	7.8	76	20.0
traders/businessmen	3		56	
handworkers	6		10	
others	1		10	
Peasants	1	0.8	2	0.5
Workers	–	–	3	0.8
Unknown	–	–	2	0.5
Total	128	100	380	100

During the first four decades of the nineteenth century representatives of the *szlachta* directed the development of the national movement. Virtually all Polish organisations – both legal and secret – acted under their direction. In the 1840s however they gradually lost their dominant position in political and social life. Polish landed society irretrievably lost its hegemony during the government of Chancellor Leo Caprivi (1890–4). Anticipating introduction of less rigid germanisation policies a majority of Polish gentry remained loyal to the Prussian state. However only insignificant and short lived concessions were made. As a consequence the authority of the landowning class was shaken. Losses incurred by landowners during the struggle with Germans over land also contributed to a decline in their social prestige. Despite relatively slow numerical growth the intelligentsia from the 1840s began to supply the Polish national movement with an increasing number of activists. This social group had its origins chiefly in the bourgeoisie and peasantry but with the passage of time it began to reproduce itself. Only about 15 per cent of the Polish intelligentsia had its origins in the *szlachta*.[27] Catholic priests were the most numerous group within the intelligentsia (470 in 1841; *circa* 700 in 1870 and 1910). Many of them participated vigorously in the national movement, directing various types of organisations. After 1870 a further considerable growth in the social activity of Polish priests took place during the *Kulturkampf* (cultural campaign). Physicians formed the second most numerous group within the intelligentsia and their numerical growth accelerated from ten in 1841 to 201 in 1912. The percentage of physicians active in the national movement was also notable. Journalists were also prominent. At the time editors of periodicals automatically had different public functions. Among the 103 journalists for whom adequate information is available as many as 88, or 85 per cent, played a significant role in the national movement.[28] Polish lawyers, apothecaries, artists and engineers were involved in small numbers. For this reason their activity in the movement was less evident.

Initially very few leading activists came from the lower middle class. This group did not begin to display larger social aspirations until the turn of the twentieth century when its economic situation began to improve and members became more successful competitors with Germans. The lower middle class began gradually to fill more positions in national organisations. In 1896 members of the intelligentsia still led 38 or 52 per cent of the 73 industrial societies whose presidents can be identified. Several years later the situation was reversed. In 1908 only 39 chairmen of these societies (30 per cent) came from the intelligentsia whereas 92 or 70 per cent were from the lower middle class.[29] The participation of handworkers and traders however remained modest in relation to their numbers.

Peasants, despite improvements in their economic situation, were underrepresented among activists. Peasant organisations (agricultural clubs) were under the control of priests and landowners. As a result of the continuous existence of these clubs and their participation in congresses and agricultural exhibits a group of peasant activists, which was 'organisationally efficient, tied to the land, the language, customs, national solidarity, and social and political conservatism', took form.[30] Yet as late as 1905 peasant farmers were the chairmen of only 84 or 30 per cent of 276 agricultural clubs. Their participation in other organisations also grew slowly.

Some urban and rural workers belonged to Polish religious, professional and educational organisations, especially Catholic workers' societies which in 1913 had a membership of approximately 30 000. At the turn of the twentieth century a group of worker activists came into existence engaging in social activity on a modest scale under the supervision of priests. The socialist movement was very weak in the Grand Duchy of Poznań and independent workers' leaders were only a tiny segment of the national movement.[31] Members of the lower middle class, peasantry and working classes had only minor positions in the leadership of the national movement. The proportion of leaders drawn from their ranks increased gradually. However by the beginning of the twentieth century this participation reached significant levels. At this time Prussian authorities drew up full lists of the Polish activists in all districts of the Grand Duchy. Lists for 12 districts have survived, and the four most representative have been scrutinised to compile the table below.[32]

Table 2.3: Professional and social profile of activists in the Polish national movement in selected districts of the Grand Duchy of Poznań in 1910

	district				
Profession	Bydgoszcz*	Moglino	Ostrów	Środa	Total
Landowners	2	2	3	6	13
Intelligentsia	25	13	27	14	79
priests	4	6	11	9	30
physicians	6	3	1	1	11
lawyers	1	–	2	1	4
journalists/writers	2	–	1	1	4
white collar workers	6	3	9	2	20
others	6	1	3	–	10
Lower middle class	16	29	20	18	83
traders/businessmen	5	9	7	5	26
handworkers	7	15	9	11	42
others	4	5	4	2	15
Peasants	–	2	18	5	25
Workers	2	–	7	1	10
Total	45	46	75	44	210

* does not include women in this district

A number of obstacles hindered the advancement of representatives of the lower middle class, peasantry and the working class into the upper echelons of the national movement. They had restricted leisure time and lacked the financial means necessary for extensive public activity. Polish members of the *Landtag* did not receive salaries and had to pay personally for their stays in Berlin which meant that only landowners, priests and lawyers were able to afford this kind of role. Furthermore the exercise of leadership functions demanded a thorough education and a good knowledge of German and of the Prussian legal system. These requirements also placed landowners and members of the intelligentsia in an advantageous position.

In terms of educational background the activists were a varied group. Members of the intelligentsia and gentry often held degrees from higher institutions of learning or at least certificates from secondary school classes. Almost all were educated in German secondary establishments and universities. Activists who had studied for a long time at the polonised universities in Cracow and Lvov or at French, Swiss or English universities were exceptional. Poles who wished to enter into a profession requiring education in the Grand Duchy of Poznań had only limited options. Only graduates of German universities were permitted to enter the law, medical and pharmacological professions. A secondary school education meant that a young man had to serve only one year instead of three in the army – a not insignificant factor. Sons of landowners who had the necessary funds for further academic wanderings studied at German universities as well. A feeling that a lengthy stay at such universities would enable the student 'to spy from within' on the organisation and functioning of the Prussian state and thus offer a good preparation for future participation in public life was very widespread among Poles. Polish activists with a higher education had most frequently studied at the universities of Breslau, Berlin, Greifswald, Halle, Leipzig and Munich. Priests were products of seminaries in Poznań and Gniezno. Only a few of them had attended universities in Breslau, Münster, Bonn, Munich and Würzburg. During their residence at German universities the majority of the activists belonged to and led Polish student organisations. Through independent study they deepened their knowledge of Polish literature and history acquiring also organisational experience which would prove useful in future social and political activity.[33]

It is difficult to establish how many of the activists could boast of a higher education and how many possessed merely a primary school certificate. Only very meagre information about many of them exists. Peasants, members of the lower middle class and those workers who were active in the lowest cells of the Polish organisational system had only a basic education which they supplemented through special courses and meetings. A majority of activists working on the district and provincial level possessed a higher education or at least a secondary school diploma. This education however was not without deficiencies, particularly in contemporary political and social studies. Not all Polish activists understood the Prussian political system thoroughly nor were they all familiar with existing legislative and economic issues. Some contemporary critics accused them of insufficient preparation for a public career and encouraged their further education through independent study. Polish activists searched for models worthy of imitation among other national minorities. In the 1820s and 1830s they followed with interest the development of the Irish nationalist movement and established contact with Daniel O'Connell. During the second half of the century they observed the activities of the Czechs. Czechs were also economic rivals to Germans and Poles sought to emulate this example. Further research is necessary in this field however.

Poznań remained the main centre of the Polish national movement. Major Polish organisations and publications had their headquarters in this city. Most important administrative departments and economic institutions also were located in Poznań, which was in addition the centre of religious life and Church administration. The significance of the city lay mainly in its geographical location in the centre of the Polish lands under Prussian rule. Activists formed significantly smaller centres in some district capitals such as Ostrów / Ostrowo, Gniezno / Gnesen, Šrem / Schrimm, Wągrowiec / Wongrowitz, Inowrocław / Hohensalza, Krotoszyn / Krotoschin, and Września/Wreschen. Local groups tended to be dominated by priests, landowners and less frequently lawyers, journalists, white collar workers, traders, wealthy artisans and peasants. In many areas individual priests or physicians directed or supported the activity of several organisations simultaneously.

The advance of the national movement in the Grand Duchy of Poznań was a consequence of the close links between the elite and the masses of the Polish population. The press had a crucial function. From the end of the eighteenth century (with a pause in the 1850s) there was a gradual escalation in the number of Polish periodicals. Between 1846 and 1848 there were 21 Polish publications in the Grand Duchy while 18 could be found in 1885. Before the outbreak of the First World War there were as many as 70 Polish dailies, weeklies and monthlies. Because of the dearth of information it is very difficult to estimate the circulation of these publications, particularly for the period before 1890. In 1898 65 000 copies of Polish periodicals were published in the Grand Duchy and 180 000 in 1906.[34] These periodicals had varying degrees of sophistication depending upon the interests and education of their readership. A majority were general information publications. Literary and satirical periodicals were scarce and did not survive for long. Periodicals aimed at the lower middle class, peasantry and working classes enjoyed the largest circulations (the *Catholic Guide* published 80 000 copies in 1910; the *Worker* published 30 000 copies in 1913). By the turn of the twentieth century Polish illiteracy had practically been eradicated. Normally several people would read each copy of a periodical, and thus the influence of the Polish press in the Grand Duchy at this time was substantial. Articles devoted to the problems of the Polish national movement, information on political and social affairs (including events in the Russian and Austrian partitions) and reports on patriotic celebrations filled the pages. In addition the press gave close attention to the activities of Polish delegates in the Prussian *Landtag* and the German *Reichstag*. It also reprinted reports released by Polish organisations. Appeals and protest actions were announced through the press. Many columns were given to legal, economic and educational advice.

After 1870 public meetings became an important means of communication for the national movement. They also represented an important form of protest against germanisation and the Prussian authorities' attack on the Catholic Church (during the *Kulturkampf*). Several thousand people from across the social spectrum participated in mass demonstrations. During such meetings many speakers denounced Prussian policies towards national minorities and reaffirmed the rights of the Poles. Appeals were made to behave in a legal fashion but also to wage their campaign in a spirit of national solidarity. Rallies served the leaders as a forum for transmitting ideals and information. For the masses they also provided a degree of moral support. Finally public meetings strengthened Polish solidarity which the propertied classes often exploited in their struggle with the workers' movement.[35]

The Polish national movement organised patriotic celebrations as a way of enhancing national sentiment. Initially these celebrations took place as religious services commemorating the deaths of outstanding Poles (such as Tadeusz Kościuszko and Adam Mickiewicz) and the anniversaries of national uprisings. Beginning in 1870 these celebrations were expanded to include speeches and artistic programmes. Large numbers of Poles participated in these celebrations. For example 6000 took part in 1894 in the Poznań centenary commemorations of the Kościuszko uprising. In small cities and villages the number of participants fluctuated between 100 and 200. Leaders of the national movement fully understood the significance of these occasions. 'National celebrations', claimed a contemporary publication, 'are the best school in which the Polish people learn to love their fatherland and to appreciate traditions and customs . . ., they [celebrations] propagate fondness for the native tongue and protect the young from denationalisation'.[36]

The Catholic Church played a crucial role as a channel of communication. A great majority of Poles regularly participated in religious observances. Priests, who were often – as mentioned above – social activists, used the pulpit to convey views on elections to the Prussian parliament, meetings and celebrations. Such priests encouraged participation in the Polish national movement. Brochures and flyers also were printed in large numbers. Such material linked national aims with religious emotions, for example the 'Ten Polish National Commandments' and the 'Seven Deadly Polish Sins'. Polish activists often met in their favourite restaurants and cafes in order to exchange opinions and news, though less so in clubs and casinos, which were usually open only for a few years (an exception here was the Scientific Circle in Poznań established in 1841). They also held meetings in the buildings of the most widely read publications in order to debate political issues and reach decisions. In small cities and villages the local elites generally met in the parish church after Sunday mass.

Political Ideas and Historical Consciousness

The vision of Poland regaining independence underlay everything the leaders of the national movement in the Grand Duchy of Poznań propagated. These leaders were divided between those advocates of an armed struggle for independence and the so-called 'organic workers' on timing and method. 'Organic workers' appealed for the implementation of the decisions by the Congress of Vienna by legal tactics and attempted to force from the Prussian authorities adherence to the promises in Frederick Wilhelm III's occupation document of 15 May 1815. Recognition that this tactic was ineffective after 1871 inspired some to ground Polish demands on the rights of Prussian citizenship. In later years an enlarging section of activists called for the middle class and the peasantry to take a greater part in public life and to become involved in the struggle with Prussia. Advocates of an armed insurrection joined 'organic workers' in emphasising the need for the masses to develop a historical consciousness. This consciousness was nurtured by circulating popular historical books, particularly those written by Józef Chociszewski which gave an easily understood version of national ideas. His writing was reinforced in other publications, for instance reproductions of historical paintings and plates by well known Polish artists. Anniversaries of important events from Polish history were celebrated, and patriotic rallies and religious nationalist Church services were organised. Formation of historical consciousness was facilitated by well known folk tales, epic poems and myths about the origins of their community.

Various periods of Polish history were attractive for different groups. In historical studies and literary and artistic works, early Slavonic themes were stressed. It was seen to provide an ancient pedigree for Polish culture and statehood and such ideals as freedom, equality and fraternity, the current preoccupations of national activists. They also turned to early Slavic times to find the bases to formulate the idea of the nation and to construct alternatively a democratic or a monarchic concept of the political system and social relations. Later periods of Polish history were alleged to demonstrate how their society was unified by an armed repulsion of foreign enemies. Examples for military victories and sacrifices made for the homeland like that of Grunwald in 1410; the Swedish invasion of 1655; the wars with Turkey in the seventeenth century; and the Bar Confederation of 1768–72 were given. Among recent events the Kościuszko Insurrection of 1794; participation of the Polish legions in the Napoleonic Wars; the November uprising of 1830–1; the events of the Spring of Nations in 1848, and the January uprising of 1863 all received special recognition.

Patriotism was exemplified by historical personalities like Stefan Żółkiewski, a *hetman* (commander-in-chief) who died in the battle of Cecora against the Turks in 1620; Stefan Czarnecki, commander of the Polish army during the Swedish invasion of 1655; King Jan III Sobieski; Tadeusz Kościuszko; Prince Józef Poniatowski; and Napoleon. Cults for these men were begun and tokens or objects that had belonged to them or had been connected with their activities as well as their portraits and miniatures were collected. For later generations of activists during Phase C examples worthy of emulation were famous early leaders of the Polish national movement in the Grand Duchy of Poznań, particularly Karol Marcinkowski, a physician who inspired and founded important institutions at the beginning of the 1840s; Hipolit Cegielski, a secondary school teacher and founder of an agricultural machinery enterprise and an active member of numerous Polish organisations; and General Dezydery Chłapowski, a landed gentleman, politician and advocate of technological progress in agriculture.

The Prussian Authorities and Polish National Activists

For an extended period the Prussian authorities regarded the Polish *szlachta* and clergy as the main element opposing the integration of the Grand Duchy of Poznań into the Hohenzollern monarchy. Even at the end of the nineteenth century they did not comprehend the danger to Prussian rule in the province posed by the small Polish middle class and the poor passive peasantry. As a result they sought to weaken numerically and economically the Polish landowners. After 1830 the Prussian authorities quickly ousted the Polish aristocracy from the position of *Landräte* (county administrators). They imposed high penalties for participation in the November uprising of 1830–1. The state also established a special fund designed to promote the acquisition of landholdings from Polish owners and accelerated land reform in an effort to win the support of the peasantry.[37] These measures, however, were not completely effective. Although the amount of land in the hands of the *szlachta* did – as has been demonstrated in the second section above – decrease rapidly, the embattled gentry retained its hegemony over Polish society and continued to form a significant portion of its elite. Relatively few of the Polish *szlachta* were denationalised and became Prussian officials or diplomats.

The Prussian authorities also did not have at their disposal means by which to limit the role of Catholic priests in the national movement. Contrary to their expectations priests were not denationalised in the largely germanised seminaries in Gniezno and Poznań or while students at German universities. Attempts to increase the number of German priests proved unsuccessful. The overwhelming majority of Germans in the Grand Duchy of Poznań were Protestant. Despite financial encouragement in the form of scholarships very few Germans attended the two seminaries. The percentage of German priests among the Catholic clergy in the Grand Duchy remained constant at about 15 per cent.[38] In this situation the Prussian authorities endeavoured to minimalise the social and political activity of Polish priests. The effectiveness of such efforts depended on the attitude of the local archbishops. Sometimes Church officials succumbed to pressure from the Prussian government and issued decrees prohibiting priests from participating in Polish organisations; however they also prevented the priests from being removed from social and political life. Church leaders simply could not violate the interests and ignore the expectations of that Polish population which represented the overwhelming majority of Roman Catholics in the province.

Within Prussian ruling circles the view that it would be impossible for Polish officials to reconcile their service to the state with representation of their own people was widespread. Thus Poles were systematically removed from the administration and judiciary. After 1870 it was impossible for Poles to enter mid and upper level government posts. Prussian authorities adopted a similar attitude towards Polish secondary school teachers. Initially they had not hindered Poles who wanted to teach in secondary schools. As a result the teaching profession had become increasingly popular among the Polish youth. In 1870 approximately 70 Poles taught in secondary schools in the Grand Duchy of Poznań. Many of them also supported the Polish national movement – to the disquiet of the Prussian authorities. Hence in 1874 they began to relocate Polish teachers to schools in central and western Germany or to encourage them to retire prematurely. Eventually they succeeded in eliminating Polish secondary school teachers entirely.[39] The Prussian authorities did not however succeed in abolishing Polish teachers from primary schools as many such positions remained vacant because this low paid sector did not attract German candidates. After denying the clergy control over primary education in 1872 Prussian authorities subjected Polish teachers to close control and forced them to carry out the germanisation decrees. A majority of Polish teachers, particularly in rural schools and fearful of 'being removed from office', eagerly carried out the authorities' instructions and often concealed their Polishness. Thus their participation in Polish public life was very modest.

The Prussian authorities exercised relatively little influence on the development of other groups within the Polish intelligentsia that encompassed the so-called free professions. Constitutional pro-visions and other laws limited interference. Physicians had the right to settle where they chose and were independent of local authorities. In 1879 lawyers also acquired this privilege. They only had to find a clientele capable of supporting them. Harassment by the Prussian authorities aimed at eliminating journalists, lower middle class or peasant activists from the national movement proved ineffectual. Thus despite intense efforts Prussia was not able to deprive Polish society in the Grand Duchy of Poznań of its leaders. Through the elimination of certain groups (particularly government officials and teachers), however, they influenced the development of the pro-fessional structure of Polish society.

State of Research

Despite the many accomplishments of Polish, German and more recently American historians, the current state of research on the Grand Duchy of Poznań is not completely satisfactory. For a long time political questions attracted the bulk of researchers' attention.[40] Historians did not begin to investigate economic transformations, ideological trends and cultural changes until after 1945. In Polish historiography and even more so in its German counterpart, works concerned with the Prussian *Polenpolitik*, Polish society's legal forms of struggle with germanisation, the Prussian Poles' participation in national uprisings and the formation of political parties occupy a dominant place. In addition researchers' efforts have been given to agricultural and industrial development, the transportation and the labour market, the workers' movement and the economic struggle between Poles and Germans. Valuable studies on literary history, painting and architecture have been published as well.[41]

To date however numerous issues have escaped systematic attention. Questions dealing with legal and political structures have been studied insufficiently. The same holds true for the examination of social and political consciousness. The history of the Catholic and Protestant Churches in the Grand Duchy of Poznań has only been examined partially. There is a serious lack of general monographs devoted to the Polish press and the development of a historical consciousness. Synthetic studies on the development of education are only partly illuminating. The results of research on the social history of Poles in the Grand Duchy are very modest. Currently only monographs concerned with the working class and the formation of the Polish intelligentsia exist.[42] The remaining social classes, in other words the gentry, the lower middle class and the peasantry, still await study. Researchers also have failed to examine the activists of the Polish national movement.

The actual quantity of the sources related to the history of the Grand Duchy of Poznań is relatively rich and varied. Over 5000 metres of archival materials located in the Regional State Archive in Poznań constitute the heart of this primary source collection, though serious gaps exist due to a fire in the building housing the archives in January 1945. A rich assembly of archival materials dealing with the north eastern part of the duchy can be found in the Regional State Archive in Bydgoszcz. Sources located in foreign archives also have significant value. The German Central State Archive in Merseburg houses an almost complete collection of documents produced by the central Prussian authorities. Thousands of documents belonging to this collection deal with all aspects of the Polish question in the eastern provinces of Prussia.[43] Documents stored in the German Central Archive in Potsdam and in the State Archive in Berlin–Dahlem contain much valuable information. Furthermore church documents from the period of Prussian rule have survived in the archdiocesan archives in Poznań and Gniezno. Other useful archival sources can be found in the library of the Poznanian Society of the Friends of Science as well as other libraries in Warzawa, Kraków and Wrocław. Among printed sources there are contemporary publications which contain articles dealing with the problems of the Polish national movement and regional reports issued by various Polish organisations. Official publications – law books, statistical collections, reports of central and provincial authorities and official announcements – are important sources of information. Memoirs are considerably less extensive.

Scholars interested in the history of the Grand Duchy of Poznań have ample sources, although wartime destruction makes it impossible to study all topics exhaustively.

Notes

1 Bernhard, p.8.
2 Hagen, p. 324.
3 Dunin-Wąsowicz, part 1, p. 575.
4 Grześ, pp. 23–4.
5 Topolski, pp. 271–82.
6 Wegener, p. 124.
7 Molik (1979), p. 67.
8 Jaworski, p. 34.
9 Jakóbczyk (1969), part II, p. 7.
10 *Ibid.*, p. 6.
11 Rezler, pp. 284–6.
12 For further information on this topic see Paprocki (1970), *passim*; Baske (1963), *passim*.
13 Trzeciakowski (1973), p. 300.
14 See Galos, *passim*.
15 Salmonowicz, p. 455.
16 Hroch.
17 Grot (1983), p. 21.
18 Kieniewicz, *passim*.
19 Grot (1963), p. 199.
20 Jakóbczyk (1951–67).
21 Jakóbczyk (1987), p. 47.
22 Seyda.
23 Paprocki (1948), pp. 26–49.
24 Jakóbczyk (1951–67), vol. III, p. 238.
25 Hagen, p. 257.
26 Source, file on Polish activists in the national movement in the Grand Duchy of Poznań that belongs to the author's private collection and *'Acta betreff. das Verzeichnis derjenigen Personen, welche als Führer und Organisationen auf politischem Gebiete in Frage kommen'*, located in the *Wojewódzkie Archiwum Państwowe w Poznaniu Prezydium Policji* [State Archive in the Adminstrative District of Poznań Presidium of the Police] (cited in future as WAPP PP) 3499, pp. 52–69.
27 Molik (1979), p. 88.
28 Molik (1983), p. 180.
29 Trzeciakowski (1964), pp. 51–73.
30 Jakóbczyk (1987), p. 46.
31 At the beginning of the twentieth century the Prussian authorities identified only 18 Polish and German socialist leaders in the Grand Duchy of Poznań; 13 of them were handworkers and four were members of the intelligentsia. In addition there was one tradesman and one worker. WAPP PP 3499, pp. 174–6.
32 *Acta betreffend die polnische Bewegung in den Kreisen: Bromberg, Mogilno, Ostrowo, Schroda,* WAPP PP 2750, pp. 85–7, 225–6, 277–8, 304–40; WAPP PP 2766, pp. 4–12; WAPP PP 2768, pp. 5–16; WAPP PP 2777, pp. 133–8.

33 Molik (1989), pp. 154–81.
34 Molik (1983), p. 136.
35 Trzeciakowski (1964), p. 149.
36 Paprocki (1973), p. 139.
37 Trzeciakowski (1973), p. 234.
38 Bończa-Bystrzycki, p. 66.
39 Molik (1991), p. 74.
40 Trzeciakowski (1984), p. 134.
41 Grot (1973), pp. 881–908.
42 Molik (1979); Szulc.
43 Paprocki (1973), pp. 855–70.

Select Bibliography

Baske, Siegfried (1963), *Praxis und Prinzipien der preussischen Polenpolitik vom Beginn der Reaktionszeit bis zur Gründung des deutschen Reiches*, Berlin.

Bernhard, Ludwig (1920), *Die Polenfrage. Der Nationalitätenkampf der Polen in Preussen*, Munich.

Blanke, Richard (1981), *Prussian Poland in the German Empire 1871–1900*, New York.

Bończa-Bystrzycki, L. (1986), *Duchowieństwo polskie Kościoła Rzymsko–Katolickiego w Wielkopolsce w latach 1815–1918* (The Polish Clergy of the Roman Catholic Church in Greater Poland 1815–1918), Koszalin.

Broszat, Martin (1963), *Zweihundert Jahre deutscher Polenpolitik*, Munich.

Buzek, Józéf (1909), *Historia polityki narodowościowei rządu pruskiego wobec Polaków. Od traktatów wiedeńskich do ustaw wyjątkowych z r. 1908* (History of the Nationalities' Policy of the Prussian Government towards the Poles. From the Vienna Conventions to the extraordinary laws of 1908), Lwów.

Dunin-Wasowicz, Karol (1960), 'Liczebność i rozmieszczenie narodu polskiego w 1864–1914' (Quantity and Distribution of the Polish People 1864–1914), in Kormanowa, Z. and Pietrzak-Pawłowska, I., (eds), *Dzieje Polski*, vol. III, part I, 1850/1864–1900, Warsaw.

Galos, Adam, Gentzen, Felix-Heinrich and Jakóbczyk, Witold (1966), *Dzieje Hakaty* (History of the *Ostmarken–Verein* (Eastern Marches Association)), Poznań.

Gentzen, Felix-Heinrich (1958), *Grosspolen im Januaraufstand. Das Grossherzogtum Posen 1858–1864*, Berlin.

Grot, Zdzisław (1973), 'Badania dziejów Wielkopolski okresu zaborów' (Studies on the History of Greater Poland in the Period of Partition), Jacóbczyk (ed), *Dzieje*.

Grot, Zdzisław (1963), *Rok 1863 w zaborze pruskim* (1863 in the Prussian Part of the Polish Territory), Poznań.

Grot, Zdzisław (1983), 'Wojskowy wkład Wielkiego Księstwa Poznańskiego w roku 1831' (The Military Contribution of the Grand Duchy of Poznań in 1831), in Trzeciakowki, L. (ed.), *Powstanie listopadowe a problem świadomości historycznej* (The November Insurrection and the Problem of Historical Consciousness), Poznań.

Grześ, Bolesław, Kozłowski, Jerzy and Kramski, Aleksander (1976), *Niemcy w Poznańskiem wobec polityki germanizacyjnej 1815–1920* (The Germans in the Region of Poznań and the Policy of Germanisation 1815–1920), Poznań.

Hagen, William W. (1980), *Germans, Poles and Jews. The Nationality Conflict in the Prussian East 1772–1914*, Chicago.

Hroch, Miroslav (1968), *Die Vorkämpfer der nationalen Bewegungen bei den kleinen Völkern Europas*, Praha.

Jaffe, Moritz (1909), *Die Stadt Posen unter preussischer Herschaft*, Leipzig.

Jakóbczyk, Witold (ed.) (1973), *Dzieje Wielkopolski* (History of Greater Poland), vol. 2 1793–1918, Poznań.

Jakóbczyk, Witold (1987), 'Jeszcze o pracy organicznej' (Still on Organic Work), *Życie i Myśl*, nos 7–8.

Jakóbczyk, Witold (1976), *Pruska komisja osadnicza 1886–1919*. (The Prussian Colonisation Commission), Poznań.

Jakóbczyk, Witold (1951–67), *Studia nad dziejami Wielkopolski w XIX wieku* (Studies in the History of Greater Poland in the nineteenth century), vol. 1–3, Poznań.

Jakóbczyk, Witold (ed.) (1969), *Wiekopolanie XIX w.* (Greater Poland in the nineteenth century), Poznań.

Jaworski, Rudolf (1986), *Handel und Gewerbe im Nationalitätenkampf. Studien zur Wirtschaftsgesinnung der Polen in der Provinz Posen*, Göttingen.

Kieniewicz, Stefan (1960), *Społeczeństwo polskie w powstaniu poznańskim 1848 roku* (Polish Society during the Poznań Insurrection of 1848), Warsaw.

Kulczycki, John J. (1981), *School Strikes in Prussian Poland, 1901–1907: The Struggle Over Bilingual Education*, New York.

Laubert, Manfred (1920), *Die preussische Polenpolitik von 1772-1914*, Breslau.

Laubert, Manfred (1923), *Die Verwaltung der Provinz Posen 1815–1847*, Breslau.

Łuczak, Czesław (1960), *Przemyst Wielkopolski w latach 1871–1914* (Industry in Greater Poland 1871–1914), Warsaw.

Mai, Joachim (1962), *Die preussisch-deutsche Polenpolitik 1885–1887. Eine Studie zur Herausbildung des Imperialismus in Deutschland*, Berlin.

Marczewski, Jerzy (1967), *Narodowa Demokracja w Poznańskiem 1900–1914* (National Democracy in the Poznań Region 1900–1914), Warsaw.

Mitscherlich, Waldemar (1913), *Die Ausbreitung der Polen in Preussen*, Leipzig.

Molik, Witold (1991), 'Der Einfluss der preussischen Politik auf die Gesellschaftsstruktur des Grossherzogtums Posen (1815–1914), Polnische Intelligenz als Vorbild', in Nitsche, P. (ed.), *Kieler Werkstücke. Reihe F: Beiträge zur osteuropäischn Geschichte Band 1*, Frankfurt am Main.

Molik, Witold (1983), 'Dziennikarze polscy pod panowaniem pruskim 1890–1914 (próba charakteryski)' (Polish Journalists during the Prussian Domination, Attempts at a Characterisation), in Czepulis-Rastenis, R. (ed.), *Inteligencja polska XIX i XX wieku. Studia, 3*, Warsaw.

Molik, Witold (1979), *Kształtowanie się inteligencji polskiej w Wielkim Ksiestwie Poznańskim 1841–1870* (The Formation of the Polish Intelligentsia in the Grand Duchy of Poznań 1841–1870), Warsaw.

Molik, Witold (1989), *Polskie peregrynacje uniwersyteckie do Niemiec 1871–1914* (The Polish Academic Migration to Germany 1871–1914), Poznań.

Paprocki, Franciszek (1970), *Wielkie Księstwo Poznańskie w okresie rządów Flotwella (1830–1841)* (The Grand Duchy of Poznań in the Period of the Flottwell Government), Poznań.

Paprocki, Franciszek (1948), 'Wykazy imienne członków powiatowych i lokalnych Komitetów Narodowych w Wielkopolsce w 1848 r.' (Register of the First Names of the Members of the District and Local National Committees in Greater Poland in 1848), *Kronika Miasta Poznania*, no. 1.

Paprocki, Franciszek (1973), 'Zródła do dziejów Wielkopolski w okresie porozbiorowym' (Sources for the History of Greater Poland in the Period after Partition), Jakobczyk (ed.), *Dzieje*.

Rezler, Julius (1980), 'Economic and Social Differentiation and Ethnicity: The Case of Eastern Europe', in Sugar, P. (ed.), *Ethnic Diversity and Conflict in Eastern Europe*, Oxford.

Rosenthal, Henry K. (1976), *German and Pole. National Conflict and Modern Myth*, Gainesville.

Salmonowicz, Stanisław (1987), *Prusy. Dzieje państwa i społeczeństwa* (Prussia. A History of State and Society), Poznań.

Seyda, Marian (1910), 'Nasze kresy' (Our Border Territories), *Kurier Poznański*, no. 104.

Streiter, Karl-Heink (1986), *Die nationalen Beziehungen im Grossherzogtum Posen (1815–1848)*, Bern.

Stüttgen, Dieter (1975), 'Provinz (Grossherzogtum) Posen', in Hubatsch, W. (ed.), *Grundriss zur deutschen Verwaltungsgeschichte 1815–1945*, Reihe A, vol. 2, Marburg.

Szulc, Witold (1970), *Położenie klasy robotniczej w Wielkopolsce w latach 1871–1918* (The State of the Working Class in Greater Poland 1871–1918), Poznań.

Topolski, Jerzy (1977), *Gospodarka polska a europejska w XVI–XVIII wieku* (The Polish and European Economies in the sixteenth to eighteenth centuries), Poznań.

Trzeciakowski, Lech (1970), *Kulturkamf w zaborze pruskim* (The *Kulturkampf* in the Part of Poland Occupied by Prussia), Poznań.

Trzeciakowski, Lech (1973), *Pod pruskim zaborem 1850–1918* (Under Prussian Occupation 1850–1918), Poznań.

Trzeciakowski, Lech (1984), 'Polityka Prus na polskich ziemiach zachodnich w XIX w. W historiografii polskiej i niemieckiej' (The Politics of Prussia in the Polish Western Territories in the Nineteenth Century. In Polish and German Historiography), *Stosunki polsko–niemieckie w historiografii* (Polish–German Relations in Historiography), part II, Poznań.

Trzeciakowski, Lech (1964), 'Towarzystwa Przemysłowe' (Industrial Association), in Grot, Z. (ed.), *Polityczna działalność rzemiosła wielkopolskiego w okresie zaborów (1793–1918)* (Political Activities of the Craftsmen in Greater Poland in the Period of the Partitions), Poznań.

Trzeciakowski, Lech (1964), *Walka o polskość miast Poznańskiego na przełomie XIX i XX wieku* (The struggle of the Polishness of the Poznańian towns at the end of the nineteenth and the beginning of the twentieth century), Poznań.

Wegener, Leo (1903), *Die wirtschaftliche Kampf der Deutschen mit den Polen um die Provinz Posen*, Poznań.

Map 2.1   The Grand Duchy of Poznań c. 1900

3 Ireland's Catholics in the British State, 1850–1922

ALAN O'DAY

Introduction

'Our rights and liberties have been trampled on by an alien aristocracy, who treating us as foes, usurped our land, and drew away from our country all material riches' declaimed the Fenian proclamation of a provisional government during the abortive and swiftly suppressed rising in 1867.[1] Near the close of the period Patrick Pearse, president of the Provisional Republic in 1916 and one of those executed for his role in the Easter Rebellion, put his country's woes down to English domination.[2] Nationalism throughout its existence in Ireland has been replete with a rhetoric blaming the physical occupation of the country by England for all manner of evils. They were not alone. Prominent British leaders frequently confirmed the Irish view. Politicians as different as David Lloyd George and Arthur Balfour acknowledged that Ireland had suffered neglect, that the Catholic Irish had not received completely equal treatment.[3]

Catholic Ireland within the British *imperium* is a classic instance of non-dominance – of a small peoples' quest to break the thraldom of a mighty neighbour. In economic, social and cultural life as well as in formal political arrangements the long shadow of British supremacy lay heavily over Ireland. But non-dominance in Ireland was above all a psychological condition. Throughout the period of the union (1801–1921) there were successive cadres of men who were determined to throw off the yoke of English rule or at the very least to modify its effect on their country. After 1867 the effort to moderate the balance between Britain and Ireland and within Ireland itself was pursued with increased intensity gaining telling results. The national struggle is a tale of how an Irish elite evolved, articulated its aspirations, persuaded and mobilised the masses and ultimately conducted a successful assault on the integrity of the United Kingdom.

Most people in Ireland perceived themselves as being in some measure colonial subjects. Non-dominance, however, has a narrower application in the Irish experience. Irish Protestants, especially those who belonged to confessions other than the Church of Ireland, were in critical respects non-dominant. Yet in general Protestants of all sorts occupied a niche in Ireland which distinguished them from Catholics. Although there were many attempts over the whole era to blend the separate religious traditions into a common nationality, relatively few found the cleavage easy to cross and on all sides there was an ambivalence about acceptance of a single ethnic identity. If the hope of unity never quite died it also was evident that after 1850, but especially from the 1880s, grass roots attitudes on the question hardened. To the extent that Irish Presbyterians were non-dominant they held a middle position between those in Britain and Ireland who were in the ascendant and Catholics clearly placed in a situation of subservience.

Three principal types of non-dominance pertained to Irish Catholics. There was of course the colonial subjugation of a small country by a greater power. Secondly Ireland had a cultural division of labour where most Catholics were clustered at the base of the social and economic pyramid. Additionally there was a profound sense of inferiority accompanied by the psychological effects of the relative deprivation syndrome. Catholics were acutely conscious of their lowly station compared with that of Irish Protestants, people in Britain and also their own kinsfolk in the USA. Lord Spencer caught the essence of the difficulty in 1887 when he observed:

> their social condition at home is a hundred years behind their state of political and mental culture. They naturally contrast the misery of many Irish peasants with the position of their relations in the New World. This cannot but embitter their views against English rulers, and strengthen their leaning to national sentiments.[4]

The appeal and success of nationalist ideas was spurred by an almost universal Catholic desire to break the bonds of non-dominance across the spectrum.

Ireland affords a convenient and important opportunity to assess the comparative methodology pioneered in a central and eastern European context. Because of the range and quality of the literature and the vast array of source material available it is possible to investigate the extent to which national activists conform to wider European patterns and in what ways they are unique. The Irish case also offers a specific environment for examination of the tensions between nationalism and ethnicity along with governmental approaches to demands arising from patriotic agitation.

General Conditions

Social, Economic and Geographical Factors

Ireland is an island situated immediately to the west of Britain having an area of 32 588 square miles.[5] The country consists of four historic provinces (Ulster, Leinster, Munster and Connaught) and is subdivided into 32 counties which are of greater importance for administration. Climate and terrain have had a significant impact on development. The climate is moist and temperatures moderate.

In many areas, notably in the south west, west, north west and parts of the east, the land is hilly, rocky and often speckled with low mountain ranges. In the east central area, the midlands and parts of the southern districts plains and fertile land are characteristic. There are few economically strategic rivers or good harbours. Mineral resources are scarce. The country has little natural timber, coal or precious metals and no important fishing industry. Construction and repair of ships developed late and was centred around Belfast. Engineering also was concentrated there and linen production in Ulster gave that region a larger stake in commerce than was evident elsewhere. Agriculture was the mainstay of the Irish economy as a whole. Overwhelmingly trade was bilateral with Britain. Relatively few people lived in towns – in 1841 merely 20 per cent resided in places having 20 or more houses and only three cities, Dublin (231 726), Cork (80 720) and Belfast (75 308), had populations over 50 000. Urban centres tended to be located in the eastern half of the island.

By the early nineteenth century population was growing swiftly. Despite periodic harvest failures and famine numbers probably reached 8.5 million by 1845. Population density was heaviest in the poorer west and on the less fertile land within regions. Few of those who toiled on the land owned their holdings. In 1870 302 proprietors or 1.5 per cent of owners claimed 33.7 per cent of the land, 750 families possessed 50 per cent, while only 20 people had ten per cent of the land.[6] Overall 4000 proprietors held 80 per cent of profitable agricultural land and some 15 527 had the remainder. In 1841 66 per cent of employed people worked in agriculture under a bewildering set of arrangements. Some were long lease tenants, others subtenants, many held land on yearly agreements and the majority toiled as labourers. Large numbers held parcels of land under different leases and even labourers had traditional rights to certain plots for their own use. But prior to the Great Famine tenants were concentrated on tiny holdings. In 1841 44.9 per cent of farms were less than five acres, a further 36.6 per cent were between five and 15 acres. Only seven per cent exceeded 30 acres. Smallholdings were most numerous on poorer land, notably in the west.

Between 1846 and 1921 the decline in population and the creation of an owner occupier class of farmers were notable transformations in the landscape. By 1851 population had fallen to 6 552 386; in 1881 to 5 174 836; and in 1901 to 4 548 775. The pattern of depopulation was uneven over time and between places. Certain periods, 1846–55 and the late 1870s and early 1880s, had exceptional emigration rates. Western counties had high levels of depopulation. Also very small tenants and agricultural labourers disappeared in disproportionate numbers. Legislation from the 1870s reduced landlord power and created peasant proprietors. By 1905 almost all agricultural land either was subject to judicial rents or in the ownership of former tenants.[7] Nearly 64 per cent of Irish farms were owned by their occupiers in 1916 though the speed of purchase differed between counties. Additionally average farm size had risen by the turn of the century. Only slightly more than 12 per cent of holdings were under five acres still and the number of farmers with at least 15 acres was nearly 58 per cent. Irish catholics were dependent on agriculture but the pace of economic improvement was erratic. Larger farmers, especially those engaged in livestock husbandry, fared best. Generally eastern, midlands and Munster farmers, and most notably the graziers, seized the bulk of the increased prosperity arising from advancing working class standards of living and enlarging demand for meat and dairy products in mainland Britain. Much of the gain was achieved in the immediate post-famine years and from around 1900.[8] Irish agriculture felt the chill of the 'great depression' during the last third of the nineteenth century, though evidence of growing agricultural wealth could be observed. Bank deposits rose, the merchant class expanded impressively and a considerable amount of new construction, particularly of an ecclesiastical variety, was visible. All of this took place against a backdrop of large scale depopulation. Irish prosperity was won in part by fewer people grasping for a slice of the economic cake though even then the rate of depopulation was insufficient to effect a universal improvement in living standards.[9] Ireland's share of the United Kingdom's economy declined after 1850. Marginal regions and individual farms were subsidised by wages from harvest labour in Britain or elsewhere in Ireland and through overseas remittances, mainly provided by children. Small western farmers were especially dependent on injections of outside cash for survival and a considerable number of Irish families found themselves breeding children with remittances in view. Despite the affluence of the north east, Ireland as a whole experienced an adverse trade balance in the last third of the century, a factor which constrained economic progress and thereby the prospects for Catholic advances in employment opportunities at home.

Unquestionably the main cleavage in Ireland was along religious lines. In 1861 Catholics formed 77.69 per cent of the population; in 1891 it was 75.40 per cent; and in 1911 it was 73.86 per cent.[10] Their distribution was uneven – Catholics in 1861 comprised 50.5 per cent of the population in Ulster; 85.9 per cent in Leinster; 93.8 per cent in Munster; and 94.84 per cent in Connaught. At county level that imbalance was magnified. In 1861 Clare in Munster had a Catholic percentage of 97.8 while that for Meath in Leinster was 93.6, both higher than the proportions of their respective provinces. Although Protestants could be found across the social spectrum everywhere, outside Ulster they were clustered in towns or in rural life as landlords, their agents, members of the households of landed families and Church of Ireland incumbents. Most parts of Ireland had scarcely any Protestants. Between 1850 and 1921 the picture hardly changed. The slight increase in the Protestant percentage resulted from greater depopulation in the overwhelmingly Catholic west, in other poor areas and shifts in Ulster. Over time Catholic proportions in the southern counties usually rose. By 1911 the percentage in Clare was 98.14, in Longford the increase over 1861 was more than 1.5 per cent. Cork, Limerick and Waterford cities all experienced rises in their Catholic proportions as well.

Though relatively scarce Protestants, especially those belonging to the Church of Ireland, exerted immense influence. They were pre-eminent in banking, large scale commerce, law, medicine, the state bureaucracy and other status occupations. They owned most of the land of course until the formation of a peasant proprietorship. Members of the Church of Ireland constituted 12 per cent of the population in 1861 and less than 14 per cent in 1911, yet until 1869 their faith was the established religion for the whole island. Over time Catholics made remarkable strides towards social and occu-pational equality though never quickly enough to satisfy inflating ambitions. Career blockage in middle class occupations was more acute in the opening decade of the twentieth century.[11]

If Irish Catholics had ample cause for disaffection and an ethno-religious basis for their grievances, social modernisation also facilitated expression of discontent. Prior to the 1840s famine dissemination of information and contact between distant places were hampered by poor transportation, illiteracy or even a common language. Between 1849 and 1879 mileage of railway track opened expanded from 428 to 2285 miles.[12] By the latter date the main towns were well served by rail and subsequent additions to lines left only remote hamlets inaccessible by train. The rail network allowed political agitators to range widely over the country and also enabled a national patriotic press centred in Dublin to penetrate into all corners of the island. Railways, furthermore, were vital to the growth of an efficient postal system. Letters per head posted rose from 2.9 annually between 1841–5 to 17.3 in the first half of the 1880s.[13] By 1885 letters posted in London normally took only 24 hours to reach Cork. Additionally the telegraph enabled messages to be transmitted quickly. By the 1870s when newspapers had been granted preferential telegraphic rates the press routinely carried reports of parliamentary speeches and the public addresses of leading patriotic figures. In 1880 more than 1.5 million telegrams were dispatched in Ireland. During the 1880s the nationalist movement relied on the telegraph to send instructions to the branches throughout Ireland and Britain.

Prior to 1831 Catholics had restricted educational opportunities. An act passed in that year provided for a state funded system of primary schools. By 1845 there were over 4500 primary schools of all sorts in operation and nearly 9000 in 1900.[14] Approximately 750 000 children were classified as in attendance in 1900. Secondary schooling advanced less impressively. In 1881 there were only 488 such schools and 489 in 1911. However the numbers of pupils at them had doubled to 40 840. During these 30 years the Catholic proportion of those receiving instruction in these establishments rose from about 50 to approximately 75 per cent, or by 1911 was slightly in excess of their share of population. Yet even in 1911 only one in 17 pupils went on to a secondary school. In the last third of the century a number of teacher training colleges and other higher education establishments were founded but they catered for comparatively small numbers as did the universities. In 1901 university students totalled merely 3200 of whom about 1000 were at the Church of Ireland institution of Trinity College, Dublin. Between the 1880s and 1901 students at Cork and Galway fell from 404 and 208 to 171 and 83 respectively. The Queen's College, Belfast, was predominantly a Presbyterian enclave. A Catholic university founded in Dublin in the early 1850s was never very healthy. Ultimately the colleges at Cork, Galway and the Catholic University were joined in the National University in 1908.

The formal obligation to maintain a secular curriculum in state funded institutions angered the Catholic clergy who referred to it as 'godless education' while patriots labelled the system 'anti-national'. Yet most National Schools were under the control of the dominant religious sect of the district and pupils were generally educated only with others of their own faith. While Irish history received little emphasis and Gaelic only attained partial recognition and that fairly late, there is ample testimony that the spirit of these schools in Catholic areas was strongly nationalist. In any case the state system was supplemented by the rapidly increasing numbers of schools run by Catholic orders, particularly the Christian Brothers.[15] Many exclusive Catholic schools for the middle class thrived, especially near Dublin, which imbued students with Catholic national sympathies. Catholic teacher training colleges and the Catholic University had a nationalist tone as well.

Access to education differed by religion, class and region but its impact in the 60 years after 1850 was impressive. In 1841 only 47.3 per cent of people over five years old could read; in 1861 that had risen to 61.3 per cent; while by 1911 illiteracy had declined to 12 per cent. However education and literacy were linked to the use of English. By 1850 only about 25 per cent of the Irish still used the vernacular tongue. Few districts with as many as 25 per cent Irish speakers survived in the eastern and northern two thirds of the country. In 1911 only 12 per cent of the people were Gaelic speaking and they were largely to be found in remote western backwaters.

Adoption of English and advancing levels of literacy created a receptive audience for newspapers and periodicals. From 1800 to 1848 no fewer than 150 periodicals were founded but most had brief existences.[16] Less than a quarter survived a year. From that time both the numbers of newspapers and their readerships increased dramatically. *The Nation*, founded in 1842 to support nationalist positions, lived on into the Edwardian years. In the 1840s and 1850s it had subscriptions of between 4000 and 7000 with many more actual readers.[17] *The Nation* was an influential weekly paper. A daily paper, the *Freeman's Journal*, also advocated moderate nationalist views becoming virtually an Irish party organ in the 1880s. It had sales of about 8500 by 1859. *United Ireland*, a weekly founded by Charles Stewart Parnell in 1881, may have sold as many as 44 000 copies of each issue in the following year. Every town of any consequence had its own local nationalist newspaper by the 1880s. Within the patriotic press all shades of nationalist opinion found expression. Richard Pigott's newspapers, notably the *Shamrock*, *Flag of Ireland* and the *Irishman*, acted as Fenian organs until he sold the titles in 1881. Later the *Leader* became a mouthpiece for Irish-Ireland opinions and *Sinn Féin* (Ourselves) also had newspapers advocating its policies. Only the constitutional nationalist press had large territory wide readerships. Irish appetites for nationalist periodicals was recognised but state officials made no more than modest infrequent efforts to curtail the activities of this lively patriotic platform.

Political Conditions

By 1850 major prerequisites for a successful national movement already existed. The Irish had a deep sense of *landespatriotismus* (territorial consciousness) which most Protestants as well as Catholics shared. Irish political awareness had two significant dimensions – the perceived degree of being part of a culture and history which differed from mainland Britain's, and an institutional framework which allowed relatively uninhibited expression of patriotic opinions. Certainly the Dublin parliament and the semi-autonomy enjoyed in the late eighteenth century formed a focus of pride and excited aspirations for the reanimation of a separate national state. Within Ireland Catholics differentiated themselves from the dominant Protestant culture and had profound feelings of having been divested of their rightful inheritance.

Irish identity was reinforced both by an emergent interest in the past and a popular sub-culture based on myths and legends. The first grew out of an eighteenth century concern for the country's Gaelic history.[18] Figures like Henry Brooke, James Barry, Charles O'Conor and Sylvester O'Halloran looked back at pre-English Gaelic society for a primordial community knit together by a heroic solidarity. They were anxious to rescue the Irish past from the grip of English and Scottish historians to show that the inhabitants of the country constituted one common people and to awaken in them that 'love of letters, Liberty and national Glory which fired our ancestors'.[19] Their vision led to the foundation of the Royal Irish Academy in 1785 with its focus on antiquarianism and investigations of the pre-English past. Leaders of the revival sought to show the Gaelic Irish as a heroic civilising people who had a readiness for self-sacrifice in defence of liberty, and were an embodiment of religious and civic virtues. This tradition was augmented through the Gaelic Society of Dublin founded in 1806; the Iberno–Celtic Society of 1818; the Celtic Society of 1843; and the Ossianic Society of 1853.[20] The Dublin University Magazine from its foundation in 1833 also sought to encourage an appreciation of Irish literature and themes. A culmination of Irish assertiveness was apparent in the Young Ireland Movement in the 1840s and through its vehicle, *The Nation*. This newspaper publicised a particular view of history as well as presenting current political intelligence. Later in the century the historical writings of the soon-to-be Unionist W.E.H. Lecky exercised a significant influence on perceptions of seventeenth and especially eighteenth century Ireland. Perhaps no one had a larger impact than Thomas Davis who through poetry and elegantly constructed essays argued for the unique values of the Irish people in contrast to the corrupting *mores* of the English.

Davis and the others formulated and codified a nationalist interpretation of history – one which was spread by the intelligentsia and firmly lodged in popular consciousness. Alongside this version of history flourished an Irish sub-culture, often anti-Protestant and always antagonistic to Britain, encapsulated in poetry, songs and celebrations. Professional ballad singers had a prominent place in pre-famine society and continued to enjoy popularity down to the 1880s.[21] Cheap patriotic song books, like the *Home Rule Songster* published in the 1870s along with pamphlets of 'Irish National Literature', encouraged a specifically Catholic nationalism. Brass bands, parades and similar forms of local political culture underlined the distinctive quality of indigenous ethnocentrism.

The formal political structure afforded an ideal opportunity for patriotic activity. In Ireland Catholics who met the property qualification could vote, though before 1829 they were barred from public offices and parliament. From 1829 they could be members of parliament and hold all but a handful of public appointments. Extension of the franchise in 1850 gave the ballot to substantial tenant farmers and thus a majority of electors in southern rural and in many urban constituencies were Catholic. Also Ireland was well represented in the House of Commons, always after 1801 having at least 100 seats, or a ratio of approximately one per 6.5 members of parliament. Before the famine Ireland was underrepresented in proportion to population but after 1885 it was always overrepresented. From 1885 the Irish franchise was equal to that elsewhere in the United Kingdom and small borough seats under Protestant influence were eliminated then. Political participation in parliament afforded very tempting possibilities.

On a restricted franchise Daniel O'Connell had been able to flex the muscle of Catholic nationalism. An Independent Irish party in the 1850s showed that Catholics could be marshalled behind a movement which sponsored a patriotic programme. When the Home Rulers emerged at the opening of the 1870s it quickly was apparent that candidates advocating patriotic aims could succeed in constituencies with majorities of Catholic voters. Though successful under open voting[22] the Secret Ballot act of 1872 further boosted Catholic potential. Passage of corrupt practices legislation in 1883 lowered the cost of elections. At the general election of 1868 Liberal party candidates advocating Irish reforms did well; in 1874 and 1880 Home

Rulers captured approximately 60 seats on each occasion, a total that increased to 85 in 1885. By the mid 1880s patriotic candidates had an iron grip on Catholic constituencies.

Municipalities, part of the Poor Law Boards and, after 1898, County Councils were elective. Each acted as a further juicy bait for those who strove to infuse public life with men supporting patriotic aims. Ireland, then, had a confluence of favourable conditions for national activism. There existed a strong sense of identity, history and destiny while the ideals of the English, American and French revolutions supplied an added source of inspiration.

Patriotic activity required an organisational apparatus.[23] In Ireland the national movement developed a rich array of organs – these can be distinguished as single issue and multi-functional groups and as moderate or constitutional and revolutionary associations. Organisations flowered early – the United Irishmen predated the Union. While in the 1820s the Catholic Association and New Catholic Association pressed the Catholic emancipation claim, that demand also served as the spearhead of other aspirations as well. In the 1840s the repeal of the Union movement sought the restoration of an Irish parliament by mutual consent with Britain, though Young Ireland, initially in alliance with Daniel O'Connell, broke off, waging the rebellion of 1848. The Catholic Associations and repeal movement were mass movements with large lists of subscribers. Young Ireland by contrast was a narrowly based collection of intellectuals. After 1850 patriotic organisations multiplied. In the 1850s tenant rights groups, clerical parties and an Independent Irish party united under a single banner for a spell but none individually, nor all collectively, were mass organisations. The Irish Republican Brotherhood founded in 1858 had more members, but was in theory at least a secret conspiratorial organisation preparing for an armed struggle. Members were grouped into circles and there was a national directory at the apex. Because of rigorous police surveillance there is a good deal of evidence for the membership, plots and programmes of the Brotherhood. It had branches in Ireland, Britain, the USA and a considerable following among Irishmen in the British army. In Ireland about 24 000 belonged to the movement in early 1867.[24] After the rebellion in that year numbers declined. Fenianism attracted the hostility of the Catholic Church which began the National Association in 1864 but it was never a mass movement and devoted itself to seeking religious and other objectives by moderate legal pressure group tactics.

Following the Fenian revolt in 1867 constitutional organisations developed and became more active. Three were of particular importance: the Amnesty Movement, the Tenant Right organisation and the Home Government Association were formed in 1869 and 1870; and each was a single issue group. The Amnesty campaign held huge demonstrations but had only a limited apparatus; the Tenant groups were comparatively few in number and under the control of large farmers; while Home Rulers pursued a restricted diet of activities due to poor funding and a desire to maximise support by limiting the scope of their demands.[25] In late 1873 the Home Rule movement was reorganised and quickly sprouted a branch network but it never had a strong centralised apparatus. Between 1879 and 1881 when it was suppressed, the Land League had pretensions of being a national organ but in fact consisted of two loosely linked sections – local branches and a central organisational umbrella. Nevertheless the League had considerable funds though these were devoured in supporting tenants in the land struggle. Charles Stewart Parnell was elected president of the League in October 1879 and became chairman of the Irish Parliamentary party in May 1880 thus linking the leadership of the two separate organisations together. In principle though they remained distinct and limited issue groups. In October 1882 Parnell founded the Irish National League which was highly centralised, indeed under the direct control of himself and his party.[26] This organisation built a large branch network and enlisted a mass membership. Through the League the party supervised candidate selection for parliamentary constituencies. Local branches had wide authority in parochial affairs though in practice they were dominated by local notables and priests. Essentially the League and its successors provided a framework for communication and conveyanced instructions between the national and the local cadres of patriots.

The Parnell divorce scandal split moderate nationalism in 1890–1 into warring factions with the result that all organisational mechanisms at national level were weakened. At the close of the century a new mass organisation, the United Irish League, established a somewhat more decentralised apparatus in succession to the various constitutional groups.[27] It remained the chief vehicle of the national movement until the First World War.

By comparison other groups after the early 1870s were small. The Irish Republican Brotherhood survived but did not thrive again until after 1916. Other combinations such as the Gaelic Athletic Association of 1884 and the Gaelic League of 1893 had limited functions and did not overtly challenge the existing national organs. In the early twentieth century Sinn Féin, which rejected the utility of Westminster parliamentarianism, provided an alternative but gained relatively few converts. Similarly the emergent socialist movement and trade unions were comparatively small and hesitant in mounting a direct challenge to the old leadership which in any event gained a fresh lease on the affections of the Irish people after 1910 when Home Rule was placed firmly back on the Liberal party agenda. Few organs were in a position of such mutual hostility that cooperation with others or working within the ambit of the parliamentary movement was impossible. There were differences in outlook and of generations between *Sinn Féin* and the United Irish League but these were not unbridgeable gulfs.

In the years after 1850 only Parnell had the prestige and charisma to hold the factions in tandem. He was aided by able organisation minded lieutenants. In retrospect it was clear that the 1880s, when a striking level of integration of various nationalist strands was achieved, had proved the exception not the rule. Even in the 1880s straddling the various objectives within the coalition composing the national movement could be an unenviable task.[28] Patriotic dissensions were laid cruelly bare after 1890. In Ireland, albeit in an attenuated form, national organisations during the mass mobilisation stage displayed the same fissurous tendencies apparent in other European national movements.

The National Movement and its Activists

Comparative analysis, especially the themes pioneered by Miroslav Hroch, are of special importance to Ireland. It was part of a politically and economically sophisticated state and a national movement emerged on Irish territory at an early date. Miroslav Hroch excluded Ireland from his treatment; in part because it did not appear to fit the pattern due, he believed, to the fact that the conflict was between a non-dominant group and a ruling nation far along the path to capitalism rather than a struggle against an old feudal regime.[29] Yet it is vital to establish accurately the degree to which Ireland fitted wider patterns considered by him and by others in the case studies. Moreover the core of the Hroch approach concerns the linkage between patriotic activism and capitalist mechanisms of exchange. The Irish example allows appropriate testing and analysis of the relationship in an instance where capitalist ideology and forms had reached an exceptional level of development.

The Irish case does not conform to the three phase typology neatly. That there was a cultural revival, attempts to widen its programme to political objectives and mass mobilisation, in Ireland as elsewhere, is unquestionably correct. But there were several cultural revivals, the last extending down to the revolutionary period, and at least two took place simultaneously with or after eras of mass mobilisation.[30]

Indeed within the period considered mass mobilisation as a concept presents difficulties for it began in the years 1820–50, experienced some pause and was then resurrected with a vengeance around 1880. At one level the peasants had been incorporated in the mass movement as early as 1798, their participation was more visible in the 1840s but perhaps not convincingly so until the Land War later in the century. Similarly, when taken from different vantage-points, the middle phase when political objectives were promulgated but the masses not incorporated as yet into patriotic agitation was either brief or very extended. Soon after the Home Rule movement was founded in 1870 the leading spokesman, Isaac Butt, made clear that neither he nor it had an immediate intention of instigating popular demonstrations. He pointed out that:

> the public did not exactly understand what was their position. The Association originated entirely in a private meeting of a few gentlemen held some time since in Dublin. They formed themselves first into a committee, and afterwards into an association – not a popular organisation – for they were not a popular organisation, but an association of a number of gentlemen who had joined together to impress on the public mind of Ireland their own opinion, and endeavour to carry them out.[31]

While he wished it were possible to dispatch deputations to explain the programme to the country, Butt reminded listeners that there had been no proposal for public demonstrations. The object was that:

> they should accustom the public mind to take in the project they had formed; and after showing that their aims were practical, they could organise the whole of Ireland, and English Ministers would think twice before they refused their demands.

Butt's apparent exposition of a non-agitational posture has to be weighed against the fact that he then also led the Amnesty Movement for release of Fenian convicts which held large public meetings and engaged in mass mobilisation of patriotic sentiment.

Cultural revivalism after 1893 presents interpretative difficulties as well. It arose very late and while some leaders eschewed political intention from the outset others always saw the movement as a vehicle for a particular vision of the nation. Most supporters wanted to create a mass organisation but until after 1916 they had little success in converting significant numbers to their position. In certain respects the Gaelic League fits the third phase when there was differentiation within the mass movement closely enough; in other ways it represents a throwback to earlier parts of the typology.

Although the Irish example might be compressed in ways to make it conform more closely to the typology it would be at the expense of some violence to the pattern of events. Yet Ireland does not vitiate the model but merely suggests a less than neat picture. Its national movement progressed through the sequence though not in the precise theoretical order and the various phases had a concurrent existence. Phases B and C in particular cannot be distinguished in an indisputably clear fashion. The question has relevance principally for an assessment of the activists who are drawn mainly from the final phase, that is, during the period of mass mobilisation. National activists in post–1850 Ireland were quantitatively numerous and drawn from more diverse social categories than was the case in most other movements investigated. However in view of the advanced stage of Irish development a wider popular basis of the agitation is what would be anticipated. Within the classification of national experiences the Irish can be placed among those movements which had to overcome two deficits. National activism emerged in the wake of the bourgeois and industrial revolutions but Irish patriots had to overcome the obstacles of not possessing political sovereignty or a completed social structure.

An outstanding virtue of the comparative approach has been the highlighting of features of national activism common to many or all such groups across Europe. Particularly notable have been the results in respect to the social and geographical profiles of agitators. Irish activists conform to the general pattern. In Ireland activists were plentiful and spread over the social and geographical landscape but with varying intensity at different times and by the character, that is, radicalisation of their programme and methods. There are two cross cutting polarities – national or territorially wide elites and local activists; and those who were essentially moderate and legal in aims and methods in contrast to those radicals prepared to employ violent means. Some activists belonged to two or more groups over time or even simultaneously but their numbers are not so extensive as to distort the picture.

Nationalist members of parliament and the small number of officials who managed the central parliamentary apparatus were at the apex of territory wide moderate activism. Members of parliament had tremendous prestige and were few in number despite the considerable Irish representation in the House of Commons. Many enjoyed lengthy political and parliamentary careers – turnover at all points between 1850 and 1918 was low. Many constituencies, particularly in the 'democratic' era after 1885, were contested only infrequently: Ireland had the highest proportion of uncontested returns of any part of the United Kingdom after 1885. Among patriotic activists, initial selection and election were moments of prime importance. Advocacy of the patriotic programme and responsiveness to local opinion, notably that of the clergy and farming interest, were essential to success but other factors also entered into the matrix. Candidates normally were expected to meet their own, sometimes substantial, election expenses and to bear the cost of spending part of the year in London as members of parliament which were unpaid until 1911, as well as to extend largesse locally. From the middle 1880s a party machine exerted more direct pressure on selection. Some candidates had their expenses paid and a bevy of members of parliament were subsidised in London but even under the leadership of Parnell, and at the pinnacle of the party's influence, the length of a man's purse was a positive commendation for selection if he met orthodox patriotic tests otherwise. A seat in the House of Commons in the patriotic interest was thus an honour restricted to a few and mainly to those of considerable reputation and

Table 3.1: Occupations of members of parliament

	1852	1874	1885	1895–1900	1910
Landowners	24	24+6	5	8	–
Rentiers and agents	–	10	–	–	2
Professions	15	27	41	44	44
Trade, industry, finance	9	12	15	16	7
				(shopkeepers inc)	
Farmers, shopkeepers (together before 1895)	–	4	22	10	12
				(farmers only)	
Working men	–	–	–	3	3

Some members of parliament were undefined and the numbers of patriotic members of parliament were larger from 1885.
Sources: Whyte, p. 90; Thornley, p. 207; O'Brien, p. 152; Lyons, p. 160; Thomas, pp. 44–5.

Table 3.2: Education of members of parliament

Highest level	1885	1892–5	1910
Primary	25	12	11
Secondary	41	35	45
University	27	29	25+13 others
Other or not reported	–	11	–

Sources: O'Brien, p. 155; Lyons, p. 165; Thomas, p. 38.

financial means. They were a genuine elite. Such men, therefore, can be traced socially, politically, territorially, by age and education.

Tables 3.1 and 3.2 provide a snapshot of the occupations and education of the apex of patriotic leadership between the early 1850s and the last general election prior to the First World War. The information has been compiled from several sources and is not equivalent for each period or category and thus provides an approximate rather than a precise picture.

Two generalisations command assent: that the social origins of patriotic members of parliament slipped over the period with the general election of 1874 marking a partial transition and that of 1885 completing the slide; and that the occupational status of these men also declined with the same dates again being turning points. In the 1850s landlords were a pronounced element but by 1900 they had been nearly eliminated. The first tenant farmer, W.H. O'Sullivan, was returned in 1874 but this class played little part in parliamentary representation until the post–1885 years. In 1906 farmers numbered 16 or just below 20 per cent of nationalist members of parliament though that total declined to merely 12 at the end of 1910. Merchants were of some consequence but manufacturers in contrast were scarcely represented. Clearly the most prominent groups, which also increased their proportion over time, were the lawyers and journalists. In 1910 they accounted for almost half of the patriotic members of parliament. Artisans and industrial workers were notable by their absence. They accounted for only three members of parliament in December 1910. Academics were also of no importance while as the clergy of both the Catholic and Church of Ireland faiths were ineligible they did not figure in the representation.

On the whole members of parliament had the advantage of a high level of formal education. In the pre-1880 years they were still drawn disproportionately from the social elite and their high educational status comes as no surprise. Democratisation in the mid 1880s scarcely altered the situation. After the general election of 1885 there were 27 members of parliament who had attended some university, including Parnell, a Cambridge man. In December 1910, despite an increase in the total of merchants, farmers and the influx of three working men, 25 members of parliament had attended a university and one more a training college. Most had received a secondary education at least, often in the later years from the Christian Brothers. In the mid 1880s men who had attended only primary school crept into the ranks but during the next 25 years their numbers actually declined. Few of these less educated members of parliament could be found among the leadership cadre at any point.

Protestants were fairly abundant even after the 1880s though their coreligionists gave the movement little support. A Protestant presence was vital to the standing of the Home Rulers in Britain and also they were more likely to have the essential characteristics of financial independence and education than middle class Catholics. The preferred route to selection obviously was through the professions, notably law and journalism, occupations which had the attributes of status, expectation of a reasonable independent income and which were usually compatible with membership of parliament. This dominance by the professions paralleled the growth in numbers and enhanced status of these occupations during the later Victorian and Edwardian years.[32] Patriotic members of parliament tended to have less exalted origins and occupational status than members of the House of Commons as a whole but they were still very much an elite. The profile of British members of parliament, particularly those of the post–1900 Liberal party, drifted towards the Irish party pattern.

Whereas parliamentarians were a small select group they were reinforced by an army of local leaders who were relatively numerous. Throughout the period local elites were a potent factor in Ireland. They dominated politics and elections. In most places they exercised significant influence over candidate selection at parliamentary elections, constituted what passed for a party machine in the patriotic interest, provided the indigenous source of finance for agitation and filled the elective positions in local government. They were, by their very character, distributed widely through the island. Prior to mass organisation local notables were necessarily the pivotal figures on the ground for patriotic activity. After complete mobilisation in the early 1880s local authority did not disintegrate but was strengthened. Local elites remained the lynchpin of organisation in an environment where the leading patriotic figures were concentrated in Dublin and London. As the movement had limited funds and mainly unpaid officials directing its machinery the labour and enthusiasm of local notables was indispensible. Local elites were channels of communication, responsible for demonstrations, the means of disseminating pamphlets and literature and ensured press support. Moreover under the cloak of the patriotic agitation local notables were able to seize and control municipal councils, the elective element of Poor Law Boards and officerships and democratic county councils following their creation under the legislation of 1898. The key moment for the extension of the authority of local patriotism was in the late 1870s and early 1880s. Local patriotic activism from that time was pervasive, if not always sustained at a high pitch, in most Catholic districts.

Local notables were generally unable to enunciate aims, order priorities or mobilise mass sentiment on their own but they could, and did, modify the policies of the central elite. The functions of all strands of the movement had to be complementary or at the very least not openly antagonistic. If local elites exerted impressive, perhaps decisive, influence on patriotic activism they have not been subjected to comprehensive investigation. Nevertheless it is possible to locate this group socially with some precision. Three major sectors comprised the elite – priests, merchants and powerful farmers. Cohesion between the sub-groups was high. Ireland was an agrarian community and outside Ulster agriculture was the main economic resource. Most parishes, for instance, served the rural community and the clergy associated themselves with the interests of the peasantry. Similarly the rapid expansion of shopkeeping in the last quarter of the nineteenth century reflected the growing prosperity and demand for goods in the rural economy. Irish towns were small and served principally as distribution centres for the agricultural sector. Even the professions in these places geared their services and conditioned their outlook to agrarian needs.

The vital role of the clergy in the national movement has been recognised. They were the one group distributed relatively equally over the land surface of the country where Catholics could be found. Priests often were the most educated Catholics in a parish while the Catholic Church remained the one truly national institution extending through the country. The Church was an ideal vehicle for the spread of patriotic propaganda, and in many places political meetings were held in churchyards following Sunday mass. O'Connell had mobilised the clergy. Between 1850 and 1852 priests gave prominent support to the new Tenant Right League. In Tipperary, a county with a pattern of patriotic agitation, 44 per cent of priests displayed support or sympathy for the League.[33] During the 1860s 25 per cent were members of the National Association. Initially few joined the Home Rule movement and leaders believed the slow progress it made could be attributed to clerical reticence. Also there was a decrease observed in direct involvement by priests in electioneering in the 1870s and 1880s. Yet it would be mistaken to view clerical participation and importance in national agitation as diminishing, rather it was less essential for the clergy to take a forward visible role. Many priests openly supported the land campaign and very few opposed the aims of the agrarian movement. Priests were very evident as patrons, chairmen and sympathisers of the National League after its formation in 1882. Few parliamentary nominating conventions functioned without the participation of the clergy.[34] During the Parnellite split priests were active in the interests of the anti-Parnellites. In the post–1891 years the protracted struggle in Westmeath between a supporter of Parnellism and the local bishop found the latter, sustained by powerful farmers, usually successful.[35] Conversion of the priests to *Sinn Féin* was undoubtedly an important stage of the Irish revolution.[36]

While the clergy obviously were a defined occupational group they were also drawn from a distinct social *milieu*. Virtually all had attended an Irish seminary, frequently Maynooth. In Tipperary an average of 52 per cent of priests had been to Maynooth, with nearly all the rest at diocesian seminaries.[37] Most were themselves from the vicinity where they served and enjoyed lengthy spells as curates, and also as parish priests if elevated to that prized dignity. It was usual for a priest to have a lifestyle at least equal – and generally superior – to that of the prominent farmers in the parish. They were not poor men and identified with the substantial tenant farmers, often having less sympathy for the material aspirations of cottiers and labourers. Perhaps their principal social attribute though is that most were sons of prosperous tenant farmers. That was the class which produced young men of devotional temperament and had the financial resources to provide an extended education and meet the considerable expenses of seminary training. The hierarchy shared the characteristics and disposition of the parish clergy. Thus priests were not so much a separate group as a differentiated section of the dominant local interest. They were men very much of the community sharing the values and reflecting the outlook of the rest of the local elite.

If lawyers and journalists were the leading sector of territory wide patriotic agitation, the most powerful farmers were its local backbone. They were numerous, had a strong sense of community, were usually devoted to the Catholic Church and wielded political weight. Farmers and their sons showed little tendency towards radicalism and ensured that the nationalist programme had a firm social platform congenial to the interests of substantial agriculturalists. Depopulation and rising average farm acreage after the famine enlarged their numbers and ensured the ascendancy of strong agriculturalists in rural Ireland.

Farmers, like other groups, experienced a degree of early mobilisation. The Tenant Right movement in the 1850s drew support from some of the newly enfranchised voters, being most successful in parts of Munster and Leinster.[38] An allied movement emerged in Ulster. Fuller participation, however, did not take place until the land war. Farmers clubs sustained activity through the 1870s but their numbers were small and membership generally confined to a tiny section of substantial tenants. Few farmers or their sons took a leading part in the Fenian conspiracy as seen in Table 3.5. They joined

Table 3.3: Elective officers, Poor Law Boards

Occupation	% 1877	% 1882	% 1886*
Landowners	87.9	65.3	38.9
Farmers	6.7	18.8	34.5
Shopkeepers	1.0	6.1	8.2
Publicans and innkeepers	0.4	1.0	2.0
Professionals	0.6	1.0	1.7
Merchants and manufacturers	0.2	1.2	0.8
Members of parliament	0.2	0.2	0.6
Land agents	0.6	0.6	0.2
Business agents	0.4	0.2	0.2
Civil servants	0.2	–	0.2
Unidentified	1.9	5.5	12.2
Total	100.1	99.9	99.5

Source: Feingold, p. 215.
*Ulster excluded

or supported the Land League and were overrepresented as an occupational group among those persons arrested under the Protection of Person and Property Act of 1881. Thereafter farmers remained a core ingredient in local activism. Already in the later 1870s but more thoroughly after 1881 the local activists attacked the traditional hold of the landlord class on Poor Law Guardianships as part of the patriotic struggle. In 1881 Parnell sanctioned an assault on these offices via the ballot box.[39] In early 1882 the nationalist newspaper United Ireland declaimed 'it's all part of one struggle – the supremacy of the will of the Irish people. Every seat of power is ours by right'.[40] By 1886 the elective element as well as Unions' officerships had slid into the hands of local patriots, especially in Munster. Table 3.3 reveals the extent of the takeover outside Ulster which is excluded from the compilation for 1886.

The table underestimates the impact of powerful farmers in that some of the Unions were urban. There was a marked tendency for counties with high densities of large farms to experience the most comprehensive takeover of the Poor Law Unions.[41] Among prominent farmers, graziers seem to have taken the lead as local leaders despite a nationalist rhetoric which was unfavourable to them. Many shopkeepers, some featuring in the table, were graziers and livestock dealers. Urban dwellers apparently took a larger part in the patriotic seizure of Unions in Connaught where large farmers were less numerous.

Whether prominent farmers, and particularly graziers, continued to occupy so pivotal a position later has been questioned.[42] Samples of members of the elective county councils for 1905 and 1908 reveal overrepresentation of traders who were most evident in Connaught and least present in Munster.[43] Some of these traders presumably were graziers as well. Farmers with holdings valued at less than £100 were underrepresented. However the expansion of *Sinn Féin* as a force after 1916 was accompanied by a moderation of the professed ambition to break up large farms and redistribute land, evidence enough of large farmer influence.[44]

Substantial merchants were the other leading element in the local elite. This group provided the parochial direction of the Land League and was overrepresented among suspects detained in 1881 (see Table 3.6), among officers of Poor Law Unions (see Table 3.3), and as County Councillors. Shopkeepers were at the centre of the distribution network and therefore were also vital in the dissemination of information. Though a distinct group many were partly engaged in agriculture as landowners, tenants, graziers and livestock dealers.[45] Merchants and prominent farmers were frequently bound together by ties of kinship. Thus in Ireland the tensions between town and country, merchant, priest and farmer were moderated even if the shopkeeper may have exhibited exploitive tendencies in his role as a provider of credit.[46]

Distinguishable from the parliamentary and local elites are the militant or revolutionary nationalists. They had rather different defining social characteristics. Class rather than the militants' religious persuasion or even the time period of the agitation seems to have been the key determinant. A profile of the largely Protestant Dublin United Irishmen of 1791 (see Table 3.4) shows the strong

Table 3.4: Dublin United Irishmen, 1791

	%
Landed gentry	0
Business, shopkeepers	52.1
Professions	22.9
Artisans	23.2
Labourers	0
Soldiers	1.8

Source: Garvin (1981), p. 23.

involvement of shopkeepers, intellectuals and artisans, the last group making its initial appearance in the list of patriotic activists.

Adherents of Young Ireland, also a movement with a marked Protestant element, displayed many of the same features in the 1840s. Those who waged the revolt of 1848 in Ireland were urban intellectuals and their rising lacked a substantial base among the peasantry.

Fenianism was more widespread and of greater significance. Its history has been dissected into three periods – 1858–79, an insurrectionalist phase; 1879–91, an agrarian era; and 1891–1923, when it adopted romantic revolutionism.[47] Throughout its existence Fenianism elicited a sympathy which extended far beyond its formal membership. The movement's importance also lay in being a nursery for many budding nationalists who subsequently moved on to other patriotic organisations.

Even at its height in the 1860s Fenianism appealed only to a tiny minority of people. Its catchment then probably was exaggerated by

Table 3.5: Fenian suspects detained, 1866–1871

Occupations	Percentage of Suspects
Agricultural sector:	21.2
Farmers	6.4
Farmers' sons	2.1
General labourers	10.6
Other agricultural	2.1
Commercial and industrial sector:	66.0
Traders and business proprietors	8.5
Shopworkers and clerks	9.2
Innkeepers and publicans	3.6
Artisans and non-farm labourers	44.7
Professional sector:	6.4
Clergy	2.1
Teachers	1.4
Newspaper editors and correspondents	2.1
Subordinate professional service	0.7
Civil service and defence sector	3.6
Domestic sector	2.8
Number of suspects	141

Source: Clark, p. 203.

the absence of effective competition. Many leaders had been famine era *émigrés* to the USA. Both earlier and subsequent revolutionaries often were drawn from the margins of the ethnic group in having foreign experience, partly non-Irish parentage or Protestant roots. The most marked characteristic, though, was the urban coloration and the high participation of artisans.[48] Farmers were greatly underrepresented. Table 3.5 based on police records of Fenian suspects between 1866 and 1871 gives evidence of these trends.

Police records additionally reveal that between 1880 and 1902 of 81 prominent Fenians under police surveillance, about 20 per cent were small shopkeepers, particularly publicans and an equivalent proportion commercial travellers, often in the liquor trade.[49] Many of the leaders seem to have been upwardly mobile.

Active involvement in the land war constituted a form of militant

Table 3.6: Land League suspects detained, 1881

Occupations	Percentage of Suspects	Percentage of Labour Force
Agricultural sector:	62.0	65.9
Commercial and industrial sector:	32.6	23.2
Traders, business proprietors and shopworkers	14.1	11.9
Innkeepers and publicans	8.1	0.4
Artisans and non-farm labourers	10.4	9.8
Other commercial and industrial	0	1.1
Professional sector:	4.6	4.4
Clergy	0.1	0.5
Teachers	1.2	0.5
Newspaper editors and correspondents	1.6	0.02
General professional	1.2	0.6
Subordinate professional service	0.5	0.2
Students	0	2.6
Civil service and defence sector	0.2	4.3
Domestic sector	0.6	2.2
Total number	845	1 571 896

Source: Clark, p. 250.

nationalism which was both more widespread and respectable. Tabulation of the occupations of men arrested under the Protection of Person and Property act of 1881 (see Table 3.6) indicates the greater presence of farmers, as might be expected, but also the over-representation of traders and publicans. Artisans and town labourers were detained but not out of proportion to their percentage of population. As usual agricultural labourers, clergy, bureaucrats and teachers took little part in this form of patriotic activity.

Activists in the Gaelic revival after 1890 tended to be young and better educated than their forebearers. Like Young Ireland in the 1840s it appealed particularly to the intelligentsia. In Ireland education was geared towards literary attainments, a preparation most appropriate to careers in commerce, clerkships, the professions and bureaucracy. Suitable employment openings did not keep pace with the rising numbers of Catholic aspirants, especially after 1900.[50] Blocked mobility was a feature of post–1900 Ireland and the Gaelic revival drew much support from teachers, professionals and civil servants along with an element of the priesthood, but failed to ignite comparable enthusiasm in rural areas and among the Irish speakers of the remote districts. However the Gaelic League declined in membership after 1906. Analysis of 304 key figures in the post–1916 *Sinn Féin* establishes that they were overwhelmingly young, Catholic and educated, often by Christian Brothers.[51] It seems most were of fairly recent agrarian background by parentage. Among the cohort farmers were less prominent than their proportion of population, professionals much more evident than their percentage.

Dissection of the social composition of patriotic activism yields significant dividends. In Ireland mass mobilisation began early and was exceptionally successful. Even so certain social groups were prominent and others were largely absent in nationalist activism. Landlords, Protestants, high state officials, judges, the urban working class, cottiers and agricultural labourers played only a tiny part. The top and bottom of the social pyramid were thus largely absent. Academics, teachers and lower civil servants, except in the Gaelic revival, were of scarcely greater importance. Artisans were numerous in revolutionary activities but insignificant elsewhere. The intelligentsia were prominent in territory wide movements yet had little role in local affairs. In contrast farmers were important locally but of little account on a broader canvas. Priests were prominent at all levels though more so locally and they seldom initiated policy or formulated tactics but rather granted or withheld approval of the secular leadership. Merchants could also be located at both levels and in moderate and revolutionary activism. Probably only large scale merchants had an impact on centrally initiated activism and then in subordinate capacities, while shopkeepers had a crucial function in local agitation.

Despite early mobilisation the pattern was far from static. It was influenced by a mass movement which until the 1870s had staccato tendencies. Irish opinion generally was firmly patriotic in outlook before 1850 but machinery to mobilise that sentiment only emerged in a comprehensive and continuous form after 1870. Priests declined in importance from the 1870s though they never ceased to be significant. Farmers and rural merchants remained relatively dormant until the close of the 1870s, thereafter playing a key role. A section of the intelligentsia only took an active part in the late stages and never exercised influence on the scale of lawyers and journalists. Protestants largely withdrew from the agitation following the land war. The social profile of activism shifted over time though perhaps never too dramatically, particularly after the early 1880s.

The territorial portrait of where leaders came from and which areas had the most intense activism exerts immense fascination. It is apparent that by the 1880s patriotic feeling had penetrated virtually

Table 3.7: Territorial distribution of activism, 1826–1889

	Leinster	Munster	Ulster	Connaught
Contributions to Catholic rent 1826	169	137	37	49
Contributions to O'Connell annuity 1833	176	157	28	20
Attendance at Repeal Meetings 1843	164	140	7	99
Contributions to Tenant League funds 1851	209	118	55	0
Attendances at Amnesty meetings 1869	180	177	8	46
Distribution of Land League meetings 1879–80	79	99	51	251
Membership of National League January 1883	120	119	79	83
Contributions to Parnell tribute 1883	170	162	31	35
Contributions to Tenant Defence fund 1889	127	171	39	77

(National Mean = 100)

Source: Hoppen, p. 480.

all of Catholic Ireland but the levels of agitation over the country varied enormously. That was true even of locally based elites' efforts to dominate institutions like Poor Law Boards. Ulster played little part in patriotic activism, either as a theatre of agitation or in the provision of leaders. Ulster reticence encompassed both Protestants, as would be anticipated, and Catholics. Table 3.7 provides a snapshot of differing types of moderate patriotic participation between the 1820s and close of the 1880s.

Territorial differences in parliamentary politics were not pronounced. Before 1850 patriotic candidates were victorious in a range of places, the chief requisite being a substantial Catholic electoral majority. By the mid 1880s only candidates who professed the national programme could hope to succeed in constituencies with Catholic majorities. Class rather than geographical origin was the key to selection, though local provenance might be an additional recommendation. Local men were probably most evident at the beginning and end of the period but members of parliament were never drawn exclusively from those who had close ties with their constituency. During its first decades the Irish party sometimes enforced outside candidates on local constituencies, Parnell's own selection for Meath in 1875 being an illustration of the practice.[52] A considerable number of members of parliament did not reside in Ireland but were longtime Londoners or from other British towns and in a few instances they were not even Irish born.[53]

Other forms of activism, however, had a notably regional flavour. Prior to the famine parts of Munster had an established pattern of social disturbance, a picture which persisted after 1850. Fenianism in the 1860s was strong in Leinster and so especially in Munster.[54] By the late 1870s its appeal was more marked in Connaught and Ulster, possibly as a response to the decaying artisan trades in those areas. The land war began in the west and unusually (see Table 3.7) the region was a hotbed of agitation. Later the United Irish League, also founded in the west, exerted a disproportionately greater attraction there.[55] At local level the earliest and most comprehensive assaults on Poor Law Boards were in Munster and certain pockets of the west.[56] *Sinn Féin* later replicated the trend. Though the centre of national organisations Dublin was not a prominent breeding ground for revolutionary leaders.[57] Between 1919 and 1921 significant Irish Republican Army operations and the responses of the crown forces through reprisals were clustered in south western districts and in parts of the west.[58] Provinces, regions and counties are extensive and conceal subtle internal differentiations. These distinctions have been less thoroughly charted. Within the large county of Cork, it is evident that certain parts only had a propensity towards patriotic involvement.[59] For Mayo, home of the Land League, it has been established that most meetings between 1879 and 1881 took place in the fertile central core of the county and scarcely any were held in the poor upland western fringe.[60] Anti-hunting incidents during the conflict were concentrated in clusters in Leinster and sections of Munster rather than throughout counties.[61]

Receptiveness to patriotic agitation was less pronounced in the most industrialised and in the poorest regions. It was most evident in districts outside Leinster associated with livestock production and dairying, that is, capitalist forms of agriculture. Leinster was an area of commercial farming but its participation was influenced by proximity to Dublin and probably the pacific historic character of the English Pale. Higher numbers of Protestants in a district did not exacerbate activism and contrary to Miroslav Hroch's hypothesis, it was not closely associated with districts of the highest population densities or abnormal levels of urbanisation,[62] though this conclusion is based on patterns from the mobilisation stage of agitation.

Patriots came from many origins and places but were distributed differently over time and type of involvement. Early mobilisation gives a picture of the post–1850 years which overrepresents activists from Phase C with its distorting effect. Yet despite parochial factors in the Irish case, patriotic agitation fits into the broad hypotheses advanced by Hroch and in the other national movements investigated.

The British Government and the Formation of National Activists

Ireland was a central motif of British politics between 1850 and 1921. Successive administrations sought to ease the sources of ethnic tension and to make the internal management of the country effective and inexpensive. Ireland was a problem because it was different, discontented and a Catholic province in a Protestant state. Over the period both assimilation and policies of special treatment were tried, though neither approach was applied consistently. Internal divisions in Ireland, even among Catholics, complicated the task of pacification but also increased the temptation to exploit differences. Initially British leaders attempted to undermine support for activists but then modified this position and saw moderate nationalists as a bulwark against extremism. The shift in approach began in the 1880s though there was a time gap between when the competing British parties altered their tactics. Part of the strategy hinged on pacifying the Catholic Church, other sections on recruiting more Catholics into the state bureaucracy, creating a peasant proprietorship and integrating Ireland into British life. Certainly the policy enjoyed some success but it was plagued by inconsistencies of application.[63] Also early mobilisation of the masses necessarily meant that the task of conciliation was both larger and more difficult.

In some parts of Europe repressive regimes were a key factor in stimulating ethnic mobilisation. Britain did not follow a repressive course. Ireland must be placed among those cases where mobilisation was a consequence of an absence of effective repression by the state. Ethnic consciousness in some instances was raised by a group being more advanced socially and economically than the dominant culture and in others by the relative backwardness of a non-dominant people. The Irish example clearly falls into the latter category. British liberal ideology acted as a bar to routinised repression but doctrines of individualism and avoidance of state interference in economic matters gave Irish patriots scope for agitation but limited government initiatives which might advance material development.[64]

State of Research

Relatively few records for the Irish national movement have been destroyed. Some loss was incurred during the civil war in Ireland following establishment of the Free State in 1922 and again from the bombing of London during the Second World War but a wide range of materials is preserved in official archives in Dublin, Belfast and England. A largely unrestricted free press and general reluctance by the British state to exercise excessive force allowed an Irish national movement to function openly and accumulate a mass of materials about itself.[65] Official commissions on Irish affairs and informal personal accounts add to the rich volume of information available. Censuses, economic and religious surveys add further dimensions to the mountain of records. The police and administrative reports on the national movement are of particular value. Leading British and Irish politicians retained their letters and papers in many instances and most of these resources are readily accessible for inspection. The proceedings of the House of Commons and the wealth of British and Irish newspapers are sources of exceptional importance. Although much information is available now in published editions the vast bulk of materials must be consulted in the various repositories. Deficiencies in the original compilation of information accounts for significant *lacuna* in the sources. There are very few obstacles in the path of addressing the Irish past.

Serious work on Irish topics was slow to get off the ground but during the past three decades there has been an explosion of interest in the field. New information and fresh perspectives characterise recent studies of Irish history. Yet despite an impressive literature, research possibilities have not been exhausted. British policy and Irish responses have been subjects of intensive investigation but the patriotic elites have evoked less attention. Parliamentary nationalists have been put under a microscope but participants of Home Rule groups in Ireland and Britain have not been accorded equally extensive treatment. Members of municipal bodies, Poor Law Guardians, County Councillors and other local authorities have attracted only limited academic inquiry. Tom Garvin's *The Evolution of Irish National Politics* and *Nationalist Revolutionaries in Ireland 1858–1912* are notable attempts to dissect the radicalised elites. William Feingold's work on tenant revolt affords an invaluable insight into the character of one local elite, the Poor Law Guardians, while J.J. O'Shea's study provides a useful glimpse of the Catholic clergy of County Tipperary. David Fitzpatrick's cameo of County Clare offers a good look into the social and mental world of one disturbed area during the revolutionary era. John Hutchinson's work on cultural nationalism is an indispensible account of the social roots of Gaelic revivalism. The work of a German scholar, Erhard Rumpf, was a pioneering application of economic and geographical analysis to Irish politics and latterly was published in a revised form in collaboration with A.C. Hepburn as *Nationalism and Socialism in Twentieth–Century Ireland*. Samuel Clark's work also utilises social development for explanation of mass agitation though the work of Paul Bew in *Land and the National Question in Ireland, 1858–82* and *Conflict and Conciliation in Ireland 1890–1910* enter important caveats and modifications and erects an impressive alternative explanatory framework built on models of internal rural class conflict in Ireland. K.T. Hoppen's analysis of Irish politics is a mine of information on many topics. A large corpus of scholarship on individuals, movements and organisations contains essential, though largely indirect, information on the composition of leadership *cadres*.

Research for this chapter has been supported by a fellowship awarded by the National Endowment for the Humanities (1980–1), grants from the British Academy and Twenty–Seven Foundation and also while a Visiting Research Fellow, St John's College, Oxford (Summer, 1985), as a Visiting Fellow, Wolfson College, Oxford (February–September 1986), Senior Associate, St Antony's College, Oxford (October 1988–March 1989), Visiting Fellow, St Aidan's College, University of Durham (April–June 1989), and a Visiting Fellowship at the Institute for Advanced Studies in the Humanities, University of Edinburgh (Summer 1989). Members of Group VI offered valuable advice. D.G. Boyce, Michael Hurst, John

Hutchinson, Roland Quinault and Ellen Wiegandt made useful suggestions. Christoph Mühlberg and Geneviève Schauinger of the European Science Foundation were a vital source of assistance.

Notes

1 *Irishman*, 9 March 1867.
2 Edwards (1977), pp. 183–4.
3 *North Wales Observer*, 10 June 1892; *Annual Register* (1899), p. 241.
4 Spencer, p. ix.
5 Statistics from, Edwards, (1973); Freeman, Vaughan and Fitzpatrick.
6 Winstanley, p. 11.
7 Crotty, p. 83.
8 Ó'Gráda, p. 130; Cullen, p. 150.
9 Fitzpatrick (1984), pp. 31–42.
10 Vaughan and Fitzpatrick, pp. 49–73.
11 Hutchinson, pp. 266–79.
12 Hoppen, p. 461.
13 *Ibid.*, p. 462.
14 Lyons (1976), pp. 82–98.
15 See Coldrey.
16 Hayley, p. 83.
17 Hoppen, p. 458.
18 Hutchinson, pp. 55–67.
19 Quoted *Ibid.*, p. 56.
20 Boyce (1982), pp. 229–30.
21 Hoppen, pp. 423–35.
22 Hurst, pp. 33–59.
23 See Alter.
24 Comerford, p. 134.
25 Thornley, pp. 174–5.
26 O'Brien, pp. 126–33.
27 Bull (1988), pp. 51–78; Bull (1972).
28 For Parnell's difficulties in the mid 1880s see O'Day (1986).
29 Hroch, p. 194, n. 11.
30 Hutchinson, p. 49.
31 *Nation*, 15 October 1870.
32 Gourvish, pp. 13–35.
33 O'Shea, pp. 51, 59.
34 O'Brien, p. 130.
35 Murray, pp. 144, 156–7.
36 Miller, pp. 391–484.
37 O'Shea, pp. 13–5, 22–3.
38 Whyte, pp. 5–13.
39 *Freeman's Journal*, 1 March 1881.
40 *United Ireland*, 4 February 1882.
41 Feingold, pp. 210, 214.
42 Jones, pp. 412–3.
43 Kennedy (1983), p. 358.
44 Rumpf and Hepburn, p. 21; Bew (1987), pp. 214–5.
45 Kennedy (1979), pp. 205–9.

46 Solow, p. 87; Bew (1979), p. 10.
47 Garvin (1987), p. 33.
48 *Ibid.*, pp. 33–40; Garvin (1981), pp. 59–65.
49 Garvin (1987), pp. 38–40.
50 Hutchinson, pp. 250–303.
51 Garvin (1987), pp. 49–56; Coldrey, pp. 248–70.
52 *Nation*, 10 April 1875; 10 and 17 January 1885; Healy, II, pp. 378–9; for the
    restrictions on the practice see Lyons (1951), pp. 146–7.
53 O'Day (1977), pp. 23–6.
54 Comerford, pp. 213–4.
55 Fitzpatrick (1978), p. 438.
56 Feingold, pp. 194–5, 202.
57 Fitzpatrick (1978), pp. 403–31; Rumpf and Hepburn, p. 56.
58 Rumpf and Hepburn, pp. 39–40.
59 Donnelly, pp. 251–376; see Geary, pp. 151–79.
60 Jordan, pp. 324–5.
61 Curtis, pp. 398–9.
62 Hroch, p. 174.
63 See Gailey.
64 O'Day (1988), pp. 229–49.
65 Townshend, p. 64.

Select Bibliography

Alter, P. (1971), *Die irische Nationalbewegung Zwischen Parlament und Revolution*, Munich.
Bew, P. (1979), *Land Question and the National Question in Ireland 1858–82*, Dublin.
Bew, P. (1987), *Conflict and Conciliation in Ireland 1890–1910*, Oxford.
Bowman, J. (1982), *DeValera and the Ulster Question 1917–1973*, Oxford.
Boyce, D.G. (1982), *Nationalism in Ireland*, London.
Boyce, D.G. (1988a), *The Irish Question and British Politics 1869–1986*, London.
Boyce, D.G. (ed.) (1988b), *The Revolution in Ireland 1879–1923*, London.
Buckland, P. (1979), *The Factory of Grievances*, Dublin.
Bull, P.J. (1972), 'The Reconstruction of the Irish Parliamentary Movement, 1895–1903: An Analysis with Special Reference to William O'Brien', Ph.D. thesis, University of Cambridge.
Bull, P.J. (May 1988), 'The United Irish League and the Reunion of the Irish Parliamentary Party, 1898–1900', *Irish Historical Studies*, XXVI.
Clark, S. (1979), *Social Origins of the Irish Land War*, Princeton.
Coldrey, B. (1988), *Faith and Fatherland*, Dublin.
Comerford, R.V. (1985), *The Fenians in Context*, Dublin.
Corish, P.J. (ed.) (1985), *Radicals, Rebels and Establishments*, Belfast.
Crotty, R.D. (1966), *Irish Agricultural Production*, Cork.
Cullen, L.M. (1972), *An Economic History of Ireland since 1660*, London.
Curtis, L.P. jnr. (1987), 'Stopping the Hunt, 1881–1882: An Aspect of the Irish Land War', in Philpin, C.H.E. (ed.), *Nationalism and Popular Protest in Ireland*, Cambridge.
Donnelly, J.S. jnr. (1975), *The Land and the People of Nineteenth Century Cork*, London.
Dudley Edwards, R. (1973), *An Atlas of Irish History*, London.
Dudley Edwards, R. (1977), *Patrick Pearse*, London.
Earl Spencer (1887), 'Preface' in Bryce, J. (ed.), *Handbook of Home Rule*, 2nd edition, London.
Feingold, W.L. (1984), *The Revolt of the Tenantry*, Boston.

Fitzpatrick, D. (1977), *Politics and Irish Life 1913–21*, Dublin.
Fitzpatrick, D. (February 1978), 'The Geography of Irish Nationalism 1910–1921', *Past & Present*, No. 78; reprinted in Philpin, C.H.E. (1987) (ed.), *Nationalism and Popular Protest in Ireland*, Cambridge.
Fitzpatrick, D. (1984), *Irish Emigration 1801–1921*, Dublin.
Freeman, T.W. (1965), *Ireland*, 3rd edition, London.
Gailey, A. (1986), *The Death of Kindness*, Cork.
Garvin, T. (1981), *The Evolution of Irish Nationalist Politics*, Dublin.
Garvin, T. (1987), *Nationalist Revolutionaries in Ireland 1858–1928*, Oxford.
Geary, L.M. (1986), *The Plan of Campaign 1886–1891*, Cork.
Gibbon, P. (1975), *The Origins of Ulster Unionism*, Manchester.
Gourvish, T.R. (1988), 'The Rise of the Professions', in Gourvish, T.R. and O'Day, A. (eds), *Later Victorian Britain*, London.
Hayley, B. (1976), 'Irish Periodicals from the Union to the Nation', *Anglo–Irish Studies*, II.
Healy, T.M. (1926), *Letters and Leaders of My Day*, 2 vols., London.
Hechter, M. (1975), *Internal Colonialism*, London.
Hoppen, K.T. (1984), *Elections, Politics and Society in Ireland 1832–1885*, Oxford.
Hroch, M. (1985), *Social Preconditions of National Revival in Europe*, Cambridge.
Hurst, M. (1965), 'Ireland and the Ballot Act of 1872', *Historical Journal*, VIII, reprinted in O'Day, A. (ed.) (1987) *Reactions to Irish Nationalism, 1867–1914*, London.
Hutchinson, J. (1987), *The Dynamics of Cultural Nationalism*, London.
Jones, D.S. (1983), 'The Cleavage Between the Graziers and Peasants in the Land Struggle, 1890–1910', in Clark, S. and Donnelly, J.S. jnr. (eds), *Irish Peasants*, Manchester.
Jordan, D. (1987), 'Merchants, "Strong Farmers" and Fenians: The Post–Famine Political Elite and the Irish Land War', in Philpin C.H.E. (ed.), *Nationalism and Popular Protest in Ireland*, Cambridge.
Kennedy, L. (May 1979), 'Traders in the Irish Rural Economy, 1880–1914', *Economic History Review*, XXXII.
Kennedy, L. (1983), 'Farmers, Traders and Agricultural Politics in Pre–Independence Ireland', in Clark, S. and Donnelly, J.S. jnr. (eds), *Irish Peasants*, Manchester.
Lyons, F.S.L. (1951), *The Irish Parliamentary Party, 1890–1910*, London.
Lyons, F.S.L. (1986), *John Dillon*, London.
Lyons, F.S.L. (1976), *Ireland Since the Famine*, 4th impression, London.
Lyons, F.S.L. (1977), *Charles Stewart Parnell*, London.
Lyons, F.S.L. and Hawkins, R.A.J. (1980) (eds), *Ireland Under the Union*, Oxford.
Miller, D.W. (1973), *Church, State and Nation in Ireland 1889–1921*, Dublin.
Moody, T.W. (1982), *Davitt and Irish Revolution 1846–82*, Oxford.
Murray, A.C. (November 1986), 'Nationality and Local Politics in Late Nineteenth-Century Ireland: The Case of County Westmeath', *Irish Historical Studies*, XXV.
O'Brien, C.C. (1964), *Parnell and his Party 1880–90*, 2nd impression, Oxford.
O'Broin, L. (1976), *Revolutionary Underground*, Dublin.
O'Broin, L. (1985), *Protestant Nationalists in Revolutionary Ireland*, Dublin.
O'Day, A. (1977), *The English Face of Irish Nationalism 1867–1894*, Dublin.
O'Day, A. (1986), *Parnell and the First Home Rule Episode, 1884–87*, Dublin.
O'Day, A. (1987), *Reactions to Irish Nationalism*, London.
O'Day, A. (1988), 'The Irish Problem', in Gourvish, T.R. and O'Day, A. (eds), *Later Victorian Britain*, London.
ÓGráda, C. (1988), *Ireland Before and After the Famine*, Manchester.
O'Shea, J.J. (1983), *Priest, Politics and Society in Post–Famine Ireland*, Dublin.
Philpin, C.H.E. (ed.) (1987), *Nationalism and Popular Protest in Ireland*, Cambridge.
Rumpf, E. and Hepburn, A.C. (1977), *Nationalism and Socialism in Twentieth-Century Ireland*, Liverpool.

Solow, B.L. (1971), *The Land Question and the Irish Economy 1870–1900*, Cambridge, Massachussetts.
Thomas, J.A. (1958), *The House of Commons 1906–1911*, Cardiff.
Thornley, D. (1964), *Isaac Butt and Home Rule*, London.
Townshend, C. (1983), *Political Violence in Ireland*, Oxford.
Vaughan, W.E. and Fitzpatrick, A.J. (1978), *Irish Historical Statistics: Population, 1821–1971*, Dublin.
Whyte, J.H. (1958), *The Independent Irish Party 1850–9*, Oxford.
Winstanley, M.J. (1984), *Ireland and the Land Question 1800–1922*, London.

Map 3.1 Ireland (1850–1920)

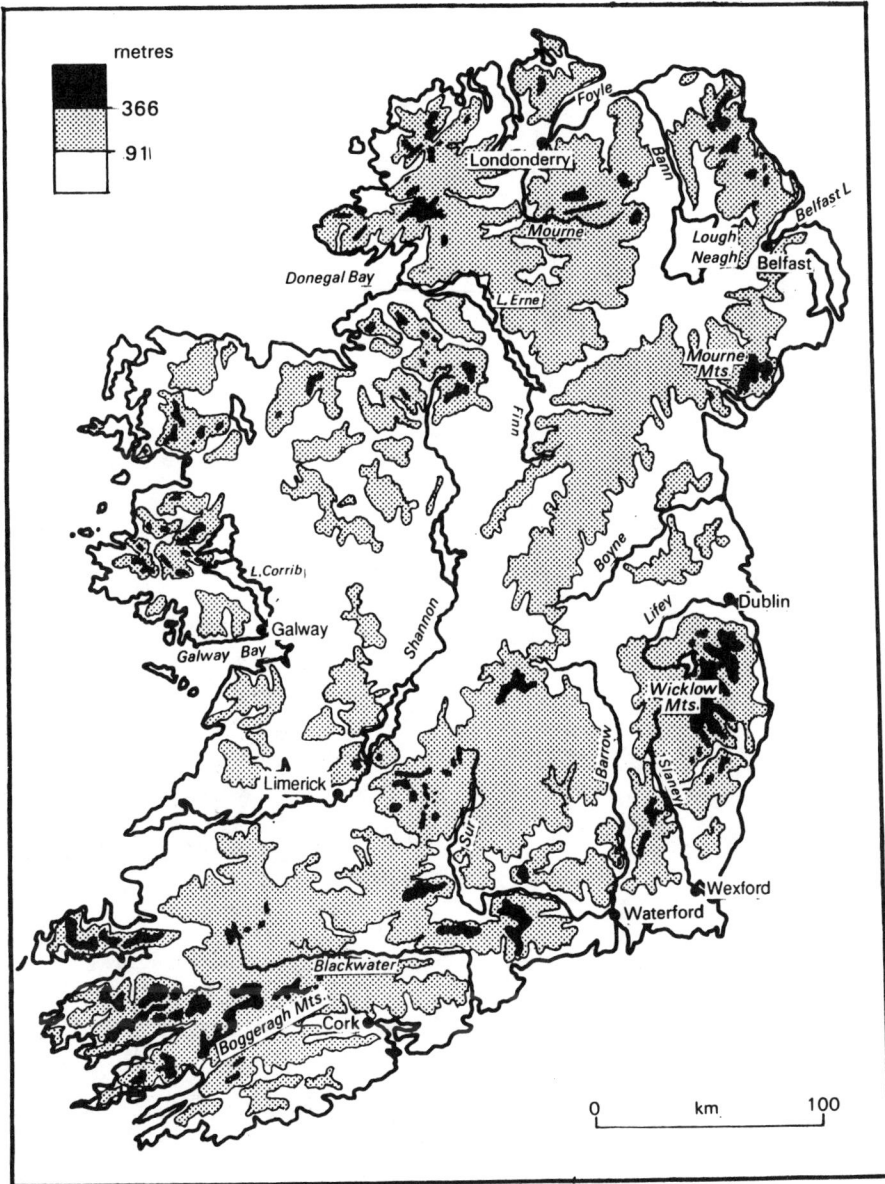

Map 3.2 Topography of Ireland, 1850–1921

4   The Czechs, 1840–1900

JIŘÍ KOŘALKA

General Conditions

Geographical Foundations

Throughout the centuries up to 1938 almost the entire territory of the Czechs was united under single rule. From 1526 this was that of the Bohemian crown worn by the Habsburg dynasty. It formed part of the non-Hungarian part of the Habsburg monarchy (unofficially called Cisleithania) after 1867, and following 1918 the Czechoslovak republic. Exceptions were separate Czech settlements in Lower Silesia under the Prussian government from the mid eighteenth century, such as the rural environs of Glatz/Kłodzko; Leobschütz/Głubczyce; Ratibor/Racibórz; and Hultschin/Hlučín – areas which did not play any part in the Czech national activities of the nineteenth century and were more or less assimilated, particularly in the political sense, by Prussian–German society. The first generation of the more than 500 000 Czech immigrants in the USA from the late 1840s onwards felt sympathy with the ideal of Czech national emancipation from the Habsburg empire although they did not significantly influence it.

Most of the Czechs lived in the kingdom of Bohemia and the markgraviate of Moravia where they made up the majority of the population: about 63 per cent in Bohemia and more than 70 per cent in Moravia. In Austrian Silesia prior to 1919–20 Czechs were only the third largest ethnic group, after the Germans and the Poles, representing 22 to 24 per cent of the population.[1] Bohemia, Moravia and Silesia were traditionally regarded by the Czech national movement as the historic provinces of the Bohemian state, to be referred to in brief as the Czech lands.

The deep political and administrative separation between Bohemia and Moravia worked as a disintegrative factor. There were two separate *diets* and two governorships, in Prague and in Brno/Brünn and after 1848–9 and 1861, a third for Austrian Silesia in Opava/Troppau was also established. Elements of *Landespatriotismus* (territorial consciousness) prevailed in Moravia and Silesia, in spite of ethno-linguistic differences and the influence of the administrative separation on the Czech national society lasted into the early years of the twentieth century. Regional differences and dialects only played a part in Moravia and Silesia, whereas the kingdom of Bohemia was characterised by a singular unity and by the dominant position of Prague, its capital.

The numbers of ethnic Czechs who lived in a few villages of Lower Austria, close to the Bohemian and Moravian border declined. Czech immigration into Vienna produced a numerous ethnic minority in the imperial capital which was important for the rise of the Czech elites. Of 340 000 persons living in Vienna in 1910 only about 98 000 stated that they spoke Czech as their *Umgangssprache* (language of daily use) even though born in Czech speaking districts of Bohemia, Moravia and Silesia. The actual number of Viennese Czechs was much higher, however, as became apparent when, less than ten years later, about 150 000 Czechs migrated from Vienna to Czechoslovakia in 1919–20.[2]

Ethno-linguistic Delimitation

Protracted controversies concerning the proper name of the ethnic and national group of *Češi* in foreign languages – whether they should be called Bohemians (*Böhmen*, in German), or Czechs (*Czechen* or *Tschechen*, in German) – was symptomatic of the ambiguous situation of the group.[3] As Bohemians they could be regarded as a historic nation like the Poles or the Hungarians, having inherited the glorious tradition of the medieval kingdom of Bohemia and being in their own eyes entitled to restore a national state of their own. As Czechs they felt themselves to be looked down upon as an unhistorical people allegedly without rights to a national state. In fact Czechs belonged to both categories in part and their status was not resolved formally until the Allies officially recognised the Czechoslovaks as forming a belligerent nation during the First World War.

The presence of German speaking people (more than 36 per cent in Bohemia and 29 per cent in Moravia) presented a crucial problem in establishing national identity in the Czech lands. Conservatives in Czech politics postulated the existence of a bilingual Bohemian nation including the Germans of Bohemia.[4] This concept failed to win acceptance like previous efforts to identify Czechs as Slavic speaking Germans, an idea which had spread in Germany during the 1840s. The German Confederation was supposed to be transformed into a German national state and since the Czech lands were to be incorporated into it, all inhabitants were declared by the Frankfurt parliament to be Germans politically.

In Moravia the Czech–German ethnic–national differentiation lasted longer than in Bohemia. Tentative attempts to create a separate

Moravian language in the early 1840s were not successful and were rebuffed by prominent Moravian born Czechs. Nevertheless most of the Moravian Czechs in 1848–9 and quite a number in the following decades did not wish to be called *Češi* (Bohemians) but Slavic Moravians or Moravian Slavs. The Moravian question was essentially the problem of the political and cultural assertion of Moravians within Czech society. Most Czechs in Austrian Silesia were distinguished by their regional and pre-national consciousness which lasted much longer and was felt more strongly there than in Moravia. They regarded themselves to be *tutajší* (from here)[5] and they remained, until 1918, an object rather than an active component of the Czech national interest.

Only a minority of the Slovaks of upper Hungary ever supported the Czech national idea. Although Slovaks were often defined by Czechs as being the Slovak or Hungarian branch of the Czech people, their representatives preferred in 1844 to create a Slovak literary language in order to unite Catholics and Protestants into a Slovak national movement. In spite of close cultural affinity, but because of their different political fortunes in the course of many centuries, Czechs and Slovaks underwent a parallel development as two closely related but diverse peoples and nations.

Demographic Conditions

Prior to the census of 1880 the ethnic composition of the Habsburg monarchy was based on a roughly calculated estimate of entire localities and parishes with scant notice taken of local minorities. In 1840 Johann Springer estimated that there were approximately 2.5 million Slavic speaking people in Bohemia and 1.5 million in Moravia[6] whereas Pavel Josef Šafařík's calculation in 1842 was of three million Czechs in Bohemia and 1.3 million in Moravia.[7] The arbitrary nature of such figures was emphasised in the work of Georg Norbert Schnabel who suggested that 66 000 Germans and 40 000 Czechs lived in Prague in 1846 by counting all well-to-do and educated persons as the former, because higher education, industry and commerce were all carried out in the German language.[8] More reliable were the official estimates of Carl Czoernig and Joseph Hain based on data provided by Catholic parishes in 1846–7.[9]

Between 1880 and 1910 Austrian official censuses did not enquire into ethnic or linguistic allegiances but rather into what language was spoken in daily life. In most cases, with the exception of the new immigration into the cities and industrial regions, this gave a reasonably accurate picture of ethnic identity in the non-Hungarian part of the Habsburg monarchy. The official estimates of 1846–7 and the censuses from 1880 to 1910 offered the following picture of Czech numbers:[10]

Table 4.1: The Czech-speaking population in the Austrian censuses, 1846–1910

	1846	1880	1890	1900	1910
Bohemia	2 598 774	3 470 252	3 644 188	3 930 093	4 241 918
Moravia	1 253 320	1 507 328	1 590 513	1 727 270	1 868 971
Silesia	93 561	126 385	129 814	146 265	180 348
Vienna	–	25 186	63 834	102 974	98 461
Lower Austria without Vienna	11 513	36 071	29 647	29 994	23 868
Other provinces of Cisleithania	2 182	15 686	14 875	18 801	22 417
Total	3 959 350	5 180 908	5 472 871	5 955 397	6 435 983

Religious Conditions

As a consequence of the counter-reformation in the seventeenth century, the overwhelming majority of the Czechs adhered to the Roman Catholic faith. The census of 1900 showed that 96.6 per cent of the Czech population in Bohemia, 96.2 per cent in Moravia, and almost 98 per cent in Austrian Silesia were Catholics. ReCatholisation of the Czechs, however, had not always been profound, particularly in central and eastern Bohemia and in several districts of eastern and western Moravia where the influence of the Hussites and the Moravian Brethren had never been destroyed completely. Traditions of late Josephinism were deeply rooted in the Czech Catholic clergy and their faith was rather rationalistic.

For Czechs the link between religion and ethnic consciousness was not as pronounced as in the Russian or Prussian parts of Poland. Percentages of both Lutherans and Calvinists using German were lower in all three provinces than their proportions of the population. Several Czech speaking judicial districts in eastern Moravia showed an unusual concentration of Protestants, such as Vsetín where Catholics totalled only 51.4 per cent. Large parts of Czech society in the nineteenth century increasingly manifested a religious tolerance and absence of interest in any religion. That is why all attempts to win at least some Slavophile Czechs for the Orthodox religion failed entirely: less than 0.01 per cent of Czechs in 1900 and 1910 belonged to the Orthodox Church.[11]

The ethno-linguistic allegiance of the Jews differed between Bohemia, Moravia and Austrian Silesia. Jewry in the Czech lands generally supported an Austro–German bureaucratic liberalism which had granted equal rights to them within the empire. Since modern Austrian statistics did not recognise the Jews as an ethnic group, they were recorded only by religion and most of them originally indicated German as their spoken language. In the 1900 census, 54 per cent of Jews in Bohemia already listed Czech as their language, particularly in rural towns of Czech Bohemia. However only 15 per cent of the Jews in Moravia indicated that Czech was their language (in spite of Czechs being 71 per cent of the population in that province) and in Silesia only two per cent of Jews opted for Czech.[12] In the Czech parts of Bohemia it became advantageous for the Jews to identify themselves as Czechs, although they themselves remained bilingual and sent their sons either to Czech or German schools. But in Moravia and Silesia social mobility continued to be associated with the German language. Anti-Semitism among Czechs had roots in traditional Christianity. It grew stronger after the mid nineteenth century because of social problems and a dislike of the Austro–German orientation of substantial numbers of Bohemian and Moravian Jews. The Czech Jewish movement and its Czech supporters in the late nineteenth century, however, managed to challenge anti-Semitism and to create a cultural partnership inside Czech society.

Economic Foundations

After the Habsburg dynasty had lost most of Silesia to Prussia in the mid eighteenth century as well as Lombardy in 1859 and Venetia in 1866 to the kingdom of Italy, the Czech lands and lower Austria became the most important area of industrial development in the empire. Bohemia, Moravia and Austrian Silesia, where the great majority of the Czechs lived, together represented approximately 25 per cent of the territory of Cisleithania and 37 per cent of its population in 1880 but about 64 per cent of its industrial production. The figures show that 93.8 per cent of hard coal; 74.5 per cent of soft coal; 83.5 per cent of cast iron; around 75 per cent of cotton textiles; 80 per cent of woollen goods; 75 per cent of chemical products; and 92 per cent of glass came from the area.[13] This predominance remained steady during the following two decades. Economic and social development however was not uniformly distributed. Up to the 1860s early industrialisation was largely concentrated in the predominantly German speaking regions from north western Bohemia to northern Moravia and Teschen Silesia and in the capitals of Prague and Brno/Brünn. During the last third of the nineteenth century though industrialisation shifted towards the interior Czech speaking regions. The iron industry originated there, the expanding engineering works and, above all, a rapidly growing food industry found in these Czech inhabited parts of the country a superior supply of raw materials and better transport facilities as well as a larger pool of cheap labour. By the end of the nineteenth century the rise of new industries, such as electrical engineering, bicycle, motorcycle and automobile manufacturing took place almost exclusively in the Czech regions and were predominantly in the hands of Czech entrepreneurs.[14] The figures for occupations were combined with those of language (ethnic linguistic affinity) in the Austrian part of the monarchy for the first time in the 1900 census.[15] At that point 43.1 per cent of the Czech working population was still in agriculture and forestry but the numbers in industry and crafts had already reached 36.5 per cent. A disproportionately high number of people worked in mining and smelting, in the building trades or in the food and clothing industries. Czechs were found in lower proportion than the Austrian average in trade and transport.

Level of Education

The educational level of the population was also recorded by ethnic–linguistic allegiance for the first time in the Austrian census of 1900.[16] It emerged that the lowest rate of illiteracy was to be found among Czech speaking Austrian subjects. In the case of Czechs over six years of age 93.8 per cent could read and write (the Cisleithanian average was 65.4 per cent); two per cent could read only; and only 4.2 per cent were illiterate. It came as a surprise to the public at the time that this educational lead of the Czechs was found at its most marked in the eldest age group: 92.8 per cent of Czech men and 80.6 per cent of women born before 1850 could read and write. The advantages of the Austrian school system were obviously more effective in Bohemia and Moravia than in most other provinces of the empire. For the Czechs the influence of the national emancipation movement which, from the end of the eighteenth century, had taken a positive attitude towards education had obviously worked. A similar influence in many respects can be said to have persisted from the tradition of the Czech Reformation in the fifteenth and sixteenth centuries.

The National Movement and its Activists

Compared to other ethnic groups of east central and south eastern Europe who had started on the road towards national political emancipation within a state of different nationality in the nineteenth century, the Czechs were a transitional and mediating type. Unlike the Magyars in Hungary or Poles in Galicia, the Bohemian and Moravian nobility with few exceptions did not identify with the Czech national movement. Significant numbers of these aristocrats, however, felt themselves to be regional patriots and by their opposition to Austrian centralisation efforts gave useful aid in some cases to the Czech national movement. Czechs had their state tradition of the kingdom of Bohemia which gave their efforts added weight; moreover the interests of Bohemian regional patriotism and Czech national movement were compatible. Slovenians, Slovaks and Ruthenians (Ukrainians) did not have this kind of internal cohesion. Throughout the nineteenth century the indigenous social and political elite of the Czechs was unequivocally non-aristocratic and civic in the widest sense. At the outset a pre-industrial strata of urban and lower middle classes, as well as members of the liberal professions and civil service originating from these groups were in the majority. After about 1860 an increasing number of self-employed entrepreneurs in agriculture, trade and industry can be found.

Social Composition and Organisational Base of the Czech Patriots During the Phase of Agitation (up to 1848)

The beginning of national Czech agitation has been placed at about 1820.[17] Even though enthusiasm for the autonomy of Czech language and culture started some decades before, only the generation born at the end of the eighteenth century succeeded in passing the line dividing scientific interest from an activism which spread the national idea successfully. Two institutions founded by the Bohemian nobility served as starting and focal points for the most successful activities of the Czech national movement before 1848. The *Vaterländisches Museum* (Patriotic Museum) in Bohemia, later the Museum of the Kingdom of Bohemia, founded in 1818, published two periodicals under the editorship of František Palacký from 1827. The German language monthly was turned into an annual almanac after three years and then discontinued in 1831. The *Časopis Českého muzea* (Journal of the Bohemian Museum) emerged as the most important periodical of the Czech national movement from the start. An influential group for furthering Czech literature and language was founded in 1830 within the museum organisation which from 1831 established a fund to pay for the editing of high quality vernacular books. This was the *Matice česká* (Czech Foundation). The Society for the Encouragement of the Trade Spirit in Bohemia also started as an aristocratic venture but Czech patriots succeeded by the mid 1840s in making their influence paramount.

Analyses of the subscription registers of the Czech museum periodical, the list of contributors to *Matice česká*, the patrons of a Catholic national editing project and the participants in a collection in aid of the Czech trade school between 1827 and 1848 show that prior to 1840 most members were priests, university students, civil servants and officials, particularly among the last those working on large country estates. While the percentage of priests declined gradually the percentage of the professional classes rose from 1837, that of artisans and tradesmen from 1841, and that of peasants from 1846. The increasing importance of the peasant population is shown by the marked rise of rural patrons of the Catholic *Dědictví Svatojánské* (Bequest of St Nepomuk). Examination of the social origins of students of Prague University and the theological seminaries in Vienna who afterwards became active Czech patriots confirm the significant percentage of those coming from the families of artisans and tradesmen. During the years of 1826–31 and 1832–7 sons of artisans, tradesmen and millers comprised nearly 48 per cent of those students successfully completing their studies in the Czech language in the Philosophy faculty of Prague University as compared to the years of 1842–7 when it had fallen to a little over 34 per cent. During the latter period the percentage of peasants' sons rose from 13 per cent to 18 per cent.[18]

It was typical of the agitation phase of the Czech national movement that the patriots were urban dwellers particularly in Prague and in medium size towns. In a topographical analysis of the distribution of patriot groups three types of areas were distinguished in Bohemia. Eastern Bohemia, the valley of the middle Labe/Elbe east of Prague and the valley of the Jizera/Iser were areas of maximum activity. In these areas all towns of more than 1000 inhabitants had an active patriot group. Amateur theatres and other cultural organisations were also most prevalent. It was a territory with a higher than average rate of artisans producing goods for the market, as well as a fertile agricultural region with effective trade and transport links and a network of schools or superior facilities for education. The second group comprised the northern part of the Czech ethnic territory and part of western and south western Bohemia where patriot groups were active only in larger towns and in some administrative centres. Lower than average activity was characteristic of southern and south eastern Bohemia and the southern part of central Bohemia.[19]

At the peak of the agitation phase of the Czech national movement in the mid 1840s, a clear regrouping of the leaders and a progressive transformation of merely cultural activities into political involvement can be identified. While a romantically inclined older generation had been preoccupied almost exclusively with the revival of Czech language and literature, a more self-confident younger generation widened the field of vision. Besides František Palacký, who significantly strengthened Czech influence in the Royal Bohemian Society of Science and in the Bohemian Museum, František Ladislav Rieger, a miller's son, and Karel Havlíček, a merchant's son, came to the forefront. In the Society for the Encouragement of the Trade Spirit in Bohemia a vigorous Czech opposition group prevailed, headed by three lawyers and a technician. Vehement discussion during the monthly meetings of the society were, for Rieger and his colleagues, a valuable nursery for their future parliamentary activities.[19] In 1845 Rieger, ably supported by Palacký, submitted a petition for permission to form a joint stock company in order to build a Czech theatre in the name of the group of well-to-do Prague citizens. When *Měšt'anská beseda* (Burgher Resource) was founded in Prague in 1846 a prestigious social centre for the Czech industrial and educated middle classes came into being. When, also in 1846, Karel Havlíček took over the editorship of *Pražské noviny* (Gazette of Prague) it was the beginning of modern Czech journalism.

After the Bohemian *diet* or *Landtag* (provincial assembly) had granted the petition of Prague citizens for the founding of a theatre an election for the planning committee was held in 1846. The results illustrated the popularity of the leading national personalities in Czech bourgeois circles. The first three positions were taken by aristocrats sympathising with the Czech effort (generous financial contributions were expected from them) and among the total of 190 names there were 45 aristocrats in all. Of the well known non-aristocratic Czechs Palacký, Rieger (still designated as 'lawyer before his final exams, and mill-owner') and some lawyers and tradesmen won significantly more votes than cultural activists of the older generation. Votes were cast for 22 burghers and homes owners (without further specification), 20 lawyers, 16 merchants, 11 brewers, ten state and country officials, seven architects and builders, six civic landowners, five professors and five millers.[20] The Czech–German differentiation was, at that time, far from complete but the social base of Czech social activities was broadened considerably even before 1848.

Establishment of the Political Identity of Czech Society in the Revolutionary Years of 1848–9

A new phase of development in the formation of the elite was opened in 1848, a 'year of many "firsts" in modern Czech history'.[21] The firsts included a Czech political programme, a free national assembly, a full scale daily newspaper, a modern constitution, elections and ideological political parties. The June rising in Prague in 1848 was the first open revolt of Czechs in two centuries to put forward political demands by force. In a preparation for the May rising in 1849 the idea of breaking up the Habsburg empire was first broached. Leaders of the Czech national movement led by František Palacký explained to the Austrian and European public that the autonomous existence of the Czech nation derived from natural law. Palacký also articulated the notion of a voluntary union of diverse nationalities in the territory between Germany, Russia and the Ottoman empire. For a number of smaller national movements, particularly the Slovaks and the Austrian south Slavs, the Czechs of 1848 became a prop and in some cases an example.

Liberal leaders of the Czech national movement in the mid 1840s enjoyed an extraordinary political authority in Bohemia. On their recommendations predominantly agrarian candidates were elected to the Bohemian *diet* in May–June 1848[22] while in June–July mainly educated persons such as lawyers and literary personalities were sent to the *Reichstag* (imperial parliament).[23] The spread of Czech national agitation from the towns into the country, already visible during the last pre-revolutionary years, gained intensity in the spring of 1848. A total of 580 petitions addressed to the *Národní výorb* (national committee) in Prague (465 in Czech) were received from more than 1200 villages, as compared to 89 petitions from middle and small towns in Bohemia.[24] After the abolition of feudal obligations by the Austrian parliament in September 1848 the political activities of the Czech agricultural population diminished visibly, but as late as 1849 the daily newspaper *Národní noviny* (National News) edited by Karel Havlíček was subscribed to by 244 Catholic priests, 65 farmers and 50 parishes in Bohemia, mostly in the countryside.[25] During the revolutionary years of 1848–9 the Czech national movement entered the stage of mass agitation and increasingly influenced some groups of farmers and skilled workers.

Despite expansion into rural areas the Czech social elite was, in 1848–9, concentrated in the towns, particularly in Prague. It was dominated by pre-industrial urban and petit bourgeois groups and also by lawyers, writers and scientists, whose life style was generally similar. Of the subscribers to *Národní noviny* in 1849, a significant number of the 46 millers and 28 brewers listed can be counted among the first Czech capitalists. It was significant however that taken together millers and brewers were more numerous than merchants or officials.[26] An analysis of the social origins of the 439 members of the sole exclusively Czech armed corps *Svornost* (Concordia), formerly the *Svatováclavské bratrstvo* (Brotherhood of St Wenceslas) in 1848 confirms the decisive role of artisans (over 27 per cent) and members of the professional class (nearly 20 per cent). The participation of others, however, must not be overlooked: there were industrialists, mostly millers and builders (five per cent) and white collar workers (3.2 per cent) and labourers (7.3 per cent).[27] It was the *Slovanská lípa* (Slavonic Lime) of the Czech national organisations in 1848–9 that achieved the most extensive popularity, having several thousand members and 66 branch offices in Bohemia and six in Moravia. As a consequence of the activities of this society in February–March 1849 addresses of support were sent to the Austrian parliament by approximately 1000 towns and parishes; of the nearly

60 000 signatures in these addresses, nearly half were collected by *Slovanská lípa*.[28] Under the neo-absolutist regime in the 1850s the unfolding of a democratic mass movement among the Czechs was brought to a halt.

Opportunities for the Social Rise of Czech Elites; Assimilation and Resistance

During the first half of the nineteenth century there were comparatively speaking many educated persons of Czech ethnic origin experiencing upward mobility towards the dominant German speaking social and cultural environment. A tendency towards assimilation was particularly apparent among Austrian civil servants in the 1850s. Many officials of Czech origin were among the pillars of the Austrian administration in Galicia; and also in Hungary after 1848 where they could give free rein to their ethnic–cultural sympathies for the Ruthenians and Slovaks. Moreover the exclusively German speaking system of secondary schools and universities in Bohemia and Moravia furthered, from the last decades of the eighteenth century, an ethnic–linguistic stratification. German was the language of administration, trade and high culture; Czech was kept for communication with the lower orders. The German speaking imperial city of Vienna was emulated socially by Prague and other predominantly Czech towns.[29] Parallel to the spread of national Czech agitation between the 1820s and 1840s a germanisation of most Bohemian towns appeared to be more successful than in the eighteenth century.

However two generations of Czech patriots devoted their greatest efforts to the renewal and the upgrading of the Czech language. Literature, theatre, balls and charity *fêtes* confined to the use of Czech spread. From about 1845 also the first Czech social clubs aided expansion of national consciousness. But German was almost exclusively used in secondary schools, business, trade schools and in the universities, so that many Czech patriots had a better command of written German than of their native tongue despite their efforts at fostering Czech. When the students of Prague University wanted to publish their political demands in both languages in March 1848 they had to ask the historian Palacký to write the Czech version as their own competence was suspect.[30] Endeavours to get a national costume recognised stemmed partly from the hope that urban men and above all women would demonstrate their allegiance to the movement even though their command of the Czech language was imperfect.

In Bohemia political assimilation was beginning by the early 1860s to work in contrary ways. As before, though to a lesser degree, advancement in the central administration, army and some economic areas meant integration into the German speaking higher society of the Austrian empire. Many German politicians in the Bohemian lands, both liberal and national, had Czech surnames and ancestry. Yet numerous Czech activists, industrial and literary personalities were from German speaking families and had some German ancestry. The last German mayor of Plzeň/Pilsen before 1868, the lawyer Franz Pankratz, was the son of a Czech hatter from Kralovice. The first Czech president of the Chamber of Industry and Commerce, the printer and journalist Ignaz Schiebl, came from a German family which had come from the Tyrol several generations earlier.[31] The leaning of most of the bilingual Jewish population in Bohemia towards the Czechs was no longer an exception, as it had been before 1848.[32]

Czech National Organisations and Means of Communication

When, after 1860–1 and even more after 1867, constitutional life was resumed in Austria favourable conditions emerged for a fresh even more intense advance of the Czech national movement. Czech elites found themselves able to utilise several institutions of self-administration promoted, or at least permitted, by the state, which had not been the case in the 1840s. The Chambers of Commerce and Industry in Bohemia were monopolised by German industrial and commercial capital until 1883–84; and even up to the dissolution of the Habsburg monarchy in Moravia. However regularly held elections furnished opportunities for the organisation of Czech parties in all areas. In the Prague Chamber of Commerce in 1864 Czechs occupied only a quarter of the seats but in the commercial section, 64 per cent of the votes went to Czech candidates.[33] It was only in 1883 that the Czechs succeeded in attaining majorities in the Chambers of Commerce of České Budějovice/Budweis and Plzeň; in June 1884, this was achieved in the Prague Chamber. Under Czech leadership all three Chambers became important bases of support for the native economy. They organised great exhibitions (which most German–Bohemian industrialists boycotted) and made it their business to further relations with other countries.

In the very first communal elections after the downfall of Austrian neo-absolutism in March 1861 the Czech candidates seized the city administration of Prague where a combined Czech–German list of candidates initially defeated the conservatives.[34] Within a short time all towns excepting České Budějovice, and communities in the Czech ethnic regions were in their hands, the last being that of Plzeň in 1868. However it took much longer to secure Czech administration in the Moravian towns; in many cases this did not happen until the 1890s.

Larger towns in Moravia such as Brno, Olomouc/Olmütz and Ostrava/Ostrau retained their purely German administration until 1918 despite having Czech majorities.[35] Towns under Czech administration, particularly the Bohemian capital of Prague, were active centres of national cultural and social life. This was particularly true of Prague after October 1882 when the last five German speaking members left the town council. The elective District government introduced in Bohemia in 1864 had an important role in the concentration of leaders at a local and regional level. Active representatives of villages were elected on to most district administrations which brought them into contact, and often conflict, with the owners of important estates and with urban representatives.[36] As early as about 1860 rather underpaid secretaries of Town Councils and Rural Councils were among the most militant activists of the Czech democratic movement.

Within a comparatively short time after 1860–1 a close network of national associations came into being, covering all areas of social life and branching into every Czech town and region. Amateur theatre clubs and choral societies were founded everywhere; almost every large and middling town had separate social *Besedas* (clubs) for the middle and artisan classes. The athletic club *Sokol* (Falcon) expanded into the largest national Czech organisation. By 1871 there were 44 *Sokol* clubs in Bohemia, five in Moravia and one in lower Austria, with a total of 10 516 members. A decline followed which was only halted in 1883, after which there was a rapid rise, resulting in 171 *Sokol* clubs with nearly 20 000 members in 1888 and 466 clubs (367 in Bohemia, 93 in Moravia/Silesia, and six in lower Austria) counting 43 870 members in 1897.[37] The catchword given out by the long time *Sokol* leader Miroslav Tyrš: 'Every Czech a *Sokol*' illustrates the mass character of the organisation and its claim to cover the entire national territory. This was only challenged when the Catholic national athletic organisation *Orel* (Eagle) and the workers' gymnastic clubs were founded at the turn of the century.

The democratic mass movement among the Czechs reached its climax after the Dual Monarchy was created in 1867. More than 100 large open air demonstrations were held in Bohemia between 1868 and 1871 and another 40 in Moravia and Silesia.[38] Initially they were called 'meetings' after their Irish counterparts but soon the term *tabor* (open air mass meeting) for them spread, which deliberately linked it to the tradition of the Hussite revolution of the fifteenth century. The total of nearly 1 500 000 people claimed by the Czech patriotic press to have taken part in the *tabors* is too high an estimate but participation of tens of thousands in a single meeting was not exceptional. The most enthusiastic participants, apart from the urban petit bourgeois, came from all levels of the rural population and the working class. Not even the failure of the Bohemian compromise in 1871, which had been attempted at a time when the democratic mass movement was already declining, could seriously slow down the swift advance of Czech activities in Austria. Lack of effective foreign support had the important result of strengthening Czech political identity internally. Around 1861–3 Czech consciousness gained a firm footing in Moravia and by the end of the 1860s even among some in Silesia.

After 1860 the most important means of communication was the independent Czech press. The leading Czech daily paper, *Národní Listy* (National News), had been under the influence of a more radical (Young Czech) wing after 1863 although conservative–liberal (Old Czech) party retained the leadership of Czech political life for another quarter of a century. Up to the beginning of the 1880s the circulation of some 4000 copies achieved in the first year did not increase significantly, but it then rose to 9744 in 1883, to 10 782 in 1890; and to 14 100 for the morning edition and 8000 for the afternoon edition in 1895. The Old Czech papers aimed at the upper classes had a much lower circulation whereas the *Politik* (Politics) in German printed more than 5500 copies in 1890. It was the popular *Národní Politika* (National Politics) which became a mass publication with 8000 copies in 1883, 17 359 in 1890, and 32 000 in 1895.[39] Because of the expensive newspaper stamp most Czech regional, artisan and workers' publications initially appeared in the form of (weekly or bi-weekly) non-political periodicals. However from the end of the 1880s the number of political newspapers and journals as well as of technical and scientific periodicals increased much faster than did non-political magazines.[40]

Table 4.2: Officially permitted Czech newspapers and periodicals in Bohemia

Year	Political	Non-political	Technical and Professional	Total
		Periodicals		
1863	10	18	17	45
1871	20	20	43	83
1879	32	30	60	122
1885	56	51	109	216
1891	102	64	153	319
1895	120	65	210	395

Social Composition of Czech Political Representation from 1861 to 1901–2

Analyses of the social and territorial origins, occupations, education and age of the Czech members of the Bohemian and Moravian *diets* provide a portrait of the composition of the Czech political elites during the four decades beginning with the reinstatement of constitutionalism and ending at the turn of the century.[41] There are advantages as well as drawbacks in concentrating on *diet* members. Not all outstanding personalities, particularly from economic, cultural and scientific groups, were elected to one of the two *diets*. But the selection is not arbitrary and the relevant data can be assembled more easily, particularly for the later period, in part from the parliamentary almanacs.[42] It is impossible to classify individual members in a social, and in some cases ethnic political sense, in the 1880s without a certain over-simplification of the transitional nature

Table 4.3: Czech deputies of the Bohemian *diet*, 1861–1901 (electoral classes of Chambers of Commerce and Industry in towns and rural communities)

Professions	Election of					
	1861	*1867/II*	*1878*	*1889*	*1895*	*1901*
Lawyers	25	24	27	24	21	18
Physicians, pharmacists	11	7	5	5	5	5
University professors	2	4	2	3	3	4
School teachers	11	8	2	5	2	1
Scholars, writers, journalists	2	7	6	3	3	2
Catholic priests	7	4	3	–	–	1
Officials, clerks	4	6	4	3	4	7
Educated middle class	62	60	49	43	38	38
Industrialists	4	6	3	5	4	3
Traders, merchants	3	4	4	8	7	3
Financiers	–	–	1	1	–	–
Engineers	–	–	–	4	2	2
Economic managers	1	1	1	1	–	2
Burghers, artisans	1	8	10	7	7	8
Business middle class	9	19	19	26	20	18
Civic landowners, peasants	6	5	10	22	36	39
Millers	2	2	4	4	2	2
Agricultural middle class	8	7	14	26	38	41
Aristocratic landowners	1	1	1	2	1	–
Total	80	87	83	97	97	97

Table 4.4: Czech deputies of the Moravian *diet*, 1861–1902 (electoral classes of towns and rural communities)[43]

Professions	Election of					
	1861	*1867/II*	*1878*	*1890*	*1896*	*1902*
Lawyers	4	6	10	12	12	13
Physicians, pharmacists	1	2	1	2	2	2
School teachers	1	3	–	–	–	–
Catholic priests	4	5	4	1	2	2
Officials, clerks	–	1	–	–	–	–
Educated middle class	10	17	15	15	16	17
Industrialists	1	1	1	1	1	2
Traders	1	–	–	1	1	–
Economic managers	–	–	–	1	2	2
Burghers, artisans	2	1	–	2	–	–
Business middle class	4	2	1	5	4	4
Civic landowners, peasants	11	7	6	13	14	13
Estate managers	–	1	–	1	1	1
Millers	1	1	1	–	–	–
Agricultural middle class	12	9	7	14	15	14
Aristocratic landowners	–	–	1	–	–	1
Total	26	28	24	34	35	36

of allegiance. Nevertheless, this method supplies a good point of departure for an analysis.

The significant proportion of educated middle class notables among the Czech members elected to the Bohemian *diet* in its first term is in sharp contrast to the social origins of the German Bohemian members. In the predominantly German speaking towns and villages of Bohemia no less than 18 factory owners were elected in 1881 and another 11 German Bohemian industrialists were sent to the *diet* by the chambers of commerce and industry. A significant number of Czech *diet* members were lawyers – mostly self-employed; a similar phenomenon can be seen in other parliamentary bodies in the nineteenth century Europe. The percentage of lawyers reached its peak in Bohemia in 1878 (33 per cent) and in Moravia in 1878 (almost 42 per cent). In the beginning the circle of politically active Czech lawyers was rather limited in both *diets*; by the end of the nineteenth century their predominance was challenged by peasant representatives, mostly elected in the rural constituencies. Delegates were counted as lawyers if they had given this profession first place in the official list even though their activities were partly of a commercial nature. In the 1880s the Old Czech leader F.L. Rieger called himself 'lawyer and landed proprietor'. Eminent owners of newspapers and printing works, such as J.S. Skrejšovský and the brothers Julius and Edvard Grégr, were included among the writers and journalists. Members of the liberal professions among the Czech delegates were the least dependent on the Austrian state or German speaking notables.

The number of university professors elected to the Bohemian *diet* remained constant. Teaching members of the Czech Technical University were habitually more active and radical than professors in the philosophy or law faculties. Secondary school teachers' involvement was limited by strong pressure from state authorities, particularly if they lived in the country distant from Prague. More independence was enjoyed in most cases by teachers at secondary or technical schools financed by the autonomous provincial or regional governing bodies. A case in point is the director of the urban secondary school in Tábor, Václav Křížek who had signed the declaration of the Czech representatives in 1868. One year later he resigned from the *diet* in order not to jeopardise the transfer of his school to state administration.[44] For these reasons the number of Czech secondary school teachers among the Czech delegates, which had been considerable during the 1860s, diminished over time; there were none at all after 1871 in Moravia. The same tendency could be seen in the case of the Catholic clergy – more clearly in Bohemia than in Moravia. A revival in the number of clerical representatives near the turn of the century was no longer due to their activity in the Old Czech movement but to the founding of new Catholic political parties.[45]

An interesting development can be seen among civil servants. Initially one *Ministerialrat* (ministry official), one mining commissioner, one *Bezirksvorsteher* (District Commissioner), and one Post Office manager were elected by Czech constituencies – all of them state civil servants. Czech civil servants in the *diet* of 1901 were quite different: two secretaries of Czech district administrations, two town secretaries, one secretary of the Czech directed Chamber of Commerce and Industry in Prague, one secretary of the Czech section of the Bohemian Agricultural Council and one Post Office director.

The continuous increase of the Czech business middle class with its growing strength and importance during the second half of the nineteenth century did not result in a proportionally large representation in the Bohemian *diet*. Nevertheless it was significant that there were two factory owners and two merchants among the 12 most important Czech personalities whose petition for the foundation of a

Czech political daily paper was submitted directly to the Emperor Franz Joseph in 1860.[46] The same industrialists, one leather manufacturer and one sugar factory owner, were among the first Czech *diet* representatives in 1861 together with a successful engine works entrepreneur and an east Bohemian proprietor of a textile mill. However most industrialists did not wish to spend their precious time in parliamentary activity. Confirmation of this fact can also be seen in a significant decrease in the numbers of German Bohemian industrial *diet* representatives. The regularly held elections for the three Chambers of Commerce and Industry in the predominantly Czech regions show, however, that for a number of years Czech economic power was concentrated in trade and small scale business. Czech majorities in the Chambers of Commerce in České Budějovice in 1883, and in Prague in 1884, were obtained with active support from Czech Jewish merchants. Those *diet* members for whom no other designations than 'town burghers' or 'mayors' could be found were included in the category 'burghers and artisans'. In Czech society, then, there was no sharply defined boundary between the lower middle class and the modern commercial bourgeoisie.

In terms of the social background of *diet* members, in both Bohemia and Moravia, the group of civil landowners and peasants showed the biggest increase. Up to the end of the 1880s representation of Czech peasants was traditionally higher in the Moravian *diet* than in that of Bohemia. However well-to-do Czech peasants worked all the more diligently in the communal and regional self-government. Up to 1884 a temporary decrease in the number of peasant members appeared in Moravia because as a rule it was only in rural constituencies that Czech candidates had an assurance of being elected. The peasants therefore elected recognised leaders of the Czech national party. In Bohemia also the authority of the Old Czech and Young Czech leaders was undiminished among the rural population. The extensive interweaving of agrarian and industrial interests in the Czech economy can be seen up to the end of the nineteenth century. Most of the early Czech limited stock companies were founded with the aid of peasant capital.[47] At that time most middle and small towns in the Bohemian lands were connected with agrarian production; on the other hand a large number of prosperous Czech peasants in the fertile regions of Bohemia and Moravia showed an unusual level of education. From the 37 *diet* representatives coming from Czech rural communities who are classed as peasants and non-aristocratic landowners in the membership lists, seven had a university education and 23 had attended secondary schools for at least four years. Of the latter half had either taken their *Matura* (final examination) or gone on to professional agricultural training.

Aristocratic owners of large estates influenced the activities of the

Bohemian and Moravian *diets* in all aspects due to their privileged electoral position. The social origins of the Czech members of the *Reichsrat* (imperial parliament) were not significantly different from those of the Bohemian or Moravian *diets*.[48] Up to the 1890s Czech political representation was formed from two important components. The decision making nucleus consisted of the comparatively small political body of the Old and Young Czechs in Prague and Brno. In contrast to the Czech representation in the parliaments of Vienna and Kremsier in 1848–9 the majority of Czech seats in the Bohemian *diet* after 1861 were the preserve of well-known town and regional leaders. Among the Czech members of the Bohemian *diet* of 1867–8 were 19 mayors of towns and 11 chairmen of district councils. During the 40 years from 1861 to 1901, 54 mayors of towns were represented in the *diet*, some of them for a remarkably long time: the mayor of Chrudim was a member for 32 years; that of Bechyně for 29 years; and of Pelhřimov for 22 years, the latter two without interruption until death. Fourteen other mayors were members for more than ten years. This tendency came to an end only with the expansion of mass political parties.

Czech National Society at the Turn of the Twentieth Century

During the nineteenth century the Czechs as an ethnic group changed fundamentally. In the socio-economic sphere the Czechs passed from the initial stages of an incomplete social structure into a society having all fundamental classes and strata of capitalism. Organisation of Czech economic life attained a high level and gave the impression of complete integration – commercial banks, credit and savings associations, industrial, trade and artisan groups, peasant organisations, trade unions and consumer cooperatives. Social changes led to an extensive differentiation of political parties and their activities. Early leaders of the Old and Young Czechs between 1897 and 1907 had to relinquish the major part of their political influence to modern democratic mass parties. In contrast to the ethnically mixed *diets* and autonomous Provincial Councils, Prague as the capital of Bohemia developed into an exclusively Czech self-governing body with maximum political activity and a foreign policy of its own. No longer did it appear necessary to direct all Czech cultural activities towards ethnic pedagogical efforts. Czech cultural and scientific leaders could participate in modern currents and innovative trends on an international scale. The entire process of education, from primary school to university, to art and technical colleges, functioned in the Czech language.

In many respects at the turn of the twentieth century the Czechs were the ethnic group on the European continent which had reached the highest degree of development but they still lacked an independent or autonomous state of their own.[49] In spite of a near complete capitalist social structure and a modern system of political parties and cultural life, all attempts at federalism, through compromise or transformation, were unsuccessful. The steadily escalating ethnic rivalry between Czechs and Germans made any fundamental solution nearly impossible. Czechs no longer wished to be an ethnic group within Austria but considered themselves to be a nation in the political sense, comparable at least to the Hungarians within the Habsburg empire; in fact a European nation like any other. On the other hand the Germans in Bohemia and Moravia were afraid of becoming an ethnic minority within a predominantly Czech state. In view of this threat they preferred a Cisleithania governed in the German interest; if necessary without Galicia, the Bukovina and Dalmatia. In this German–Austrian nucleus they would have the majority over the Czechs (and the Slovenes). The complicated international position of Czech society in the centre of Europe, in close proximity to the German *Reich*, was the main reason why the great majority of Czech politicians prior to 1917—8 did not work towards separation from the Austrian state.

The Austrian Government and the Czech Social Elites in the Nineteenth Century

The Austrian system of government was, for the second half of the eighteenth century, German in language, culture, administration and military matters. Up to 1866 this position was emphasised by the Austrian claim to leadership in Germany. It was inimical towards the endeavours of Italians and Poles to achieve their own national state as well as towards similar tendencies of liberal and democratic Germans. Within this framework the Austrian government after 1815 was prepared to tolerate the ethnic identity of the Czechs in Bohemia and the Slav dialects in Moravia and even to offer the linguistic movements moderate support. The Austrian state expected to gain from the literary movements of western and southern Slavs a counterbalance against a possible orientation of the Austrian Slavs towards Russia. Czech endeavours were supposed to be confined to an ethnic, fundamentally non-political level. The Austrian Chancellor, Prince Metternich, insisted on distinguishing between encouragement of ethnic identity and the fostering of nationalism in the political sense. In his opinion a good government ought to be able to discern the moment for intervention necessary for keeping national development on the right track.[50]

The idea of an Austrian identity faithful to the emperor and supra-

ethnic influenced a significant part of the Czech population during
the whole of the nineteenth century. This was more evident in
Moravia and Austrian Silesia than in Bohemia. In resisting the
German revolution in 1848–9 the Austrian governments were
interested to some extent in a participation of Czech political
representatives friendly to Austria. The attempt of the Governor,
Count Leo Thun, to appoint a provisional Bohemian government at
the end of May 1848 was not recognised in Vienna however and all
endeavours towards the political autonomy of Bohemia or the Czech
lands failed.[51] The resulting Austrian neo-absolutism of the 1850s
was the last attempt to build a homogenous modern society under
German rule on a diversity of ethnic territories within the Habsburg
monarchy.[52] After this concept had broken down, because of
inherent weakness and contradictions coupled by defeats on the
battlefields of 1859 and 1866, the Cisleithanian non-Hungarian part of
the Habsburg monarchy developed into a multi-ethnic state comprising several nationalities with recognition of equal rights.[53] The
rise of the Czechs between the 1860s and 1914 did not meet with any
serious opposition from the Austrian state. On the contrary it
encouraged a number of legislative, economic, social and cultural
measures and policies.

Czech social and political elites were connected to the Austrian
state by many ties. They had adopted some characteristic aspects of
Austrian social and political life but others had been formed through
opposition and resistance to Austrian rule. In a certain sense the
Czechs occupied an advantageous position. Though in diplomatic
circles and in influential state and army positions, the Czech share of
power was so negligible as to be practically non-existent, they moved
to the front in democratic mass movements, in culture and sports.
Czech society could take advantage to a large extent of the economic,
socio-political and cultural facilities of the state without having to
assume responsibility for its management.[54] The extensive system of
Czech political, economic, cultural and other organisations was to
some extent a substitute for political self-government. Moreover the
efficient communal and regional self-administration was quite
capable of defending specific interests of Czech society and its elites
against the state. There remained, however, the fundamental difference between a dynamic national society and an authoritarian
government in the areas of foreign and military affairs.

State of Research

Until a few years ago there had been relatively little research concerning the rise of the Czech social and political elites after 1848–9. Studies

of economic history and demography undertaken from the early 1950s in most cases took no notice of the ethnic aspect, whereas the treatment of the nationality question in the Bohemian territories took insufficient notice of social history. For the period up to 1848 the methodically impressive analyses of Miroslav Hroch were pioneering. A historiographic assessment of the research into the Czech bourgeoisie, closely connected to the problem of modern Czech elites, can be found in the works of Jiří Kořalka of 1989 and 1991.

Notes

1 See the statistical survey by Urbanitsch in Wandruszka and Urbanitsch, vol. I, table 1, after p. 38.
2 Brousek, pp. 23, 31–2.
3 Kořalka (1980), pp. 208–9; see also Kořalka and Crampton, vol. 1, pp. 489–90.
4 Kořalka (1988), pp. 33–6.
5 Kolejka (1960), pp. 348–59; Pallas, pp. 49–54.
6 Springer, p. 139.
7 Šafařík, pp. 94–5.
8 Schnabel, table 8.
9 Hain, pp. 204–6.
10 Ibid., pp. 205, 224, 231, and 234; Wandruszka and Urbanitsch, table 1 following p. 38.
11 See Živanský, pp. 700–12.
12 Bihl, pp. 904–6.
13 See Říha and Mésároš, pp. 501–4.
14 Horská-Vrbová (1965), pp. 58–61.
15 Österreichische Statistik, vol. 66, no. 1, Vienna 1905.
16 Österreichische Statistik, vol. 63, no. 3, Vienna 1903.
17 Hroch (1968), p. 41; Purš and Kropilák, pp. 514–6.
18 Hroch (1968), pp. 41–50, 57–60; Hroch (1971a), pp. 128–31; Hroch (1985), pp. 44–61.
19 Hroch (1968), pp. 50–3. See also Hroch (1971b), pp. 513–36.
20 Rak (1985), p. 50–1.
21 Pech, p. 333.
22 Heidler, pp. 36–59; see also Pech, pp. 104–5.
23 Spáčil, p. 175.
24 Roubík (1954); see also Pech, p. 114.
25 Roubík (1930), pp. 40–1; Havránek (1983), pp. 112–3.
26 Havránek (1983), p. 113.
27 Moravcová (1981), pp. 34–42; Moravcová (1986), pp. 42–8.
28 Novotný, pp. 45–8.
29 See Raupach, pp. 26–7.
30 Havránek (1986), p. 38.
31 Moravcová (1986), pp. 62–72, 158–61.
32 See Čepelák, pp. 95–9, 105, 176.
33 Horská-Vrbová (1962), p. 266.
34 See Cohen, pp. 46–51.
35 Glassl, pp. 21–3.
36 Heumos (1979), pp. 38–43, 62–3.

37 Nolte, p. 138.
38 Purš (1958), p. 661; Říha and Mésároš, p. 413.
39 Roubík (1936), pp. 130 and 169.
40 *Ibid.*, p. 268.
41 Preliminary papers by Kořalka (1990), and Malíř were presented at an international conference 'Bürgertum in der Habsburgermonarchie' 1988. Tables 3 and 4 are based on both papers.
42 Navrátil (1902); Navrátil (1900). See also Fiala and Malíř (1990).
43 There were no Czech deputies elected by the Chambers of Commerce and Industry in Brno/Brünn and Olomouc/Olmütz.
44 See Kořalka (1978), pp. 19–22.
45 Malíř (1990), pp. 67–8, appendix.
46 Tobolka, p. 21.
47 Horská-Vrbová (1962), pp. 259–60.
48 See Navrátil (1903).
49 See Kořalka (1986), p. 170.
50 Haas, p. 132.
51 See Kazbunda, pp. 212–23; Pech, pp. 102–3.
52 Helfert, used the word 'national' in the sense of *gesamtösterreichisch* (all-Austrian).
53 See Stourzh, pp. 975–1206.
54 Kořalka and Crampton, pp. 517–8; Megner, pp. 262–8.

Select Bibliography

Bihl, W. (1980), 'Die Juden', in Wandruszka, A. and Urbanitsch, P. (eds), *Die Habsburgermonarchie 1848–1918*, vol. 3, part 2, Die Völker des Reiches, Vienna.

Brousek, K.M. (1980), *Wien und seine Tschechen: Integration und Assimilation einer Minderheit im 20. Jahrhundert*, Schriftenreihe des Österreichischen Ost– und Südosteuropa–Instituts, vol. 7, Vienna.

Čepelák, V. (ed.) (1967), *Dějiny Plzně* (A History of Plzeň), vol. 2: 1781–1918, Plzen.

Cohen, G. B. (1981), *The Politics of Ethnic Survival: Germans in Prague, 1861–1914*, Princeton.

Fiala, P. (1988), 'Zastoupení českých politických stran na moravském zemském sněmu na konci 19. století' (The Representation of Czech Political Parties in the Moravian *Diet* at the End of the Nineteenth Century), *Časopis Matice moravské*, vol. 107, Brno.

Garver, B.M. (1978), *The Young Czech Party 1874–1901 and the Emergence of a Multi-Party System*, Yale Historical Publications, New Haven.

Glassl, H. (1967), *Der Mährische Ausgleich*, Veröffentlichung des Sudetendeutschen Archivs, Munich.

Haas, A.G. (1968–9), 'Metternich and the Slavs', *Austrian History Yearbook*, vol. 4–5, Houston.

Hain, J. (1852), *Handbuch der Statistik des österreichischen Kaiserstaates*, vol. 1, Vienna.

Havránek, J. (1967), 'The Development of Czech Nationalism', *Austrian History Yearbook*, vol. 3, part 2, Houston.

Havránek, J. (1983), 'Předpoklady působení české kultury v Čechách v 19. století' (Preconditions of the Impact of the Czech Culture in Bohemia in the Nineteenth Century), *Město v české kultuře 19. století* (The Town in the Czech Culture of the Nineteenth Century), Studie a materiály Národní galerie, vol. 1, Praha.

Havránek, J. (1986), 'Karolinum v revoluci 1848' (The Carolinum in the Revolution of 1848), *Acta Universitatis Carolinae, Historia Universitatis Carolinae Pragensis*, vol. 26, no. 2, Prague.

Heidler, J. (1907), 'Český sněm ústavodárný 1848' (The Constituent of Bohemia in 1848), Český časopis historický, vol. 13, Prague.

Helfert, J.A. (1853), Über Nationalgeschichte und den gegenwärtigen Stand ihrer Pflege in Österreich, Prague.

Heumos, P. (1979), Agrarische Interessen und nationale Politik in Böhmen 1848–1889: Sozialökonomische und organisatorische Entstehungsbedingungen der tschechischen Bauernbewegung, Quellen und Studien zur Geschichte des östlichen Europa, vol. 11, Wiesbaden.

Heumos, P. (1983), 'Kleingewerbe und Handwerk in Prag im späten 19. und frühen 20. Jahrhundert', Bohemia, vol. 24, Munich.

Horská-Vrbová, P. (1962), 'K otázce vzniku české průmyslové buržoazie' (Problem of Origin of the Czech Industrial Bourgeoisie), Československý časopis historický, vol. 10, Prague.

Horská-Vrbová, P. (1965), Český průmysl a tzv. druhá průmyslová revoluce (The Bohemian Industry and the so-called Second Industrial Revolution), Rozpravy Československé akademie věd, řada společenských věd, vol. 75, no. 3, Prague.

Horská, P. (1972), 'Pokus o využití rakouských statistik pro studium společenského rozvrstvení českých zemí v 2. polovině 19. století' (An Attempt at Using the Austrian Statistics for the Investigation of the Social Stratification of the Czech Lands in the Second Half of the Nineteenth Century), Československý časopis historický, vol. 20, Prague.

Hroch, M. (1968), Die Vorkämpfer der nationalen Bewegung bei den kleinen Völkern Europas. Eine vergleichende Analyse zur gesellschaftlichen Schichtung der patriotischen Gruppen, Acta Universitatis Carolinae Philosophica et Historica, Monographia 24, Prague.

Hroch, M. (1971a), 'Das Erwachen kleiner Nationen als Problem der komparativen sozialgeschichtlichen Forschung', in Schieder, T. (ed.), Sozialstruktur und Organisation europäischer Nationalbewegungen, Studien zur Geschichte des neunzehnten Jahrhunderts, vol. 3, Munich.

Hroch, M. (1971b), 'K otázce územní skladby národního hnutí' (Problem of the Territorial Structure of the National Movement), Československý časopis historický, vol. 19, Prague.

Hroch, M. (1985), Social Preconditions of National Revival in Europe: A Comparative Analysis of the Social Composition of Patriotic Groups among the Smaller European Nations, Cambridge.

Kazbunda, K. (1929), České hnutí roku 1848 (The Czech Movement of 1848), Prague.

Klíma, A. (1979), Na prahu nové společnosti 1781–1848 (On the Eve of a New Society, 1781–1848), Prague.

Kolejka, J. (1960), 'České národně politické hnutí na Moravě v letech 1848–1874' (The Czech National–Political Movement in Moravia in 1848–1874), Brno v minulosti a dnes, vol. 2, Brno.

Kořalka, J. (1978), Vznik táborského muzea roku 1878 (The Foundation of the Museum of Tabor in 1878), Tabor.

Kořalka, J. (1980), 'Fünf Tendenzen einer modernen nationalen Entwicklung in Böhmen', Österreichische Osthefte, vol. 22, Vienna.

Kořalka, J. and Crampton, R.J. (1980), 'Die Tschechen', in Wandruszka, A. and Urbanitsch, P. (eds), Die Habsburgermonarchie 1848–1918, vol. 3, part 1, Die Völker des Reiches, Vienna.

Kořalka, J. (1986), 'Aufstieg moderner Nationalgesellschaften in Österreich', in Berner, P., Brix, E. and Mantl, W. (eds), Wien um 1900: Aufbruch in die Moderne, Vienna.

Kořalka, J. (1988), 'K pojetí národa v české společnosti 19. století' (Concept of Nation in the Czech Society of the Nineteenth Century), Povědomí tradice v novodobé české kultuře (the Consciousness of Tradition in the Modern Czech Culture), Studie a materiály Národní galerie, vol. 3, Prague.

Kořalka, J. (1989), *Die tschechische Bürgertumsforschung*, Universität Bielefeld, Sonder-forschungsbereich 177, Arbeitspapier 5, Bielefeld.

Kořalka, J. (1990), 'Tschechische bürgerliche Landtagsabgeordnete in Böhmen 1861–1913', in Bruckmüller, E., Döcker, U., Stekl, H. and Urbanitsch, P. (eds), *Bürgertum in der Habsburgermonarchie*, Vienna.

Kořalka, J. (1991), *Tschechen im Habsburgerreich und in Europa 1815–1914. Sozial-geschichtliche Zusammenhänge der neuzeitlichen Nationsbildung und der Nationalitäten-frage in den böhmischen Ländern*, Schriftenreihe des Österreichischen, Ost- und Südosteuropa-Instituts, vol. 18, Vienna and Munich.

Malíř, J. (1985), *Vývoj liberálního proudu české politiky na Moravě. Lidová strana na Moravě do roku 1909* (The Development of the Liberal Current of the Czech Politics in Moravia: the People's Party in Moravia until 1909), Opera Universitatis Purkynianae Brunensis, Facultas philosophica, vol. 258, Brno.

Malíř, J. (1988), 'Zu einigen Entwicklungszügen der tschechischen liberalen Parteien vor 1914', *Sborník prací filozofické fakulty brněnské univerzity*, C 35, Brno.

Malíř, J. (1990), 'Zur Problematik der tschechischen bürgerlichen Vertretung im mährischen Landtag in den Jahren 1861–1913', in Bruckmüller, E., Döcker, U., Stekl, H. and Urbanitsch, P. (eds), *Bürgertum in der Habsburgermonarchie*, Vienna.

Megner, K. (1985), *Beamte. Wirtschafts- und sozialgeschichtliche Aspekte des k.k. Beamtentums*, Studien zur Geschichte der österreichisch-ungarischen Monarchie, vol. 21, Vienna.

Moravcová, M. (1981), 'Sociální složení členů pražského sboru "Svornost" v roce 1848' (The Social Structure of the Members of the Prague Corps 'Concordia' in 1848), *Český lid*, vol. 68, Prague.

Moravcová, M. (1986), *Národní oděv roku 1848. Ke vzniku národně politického symbolu* (The National Costume of 1848: Origins of a National–Political Symbol), Prague.

Navrátil, M. (1900), *Almanach sněmu Markrabství moravského 1896–1902* (Almanac of the *Diet* of the Margraviate of Moravia, 1896–1902), Prague.

Navrátil, M. (1902), *Nový český sněm 1901–1907* (The New Bohemian *Diet*, 1901–1907), Prague.

Navrátil, M. (1903), *Čechové na říšské radě 1879–1900* (The Czechs in the Imperial Parliament, 1879–1900), Tabor.

Nolte, C. (1986), '"Our Task, Direction and Goal": The Development of the Sokol National Programme to World War I', in Seibt, F. (ed.), *Vereinswesen und Geschichtspflege in den böhmischen Ländern*, Bad Wiesseer Tagungen des Collegium Carolinum, Munich.

Novotný, J. (1976), 'Slovanská lípa 1848–1849. K dějinám prvního českého politického spolku' (The Slavonic Lime 1848–1849: Towards a History of the First Czech Political Association), *Acta Musei Pragensis*, Prague.

Österreichische Statistik, vol. 63, no. 3 (1903), Vienna.

Österreichische Statistik, vol. 66, no. 1 (1905), Vienna.

Pallas, L. (1970), *Jazyková otázka a podmínky vytváření národního vědomí ve Slezsku* (The Language Question and Conditions of Forming the National Consciousness in Silesia), Ostrava.

Pech, S.Z. (1969), *The Czech Revolution of 1848*, Chapel Hill.

Polišenský, J. (1975), *Revoluce a kontrarevoluce v Rakousku 1848* (The Revolution and Counterrevolution in Austria, 1848), Prague.

Purš, J. (1960), 'The Industrial Revolution in the Czech Lands', *Historica*, vol. 2, Prague.

Purš, J. and Kropilák, M. (eds) (1982), *Přehled dějin Československa* (Survey of the History of Czechoslovakia), vol. I, part 2, 1526–1848, Prague.

Purš, J. (1987), *Volby do českého zemského sněmu roku 1872* (The Elections for the Bohemian Provincial *Diet* in 1872), Prague.

Rak, J. (1985), 'Divadlo jako prostředek politické propagandy v první polovině 19. století' (The Theatre as a Medium of Political Propaganda in the First Half of the Nineteenth Century), *Divadlo v české kultuře 19. století* (The Theatre in Czech Culture of the Nineteenth Century), Studie a materiály Národní galerie, vol. 2, Prague.

Raupach, H. (1939), *Der tschechische Frühnationalismus. Ein Beitrag zur Gesellschafts – und Ideengeschichte des Vormärz in Böhmen*, Volkslehre und Nationalitätenrecht in Geschichte und Gegenwart, series II, vol. 3, Essen.

Říha, O. and Mésároš, J. (eds) (1960), *Přehled československých dějin* (Survey of the Czechoslovak History), vol. II, parts 1–2: 1848–1918, Prague.

Roubík, F. (1930), *Časopisectvo v Čechách v letech 1848–1862* (The Periodicals in Bohemia, 1848–1862), Prague.

Roubík, F. (1936), *Bibliografie časopisectva v Čechách z let 1863–1895* (A Bibliography of Periodicals in Bohemia, 1863–1895), Prague.

Roubík, F. (1954), *Petice venkovského lidu z Čech k Národnímu výboru z roku 1848* (Petitions of the Rural Population from Bohemia to the National Committee of 1848), Prague.

Šafařík, P.J. (1955), *Slovanský národopis* (The Slavonic Ethnography), Hynkova, H. (ed.), Prague.

Schnabel, G.N. (1846), *Tafeln zur Statistik von Böhmen*, Prague.

Schránil, R. and Husák, J. (1911), *Der Landtag des Königreichs Böhmen 1861–1901: Personalien*, Prague.

Spáčil, J. (1948), *Veškerá moc ve státě vychází z lidu. Kronika o kroměřížském sněmu 1848–1849* (All Power in the State Comes from the People: Chronicle on the Parliament of Kremsier, 1848–1849), Kroměříž.

Springer, J. (1840), *Statistik des österreichischen Kaiserstaates*, vol. I, Vienna.

Stourzh, G. (1980), 'Die Gleichberechtigung der Volksstämme als Verfassungsprinzip 1848–1918', in Wandruszka, A. and Urbanitsch, P. (eds), *Die Habsburgermonarchie 1848–1918*, vol. 3, part 2, Die Völker des Reiches, Vienna. Also as a book (1985), Vienna.

Tobolka, Z. (1933), *Politické dějiny československého národa od r. 1848 až do dnešní doby* (A Political History of the Czechoslovak Nation from 1848 up to Our Times), vol. 2: 1860–1879, Prague.

Urban, O. (1978), *Kapitalismus a česká společnost. K otázkám formování české společnosti v 19 století* (Capitalism and Czech Society: Problems of the Formation of Czech Society in the Nineteenth Century), Otázky dějin, Prague.

Urban, O. (1982), *Česká společnost 1848–1918* (Czech Society 1848–1918), Prague.

Wandruszka, A. and Urbanitsch, P. (eds) (1980), *Die Habsburgermonarchie 1848–1918*, vol. 3, parts 1–2, Die Völker des Reiches, Vienna.

Živanský, T. (1906), 'Náboženská a církevní statistika Rakousko–Uherska' (The Religious and Church Statistics of Austria–Hungary), in Tobolka, Z. (ed.), *Česká politika* (The Czech Politics), vol. 1, Prague.

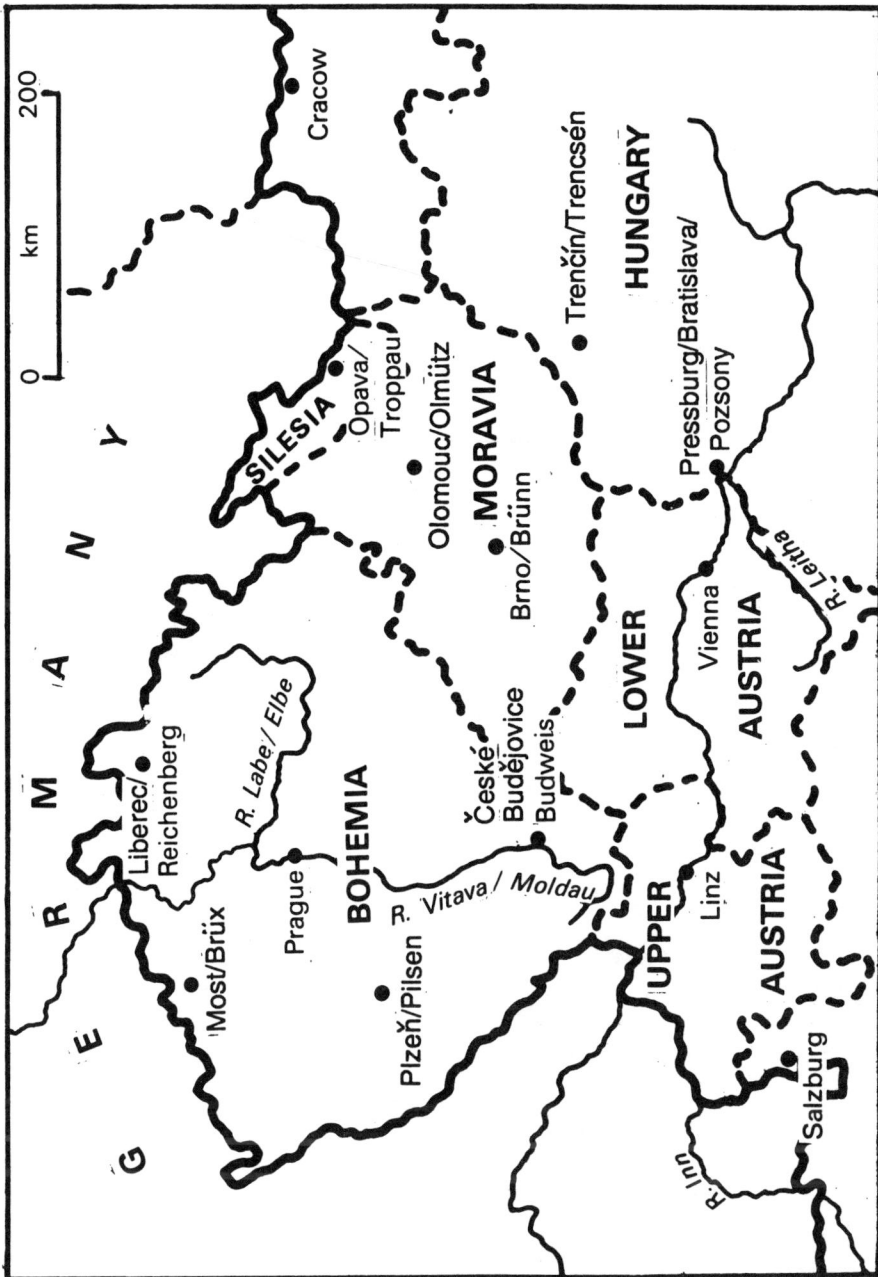

Map 4.1   The Bohemian lands in the Habsburg empire
Source: Robert A. Kann, Das Nationalitätenproblem der Habsburgmonarchie, Bd.
1. *Graz*, Köln, 1964.

5 The Ukrainians of the Russian Empire, 1860–1914

ANDREAS KAPPELER

Preliminary Remark

This case study deals with a non-dominant ethnic group using an eastern Slavic language which was known to history as the Rus', Rusyny, Ruthenians, Little Russians and – in modern times – as Ukrainians. The history of the Ukrainians developed in the framework of the *Kievan Rus'*, the great principality of Lithuania and the kingdom of Poland–Lithuania (since 1569). In the middle of the seventeenth century the majority of Ukrainians became part of the independent state of the Dnepr Cossacks (*hetmanate*). After the partition of Ukraine between Poland–Lithuania and the Muscovite state in 1667 the eastern part of the Ukrainian polity was able to maintain an autonomous position in the Russian empire for a century. After 1764 the *hetmanate* was integrated into the administrative and socio-political structure of the Russian empire, as were those parts of the Ukraine which came under Russian rule following the partitions of Poland. Thus in the nineteenth century the overwhelming majority of Ukrainians lived in Russia with the exceptions of the so-called Ruthenians of eastern Galicia, those of Bukovina and the Rusyny of Transcarpathia who became subjects of the Habsburg emperors.

This study deals only with the Ukrainians of the Russian empire. The Ukrainians of the Habsburg empire lived under different political conditions and had a separate social structure, religion and cultural tradition. Although the national movements of the Ukrainians on both sides of the Austro–Russian border were interrelated, they need to be analysed separately. The chronological limits of the study are set by the beginning of a broader national agitation around 1860 and the outbreak of the First World War which opened a new chapter in the history of the Ukrainians.

General Conditions

Social Conditions

The 22.4 million Ukrainians[1] who lived in the Russian empire in 1897 were at that time numerically the largest non-dominant ethnic group in Europe.[2] There were also 3.8 million Ukrainians in Austria–Hungary but they are outside the bounds of this study. At the end of the nineteenth century the Ukrainians composed 17.5 per cent of the total population of Russia. They spoke Ukrainian, a distinct Slavic language related to Russian, and like the Russians were almost all members of the Orthodox Church. A large proportion of the Ukrainians in the Habsburg empire were followers of the Uniate Church, which was proscribed in Russia.

More than three-quarters (17 million) of the Ukrainians in Russia lived in the Ukraine; that is, in the nine *gubernii* (provinces) in the south-western part of the empire where they constituted 73 per cent of the population (see Table 5.1). The Ukraine was divided into three regions each with its own historical tradition: the 'left bank' Ukraine comprising the provinces of Poltava, Chernigov/Chernihiv and Khar'kov/Kharkiv[3] which had been under Russian rule since the seventeenth century – most of it initially as an autonomous *hetmanate* – where the highest concentration of Ukrainians (81 per cent of the total population; in the province of Poltava it was as high as 93 per cent) lived. The remaining population was primarily Russian. The 'right bank' Ukraine comprised the provinces of Kiev/Kyiv, Podolia and Volhynia which had been annexed by Russia in the course of the partitions of Poland at the end of the eighteenth century (with the exception of the city of Kiev which had been part of Russia since the seventeenth century). The 1897 census showed that 77 per cent of the population of the 'right bank' Ukraine were Ukrainians; 12.5 per cent Jews; 4.3 per cent Russians; and 3.4 per cent Poles. The third region comprised the southern Ukraine, the so-called New Russia or the provinces of Ekaterinoslav/Katerynoslav, Kherson and Tauria, the large steppes north of the Black sea which had been colonised gradually since the end of the eighteenth century. The major ethnic proportions in this area were 56 per cent Ukrainians; 21.4 per cent Russians; 7.6 per cent Jews; and 4.5 per cent Germans.

Despite the numerical preponderance of the Ukrainians, the society, economy, politics and culture of the Ukraine were all dominated by other ethnic groups. Although a numerical majority the Ukrainians were in every other respect a non-dominant ethnic group and had the typical characteristics (such as the incomplete social structure) of 'small' peoples as defined by M. Hroch.[4] This is apparent from the ethnic composition of the urban population[5] in the

Table 5.1: The various ethnic groups in the general population and in the urban population of the Ukraine 1897 (in %)

	1	2	1-2	3	City Khar'kov	4	City Kiev	5	6	4-6	7	8	City Odessa	9	7-9	1-9
	Gouv. Chernigov	Gouv. Poltava	heartland left bank Ukraine	Gouv. Khar'kov		Gouv. Kiev		Gouv. Podolia	Gouv. Volhy.	right bank Ukraine	Gouv. Ekaterin.	Gouv. Kherson		Gouv. Tauria	Southern Ukraine	UKRAINE
Ukrainians	66.4	93.0	81.0	80.6		79.2		80.1	70.1	76.9	68.9	53.5		42.2	56.1	72.6
Urban Pop.	48.8	57.1	53.5	54.1	25.9	28.2	22.2	32.5	19.7	27.1	27.0	17.2	5.7	10.4	17.5	30.4
Russians	21.6	2.6	11.2	17.7		5.9		3.3	3.5	4.3	17.3	21.0		27.9	21.4	11.8
Urban Pop.	23.2	11.4	16.5	39.6	63.5	33.1	54.2	15.0	19.0	25.1	40.7	45.0	50.8	49.1	45.1	34.0
Jews	2.8	4.0	3.5	0.5		12.1		12.2	13.2	12.5	4.7	11.8		3.8	7.6	8.1
Urban Pop.	2.8	29.3	17.9	3.2	5.7	31.0	12.1	46.1	50.8	39.7	26.0	28.4	32.5	11.8	22.0	26.9
Poles	0.1	0.1	0.1	0.2		1.9		2.3	6.2	3.4	0.6	1.1		0.7	0.8	1.7
Urban Pop.	0.6	1.1	0.9	1.3	2.3	4.7	6.7	4.9	7.6	5.5	1.8	3.1	4.5	2.5	2.8	2.9

Ukraine where in 1897 the Ukrainians constituted only 30 per cent compared with 34 per cent Russians and 27 per cent Jews (see Table 5.1). In the southern Ukraine, the most urbanised area, and in the cities of Odessa, Kiev, Khar'kov and Ekaterinoslav their percentage was even lower. Only a few relatively small cities in the 'left bank' Ukraine had Ukrainian majorities. An extremely low percentage of Ukrainians lived in cities – 5.5 per cent as compared with 13 per cent for all of the Ukraine, 38 per cent for Russians and almost 44 per cent for Jews. Urbanisation in the Ukraine made great progress during the last decades of tsarist rule but the percentage of Ukrainians in the cities successively decreased, as can be demonstrated by the case of Kiev: from 32 per cent in 1874 to 22.2 per cent in 1897 and down to 16.4 per cent in 1917.[6]

Data on the social and occupational structure collected in the 1897 census revealed a division of labour among the larger ethnic groups in the Ukraine. Agriculture was the particular domain of the Ukrainians in which they constituted 85 per cent of the work force. In some provinces such as Poltava and Podolia virtually all the peasants were Ukrainians. In almost all other occupations and social estates the Ukrainians were grossly underrepresented. In the cities and the countryside the Jews were concentrated in their traditional roles as merchants, traders, craftsmen, innkeepers or managers. Jews were strongly represented among the lower urban classes and (richer) merchants and the professions. The Russians constituted a large portion of the landowning nobility – in the 'right bank' Ukraine together with the Poles – and the urban upper classes (civil servants, merchants, entrepreneurs, members of the professions). Russians also made up the great majority of the industrial workers, of the urban lower classes and in some areas of the rural lower classes as well.

Generally speaking the socio-ethnic structure of the Ukraine at the end of the nineteenth century was characterised by a Russian upper class in the cities and the countryside, while the urban middle and lower orders were made up of Jews and Russians, and the peasant lower class was Ukrainian. Important regional differences must however be considered: in the 'left bank' Ukraine, especially in the province of Poltava, the nobility, the urban middle and lower classes, the professions and the civil servants were mostly Ukrainians. In the 'right bank' Ukraine there were also Poles in the upper class; and in the southern Ukraine the rural middle and upper strata included German colonists.

The socio-ethnic structure of the Ukraine was of crucial importance for the history of the Ukrainians in the Russian empire. As a predominantly agrarian population which until 1861 consisted to a large extent of enserfed peasants subject to *corvée*, the Ukrainians played only a marginal role in the economic, political and social developments that took place in the large cities. The strong presence of non-Ukrainian ethnic and religious groups in the upper and middle classes restricted the social mobility of the Ukrainian peasants who could not compete with the Russians, Jews, Poles and Germans. When a Ukrainian peasant moved to the city or managed to climb up the social ladder, he found himself in a strange environment and was subject to a strong assimilationist pressure. Usually he preferred to stay in his Ukrainian village. As one contemporary observer put it, in the eyes of the Ukrainian peasants, the city was 'great Russian, Jewish, Polish, but not ours, not Ukrainian'.[7]

The interethnic division of labour explains the fact that the hectic socio-economic development in parts of the Ukraine at the end of the nineteenth and the beginning of the twentieth century took place largely without the participation of the Ukrainians. It is true that the southern Ukraine became the most important centre of mining and heavy industry in Russia, but there were very few Ukrainians among the entrepreneurs or the skilled industrial workers. There were more Ukrainians in the sugar industry located in the 'right bank' Ukraine. The southern steppe regions became the scene of commercialised export orientated agriculture, but those who profited from this development were not so much the Ukrainian peasants who owned little land but rather the large Russian landowners and the affluent German colonists.[8] The educational system also was expanded in the last decades of the tsarist regime, but the illiteracy rate among the Ukrainians above ten years of age remained 76 per cent in 1897, more than one and half times as high as that of the Russians of the Ukraine, not to mention the much lower rates among the Jews and Germans.

Thus urbanisation, industrialisation, improvements in literacy and the development of trade and transportation which took place in the Ukraine during the last three decades before 1914 had only a marginal impact on the Ukrainians themselves. Social mobilisation and the complementary development of social communications – according to Karl W. Deutsch the decisive preconditions for a national movement – had a limited effect on the Ukrainians of the Russian empire up to 1914 as is apparent from the social structure of the Ukrainians detailed in the 1897 census. Over 90 per cent of the Ukrainians still belonged to the peasant estate, and 87 per cent earned their livelihoods in agriculture as illiterate peasants with little land. Furthermore in the countryside there were only small non-peasant groups such as people involved in trade and industry, the Orthodox clergy and a small group of nobles who spoke Ukrainian. Of the Ukrainians in the cities (five per cent), many belonged to the peasant estate and maintained ties with their villages. The other Ukrainian urban dwellers – small traders, craftsmen, day labourers and workers – lived in an environment under a powerful Russian influence, as did groups of the nobility and the intelligentsia. It was only in the 'left bank' Ukraine (above all in the province of Poltava) that the situation was different. There the social structure of the Ukrainians was largely 'complete'. In general however the Ukrainians were a peasant people and their social structure did not change substantially during the period of industrialisation before the First World War.

Political Conditions

The delayed social mobilisation of the Ukrainians in the Russian empire was the result not only of the socio-economic conditions but also of the autocratic system of rule and of government policy towards the Ukrainians. Autocracy, which theoretically implied the absolute monopoly of power by the ruler, did not permit any institutionalised political participation until 1905. There were no legal parties, no parliament, no constitution, no guarantee of civil rights or liberties and no free press. Autonomous social forces and organisations which acted outside bureaucratic controls were suppressed or rigorously supervised either by the police or through censorship. However, the reforms of the 1860s did bring about a degree of liberalisation. In addition to the long overdue emancipation of the serfs, the *zemstvo* reform granted rights of self-government at the provincial level (in the 'right bank' Ukraine this was not established until 1911). But political reaction set in, soon reaching its climax in the last two decades of the nineteenth century. From the 1860s an opposition movement to the tsarist autocracy arose. It was led by the Russian intelligentsia which, from the 1870s, had been strongly influenced by populist and agrarian socialist tendencies. At the end of the nineteenth and the beginning of the twentieth century the liberal and radical intelligentsia formed a constitutionalist movement. One consequence of accelerated industrialisation was that social democracy gained ground.

The 1905 revolution forced the government to make basic concessions: a constitution was granted, a parliament was elected and civil rights and liberties were guaranteed for the first time. However after 1907 some of these concessions were rescinded. Up to 1917 the political system remained a mixture of traditional bureaucratic autocracy and constitutional parliamentary monarchy. For the multi-national state with its great Russian minority of no more than 44 per cent in 1897 policy towards the nationalities was crucial. Premodern Russia had followed basically a flexible, pragmatic and tolerant policy towards nationalities, especially when it could co-operate with loyal non-Russian elites. But in the second half of the nineteenth century repressive and aggressive tendencies increased, culminating in the 1880s and 1890s in an assimilatory policy of russification, particularly towards some nationalities in the western part of the empire. The most important factors of this reorientation were as follows:

- The desire to adjust the administrative, social and to a certain extent also, the cultural conditions in the peripheral regions to those of modernising Russia;
- the wish to counter the national movements of the non-Russian peoples, in particular that of the Poles, who were considered a danger to the integrity of the multi-national empire;
- the emergence of Russian nationalism in reaction to the gradual social and economic modernisation and to the demands of the individual nationalities.

However Russian nationalism did not become the official ideology of tsarism. The autocratic government continued to mistrust all social forces which aimed at limiting the state's monopoly of power, and any such movements were viewed as a fundamental threat to the system. Policy towards nationalities in the late Russian empire was not always repressive nor did it always seek to impose assimilation, and it often made concessions, especially during the 1905–7 revolution.

Nevertheless the policy towards the Ukrainians from the 1860s was particularly repressive. This was due to the economic and strategic importance of the Ukraine as well as its ethnic mixture, with the substantial percentage of Russians. The Ukrainian national movement was also considered particularly dangerous because the government saw it in connection with the Polish question and Russian–Austrian relations were affected as well. Russians blamed the Austrians for acting in concert with the 'Ruthenians' in Galicia to stir up the Ukrainians in Russia against the government. Finally since the Orthodox Ukrainians were so closely related to the Russians in language, culture and historical tradition, the government and Russian society considered the Ukrainians an offshoot of their own people. Ukrainian national stirrings were considered therefore a betrayal of the bonds of brotherhood between 'Little' and 'Great' Russians, a matter dear to both the government and Russian nationalist public.

The National Movement and its Activists

The History of the National Movement

As was the case with many other peoples in Europe, at the end of the eighteenth century the Ukrainians of Russia became interested in their language, literature, folklore and history. This first phase of the national movement had its social base in the nobles of the 'left bank' Ukraine and of Kiev. Typical of the movement was its literary, scientific and regional character in which, apart from the Ukrainians, Russians and Poles also participated. The climax of this first phase (Phase A of Hroch's typology) was reached in historical writings about the Cossack era and in the early poetry of the ex-serf Shevchenko. This literature laid the foundations for a historical and national consciousness, which clearly distinguished the Ukrainians from the Poles and the Russians. Cultural and scholarly contributions on the past and the present of the Ukrainian people remained an important part of the national movement until the First World War.

In the 1840s the beginnings of a transition to the second phase (Phase B) became apparent. This was the phase of active national agitation by a group of patriots who no longer followed cultural goals alone but also sought political ends and who additionally wanted to spread national consciousness among all classes of the people. One such group was the 'Brotherhood of Saints Cyril and Methodius', a small circle at the University of Kiev. It had idealistic goals which included elements of a national programme. In 1847 the police uncovered this secret organisation and its members and sympathisers, including Shevchenko, were arrested and later proscribed.

Further movement towards Phase B can be discerned during the relatively liberal years preceding the emancipation of the peasantry. It was initiated on the one hand by a few outstanding men of letters and historians in St Petersburg. On the other hand, national Ukrainian groups were formed at the University of Kiev which at that time was very much under the domination of Polish students. These groups were called the *hromady* (communes or societies) and had the goal of enlightening Ukrainian peasants. However even such moderate activities aroused the suspicion of the government and the January uprising in Poland prompted a strong reaction by officialdom against this embryonic 'Ukrainophile' movement, which was wrongly accused of being a 'Polish intrigue'. In June 1863 the Minister of the Interior, Valuev, issued a circular which denied the existence of the Ukrainian language and forbade the printing of books, with the exception of *belles lettres*, in this non-existent language. In view of the generally liberal policy at that time this was an unusually severe measure.

A third attempt by the Ukrainians to establish a national movement followed a relaxation in the repressive policy of the government in the first half of the 1870s. The *hromady* were reactivated. In Kiev a group of intellectuals joined together in the 'south western section of the Imperial Geographical Society', which though pursuing primarily cultural aims (V. Antonovych) also had socio-political goals (M. Drahomanov). The more radical so-called 'Young *hromada*' sought contact with the populist movement of the Russian *Narodniki* (populists). Again officials reacted quickly and energetically. In the act of Ems of 1876 Alexander II confirmed the prohibition of Ukrainian publications and extended the ban to include dramas and songs. These measures and the political reaction after 1881 brought about a new period of stagnation for the Ukrainian national movement in Russia.

In the 1880s the centre of Ukrainian national activity shifted to Austrian Galicia where the political conditions for national development were much more favourable. Ukrainian schools, theatres, national organisations and periodicals, and after 1890 nationalist parties, made Galicia, L'viv/Lwów/Lemberg in particular, the Piedmont of the Ukrainian national movement.

The Ukrainians of Russia finally entered Phase B in the 1890s, later than the Ukrainians of Austria, at a time when the Ukraine was already experiencing industrialisation and the beginnings of a labour movement. After a few forerunners the first national political parties were founded illegally at the turn of the century; the two important ones were the Revolutionary Ukrainian party established in 1900 with national revolutionary and socialist goals (after 1905 it became the Ukrainian Social Democratic Workers' party) and the moderate liberal Ukrainian Democratic Radical party which came into being between 1903–5: the nationalist Ukrainian People's party and the Ukrainian Social Revolutionary party remained insignificant.

The 1905 revolution, simultaneously bourgeois–democratic, agrarian, proletarian and national, produced a *Völkerfrühling* among the nationalities of Russia. The prohibitions of 1863 and 1876 were nullified and many Ukrainian periodicals and books could be printed for the first time. Parties were legalised temporarily and new national organisations were founded similar to those in Galicia, such as *Prosvita* (the Society of Enlightenment) with over 100 branches, many student organisations, scholarly societies, a Ukrainian peasants' union and peasant cooperatives. Sixty-three Ukrainians were elected to the first *duma* (the Russian parliament) and 46 to the second *duma*, and most of them joined together in a Ukrainian *hromada*. But by 1907 political reaction had set in again. Many Ukrainian organisations were forced to go underground, most publications were banned and the dynamism of the movement was broken. These political changes could not turn the Ukrainian national movement back to Phase A but it prevented its further development to Phase C in which the masses are mobilised. The Ukrainian national movement did not reach this stage until the First World War when new possibilities opened up in

1917. The Ukrainian national movement in Galicia by contrast had completed the transition to Phase C by 1914.

In the following study of the formation of a nationally conscious elite particular concentration has been given to the fully developed Phase B in the years 1900–14, reference to the previous attempts at national agitation and organisation which were repeatedly interrupted is, however, essential for understanding the situation.

The Evolution of National Activists

The section on social conditions makes it plain that it is essential to ask which social groups can be considered as national activists. In contrast to many other non-dominant ethnic groups the Ukrainians of Russia had their own property owning nobility. It was under-represented when compared with the Russian nobility and when compared with the Polish nobility in the 'right bank' Ukraine. Over the centuries this Ukrainian nobility had become strongly polonised but by the nineteenth century it felt Russian. Despite this many nobles had also a consciousness of territorial patriotism that permitted them to become the supporters of the national movement during Phase A. At the end of the nineteenth century they had still not become fully assimilated as Russians or Poles but instead maintained a double or multiple loyalty and identity. This explains why in the 1897 census a total of 56 808 hereditary nobles (with their families) stated that Ukrainian was their mother tongue.[9] The term nobility is not to be taken here in the strict sense of the word, that is of a property owning upper class. It also included nobles who had other, usually urban, occupations. This nobility looked like a nascent national elite but the social interests of the Ukrainian nobility bound it to the autocratic system. The nobility would have something to lose by involvement in the national movement.

The middle classes in the cities as well as in the countryside counted for little as national activists. Only the small group of Ukrainian craftsmen and merchants in the cities of the 'left bank' Ukraine need be considered in this connection since the national movement could exploit their conflict of interest with Jews and Russians. The Ukrainian peasants were socially almost homogenous as there were no groups of well-to-do farmers. Most Ukrainian peasants were socially immobile and illiterate. Only among the Ukrainian peasants of the 'left bank' Ukraine can an embryonic national consciousness be identified. Their primary concern was the agrarian not the national question. They wanted more land, as was clearly expressed in the agrarian revolts between 1902 and 1906. However since most of the landowners were Russians and Poles there was a possibility of linking the dominant social interests of the peasants with national aims.

The clergy had a leading role in many national movements, for example among the Ukrainians of Galicia. Although in the Russian Ukraine approximately half of the poor Orthodox clergy were Russians the other half, approximately 50 000 (with families), represented a group with sizeable potential for the Ukrainian movement especially since they lived in close contact with the peasants in the villages and were also teachers in the primary schools run by the Orthodox Church. But the clergy were not highly motivated towards participation in the Ukrainian movement in the Russian empire since they had no confessional differences with the state and the dominant national group. The clergy were a loyal part of the Orthodox Church and as such were supporters of the Russian Orthodox state.

Finally there were the secular intelligentsia whose importance in national movements, according to H. Seton-Watson, was in inverse proportion to the degree of economic development of the society and of political freedom.[10] The number of educated persons in the Ukraine was quite small however. In 1897 47 000 Ukrainians were recorded as having secondary or higher education, more than half of whom lived in the 'left bank' Ukraine, but this represented less than 0.3 per cent of the Ukrainian population. By comparison 143 000 Russians in the Ukraine had a similar education (five per cent of the Russian population of the Ukraine), a clear indication of Russian domination of Ukrainian intellectual life.

A collective biography of 209 activists of the Ukrainian national movement was prepared for this study.[11] The data collected supports Seton-Watson's theory regarding the dominance of the intelligentsia: more than three-quarters of the national activists had attended an institution of higher learning. Their percentage decreases gradually from period one (1860–4) through period two (1870–76) to the crucial period three (1900–14) (see Table 5.2). The percentage of persons with higher education among the 116 leading members of the Revolutionary Ukrainian party in the years 1904–5 investigated by Boshyk (65 per cent) confirms the result.[12] The great majority of the rest of the national activists had at least spent some time at a secondary school and thus belonged to the meagre 0.3 per cent of well educated Ukrainians. Considering the very low level of education of the general population this – even when compared to the Russian revolutionary movement[13] – extraordinarily high percentage of intellectuals is the most important characteristic of the Ukrainian national activists in Russia. The intelligentsia considered themselves the personification of the entire nation, above all social classes, and as men predestined to be the leaders of the national movement.[14]

What were the occupations of the activists in the Ukrainian

Table 5.2: Level of education of the national activists (including non-graduates, in %)

	Total n=215*	Period 1 n=65	Period 2 n=56	Period 3 n=94
University	53.0	73.9	44.6	43.5
Religious seminary	4.2	3.1	5.4	4.3
Others of unspecified institutions of higher learning	25.1	21.5	26.8	27.7
Total higher education	82.3	98.5	76.8	75.5
Secondary education	11.6	1.5	19.6	13.9
Primary education	5.6	–	3.6	10.6

*30 are mentioned more than once; for sources and explanations see note 11.

Table 5.3: Occupational distribution of the national activists (in %)

	Total n=253*	Period 1 n=64	Period 2 n=57	Period 3 n=132
Students	25.4**	54.6	28.1	9.8**
Communication specialists (press, theatre, literature)	21.0	9.4	15.8	28.8
Teachers at institutions of secondary and higher learning	15.5	12.5	24.6	12.9
Professionals	12.0	4.7	10.5	15.9
Medium and low level civil servants and white collar workers	10.8	7.8	12.3	11.4
Upper class (landowners, high level civil servants, entrepreneurs)	6.7	7.8	3.5	9.8
Primary schoolteachers	5.5	1.6	3.5	6.8
Peasants, workers	2.4	–	1.7	3.8
Clergy	0.8	1.6	–	0.8

*   53 are mentioned more than once.
** The percentage of students in Period 3 is too low because the study was not confined to a fixed year but covers 14 years. Therefore it lists many activists under their later occupations, not as students.

For sources and explanations see note 11.

national movement? In the first place most of them had been students. In the movements during period one (see Table 5.3) which were dominated by young people and in the Revolutionary Ukrainian party during the years 1904–5 the majority of the supporters were students from secondary schools or colleges. In all three periods the percentage of students was high and in period three it was considerably greater than the figures in Table 5.3 suggest.[15] Even more important than the socially transient group of students were educated persons such as the teachers at secondary and higher schools, 'communication specialists' such as editors, journalists, writers and actors as well as professionals, primarily physicians and lawyers. Taken together they constituted almost half of the national activists. During period three when employment opportunities improved the percentage of journalists and professionals increased markedly. It was from these circles of intellectuals that the leaders of the national organisations, the ideologues and the politicians of the movement were recruited.

In addition to this 'upper' intelligentsia there also were members of a 'lower' intelligentsia, often of rural origin, who spread the national idea among the peasants. They were usually lower or middle grade civil servants, white collar workers (especially in the framework of the *zemstvo*) and primary school teachers. This group increased steadily and after 1900 must have had a higher representation, especially among the sympathisers of the national movement, than the 18 per cent shown in Table 5.3. Teachers and employees of the *zemstvo* were civil servants and therefore could often only work clandestinely. Moreover nationalist activities in urban centres were recorded more often than those in the countryside. These two groups of intelligentsia together with the students composed 90 per cent (in period three approximately 85 per cent) of the activists and over 95 per cent of the leading members of the Ukrainian national movement. A fourth of the remaining ten per cent were peasants and workers who played only a marginal role as representatives to the first and second *duma*. In the sample the economic middle class (merchants, craftsmen, manufacturers) did not supply a single activist in any of the three periods.

The analysis above answers the question of whether the nobility or the clergy was in a position to form the new national elite. Obviously the Orthodox clergy played only a marginal role in the national movement. The clergy, although the largest social group with a certain amount of education and in continual contact with the Ukrainian speaking illiterate peasants, must be seen as having a minimal direct contribution to the rise of Ukrainian nationalism. Likewise only a small group from the noble upper class consisting of landowners, civil servants and officers was committed to the national movement. As a rule they acted as patrons, like the Simirenkos, sugar factory owners whose fathers had been serfs. The vast majority of nobles, even if they identified themselves with the vernacular mother tongue, were not willing to give up their loyalty to the state and to Russian or Polish values for the sake of the Ukrainian cause. E. Chykalenko, one of the few prominent activists from the ranks of the landowning nobility, commented on the attitude of his peers by criticising their self-interest: 'It is no wonder that our nobles hardly produced a single Ukrainian patriot for in this field no favours are to be obtained from the Tsar.'[16]

By referring to the incomplete data available regarding the social background of the activists, it can be assumed, however, that the nobility and the clergy contributed indirectly to the Ukrainian national movement.[17] The majority were of noble origin although their percentage gradually decreased, as was the case also with the Russian revolutionaries. Even though their fathers were often no longer landowners but rather intellectuals serving the state or the *zemstvo*, being a member of the nobility was the surest way of entry into schools of higher learning. Thus the Ukrainian nobility did not take over the leadership of the national movement as was the case among the Poles or the Hungarians. However nobles stemming from the Cossack officers (*Starshyna*) of the *hetmanate* in the 'left bank' Ukraine maintained the tradition of Ukrainian independence – by reviving it in Phase A during the first half of the nineteenth century and later by transmitting this tradition, via the intelligentsia of noble origin, to the modern national movement.[18] The clergy also exercised an influence indirectly on the national movement through their sons who obtained higher education. Even though Chykalenko's statement seems exaggerated – namely that 'among the activists of the national renaissance the sons of priests were most numerous and [they were] the only intellectual group who had been since youth close to the people and familiar with its way of life and language'[19] – still a fifth of the national activists were of clerical origin.

The percentage of the activists of peasant origin increased noticeably only after 1900 (Shevchenko was an exception) ultimately rising to 25 per cent. This reveals a process of democratisation: persons of rural background constituted half of the activists in the important third period.[20] It becomes clear that the Ukrainian peasants, the only large social group whose primary interests were in opposition to the (Russian) state and the (Russian or Polish) upper classes, were slowly being incorporated into the Ukrainian national movement.

An evaluation of the birthplace of 207 activists (Table 5.4) indicates a preponderance from the provinces of Poltava, Chernigov and Kiev in which about 40 per cent of the Ukrainian population lived. Roughly two thirds of the activists and 85 per cent of the leaders of the

Table 5.4: The geographic origin of the national activists (place of birth, in %)

Region	Total n=207	Among them, individual provinces with over 10%
Left bank Ukraine	46.9	Poltava 27.1; Chernigov 16.0
Right bank Ukraine	35.8	Kiev 23.7
Southern Ukraine	13.1	
Rest of Russia	4.2	

national movement came from towns and villages in these three provinces.[21] As discussed in the section on social conditions this was the region with the highest concentration of Ukrainians (except for Kiev) where Ukrainians had a 'complete' social structure, with a relatively high proportion of nobles, city dwellers, clergy and intellectuals. The provinces of Poltava and Chernigov had formed the heartland of the Cossack *hetmanate*, the traditions of which were still alive. The centre of the *hetmanate* had been Kiev, located on the right bank of the Dnepr. During the nineteenth century the 'left bank' Ukraine, which had no large urban centre, remained oriented toward Kiev, not toward Char'kov. Kiev was the old centre of Ukrainian culture, the seat of a university and on account of its geographical location, it was predestined to be the centre of the national renaissance. This might further explain why a high percentage of the activists came from the province of Kiev. Remaining areas of the 'right bank' Ukraine which had a comparable socio-ethnic structure, and the southern Ukraine with its developed industry and agriculture where the competition of the Russian socialist movement was strong, were less important. Finally not a single activist in the sample came from Austrian Galicia.

The results of this study of collective biography permit a description of the ideal type of Ukrainian national activist. Typically the activist was the son, rarely the daughter, of a minor noble, an intellectual of noble origin or a priest, though later more often the scion of a peasant. He grew up in a village or a small town in one of the provinces of Poltava, Chernigov or Kiev and as a rule had attended a secondary school, less often a religious seminary, a technical school or a teachers' training college. Secondary education in the Ukraine was under a strong Russian influence, its main purpose being the socialisation of the youth of the area into accepting the values of Russian culture. Nevertheless these institutions developed, especially from the 1890s, into centres of the Ukrainian national movement. Later activists often made their first contact with the national movement in such schools in Kiev, Poltava and other cities. Most activists had attended a university. The University of Kiev had the greatest attraction: more than half of the activists with a university education had studied there, especially in the historical–philological faculty, and an increasing number came from the faculty of law. Also of importance (in the order given) were the Universities of Char'kov, St Petersburg and Odessa, some religious academies and, after 1900, certain technical colleges (see Table 5.2). Few came from universities outside Russia, including the University of L'viv.

In the university cities the Ukrainian young people were strongly influenced by the Russian language and culture. Many of them chose to make a career in Russian society while others joined Russian revolutionary groups at the universities. Only a small percentage developed a specific Ukrainian identity as a result of their confrontation with Russian society. At almost all universities secret patriotic societies developed, in some cases with active assistance of university professors. Despite the repressive regime between 1884 and 1905 the Russian universities along with the *zemstvo* were virtually the only institutions which enjoyed a certain degree of freedom of action from officials and police. They became the breeding ground not only for the modernising Russian state and the revolutionary movement, but also for the Ukrainian national movement. The cultural interests of individual university professors were fused with the more radical goals of the students. Student organisations, which often worked together with the Russian revolutionaries, belonged to the driving forces of the national movement both in the early period around 1860 and at the beginning of the twentieth century.[22]

Young intellectuals were active in national organisations both during and after their studies. The younger and older generations met in these associations. A small number of students became professional activists; a larger number took up urban professions as lawyers, engineers, teachers, civil servants and white collar workers. Some graduates of the secondary schools and universities returned to the countryside as teachers or as employees of the *zemstvo*. They tried to found branches of national organisations in order to spread its ideology in the rural areas. For professional or political reasons some had to go to other parts of Russia or abroad. Although M. Drahomanov made Geneva a spiritual centre of the Ukrainian national movement for a few years with his periodical *Hromada* (1878–82) and despite outstanding leaders of the third period such as M. Hrushevs'kyj being active in Galicia for a longer period, on the whole *émigrés* did not play a decisive role in the Ukrainian movement.

Kiev remained the undisputed centre of the Ukrainian national movement in Russia from the 1840s to 1914, though only 22 per cent of the city's population in 1897 were Ukrainians, and of these three fifths belonged to the peasant estate. Only a small proportion (five per cent) of the Ukrainians in Kiev had a secondary or higher education. Among these 2734 men and women, who represen'ed a small minority compared with the 20 000 educated Russians in the city, were many national activists. They met regularly in Ukrainian clubs and conducted national organisations or periodicals. Some provincial towns such as Poltava and Chernigov were also seats of a nationally conscious active elite during all periods.

Next to Kiev the only urban centres with supra-regional import-ance for the Ukrainian movement were St Petersburg, Khar'kov for a time and, in the third period, L'viv. In L'viv the activists from the Dnepr Ukraine met the Ukrainians from Galicia and many publi-cations could be printed there which were prohibited in Russia. On the whole it becomes clear that the national activists and the entire Ukrainian movement were mainly concentrated in the cities, whereas the rural population, 95 per cent of the total, remained largely indifferent.

The decisive phase in the formation of the national activist was therefore the period when he or she was in Kiev or in some other city, usually as a young student, where he or she could be won for the movement. The sources are not very revealing about this decisive step towards acquiring national consciousness and becoming a national activist. In some cases it seems that it was a gradual process which began in early youth and was intensified at the university.[23] There are a few memoirs by famous leaders of the national move-ment which describe their conversion to the cause of Ukrainian national identity. The best known example is the 'Confession' of V. Antonovych, written in 1862, in which the 'repentant' Polish (or polonised) young noble professes his allegiance to the Ukrainian nation in order 'to atone with perseverance for all the wrongs done by those of his class to the people'.[24] Alexander and Sofia Rusov, both of Great Russian background, came into contact with the movement in Kiev, were converted to Ukrainianism, began to speak and write in Ukrainian and remained activists until their deaths.[25] The fact that there were many Poles, Russians, Jews and Germans among the Ukrainian activists underlines the importance of subjective commit-ment to the nation.

A majority of the socially mobile Ukrainians succumbed to the acculturation pressure of the Russian urban background. If someone were career orientated, regardless of whether he was employed in the civil service, army, commerce or the sciences, he almost auto-matically became russified. Russian society and economy were undergoing a process of modernisation, Russia's science and culture were blossoming, and these exercised a great attraction for young Ukrainian intellectuals. What did the Ukrainian language and the provincial culture have to offer by contrast? The Ukrainian activists lamented russification but this process was not only the result of the assimilatory policy of the government and could not be ascribed merely to the desire for a career. It was to a certain extent a natural process of acculturation. Not only official Russia but also the Russian opposition movements had a powerful influence on Ukrainian intellectuals.

A danger exists, then, of making assimilatory processes appear abnormal. Writings on nationalism have tended to assume that national exclusiveness was normal but such a narrow perspective cannot do justice to the conditions in the multi-ethnic empires of eastern Europe, which were deeply rooted in pre-national traditions. Thus nationalist Ukrainians often accused russified Ukrainians of being traitors to the cause. But what does 'russified' mean and what were the criteria for the assimilation of the middle and upper classes who were naturally multi-lingual and who had not just one, but two or even three loyalties? It is more rewarding, as suggested by Paul R. Magocsi,[26] to trace conversion from traditional multi-affiliation to the new national principle of exclusive loyalty. The majority of the Ukrainian speaking elite maintained a dual loyalty and had simultaneously a Ukrainian and a Russian or Polish identity. This is evident from the complaints in the national press about the exclusively cultural interests of the pro-Ukrainian nobles and the inadequate knowledge of the Ukrainian language even among activists and from works by Russian scholars of Ukrainian origin.[27] Only a small minority opted for an exclusive Ukrainian identity. Survival of this concept of multiple loyalty was not only an expression of the relatively delayed Ukrainian national development but was also a recognition of the socio-ethnic structures and the socio-cultural realities of the multi-national Russian empire.

The small nationally conscious and active elite which came into being in the Ukraine created organisations and channels of communication with the aim of influencing larger sections of the population. To a certain extent they followed the example of the Ukrainians in Galicia whose national movement had developed under more favourable political conditions. A natural consequence of the dominance of the intelligentsia among the activists was that nationalist organisations were interested primarily in promoting language, culture, history and popular education, whereas groups with economic goals (except for the cooperatives) or popular recreation clubs were absent. This was not the case in Galicia. After the turn of the century the Ukrainian political parties began to play an important role in the formation of a national elite and the spreading of patriotic ideas. Most national organisations remained small coteries of intellectuals or students. Only in 1906 and 1907 did the *Prosvita* societies and the Ukrainian Social Democratic Workers' party succeed in gaining a membership of a few thousand and in extending their activities all over the Ukraine. Ukrainian peasants were mobilised for the national cause for the first time but the percentage of the over 25 million Ukrainians in Russia who took part was very small.

During the repressive era before 1905 *belles lettres*, particularly the works of Shevchenko, and the Ukrainian theatre companies spread national ideas among the masses. Liberalisation in the aftermath of the 1905 revolution permitted activists to publish several newspapers and periodicals which were to become important channels of communication. However the 19 Ukrainian periodicals in print in 1913 with a circulation of only a few thousand copies were a modest beginning when compared with the 226 Russian publications appearing in the Ukraine or with the 66 Ukrainian periodicals published in Galicia or the 234 Polish magazines printed in Russia.[28] The publisher of the only Ukrainian daily newspaper that appeared continuously over a longer period of time, *Rada* (1906–14), complained repeatedly about financial problems, the lack of subscribers, its constant battle with the authorities, censorship, police interference, a lack of skilled labour and the overwhelming competition of the Russian press.[29] In addition Ukrainian was not yet a standardised literary language thus posing a further difficulty in communication. Yet it is true that the communications network spread its net widely and the few national publications played a vital role that should not be underestimated. They facilitated the exchange of opinion among the activists and the formation and confirmation of national values and political goals. Apart from periodicals the national activists tried, especially after 1905, to reach broader sections of the population by way of Ukrainian popular pamphlets and books.

What were the ideas propagated? In the first place the historical consciousness formed during the first phase had helped them to dissociate themselves from the dominant Russian ideology of integration or the still influential Polish one, both of which tried to win over the Ukrainians. A decisive component was the idealised Ukrainian Cossack past as a symbol of freedom and equality in contrast to Muscovite despotism and the rule of the Polish aristocracy. As contrasted with the glorification of the Cossack *hetmanate* and its leaders as handed down by the Ukrainian nobility, the former serf Shevchenko had a populist picture of history that idealised only the ordinary simple free Cossack, not the upper class. His outstanding literary work created a national myth.[30] This populist consciousness of history was taken over by the majority of the national activists during the second half of the nineteenth century. It was not a coincidence that historians like M. Kostomarov,

V. Antonovych and M. Hrushevs'kyj became leading personalities of the national movement. Shevchenko, by virtue of his banishment and early martyrdom, became a national symbol and the key unifying figure in the Ukrainian movement. Annual commemorations of his death were national demonstrations, the most impressive with tens of thousands of demonstrators in March 1914.

Although Shevchenko's literary work and Drahomanov's political thought already had integrated radical socio-political elements into the Ukrainian consciousness, the goals of the national activists were still primarily cultural and linguistic. Even after 1905 the main demands were equal rights for the Ukrainian language, its introduction into schools and courts, the establishment of Ukrainian professorships at the three universities in the Ukraine and the construction of monuments and museums for the poets Shevchenko and Kotlyarevsk'yj. In addition there were rather moderate political goals such as autonomy for the Ukraine within the framework of a federated Russian empire or, more generally, a democratic reform of Russia. Most young Ukrainian intellectuals who had socialist ideas joined the Russian revolutionary movement: in the 1870s the *Narodniki* and after 1900 the social revolutionaries or the social democrats.

Within the national movement there was a constant tension between the culturally orientated 'older' and the 'younger' generation. The latter was more radical, under the influence of Russian populism and Drahomanov's thinking, and became increasingly aware that the mass of the Ukrainian peasants could not be mobilised by cultural programmes. Only after the turn of the century did young intellectuals in the Revolutionary Ukrainian party begin to link urgent social problems (foremost a radical solution of the land question) with national goals. They now began to agitate among the peasants. (It was not by chance that the sons of two of the leaders of the 'old *hromada*', D. Antonovych and M. Rusov, and several peasants' sons were among them.) It is true that the Revolutionary Ukrainian party tried eventually to win over the workers but suffered from the competition of the larger Russian parties, namely the social revolutionaries and the social democrats. This is evident in the formation of a splinter group – the *Spilka* (Ukrainian Social Democratic Union) – which joined the Russian social democrats in 1905 and had more success in the Ukraine in the following years than the Ukrainian Social Democratic Workers' party. However the inclusion of populist and agrarian–socialist goals in the national programme was imperative as had already been pointed out by Shevchenko and Drahomanov. This was the only way the national movement, led by a small group of intellectuals, could win the support of the vast majority of the population, the Ukrainian peasants. After the February revolution this problem became even more urgent.

By 1917, however, the activists had still not succeeded in mobilising the mass of the Ukrainian peasants for the national cause. Nationally mobilised groups represented only a small portion of all social classes, including the intelligentsia. In the multi-ethnic Ukrainian society the Ukrainian patriots remained a marginal group. They did not become part of the social elite of the country, since that was incompatible with their primary Ukrainian loyalty. On the other hand the Ukrainian intelligentsia had initiated a national movement under extremely difficult social and political conditions and, despite serious setbacks, had created a preliminary infrastructure for a national Ukrainian culture and society. It established itself at the beginning of the twentieth century as the new national elite at the expense of the nobility which remained loyal to the autocracy and to Russian aristocratic society. This new elite remained a small yet divisive group, unevenly spread over the country, with only limited influence. But it was important – especially for the period after 1917 – that it existed at all.

The Russian Government and the Formation of a Ukrainian Elite

From the 1860s the Russian government tried to assimilate the Ukrainians through policies of national discrimination. Propagation of the 'little Russian dialect' was to remain confined to the peasants. Those who were socially mobile had to use the Russian language, had to profess loyalty to the Russian nation and were required to accept assimilation. This was particularly true for civil servants, teachers and priests. Ukrainians were not discriminated against as citizens – in contrast to the Jews; neither their religion, outward appearance nor their social status set them apart from the Russians. If they spoke Russian and remained politically loyal they had every opportunity to become a part of the social, political and intellectual elite of the empire.

This policy was implemented with the exception of the years 1905–6 by the traditional methods of bureaucratic despotism and police repression. However the majority of socially mobile Ukrainians voluntarily accepted assimilation while the Ukrainian lower classes remained indifferent. Only a small group of intellectuals resisted russification and tried to initiate a national Ukrainian movement. The Russian government observed the activities of these 'Ukrainophiles' with suspicion. They were considered a danger not only for the socio-political stability of the empire but also a threat to the unity of a Russian nation embracing not only the great Russians but all eastern Slavs including the Byelorussians and Ukrainians.

Thus the authorities in St Petersburg and the Ukrainian cities suppressed even the modest cultural activities aimed at revival of the Ukrainian language and the founding of national organisations and periodicals. Police watched the activists closely and persecuted them, imposing fines and terms of imprisonment. Reactions to political activities were even sharper, especially to agitation in the countryside or to socialist tendencies among Ukrainian students. In executing government policy towards the Ukrainians, which was much more repressive than the policy towards most of the nationalities of the Russian empire, government and society, including most of the opposition groups, were in fundamental agreement. On occasion measures against small groups of 'little Russians', who favoured secession from the 'great Russian' people, were approved. It is true that among the Russian intellectuals and opposition groups there was some sympathy for the 'Ukrainophiles', but in pre-revolutionary Russia other matters had a higher priority.

What role did government policy play among the factors which hindered the formation of a Ukrainian elite? Ukrainian historians usually considered the repressive policy of the tsars to have been most important in delaying the national movement. The fact that Ukrainian nationalism flourished and stagnated, corresponding to the relatively liberal and repressive phases of government policy, supports this hypothesis. In comparing the situation in Russia with that of the Ukrainians in Galicia the importance of government policy becomes even clearer.

The socio-economic starting point of the Ukrainians in Galicia was no better than in Russia but, because of the more liberal Austrian policy, they experienced social emancipation earlier and had greater opportunities for national development. Recent research, for instance by Krawchenko, has emphasised socio-economic conditions, although it is admitted that these were a long term result of a repressive Russian policy against Ukraine. As has been shown in this study the socio-ethnic conditions in the Ukraine played a decisive role in delaying the formation of a national elite.

A third factor was the great attraction that a modernising Russian society and culture exercised on Ukrainians. They had no confessional barriers to overcome as was the case in Galicia and they were accepted by the Russians. The common religion and the linguistic and cultural proximity to the ruling nation proved to be a restraint on national consciousness. Nonetheless there can be no doubt that the autocratic form of government and the unusually repressive policy from the 1860s towards any and all Ukrainian cultural and linguistic effort did substantially delay the formation of a national elite. Prohibition of Ukrainian in school and of a vernacular press prevented the development of the necessary means for national communication. But government policy was not solely responsible. The interaction of the three factors mentioned ensured that the approximately 30 million Ukrainians of the Russian empire before the First World War not only remained a non-dominant ethnic group but also produced only a small national elite.

State of Research

Source material for the study of the Ukrainian national movement in the Russian empire in general and the formation of a national elite in particular has not been readily available until recent times. Material on this question in the Soviet archives was not accessible to western researchers. Therefore the most important sources are the Ukrainian periodicals and pamphlets which appeared in Russia – especially after 1905 – and in Galicia.[31] In addition material was published during the interwar period in the Ukrainian Soviet republic and in Poland and there are sources, in particular memoirs, which were published by Ukrainian emigrants. All this material has to be viewed very critically, either because the sources were published under conditions of oppressive rule or because of the biased viewpoint of those who produced it.

This difficult source situation accounts in part for the inadequate state of research. Whereas there are several excellent scholarly works about the Ukrainian national movement in the Habsburg empire,[32] the same cannot be said for more current literature on the movement in the Russian empire. Since the mid 1930s the subject has been more or less taboo for Soviet researchers and only a few politically 'safe' aspects have been treated in any way.[33] Until now Polish and western students of Ukrainian history have concentrated on other questions. However several surveys have appeared which can serve as an introduction to this complex problem.[34] A few unpublished dissertations are the only recent treatments of the Ukrainian national movement in the Russian empire. Of special interest is the carefully researched and richly documented work on the Revolutionary Ukrainian party by George Boshyk[35] who also addressed the specific question of the formation of national activists.

Notes

1 In this study I use the modern term 'Ukrainians' and not the terms common at that time: 'little Russians' in the Russian empire and 'Ruthenians' in the Habsburg empire.
2 The following statistics were extracted from material on the 1897 Russian census to which I refer for this entire chapter: *Pervaia vseobshchaia perepis' naselenia*

Rossijskoj imperii [The first general census of the population of the Russian empire], 1897 g. vols 8, 13, 16, 32, 33, 41, 46, 47, 48 (*Sanktpeterburg*, 1903–5). Consult the data relevant to this study in Tables XIII, XV, XXII, XXIV – this material was prepared in the framework of a project at the Cologne Seminar for Eastern European History which was supported by the *Deutsche Forschungs-gemeinschaft*; I would like to thank members of this project for their assistance. It is not possible to discuss here the value of this source material. Compare now: H. Bauer, A. Kappeler and B. Roth (eds) (1991), *Die Nationalitäten des Russischen Reiches in der Volkszählung von 1897*, 2 vols. Stuttgart. One point should be mentioned however: the ethnic composition of the population in 1897 was determined from data based on the mother tongue. Individual data is also available in Krawchenko; Bruk, Kabuzan, pp. 15–31.

3 Here and in the rest of the study I use the official Russian name for provinces, towns and rivers, not the Ukrainian form, which was not recognised by the tsarist authorities.

4 Hroch, pp. 8–9.

5 That the administrative definition of city in the census of 1897 does not coincide functionally with the modern term does not prejudice the following analysis.

6 See Herlihy, pp. 135–55; Bisk, p. 3.

7 Quotation from Weinstein (1942), p. 31.

8 Compare Neutatz (forthcoming).

9 See also for the following the material from the 1897 census cited in note 2.

10 Seton-Watson, pp. 343, 338.

11 The study was made possible by a European Science Foundation research grant and important sections were prepared by Brigitte Roth, MA, with the support of Sabine Heinzel. This study can only be summarised and results are partial. We have analysed the biographical data of 66 national activists in period one (1860–4), members of *hromady*, signers of petitions; of 60 activists in period two (1870–6), *hromady* in Kiev and other cities; and of 106 activists of period three (1900–14), publishers and editors of Ukrainian periodicals, leading members of the national parties and the Ukrainian *hromada* in the first and second *duma*. In addition the activists were divided into three groups according to their importance. The material used is not always representative, both with respect to the people selected and completeness. The biographical data were taken primarily from encyclopedias such as *Encyklopedia Ukrainoznavsta*, vols 1–9; *Encyclopedia of Ukraine*, vol. 1; *Radyanskaia encyklopedia istorii Ukrainy*, vols. 1–4; *Dejateli revoljucionnogo . . .*, vols. 1–5; Pavlovskij. For period one see Zhytec'kyj; for period three see *Chleny 2–oj*; Bojovich. In addition obituaries in periodicals and memoirs were consulted.

12 Boshyk, pp. 415–25.

13 For example, see Kappeler (1979); 55 per cent graduates of universities, 74 per cent with secondary or higher education (pp. 537–41).

14 See declarations by the 'Ukrainian intelligentsia' in 1905 (*Kievskaja Starina* 24, 88, 1905, mart, II, p. 253 and already in 22, 83, 1903, I, p. 200–1), and in general Doroshenko (1907), pp. 1–29, particularly 5–6.

15 See note ** to Table 5.3.

16 Chykalenko (1931), p. 70.

17 The criterion 'estate' does not permit the drawing of conclusions regarding social status. It is just a rough social classification.

18 Refer to Rudnytsky, p. 200; Kohut (1981), pp. 103–119, especially 114–15; Kohut (1988), pp. 264–76, 304–05.

19 Chykalenko (1931), p. 70; Chykalenko (1955), p. 348.

20 Refer to Boshyk, pp. 282, 423–4, and Duchyns'kyj, pp. 283–320, both with similar data.

21 According to Boshyk, p. 424, 71 per cent of the *Revoljucijna Ukrainsk'ka Partia* members came from the three governments.
22 Unfortunately, more detailed investigations about Ukrainian students have not been made. For period 1 see Serbyn, pp. 197–212.
23 For example in Chykalenko (1955), pp. 75–127; Hrushevs'kyj (1979), 16, pp. 82–5; Doroshenko (1949), pp. 5–33.
24 Antonovich, p. 94.
25 Rusov, pp. 40–9; Rusova, pp. 150–5.
26 Magocsi (1989). For the preconditions of dual loyalty among Ukrainian nobles in Phase A compare Kohut (1981), pp. 257–76; Saunders.
27 Chykalenko (1931), pp. 67, 70, 91, 221, 334; Rudnytsky, pp. 207–8; compare the answer of the well known economic historian Tugan-Baranovskij to an enquiry by the periodical *Ukrainskaia Zhizn'* (1914), 1, pp. 15–6.
28 Ukraine (1976), vol. 2, p. 488. See Ihnatienko; Domanyts'kyj, pp. 48–65.
29 Chykalenko (1931), *passim*.
30 Grabowicz.
31 These sources are difficult to find in western Europe. Thanks to a European Science Foundation grant I was able to consult several contemporary Ukrainian periodicals in the Slavic section of the university library in Helsinki.
32 Compare the titles in: Magocsi (1983), pp. 116–67 and more recently Himka.
33 Compare, for example, Borysenko; Voloshchenko; Marachov.
34 Krawchenko, Chapter 1, especially pp. 29–39; Rudnytsky; Subtelny, pp. 221–42, 279–306; Borschak; individual articles in *Ukraine* (1963, 1976).
35 Boshyk. I would like to thank Dr Boshyk for sending me a copy of his dissertation. See also Ivancevich and Voskobiynyk.

Select Bibliography

Antonovych, V. (1862), 'Moja ispoved'. Otvet Panu Padalitse' (My confession. Answer to Mister P.), *Osnova*, sichen'.
Bisk, I. (1920), *K voprosu o sotsial'nom sostave naselenia Kieva (po dannym perepisi 1917 goda)* (On the question of the social composition of Kiev (the results of the 1917 census)), Kiev.
Boiovich, M.M. (1906), *Chleny Gosudarstvennoj Dumy (Portrety i biografii). Pervyj sozyy 1906–1911 gg.* (The members of the state *duma*. Portraits and biographies), Moscow.
Borschak, E. (1930), 'Le Mouvement national ukrainien au XIXe siècle', *Le Monde Slave* III, IV and V.
Borysenko, V.I. (1980), *Borot'ba demokratychnykh syl za narodnu osvitu na Ukraini v 60–90–kh rokakh XIX st.* (The struggle of the democratic forces for the education of the people in the Ukraine from the 1860s to 90s), Kiev.
Boshyk, G.Y. (1981), *The Rise of Ukrainian Political Parties in Russia, 1900–1907: With special reference to Social Democracy* (Unpublished Ph.D. thesis), University of Oxford.
Bruk, S.I. and Kabuzan, V.M. (1981), 'Chislennost i rasselenie ukrainskogo etnosa v XVIII – nachale XX v.'. (The number and the distribution of the ethnic Ukrainians from the Eighteenth Century to the beginning of the Twentieth Century), *Sovetskaia Etnografiia*, 5, pp. 15–31.
Chleny 2–oj Gosudarstvennoj Dumy (The members of the second *state duma*) (1907), St Petersburg.
Chykalenko, Ie. (1931), *Shchodennyk* (Diary), 1907–1917, Lviv.
Chykalenko, Ie. (1955), *Spohady* (Memoirs), *1861–1907*, New York.

Deiateli revoliutsionnogo dvizhenija v Rossii. Bio-bibliograficheskij slovar' ot predshestvennikov dekabristov do padenija tsarizma (The activists of the revolutionary movement in Russia. Bio-bibliographical dictionary from the predecessors of the Decembrists to the fall of tsarism), vols 1–5 (reprint from Moscow 1927–33), 1974, Leipzig.

Domanyts'kyj, V. (1907), 'Ukrains'ka presa v 1906 r' (The Ukrainian Press in 1906), *Ukraina*, 1, pp. 48–65.

Doroshenko, D. (1907), 'Ukraina v 1906 rotsi' (The Ukraine in 1906), *Ukraina*, 1, pp. 1–29.

Doroshenko, D. (1949), *Moi Spomyny pro davnie–mynule* (My reminiscences about times long past), 1901–1914, Winnipeg.

Doroshenko, D. (1957), *Survey of Ukrainian Historiography* V–VI, The Annals of the Ukrainian Academy of Arts and Sciences in the US; New York.

Doroshenko, V. (1917), *Ukrainstvo v Rossi. Noviishi chasy* (Ukrainiandom in Russia. The modern times), Videń.

Drahomanov, M.P. (1906), 'Avtobiografija' (Autobiography), *Byloe*, I, pp. 182–213.

Drahomanov, M.P. (1970), 'Avstro–rus'ki spomyny' (Austro–Ruthenian memoirs), 1867–1877, in Drahomanov, M.P., *Literaturno–publistychni pratsi*, II, Kyiv.

Duchyns'kyj, A. (1928), *Revoljucijna Ukrains'ka Partia (RUP) na Poltavshchyni za arkhivnymy materialamy 1901–1905 rokiv* (The Revolutionary Ukrainian party in the region of Poltava from archival material for the years 1901–1905), Za sto lit 2.

Encyclopaedia of Ukraine, vol. 1 (1984), Toronto.

Encyklopedia Ukrainoznavsta (Encyclopaedia of Ukrainian Studies), vols 1–9 (1953–80), Paris.

Grabowicz, G.G. (1982), *The Poet as a Mythmaker. A Study of Symbolic Meaning in Taras Ševčenko*, Cambridge, Massachusetts.

Herlihy, P. (1981), 'Ukrainian Cities in the Nineteenth Century', in Rudnytsky, I.L. (ed.), *Rethinking Ukrainian History*, Edmonton, pp. 135–55.

Himka, J.P. (1988), *Galician Villagers and the Ukrainian National Movement in the Nineteenth Century*, London.

Hroch, M. (1985), *Social Preconditions of National Revival in Europe. A Comparative Analysis of the Social Composition of Patriotic Groups Among the Smaller European Nations*, Cambridge.

Hrushevs'kyj, M. (1979), 'Avtobiohrafija' (Autobiography), 1926, *Ukrains'kyj Istoryk*, 16, pp. 79–87.

Hrushevs'kyj, M. (1980), 'Avtobiohrafija' (Autobiography), 1926, *Ukrains'kyj Istoryk*, 17, pp. 71–88.

Ihnatienko, V. (1930), *Bibliohrafia ukrains'koj presy* (Bibliography of the Ukrainian Press), 1816–1916, Kharkiv.

Ivancevich, A. M. (1976), *The Ukrainian National Movement and Russification*, Ph.D. diss., Northwestern University; Xerox Ann Arbor.

Kappeler, A. (1979), 'Zur Charakteristik russischer Terroristen (1878–1887)', *Jahrbücher für Geschichte Osteuropas*, 27, pp. 520–47.

Kappeler, A. (1982), 'Historische Voraussetzungen des Nationalitätenproblems im russischen Vielvölkerreich', *Geschichte und Gesellschaft*, 8, pp. 159–83.

Kohut, Z.E. (1981), 'Problems in Studying the Post-Khmelnytsky Ukrainian Elite (1650s–1830s)', in Rudnytsky, I.L. (ed.), *Rethinking*, pp. 103–19.

Kohut, Z.E. (1988), *Russian Centralism and Ukrainian Autonomy. Imperial Absorption of the Hetmanate 1760s–1830s*, Cambridge, Massachusetts.

Krawchenko, B. (1985), *Social Change and National Consciousness in Twentieth Century Ukraine*, London.

Magocsi, P.R. (1983), *Galicia. A Historical Survey and Bibliographical Guide*, London.

Magocsi, P.R. (1989), 'The Ukrainian National Revival: A New Analytical Framework', *Canadian Review of Studies in Nationalism*, 16, pp. 45–62.

Marachov, G.I. (1981), *Sotsial'no–politicheskaja bor'ba na Ukraine v 50–60–e gody XIX veka* (The social–political struggle in the Ukraine in the 1850s and 1860s), Kiev.

Neutatz, D. (1990), *Die deutsche Frage in Süd- und Südwestrussland. Kolonisten im Spannungsfeld russischer und deutscher Politik 1861–1914*, Diss., Salzburg.

Pavlovskij, I.F. (1912), *Kratkij biograficheskij slovar' uchenykh i pisatelej Poltavskoj gubernii s poloviny XVIII veka* (Short biographical dictionary of scholars and writers of the Poltava province since the middle of the Eighteenth Century), Poltava.

Radyanskaia encyklopedia istorii Ukrainy (Soviet Encyclopaedia of the history of the Ukraine), vols 1–4 (1969–72), Kiev.

Rudnytsky, I.L. (1963), 'The Role of the Ukraine in Modern History', *Slavic Review*, 22, pp. 199–216, discussion pp. 217–62.

Rudnytsky, I.L. (1977), 'The Ukrainian National Movement on the Eve of the First World War', *East European Quarterly*, 11, pp. 141–54.

Rusov, A. (1913), 'Kak ja stal chlenom "Gromady"' (How I became a member of the *Hromada*), *Ukrainskaia Zhizn'*, 10, pp. 40–9.

Rusova, S. (1928), 'Moi spomyny rr. 1861–1879, 1879–1915' (My reminiscences of the years 1861–1879, 1879–1915), *Za sto lit*, 2 and 3.

Saunders, D. (1985), *The Ukrainian Impact on Russian Culture 1750–1850*, Edmonton.

Savchenko, F. (1970), *Zaborona ukrainstva 1876 Vr.* (The prohibition of Ukrainiandom in 1876), reprint of the Kiev 1930 edition, Munich.

Serbyn, R. (1984), 'Les étudiants de Kiev d'après les registres académiques, 1858–1863', *Studia Ucrainica*, 2, pp. 197–212.

Seton-Watson, H. (1962), ' "Intelligentsia" und Nationalismus in Osteuropa 1848–1918', *Historische Zeitschrift*, 195, pp. 331–45.

Shevelov, G.Y. (1986), 'The Language Question in the Ukraine in the Twentieth Century (1900–1914)', *Harvard Ukrainian Studies*, 10, pp. 71–126.

Subtelny, O. (1988), *Ukraine. A History*, Toronto.

Ukraine. A Concise Encyclopaedia (1963–76), 2 vols, Toronto.

Voloshchenko, A.K. (1974), *Narysy z istorii suspil'no–politychnoho rukhu na Ukraini v 70–kh – na pochatku 80–kh rokiv XIX st.* (Outline of the history of the socio-political movement in Ukraine in the 1870s and the beginnings of the 1880s), Kiev.

Voskobiynyk, M.H. (1982), The Nationalities Question in Russia in 1905–1907: A Study in the Origin of Modern Nationalism, with special reference to the Ukrainians (Ph.D. diss. University of Pennsylvania, Xerox Ann Arbor).

Weinstein, H.R. (1942), 'Land Hunger and Nationalism in the Ukraine 1905–17', *Journal of Economic History*, 21, pp. 24–35.

Zhytec'kyj, I. (1928), 'Kyivs'ka hromada za 60–ykh rokiv' (The Hromada of Kiev in the 1860s), *Ukraina 26*, 1, pp. 91–125.

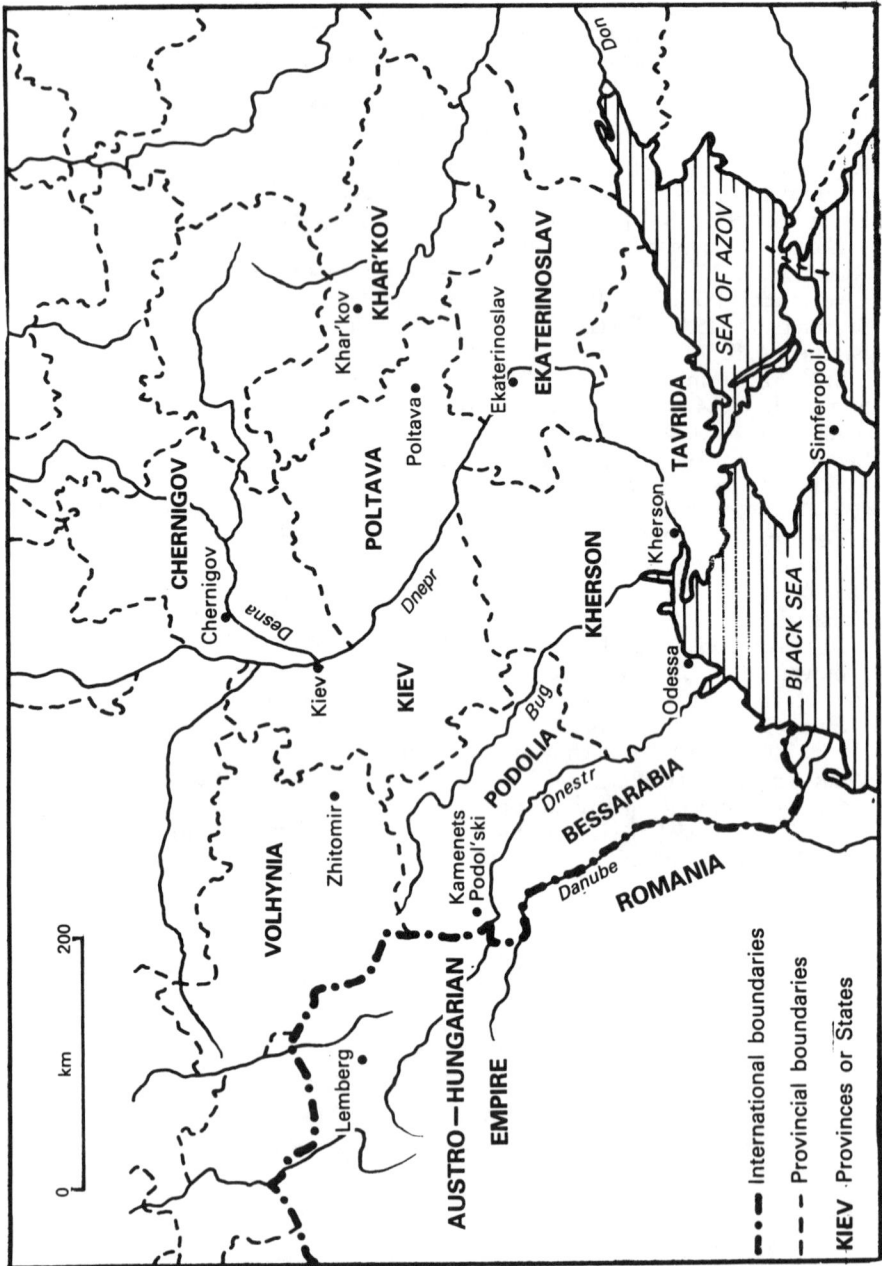

Map 5.1   Ukraine in 1900
Source: P.R. Magocsi, Ukraine. A Historical Atlas, Toronto, 1985, page 17.

6 The Catalans within the Spanish Monarchy from the Middle of the Nineteenth to the Beginning of the Twentieth Century

GERHARD BRUNN

Introduction

Compared to other European countries, the Spanish monarchy was successful relatively early in laying the foundations for a firmly structured unitary state. From the eighteenth century there was a well established trend towards standardisation which was reinforced by the example of the French Revolution. During the first half of the nineteenth century this practice continued. But, while some other European countries succeeded in transforming a specific administrative unit, the 'state' into a special community of common interests, carried by the consensus of its citizens, the 'nation', the Spanish monarchy experienced a counter movement. Not only did regional loyalties persist but they gained new and unexpected momentum in the nationalism of the Basque country and Catalonia. With Catalan reawakening, in particular, an exemplary national movement disassociating itself from the existing state as a whole made an appearance. Beginning with the revival by a few intellectuals of autonomous cultural and historical particularities, Catalan aspirations as formulated by a regionalist group with a small social base grew into a mass movement at the turn of the century. What distinguished Catalanism from other national movements was that it never aspired to complete separation but sought to attain, within the Spanish state, a far reaching autonomy. The autonomy was eventually granted, initially during the Spanish republic (1932–9) and most recently within the period of the new Spanish democracy.

General Conditions

Social and Economic Conditions

Catalonia, in the north east of the Spanish peninsula, has been a part of the Spanish state since 1469. With its territory of 31 980 sq km, distributed between the four administrative provinces of Gerona, Lerida, Barcelona and Tarragona, it occupies 6.3 per cent of Spain's total area but is comparable in size to Belgium. Catalonia, as a political and judicial unit with its own linguistic–cultural identity, can be traced back to the middle ages. Lawyers first used the term *Principat de Catalunya* (principality of Catalonia) in the fourteenth century and a political consciousness has been formed within this specific territory. Catalonian identity is a remarkable occurrence as the movement has seen itself as being mostly defined by linguistic–cultural factors,[1] whereas the political frontiers of the *Principat de Catalunya* are not coterminous with the region where the Catalan language is spoken. Catalan speaking areas extend into the Valencia region, to the Balearic Islands and to a strip of Aragon bordering on Catalonia. Beyond the frontiers of Spain the language is spoken in Andorra, in the French Roussillon and in the Sardinian town of Alghero. Due to the problem in defining the term 'Catalonia', since the 1960s it has become increasingly common to speak of the Catalan speaking areas as the *Països Catalans* (Catalan lands).[2]

In 1860 the four Catalan administrative provinces had a population of 1 674 000 which rose to 1.966 million towards the end of the century and to 2.6 million in 1920. As the Spanish census does not include a language enumeration there are no exact data on the numbers using Catalan as their mother tongue. Judging from available reports, however, it can be presumed that the overwhelming majority of the people spoke Catalan in daily life even though, in official and judicial matters, Spanish was used almost universally.[3] General use of Catalan can be deduced from the fact that as late as 1860 the illiteracy level was still 80 per cent and only fell to 40 per cent in 1920. School instruction and informal teaching of reading and writing was exclusively in Spanish. It was through literacy by and large that Spanish found its way into daily life.

Economically and socially Catalonia had a key position within Spain. Spanish trade and industrial production was concentrated there to a high degree, particularly in the city and province of Barcelona. Industrialisation was uneven however. From proto-industrial beginnings until the end of the nineteenth century its economy was based very substantially on textiles. Up to 1909 invested capital and the value of the output from the textile industry surpassed all other industries combined. At this date though overall economic development stagnated, modernising tendencies were on the way to shifting production from consumer items to capital goods such as the metal, chemical and electrical industries. Lack of energy, raw materials and capital plus antiquated forms of finance, organisation and production restricted the international competitiveness of Catalan industry. It was dependent on the poor and fluctuating Spanish market. In spite of all these defects Catalonia was in 1900 the leading industrial region. As early as 1856 25 per cent of the Spanish tax revenue derived from industry came from Catalonia and this percentage rose to more than 38 per cent by 1900. Around 1900 Catalan industry held the leading position in nearly all areas of Spanish production.

Catalan agriculture, despite problems (such as destruction of the vines by phylloxera), was healthier than in other parts of the country. A larger percentage of medium sized units and independent farmers, longer leases and competitive products gave to Catalan agriculture a greater degree of prosperity, technical improvement and social stability than was usual elsewhere.[4] Increasing numbers of people were drawn to Barcelona and to the smaller industrial towns within its ambit. Barcelona's numbers rose from 175 000 to 545 000 equalling more than 27 per cent of the population of Catalonia. Prior to the 1920s most migrants to Barcelona came from other parts of Catalonia. Even in 1920 68 per cent of the population were born in Catalonia and a high percentage of the immigrants came from the other *Països Catalans*. As a recent study shows the immigrants were assimilated into the dominant Catalan *milieu*. Thus there could not really be a question of destruction of Catalan culture though Catalanists raised that spectre.[5]

Rapid economic growth created a fully developed, socially and politically differentiated society minus a state in Catalonia. In 1900 manufacturing gave employment to 27 per cent of the work force in Catalonia, 11 per cent more than in the whole of Spain including Catalonia. The difference in structure can be made even more striking by comparing the figures for the province of Barcelona with those for all Spain. As early as 1872 only 34 per cent of the working population in Barcelona were engaged in agriculture, 20 per cent in industry and 17 per cent in crafts. Elsewhere in Spain – excluding Catalonia – 72 per cent were occupied in agriculture, two per cent only in industry and seven per cent in craft work.[6]

A characteristic of Catalan industrialisation was the existence of numerous medium and small independent business enterprises as well as large industrial concerns. Thus there was not an upper bourgeoisie on one side and the industrial proletariat on the other but rather, extensive middle classes, petit bourgeois, shopkeepers, craftsmen – *menestralia* (middle sorts) in Spanish terms. These middle classes were gaining even more importance from the considerable increase in number of white collar workers arising out of the differentiation and expansion of economic activities especially the growing service sector.

The Catalan upper bourgeoisie as a clearly definable group comprised some large scale bankers, commercial and textile magnates. Politically conservative – even reactionary, organised in powerful pressure groups, they exercised considerable economic and political influence in Catalonia. They tenaciously resisted social reforms and thereby gave impetus to the violent labour conflicts which progressively characterised the region.[7] At the bottom of the differentiated industrial society of the city of Barcelona and its environs in 1907 were concentrated 84 000 industrial workers.[8] The working conditions and the living standards of this industrial proletariat were below western European standards. For instance, employers disregarded legal restrictions on the employment of women and children. Moreover the actual purchasing power of wages diminished at the turn of the century.

Between the upper bourgeoisie and the proletariat there was the comparatively extensive stratum of the middle and lower middle classes. The proportion of the traditional middle classes – professionals and medium sized land owners for example – both in the Catalan hinterland and near Barcelona hardly differed from that elsewhere in Spain. There was, however, a remarkable concentration of professionals in Barcelona. Barcelona's exceptional position is evident in the percentage of people engaged in manufacturing. In 1905 10 754 independent businessmen were listed in Barcelona alone. White collar employees also belong in these specific social strata. In 1907 the insurance lists for Barcelona record 11 980 in the service sector. If the 1000 teachers, 250 commercial travellers, 1850 musicians, 300 singers and variety artists, 370 journalists, 124 photographers, and 100 draughtsmen are added to this new middle class emerging in Barcelona, a clearer view of a society unique within Spain can be obtained.[9]

Beyond the modern community around Barcelona there existed a traditional rural society in the remote districts. In contrast to other parts of Spain rural society did not set Catalonia's tone. Agrarian society was oriented towards Barcelona which determined the direction and rhythm of economic, social, political and cultural development and drew the whole of Catalonia under its spell. Spain was inward looking; bound up in local isolation, traditionalism, with a political routine not greatly touched by things happening in the outside world. Catalonia however was quite the opposite. There economic development freed a growing number of people from old ties and ancient habits, necessitating their assimilation or integration into new forms of social communication, behaviour, groupings, organisation and obligations. Spain and Catalonia thus drifted farther apart. Separate patterns of social communication and values developed in Catalonia. An autonomous culture emerged open to modern European currents and receptive to these outside cultural changes. Moreover this segregation gave support to the development of a Catalan consciousness which could rest on structural differences, on established and historical traditions and an indigenous language.

Political System, Government and Administration

In the eighteenth century in Spain as in France, the Bourbons had begun to impose a centralised monarchy. Gradual abolition of traditional privileges and the introduction of a judicial system applicable to all citizens were vital aspects of Spanish liberalism which succeeded, in spite of violent counter movements, in leaving its mark on politics. Gradually liberal demands were realised during the nineteenth century, abolishing in Catalonia as elsewhere the remaining separate political and judicial privileges and institutions. In 1822 the Catalan criminal law was abolished; in 1829 the trade law; and in 1834 the separate jurisdiction was dissolved. As early as 1833 the region, which had hitherto been treated as a single unit, was divided into four administrative provinces in the French manner. In 1845 the provinces were integrated into a uniform tax system and also had to accept conscription which prior to that time had not been extended to Catalonia. These measures were accompanied by a policy establishing Spanish as the sole official language for the country. In 1825 state schools were prohibited from teaching in Catalan and until after the turn of the century there was a host of other laws and decrees enforcing Spanish as the sole language within state institutions, education and in legal affairs.

Measures of centralisation and standardisation did not spring from a minority policy directed against Catalonia or, later, against the Basque country. Rather there was no official consciousness that ethnic minorities existed in Spain. Even when a strong Catalan movement developed its existence was ignored. Measures of centralisation were intended to lay the foundations for a bourgeois national state. Moreover a centralised national state was on the whole accepted and supported in Catalonia despite occasional opposition because it suited the interests of Catalan middle classes involved in industrialisation and striving for a national market. Liberal centralism promised prosperity for factories, including a wide market for their goods, made possible through the construction of railways.[10]

A centralised state did not lead directly to a development similar to that taking place north of the Pyrenees. Elites reigning in Madrid lacked the will to pursue a policy which would have made such a course possible. At the time of the emergence in the progressive European states of a new economically orientated class, the Castilian Spanish centre of power in Madrid was dominated by elites rooted in pre-industrial culture. Owners of large estates, aristocrats of old or new creation, the minor nobility, academics in search of a career within the state apparatus and trade or financial speculators made up the groups exercising influence in an agrarian feudal Spain dominated by a rural and commercial oligarchy.

After decades of violent political strife in 1876 Spain attained a political equilibrium which for a quarter of a century ensured quiescence and a certain material progress. It happened, however, at the cost of social development because the country's structures and institutions reinforced a static society. Theoretically after 1876 Spain had one of the most liberal and democratic constitutions in Europe, especially after 1890 when universal male suffrage was granted. In practice, though, the potential political mobilisation of the people through the ballot was thwarted by a silent agreement between the two main dynastic parties. Manipulated elections and regular exchanges of power by mutual agreement within small groups of local notables restricted mass influence on politics. Control of the political structure was managed with the aid of so-called *Caciques* or local political magnates who manipulated elections using a rich arsenal of inducements and intimidation.

The Catalan upper classes were integrated into this political system. Dominance of the political machinery was maintained by a leadership who promoted a policy furthering specific Catalan interests and demands. But 'Catalan egotism' met with strong resistance in Madrid and was only partially successful, as for instance in the case of protective tariffs. Because of this limited success a latent estrangement between Catalonia and the central political authority in Madrid began to alienate the Catalan upper classes from the dynastic parties and made possible their growing integration into the national movement after 1900.[11]

Spain's constitution was favourable to divergent political movements. When adopted on 30 July 1876 it guaranteed classic civil rights – freedom of opinion, printing, the press, assembly and association. These rights, however, were granted on the condition that they were not used for agitation and actions against the existing social or political order. Considerable powers of intervention remained in the hands of the state administration. Moreover the government had in article 17 a useful tool to prevent unrestricted use of civil liberties. Declaration of a state of emergency was one of the standard measures available to every successive government to preserve peace and order, particularly when threatened by disruptive strikes and the waves of political assassinations at the turn of the century. These powers were employed against Catalanism as well.[12]

The National Movement and its Activists

The History of the Catalan Movement

The beginnings of a Catalan movement in the form that gained ascendancy around 1900 can be traced back to the second half of the nineteenth century. Its nucleus was in linguistic–cultural movements. The nineteenth century was generally a time of revival in the spheres of languages and literatures, and Catalonia was no exception. While the Catalan language 'was, up to the eighteenth century, used by clergymen from the pulpit, by merchants in the exchange, in letters, in social intercourse, in the assemblies and in education'[13] it became restricted to colloquial use about the middle of the nineteenth century. Formal education could be pursued only in Spanish. Poets and writers, even in Catalonia, used Spanish exclusively. Administration was conducted in Spanish. Perfect command of Spanish was imperative for anybody wishing to rise socially.

Around the middle of the nineteenth century a change became apparent. Catalan was rediscovered as a literary language. It found, from 1859, its first institutional nurturing place in literary contests. These *Jocs Florals* (flower games) were based on medieval models. Plays in Catalan enjoyed great popularity in the 1860s. For the first time also periodicals in Catalan found a market. In 1880 an expert with intimate knowledge of the Catalan literary scene listed more than 500 poets and writers using the vernacular language. Within a few years the new flowering of Catalan literature had spawned a remarkable theatre, a great epic – the *Atlantida*, prose writers, novels of every description, scientific works, periodicals and newspapers.[14]

A young generation of intellectuals, strongly influenced by the German and Scottish Romantic movements, looked for a new spiritual home in the region. Catalan lawyers were influenced deeply by the German historical law school, finding in it the arguments for their fight against the standardisation of Spanish jurisprudence and the preservation of regional legal traditions. Catalan medieval history was rediscovered and, in voluminous historical works, presented to readers through a romantic haze.[15]

This movement was initially one of cultural self-assertion. 'Why', wrote Rubio i Ors, one of the most eminent exponents of the restoration of Catalan poetry, 'should Catalonia not abandon the humiliating role of pupil or imitator and create for itself an independent literature distinguishable from the Castilian one?'[16] *Refer una patria*, the recreation of a 'mother country' for the soul and the spirit was the concern of the *renaixença* or cultural rebirth. Initially it had been filled with Christian medieval Romanticism and critics had remarked that a mummy had been resurrected to be displayed as a holy relic. Very soon however the flourishing Catalan culture had become influenced by the radical changes taking place in Europe and attained, by the turn of the century, a majestic and unique quality. By then it was no longer restricted to art as such but had become an instrument of political debate and spiritual modernisation. 'Modernism' in particular became the manifestation of a cultural elite wanting to achieve for itself a new way of living similar to that of people in the more advanced European nations to the north. This elite was democratic, industrially orientated, open to education and culture and it believed in progress.[17]

Political Catalanism advanced on the back of this cultural movement. So far the Catalanist movement fits nicely into the schedule devised by Miroslav Hroch. The Catalan movement had its Phase A in which learned individuals or those interested in culture, art, history and folklore began to occupy themselves with the heritage of the regional civilisation. Phase B followed in which a minority started systematic agitation, and this was followed by Phase C in which Catalanism became a mass movement. Chronologically Phase A may be said to comprise the years from the 1830s or 1840s to 1880 when the first Catalanist congress met. Phase B ended around the turn of the century, with Phase C following after 1900 with mass agitation and successful electoral campaigns. Catalanism, however, can not be explained completely by reference to the Hroch model. Catalanism was not entirely new, going back to the political currents and opposition movements of Carlism or federalism which had thrived in the first half of the nineteenth century. All these movements had presented, though with differing goals and rationale, modes for state organisations aiming at comprehensive self-government by regions rather than Spanish centralism. Catalanism not only took over regionalist ideas but also integrated members from the ideologically differing movements. Ambitions to comprehensiveness along with the varieties of social and political interests in a modernising society led to an early split of Catalanism into political wings.[18]

An initial impetus to make Catalanism a political movement came from the former federalist Valentí Almirall. He founded the first Catalan newspaper, the *Diari Català*. He was also the driving force behind the first Catalan congress which resolved to create a central scientific and artistic association and he organised the first effective political action. He gained the support of the so-called 'living forces', that is a significant section of leading economic and intellectual figures of Catalonia, for a memorandum protesting against the lowering of tariffs, demanding Catalan civil law, accusing centralism of neglecting their interests and demanding farreaching regional self-government.[19]

In 1887 the unity of Catalanism was broken. Conservative representatives turned against the 'democratic' social ideas of Valentí Almirall and founded a separate alliance, the *Lliga de Catalunya* (the Catalan League). It represented a Catholic conservative Catalanism and dominated the movement until the turn of the century, particularly because it won the support of university students in the *Centre Escolar Catalanista* (Catalan Study Centre). This was in the 1890s the spearhead of Catalanism and it nurtured the leaders who were to determine policy in the new century.

Around 1890 Conservative leaders organised the first comprehensive agitation, thereby helping to thwart complete standardisation of Spanish civil law. Out of this experience the *Unió Catalanista* (Catalan Union) formulated a list of demands which included the basic elements of a Catalan regional constitution, by which Catalonia would be a separate state within a loose Spanish federation.[20] The breakthrough to becoming a political force took place around 1900. After the loss of its last colonies Spain experienced a deep crisis in domestic politics. The loss of colonies was also a severe blow for Catalan industry. Markets which had absorbed more than 30 per cent of regional industrial production disappeared. In this critical situation that group of resourceful intellectuals, highly gifted in politics and organisation, which had up to then worked within the *Unió Catalanista*, succeeded in winning over the upper bourgeois classes with its political, economic and social influence, as well as large parts of the middle classes without fixed political loyalties, to support Catalanist goals. Whereas the *Unió Catalanista* had been strictly an extra-parliamentary opposition these young intellectuals eagerly pressed into parliament in order, step by step, to gain power by evolutionary constitutional methods. The reform conscious upper bourgeois class and the young intellectuals formed an alliance, sponsored candidates for the coming parliamentary elections and achieved victories for the first four candidates standing on a Catalanist programme.[21]

With the act of 1901 Catalanism gained a firm political footing. During the following years it rose with the aid of political parties – the first of which, the *Lliga Regionalista* (Regional League), was founded in 1901 – to become the prime mover in politics in Catalonia. It gained places on self-governing bodies and in 1913 achieved the vital initial step towards official recognition of Catalonia as a regional political entity with the amalgamation of the four Catalan administrative provinces into a single administrative unit. But Catalanism was not a cohesive movement. It was split into several socially divergent right and leftist currents. Furthermore its constituency was contested by other parties, primarily the radical republicans led by Alejandro Lerroux, which were able to enlist and mobilise a significant electorate and prevented Catalanism gaining an unchallenged hegemony. Until after the First World War Catalanism remained dominated by the conservative *Lliga Regionalista*, controlled by the upper middle and upper classes. During the socially and politically tumultuous years preceding the dictatorship of Primo de Rivera in 1923, when the *Lliga* sought government support to combat the danger of social upheaval, it lost much of its support. In the turmoil the left wing Catalanist parties seized their opportunity. They shaped programmes and strategies which in the 1930s enabled them to unite the region's middle classes and workers in both town and country behind Catalanist goals, thus achieving a farreaching autonomy within a Spain which up to then had been centralist. Franco's victory in 1939 in the civil war put an end to Catalanist activity. That Catalanism had developed deep and ineradicable roots however became obvious after Franco's death. It revived then with un-diminished force and achieved, in the new Spanish democracy, its goal of autonomy.

The Elites of Catalanism

An enquiry into Catalan political elites must take into account two coexisting communities – a traditional agrarian society and an industrial world around Barcelona. Elites in the smaller towns of the rural hinterland belonged to the tiny stratum of traditional notables – mostly landowners, an occasional manufacturer, shopkeepers, craftsmen, lawyers, physicians, apothecaries and priests. In industrial towns a different picture emerges. Large scale merchants, industrialists and middle class leaders of trade and commerce were dominant. The professional class, of course, also was present but its members to a large extent rendered services to commerce and they were integrated into the industrial society. In addition there were the groups which were absent in rural society – members of the new technical professions, architects, engineers, steadily growing numbers of white collar workers and the numerous intellectuals all combining to set the tone for the lively cultural life of Barcelona. Alongside the traditional commercial middle class elites was a new spiritual and cultural intelligentsia capable of producing leaders for the Catalanist movement. However generally it was only after 1900 that this occurred.[22]

Catalonia's elites were generally indigenous to the region. There were no specific obstacles to the rise of Catalans. But command of

Spanish was imperative, for all social mobility required competence in Spanish. Spanish was obligatory of course in the educational system. The educated middle classes studied at the University of Barcelona which had 2000 students around 1900. To obtain a degree in one of the five faculties it was necessary to pass a final examination in Madrid. Nevertheless the newly emerging elites were for several reasons oriented to a large extent towards the region. Catalonia had a distinct character, it possessed an economic and cultural centre and its expanding industrial society was able to absorb the upwardly mobile. The ambitious sought to fulfil their aspirations outside the state apparatus. A prospering economy and the exciting cultural atmosphere encouraged, moreover, a feeling of superiority *vis à vis* the rest of Spain, particularly Castile.

Emerging Catalanism has been defined already as a literary–cultural movement. It is therefore not surprising that early participants were from the Catalan educated classes. There were also professors from the university which had been restored in Barcelona around 1830.[23] Two anthologies of Catalan poetry for 1858–9 list the social status of the authors. The overwhelming majority came from 'good society'. Academically educated middle class authors predominate. Lawyers, professors and physicians are in the majority but there were also industrialists and leading civil servants from cultural institutions. If the pattern is predictable, does this group bear comparison with those responsible for the converting Catalanism into a political movement? Evaluation of the editorial lists of the first Catalan daily paper and of participants in the first Catalan congress show that the leading figures did not spring from the emerging industrial middle classes. This Catalanism was dominated by intellectuals. Such intellectuals however were not well-to-do members of the upper classes, enjoying economic independence, but belonged to the professional classes, often having had an academic education, though few roots in the old propertied society. They were upwardly mobile, connected with the cultural scene, without private means and bound to the town, having to earn their living.[24]

This pattern also is not surprising. After all Valentí Almirall, the leader, had been converted from the democratic–federal movement to Catalanism. Federalism itself also had key support in the lower middle classes, the petit bourgeoisie. The group surrounding Valentí Almirall along with the 'progressive' Catalanism that it represented actually withdrew into the background after a few years as Catholic conservative Catalanism began to set the tone.

A recent enquiry throws light on the origins of conservative Catalanism, its importance for the movement as a whole plus its participants and ideological framework. Analysis of the most important 'picked troup' of this Catalanism, the 'Group of Vic' gathered round Canon Collell and the periodical *La Veu de Catalunya*, shows it was drawn from three interdependent professional groups: clerics, lawyers and other learned professions, and rural landowners. It also included some freelance writers more or less dependent on commissions for their livelihood. Men with higher education and members of the professional classes were overrepresented. Participants had a common characteristic: they were still bound up in the rural world. Either the father had been a landowner or they had become landowners themselves through inheritance or purchase. None came from industrial origins. Their taxed property tied them to the reigning oligarchy in the hinterland of Barcelona from which they came.[25]

The most precise pointers to the social profile of activists before the breakthrough to a mass movement can be gathered from the lists of delegates who were sent by associated organisations to the main assemblies of the leading Catalan organisation, the *Unió Catalanista* which had branches throughout the whole province. Various bourgeois professions make up a majority but it is also apparent that the Catalan elites were still from the traditional dominant rural classes. The pattern remained relevant for the years between 1892 and 1904. Landowners and members of the professional classes obtained an undisputed predominance in the first assemblies. They provided 62 to 67 per cent of delegates. There were also a disproportionate number of the upper bourgeoisie of the towns and the rural agrarian oligarchy present. Artists also appear on the lists in greater numbers than their percentage in the population as a whole. This is the case for teachers and academics as well but they were not nearly as numerous as artists. Clergymen, students, civil servants and white collar workers participated in much smaller numbers but it would certainly be wrong to deduce from their small representation that their influence was weak. Studies of conservative Catalanism in particular show that priests exercised an extraordinary influence, particularly on its ideology. Nor do the lists show the enormous importance the student activists had in the 1890s.

From 1901 a radical change in the background of the delegates can be detected. Those dominating strata of the bourgeoisie, the agrarian middle and upper classes, declined swiftly. Craftsmen, tradesmen and students, but above all white collar employees and workers, increased sharply. Thus the lists clearly show that by the opening of the twentieth century a new social strata was incorporated into Catalanism.

Werner Conze has postulated that national movements are instruments of the new industrial middle classes, but his hypothesis does not fit into the first phases of development of Catalanism. In the first two phases the chief activists were landowners, members of the

Table 6.1: Professional structure of the delegates of the *Unió Catalanista* (1882–1904) in percentages

	1892	1893	1895	1897	1901	1904
Manufacturers and bankers	9.8	10.3	9.3	6.6	4.6	4.5
Merchants	5.1	12.2	12.4	12.7	9.0	5.6
Owners of large estates	10.6	8.8	8.6	3.5	7.0	4.4
Landowners	27.7	30.9	33.3	39.6	31.2	19.2
Artisans and tradesmen	4.1	3.5	3.0	10.1	10.2	12.5
Liberal professions	39.1	32.9	32.2	21.7	26.7	27.3
Teachers, professors	4.8	7.6	3.3	2.8	4.7	4.0
Priests	1.7	1.5	0.4		0.8	0.5
Artists	6.8	9.5	10.0	10.8	5.8	6.1
Students					1.5	4.7
Civil servants					1.3	0.8
Farmers					0.8	2.1
Employees and workers	1.3	0.8	1.4	0.3	7.7	11.7
Basic number of delegates	235	262	267	316	949	609

Note: Because of double entries the total exceeds 100 per cent.
Source: Brunn (1978a), p. 450.

liberal professions and small merchants; that is, mostly middle class small town notables and people with private means – the classic Spanish *classes medias* (middling orders). Calling them middle classes in the present meaning of the term certainly would be inappropriate. Quantitative date, though it must be employed with caution, clearly shows the extent to which traditional elites based on rural traditions supported Catalanism. The importance given to and the weight carried by certain persons and by strategically important minorities is far greater than can be demonstrated by analysis of quantitative data alone. Overrepresentation of rural delegates in the assemblies of the *Unió Catalanista* for instance obscures the influence of the cultural elite and intellectuals of Barcelona.

As late as at the beginning of the third phase of Catalanism the industrial middle classes as well as the upper bourgeoisie were a determining factor in the leading circles of activists. This can be demonstrated by analysing the Catalanist candidates for the Spanish parliament. Significant differences exist between the candidates of the dominant force founded in 1901, the *Lliga Regionalista*, and the so-called Catalanist left wing parties. Twenty-five per cent of the candidates put up by the *Lliga Regionalista* were manufacturers, bankers, and top managers, 12 per cent were board members of economic associations; in other words, elites which had up to then appeared on the lists of candidates of the two great dynastic parties, oriented towards Madrid and directed from the capital. The upper middle classes, allied to the owners of large estates, also exercised their influence through lawyers who, as can be proved in certain cases, were nominated expressly because they meant to act in the interests of the monied classes. Once having become the leading political power in Catalonia the *Lliga Regionalista* had the reputation of being a careerist party.[26]

It is vital to look beyond the narrow strata of the upper bourgeoisie and their dependents. Further insight is gained through examination of the parliamentary candidates of the Catalanist left which was, until the beginning of the 1920s, organised in consecutive parties, particularly *Centre Nacionalista Republicá* (Nationalist Republican Centre) and *Unió Federal Nacionalista Republicana* (Federal Nationalist Republican Union). They were liberal non-socialist left of centre parties in their programmes and politics. A recent study postulates that these parties were the political manifestations of the Catalan intelligentsia, ranging from bohemian newspaper reporters to the educated professional classes.[27] The social status of the candidates of these parties for Spanish parliamentary elections modifies the picture however. The intelligentsia was drawn to these parties in larger numbers though the data does not show meaningful differences. The proportion of scientists, artists and journalists was four per cent higher than in the *Lliga*; representation of physicians, architects and engineers was two per cent greater. However lawyers who, after all, might be counted partly among the intelligentsia are 20 per cent lower. Thus it seems that lawyers were strongly bound up in the interests of the bourgeois class and agrarian oligarchy, groups almost absent in the left wing parties. Owners of large estates, supplying 12 per cent of the candidates for the *Lliga*, were non-existent in the left wing parties. The elite of the left wing parties was drawn from the old and new middle classes: 20 per cent of the candidates were merchants and tradesmen (there were only five per cent of these in the *Lliga*) plus 9.5 per cent white collar and skilled workers, not present at all in the *Lliga*.

Analysis of the data confirms that from its entry into the political arena in 1901, Catalanism had been an instrument of the differentiated industrial middle classes and the traditional upper classes and that it no longer embraced all strata. The common goal –

Table 6.2: Distribution of candidatures for the *Lliga Regional-ista* and the *Centre Nacionalista Republicá/Unió Federal Nacionalista Republicana* within different occupations

	Lliga Regionalista	*CNR/UFNR*
Candidatures, absolute numbers	121	63
Lawyers	52.1	30.2
Journalists, artists, writers, scientists	8.3	12.7
Physicians, architects, engineers	5.8	8.0
Owners of large estates	12.4	–
Manufacturers, bankers, businessmen	25.6	14.3
Merchants, tradesmen	5.8	19.8
Landowners	10.7	10.3
Farmers	–	2.9
Skilled workers, employees	–	9.5
Representatives of economic associations	12.1	–

Note: Because of double entries the total exceeds 100 per cent.
Source: Brunn (1978), p. 456.

autonomy for the Catalan region – still existed but the remaining political and social goals were too disparate. Catalanists congregated in separate political parties which, though cooperating on some issues, were otherwise mutually hostile. The conservative upper classes, the traditional oligarchies and their allies found their home in the *Lliga Regionalista*. Those social strata newly created by the urban and industrial development, including the emergent intelligentsia together with the traditional middle classes, became active in the 'left wing' parties.

Catalanist Elites: Their Organisations and Channels of Communication

Catalanism generated an extensive network of associations and channels of communication.[28] The tendency to found many independent or loosely interdependent associations instead of a few rigid and hierarchical mass organisations was a characteristic of the Catalan movement. Prior to 1892 only 77 societies had been founded. During the 1890s 141 further societies were created but the real upward swing occurred in the first 20 years of the new century with more than 1100 societies being created, demonstrating that after a push in the 1890s the movement reached an advanced stage of development with the opening of the new century.

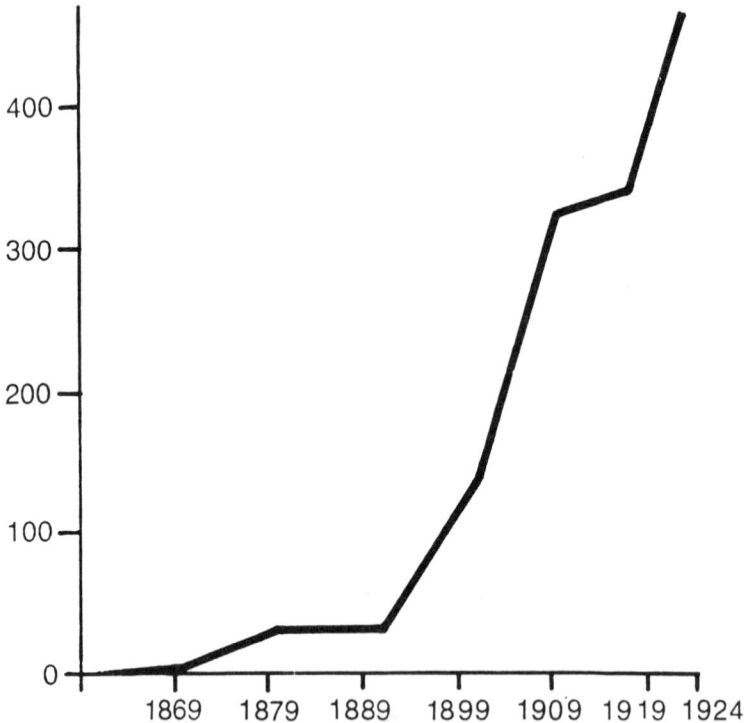

Figure 6.1: New Catalanist societies (1859–1923) absolute numbers
Source: Brunn, p. 343

A clear sequence of societies ranging from cultural–national to those geared to agitation, including political parties, can be distinguished. If the purpose of the early societies had been the cultivation of language, literature, music and history, the later ones engaged in political agitation outside parliament. Political parties appearing after 1901 undertook in their turn to penetrate self-governing administrative bodies and to advance their aims through membership in the Spanish parliament. All three types of ethnic associations, as in Ireland, Macedonia and elsewhere, existed simultaneously after 1900, supplementing each other in their forms of organisation and activities and creating a firm base for the propagation of Catalanist aspirations in public. The promotion of Catalanist goals, the forms of communication, the exercise of influence in public, also from the very beginning, were increasingly varied and effective.

During the early phase the medium of communication was mainly literature, poetry and plays plus scientific and above all historical works. When the movement began to become more political, congresses were held and petitions used. Finally there was a move towards frequent large scale public events. After the turn of the century mass demonstrations brought hundreds of thousands of people together. Oral forms of communication were supplemented by a great variety of publications. Propagandist publications for instance sold more than 100 000 copies as early as the 1890s.

Newspapers and periodicals are vital channels of communication for all modern political movements and this has proved the case in Catalonia as elsewhere from the 1880s. However a peculiar incongruity exists. Periodicals written in Catalan led a marginal existence in the publishing world of the region before the 1920s. In spite of the rapid advance of Catalan as a literary language it held only a minority position in the print media prior to 1923. Before 1923 the total number of Catalan newspaper sales did not exceed 20 per cent of the newspaper market in Barcelona.[29] In view of the overwhelming predominance of the Spanish language press it is remarkable that the Catalan movement succeeded in achieving such a dominant influence in political life.

Political Ideas of Catalan Elites

An important factor in the development of a separate consciousness among Catalan elites was the difference in structure, both economic and social, of agrarian Spain and industrialised Catalonia. The Spanish state failed to act as an integrating force, being unable to satisfy the desires of the Catalan bourgeois classes for a modern state and society.

Ideologues of Catalan nationalism derived their ideas from different European philosophical currents. Whereas conservatives followed German Romanticism, liberals drew their inspiration from French writings. Philosophers explained the special position of Catalonia in a very personal manner, suggesting a difference in the nature of Catalans from other Spaniards.[30] Catalans were attributed with a specific form of civilisation. In this ideology they were practical, economical, realistic people possessing a work ethic. Such Catalan ideology was strengthened by resort to history. In the 1850s the first historical works designed to recreate a collective memory appeared. From that time Catalan historical writing was no longer understood to concern a province of Spain but to act as national history on its own merits. History showed that Catalonia was a country equal to the dominant Castilian nation. A new myth was being fostered that the Catalan past was the history of a liberation movement. Catalonia was represented as a nation, as a country with a long democratic and freedom loving tradition. It was a self-conscious myth in which the particular personality of Catalonia, its nationality, manifested itself.

According to this legend Catalonia had been deprived of its independence by Castile and had been made a cultural slave to dominant Castilian values. It also prophesied imminent liberation of Catalonia. Catalonia had to regain its identity and soul by throwing off the Castilian yoke. The nation, conservative Catalanists emphasised, was an eternal, indestructible and fundamentally unalterable personality above differences of class, moulding its members into a single entity and binding them together for a common destiny which had to be restored fully again.[31]

Catalanist liberal nationalism stressed the voluntary bonds of the nation. Conservative and liberal visions also differed on the function of nationalism, on the appropriate forms of government in Spain and Catalonia, on the internal condition and organisation of the nation, on the position of the individual, and on the social question. The aim of a socially conservative Catalanism pledged to corporatist ideas was the defence of the existing order, of religion, the family, judicial institutions and property. For the Catalan left, in marked contrast, the idea of freedom took a central position. It saw itself as being nationalist, social, democratic and republican. Not only was Catalonia as a nation meant to obtain self-determination in the spiritual, social, economic and political fields but liberation also necessitated the release of the individual from unjustified obligations in order for him to achieve self-fulfilment. Consequently separation of Church and State had a high priority.[32]

The Spanish Government and the Catalans

To date there has been no systematic investigation of the responses of the Madrid government to Catalanism. Neither are there any archive based studies published on the policy of the state administration in Catalonia. However as the leading personalities, patriotic societies, meetings and publications were subject to police surveillance, much material exists on them.

No systematic policy of suppression existed before 1923. Endeavours to reorganise Spain into a centralist uniform state during the course of the nineteenth century were not directed against Catalonia specifically but were part of the drive for a united, uniform and indivisible national state, a concept derived from French ideas. This policy of unification was implemented without significant reservations until the 1860s. Only the last great project, codification of a civil law valid for the whole of Spain, met with embittered resistance (with national overtones) in Catalonia.[33]

Still neither the government in Madrid, the administration in Catalonia, nor the Castilian intellectuals were visibly hostile to the revival of a literary and cultural tradition based on the vernacular language. On the contrary the local administration took a benevolent interest in these activities. The annual festive flower games were a society event.[34] During the World Exhibition in Barcelona in 1888 the Spanish queen, Maria Christina, was festival queen. It was only when leaders began to use cultural activities as a foundation for more extensive Catalan nationalism that disputes arose, intellectually and politically, in literary and scientific circles in Madrid between those defending the cultural unity of the Spanish nation and advocates of pluralism within Spain.[35]

Up to the turn of the century there were few occasions for repressive measures against Catalanist activists. They led a minority movement without political implications and stayed within the established constitutional order and did not, in their demands, attack the legitimacy of the existing state. Certainly Catalanists did not attack the social fabric of the state. As Spain was, in spite of some reservations, a constitutional state and neither Catalanists nor other opposition movements met with severe restrictions provided that they did not assault the state overtly. From the turn of the century changing attitudes emerged. Catalanists grew more radical which in turn led to violent reactions. In 1897 when the *Unió Catalanista* compared the Catalan endeavours to the fight of Crete against Turkish rule in a manifesto to the Greek king, the first repressive measures of some harshness were imposed. Newspapers were proscribed and editors sent to prison for 'insulting the nation'.[36]

The actual turning point came after the loss of the last colonies. As Catalanist leaders met with a greater response within the region they stood for elections and became important politically. Moreover Madrid had the precedent of Cuba before its eyes. Cuba had only demanded autonomy at first, but that had been only the initial step towards separation. With the motto 'stop the beginnings' the government acted against similar tendencies in Catalonia. On 1 January 1900 the first law designed to ward off the Catalan danger was promulgated. Previously only the worker's movement had been the object of special legislation, in the form of legal elastic clauses open to wide interpretation but aimed to hamper its spread. Now 'Attack on the Integrity of the Nation' was made a punishable offence.[37]

Available research does not permit as yet a comprehensive assessment of the lengths to which the administration was prepared to go in suppressing Catalanism. However one example will serve to illustrate the situation: the government in Madrid had a deciding influence on filling bishoprics in Catalonia. Whereas during the nineteenth century the Catalan question did not play a part in the selection, in the new atmosphere non-Catalan bishops were automatically appointed.[38] The state sought to ensure the use of Spanish in spiritual matters and to control the clergy in order to discourage participation in the Catalanist movement. Language policy, in sermons for instance, became the instrument of a repressive policy, something unknown earlier.[39]

The sensitivity of the authorities in Madrid and the severity of their reaction when a suspicion arose that the integrity of Spain or its most important institutions were threatened became obvious in 1904. Officers in Barcelona thought the honour of the army had been defiled by a caricature in a Catalan periodical. They retaliated by storming and wrecking the editor's office. It was not the officers but the editors responsible for the caricature who were punished by the court. Moreover after this incident the Spanish parliament included the offence of 'insult to the nation' in the penal code. Libelling of the army and all offences concerning the honour and integrity of the nation became subject to military jurisdiction. The new laws set in train frequent trials and sentences and the voluntary preventive exile of such Catalanist activists as were threatened with prosecution.[40] Nevertheless legal prosecution of Catalanists was still kept within strict bounds, not least because they were not radical revolutionaries.

In Madrid the Catalan political representatives met with an inimical climate. In his biography of Josep Cambó, the leading Catalan member of parliament, Jesus Pabón has offered much evidence that shows the political manoeuvres of different governments aimed at the elimination of the movement.[41] Other evidence also suggests that the politicians of both the governments in Madrid and the subordinate administrations fought the Catalanists by subversion, by force and through tolerating strong arm tactics used by others. Catalans frequently voiced their suspicions that the most successful rival of Catalanism, the Radical Republican party under the notorious Alejandro Lerroux, was financed by Madrid in order to offer an effective counterbalance to their parties. Lerroux did in fact receive subsidies from Madrid. Another party, the *Unión Monárquica Nacional* (Monarchical National Union), was indisputably inspired and financed from Madrid where there was a hope it would entice away the *Lliga Regionalista*'s most valuable supporters, the upper classes. Moreover suspicions in this respect are strengthened by some indications that the governments in Madrid used anarchist violence in Barcelona for their own purposes, employing hired criminals and agents provocateurs, particularly during the time when the infamous La Cierva was Home Secretary but also after 1917.

It was hoped that citizens would ask for official protection. By calling a self-provoked state of emergency an excuse would be available for restricting political activities.[42]

Though there was a tenacious resistance against the political demands of the Catalanists in Madrid there were also politicians who wished to grant concessions which would avoid the ultimate alienation of the Catalan middle classes from the Spanish centre. On the question of protective tariffs Catalan interests had already been considered before the turn of the century. In 1906 a protective tariff was granted which fully satisfied Catalan desires. Resistance against the standardisation of civil law had been successful in the 1890s. A further concession was the amalgamation of the four Catalan provinces into a single administrative unit. From 1913 the administrative duties which previously had been performed by the separate provinces were delegated to an administrative centre, the *Mancomunitat*, in Barcelona. The first director of this *Mancomunitat*, Prat de la Riba, ran his administration like that of a small national state and achieved, with the aid of war profits, a rapid modernisation of the region.[43] It was only when the dictatorship of Primo de Rivera was proclaimed in 1923 that the government in Madrid adopted a policy of systematic suppression which, however, did not have a lasting effect. Catalanism had deep roots and could not be suppressed easily especially when repression, even during the dictatorship, was not really harshly prosecuted.[44]

State of Research

Research materials for Spanish state authorities, for autonomous bodies in Catalonia, for private institutions, as well as for leading personalities, were unknown or unaccessible to a large extent until recently.[45] Research has therefore been based mainly on contemporary publications, periodicals and brochures which have been available in quantity.[46] Up to about 1970 the censorship of Franco's government prevented detailed studies of Catalanism. Nevertheless during the 1950s and the 1960s some standard works were published; for instance the monumental biography of the leading Catalanist politican Cambó by Jesus Pabón, and the analyses of Catalan history, mainly during the nineteenth century, by Pierre Vilar and Vicens i Vives. These works remain the starting point for all interpretations of the rise of Catalanism during the second half of the nineteenth century.[47]

Subsequently an extensive literature comprising all areas of Catalan history has flowered, which is summed up in the latest multivolume general history of Catalonia under the direction of

Pierre Vilar. Beside the political development both economic and social events[48] have been studied extensively. There are also many separate investigations of industrial and agrarian development along with political and social problems arising from it. The organisation of employers and workers has been assessed as well.[49] Cultural development, particularly the part Catalanism played in the radical turn towards European modernism, is still one of the most important areas of study. An omnibus volume published in 1986, *History and the Young Catalan Historians*, shows the direction taken by current historical writing.[50] On the whole the economic and social framework within which Catalanism flourished has been illuminated so effectively that the origins of the movement have become vivid. However there is a lively debate at the moment on why the political and social foundations of Catalanism made success possible after 1900.[51] Catalanism itself has been treated in many studies. Research has concentrated above all on political developments. The history of the most important party of Catalanism, the *Lliga Regionalista*, has been examined. The works of the specialist in this area, Borja de Riquer, are of special value because they are among the few available at present based on archive material. Research on sources for the history of the Catalanist left wing parties are also under way.[52]

The state of research on the policy of Madrid in dealing with Catalonia and Catalanism is unsatisfactory. To date only those aspects which became obvious during the conflict with Catalanism have been treated. Neither the debates of the Spanish parliament nor the policy of successive governments in Madrid have been a subject of investigation nor has there been a thorough evaluation of materials contained in the ministerial archives in Madrid or of those from government institutions in Barcelona. In spite of the extraordinary intensity of historical writing which has taken place during the last ten years many problems remain for which only tentative assessment can be offered.

Notes

1. Nagel (1988), p. 55.
2. 'Catalunya', *Gran Enciclopedia Catalana*, vol. 4, pp. 691–2.
3. In 1808 even in the French part of Catalonia nearly all people used the Catalan language exclusively. See *Patois de France* (Bibliothèque National Paris, MS. franç nouv.–acqu. 5912). I am indebted to Dr Pabst (University of Cologne) for this reference.
4. Garabou.
5. Nagel (1989).
6. For the whole passage and all quantifications, see Brunn (1978b), pp. 162–5; also Nagel (1983), pp. 6–11.
7. Vicens i Vives and Llorens; Jutglar.

8   Riquer (1979), p. 12.
9   Instituto de Estadística y politica social, Barcelona, *Estadísticas sociales* (1921), p. 27–36; Ucelay Da Cal, p. 135.
10 Brunn (1978a), pp. 285–7.
11 *Ibid.*, pp. 292–3; Riquer (1987), pp. 19–56.
12 Brunn (1978a), pp. 325–8.
13 Fastenrath, p. XXXIII.
14 *Ibid.*, pp. XVI–XVII.
15 Hina, pp. 66 *passim*.
16 *Catalanische Troubadoure*, p. XXIV.
17 Basegoda *et al.*
18 Camps i Giró; Vidal and Terrades; Termes, pp. 177–87.
19 Vejarano; Nadal *et al.*; text of the memorial in González Casanova, pp. 494–518.
20 *Ibid.*, pp. 536–9.
21 For a survey of the beginnings of political Catalanism and its evolution after the turn of the century see Ardit *et al.*, pp. 358–66; Brunn (1978a), pp. 295–300; Izard; Riquer.
22 Casassas i Ymbert (1979); Ucelay Da Cal, p. 132.
23 Ardit *et al.*, pp. 248–54. The following passage rests upon the findings of three studies: Brunn (1978a); Brunn (1978b); Brunn (1973), pp. 186–203.
24 Figueres, pp. 73–93.
25 Ramisa, pp. 67–70.
26 Riquer (1987), pp. 83–4. The integration of professionals and intellectuals into the ranks of the *Lliga Regionalista* is documented by Casassas i Ymbert (1983), pp. 7–32; Casassas i Ymbert (1979), pp. 103–31.
27 Ucelay Da Cal, pp. 131–2.
28 Brunn (1978a), pp. 340 *passim*.
29 Solà i Dachs; Torrent and Tasis; Rovira i Virgili (1916), p. 1.
30 For the following see the excellent study of Hina; also Brunn (1978a), pp. 329–39.
31 Mañé y Flaquer; Torras i Bagès; Prat de la Riba; Llobera, *passim*.
32 Brunn (1978b), pp. 161–2.
33 For certain aspects of this controversy see Comalada i Negre, pp. 57–86; Verdaguer i Callís.
34 Miracle.
35 Hina, pp. 189–257; Reglá, pp. 177–82.
36 Riquer (1979), pp. 22, 42; Brunn (1978a), pp. 326–8.
37 Hernández, pp. 228–34.
38 Petschen.
39 Milan i Massana, pp. 7–11; Ferrer i Gironès, pp. 62 *passim*.
40 Artola, vol. 1, p. 146; Rovira i Virgili (1970). In 1909 the Catalanist newspaper *El Poble Català* counted 15 Catalanists in exile, three in prison and seven who were put on trial. *El Poble Català*, 29 March 1909.
41 See Pabón (1952), vol. I, pp. 205 *passim*.
42 Brunn (1978a), pp. 304–5; Culla i Clarà; Manjou, pp. 53–62.
43 Ainaud and Jardi; Camps i Arboix.
44 Ardit *et al.*, pp. 484–8, 493–501.
45 Simon i Tarrés, pp. 15–31; Jaume Sobrequés i Callicó.
46 Brunn (1978a).
47 Jesús Pabón (1952–69); Vilar; Vicens i Vives and Llorens.
48 Volumes V and VI are of special interest here: Fontana; Termes. For the latest developments see Alcoberro i Pericay, pp. 62–102; Termes, p. 177– 187 and his extensive bibliography in Termes (1987), pp. 423–47.
49 Alcoberro i Pericay, pp. 71–84; Ardit *et al.*; Izard and Riquer, vol. 4.
50 See note 48; and Josep Termes *et al.* (1986). *Catalanisme*.

51 Termes.
52 Riquer (1977); Molas; Ucelay Da Cal, pp. 129–45.

Select Bibliography

Ainaud, Josep Maria and Jardi, Enric (1973), *Prat de la Riba, home de govern*, Barcelona.
Alberti, Santiago (1972), *El republicanisme català i la restauració monàrquica 1875–1923*, Barcelona.
Alcoberro i Pericay, Agustí (1986), 'La Història contemporània dels països catalans als darrers cinc anys. Per un balanç historiogràfic', in *La Història*, pp. 62–102.
Ardit, M. *et al.* (1980), *Història dels Països Catalans de 1714 a 1975*, Barcelona.
Artola, Miguel (1974), *Partidos i programas politicos 1808–1936*, Madrid.
Balcells, Albert (1977), *Cataluña contemporánea I (Siglo XIX)*, Madrid, 2nd edition.
Balcells, Albert (1984), *Cataluña contemporánea II (1900–1939)*, Madrid, 5th edition.
Basegoda, J. *et al.* (1976), *Modernismo en Cataluña*, Barcelona.
Berkenbusch, Gabriele (1988), *Sprachpolitik und Sprachbewußtsein in Barcelona am Anfang dieses Jahrhunderts*, Frankfurt/Main, Bern, New York.
Bonet, J. (1984), *L'església catalana, de l'illustració a la Renaixença*, Montserrat.
Brunn, Gerhard (1978a), 'Die Organisationen der katalanischen Bewegung 1859–1923', in Schieder, Theodor and Dann, Otto (eds), *Nationale Bewegung und soziale Organisation I. Vergleichende Studien zur nationalen Vereinsbewegung des 19. Jahrhunderts in Europa*, München, Wien, pp. 285–7.
Brunn, Gerhard (1978b), 'Regionalismus und sozialer Wandel Das Beispiel Katalonien', in Dann, Otto (ed.), *Nationalismus und sozialer Wandel*, Hamburg, pp. 161–5.
Camps i Arboix, Joaquim de (1968), *La Mancomunitat de Catalunya*, Barcelona.
Camps i Girò, Joan (1973), *La guerra dels Matiners i el catalanisme polític, 1846–1849*, Barcelona.
Casassas i Ymbert, Jordi (1983), 'Els quadres del regionalisme. L'evolució de la Joventut Nacionalista de la Lliga fins el 1914', in *Recerques* 14, pp. 7–32. idem, 'Configuració del sector "intel.lectuel-professional" a la Catalunya de la Restauració' (a propòsit de Jaume Bofill i Mates), in *Recerques* 8 (1979), pp. 103–131.
Catalanisme, història, política i cultura (1986), Josep Termes *et al.*, Barcelona, *idem* (1989), 'Intel.lectuals, professionals i polítics a la Catalunya contemporània' (1850–1920), Barcelona.
Catalunya i Espanya al segle XIX (1987), Josep Fontana *et al.*, Barcelona.
'Catalunya' (1968), in *Gran Enciclopedia Catalana*, vol. 4, Barcelona.
Comalada i Negre, Àngel, 'L'aspecte jurídic del Memorial de Greuges', in Nadal, Joaquim *et al.* (1986), *El memorial*.
Culla i Clara, Joan B. (1987), *El republicanisme lerrouxista a Catalunya (1901–1923)*, Barcelona.
Duarte, Angel (1987), *El Republicanisme català a la fi del segle XIX*, Vic.
Estadisticas sociales. Monografia Estadistica de la clase obrera (1921), Barcelona.
Fastenrath, Johannes (collater) (1890), *Catalanische Troubadore der Gegenwart. Verdeutscht und mit einer Uebersicht der catalanischen Literatur eingeleitet von. . .* Leipzig.
Ferrer i Gironès, Francesc (1986), *La persecució política de la llengua catalana*, 2nd edition, Barcelona.
Figueres, Josep Maria (1986), 'El Diari Català (1879–1881); plataforma d'exposició del pensament catalanista', in *Catalanisme, història, política i cultura*, Barcelona.
Fontana, Josep (1988), 'La fi del'antic règim i la índustrialització (1787–1868)', in Vilar, Pierre (ed.), *Història de Catalunya*, vol. V, Barcelona.
Gali, A. (1978), *Història de les institucions i del moviment cultural de Catalunya*, vols I–III, Barcelona.

Garrabou, R. (1983), *El camp català als segles XIX i XX, a estructura social i econòmica del camp català*, Barcelona.

González Casanova, J.A. (1974), *Federalisme i autonomia a Catalunya 1869–1938*, Documents, Barcelona.

Gran Enciclopedia Catalana, vol. 4 (1968), Barcelona.

Harrison, Joseph (1978), 'El món de la gran indústria i el fracàs del Nacionalisme català de dreta (1901–1923)', in *Recerques*, 7, pp. 83–98.

Hina, Horst (1978), *Kastilien und Katalonien in der Kulturdiskussion 1714–1939*, Tübingen.

La Història i els joves historiadors catalans. (1986), Ponències i communicacions de les primeres jornades de joves historiadors catalans. Pòrtic de Jaume Sobrequés i Callicó, Barcelona.

Histoire de la Catalogne (1982), Sous la direction de Joaquim Nadal Ferreras et de Philippe Wolff, Toulouse.

Izard, Miquel and Riquer, Borja de (1983), *Conèixer la història de Catalunya. Del Segle XIX fins a 1931*, vol. 4, Barcelona.

Izard, Miquel (1979), *Manufactureros, fabricantes y revolucionarios. Las burgesías industriales catalanas y el control del poder en España. 1868–1875*, Barcelona.

Izard, Miquel (1978), *El segle XIX. Burgesos i proletaris*, Barcelona.

Jutglar, Antoni (1972), *Història crítica de la burgesia a Catalunya*, Barcelona.

Linz, J. (1973), 'Early state-building and late peripheral nationalisms against the state', in S.N. Eisenstadt and S. Rokkan (eds), *Building States and Nations*, Beverly Hills, pp. 32–116.

Llobera, J.R. (1983), 'The idea of "Volksgeist" in the formation of Catalan nationalist ideology', in *Ethnic and Racial Studies* 6, pp. 332–50.

McDonagh, Gary Wray (1986), *Good Families of Barcelona: A social history of power in the industrial era*, Princeton.

Mañé y Flaquer, Juan (1887), *El regionalismo*, 2nd edn., Barcelona.

Milan i Massana, Antoni (forthcoming), 'The Catalan Language in the Conflict between Centralism and Autonomism', in Sergij Vilfan (ed.), *Ethnic Groups and Language Rights*, Aldershot: Dartmouth.

Miracle, Josep (1960), *La restauració dels Jocs Florals*, Barcelona.

Molas, Isidre (1972), *Lliga Cataluña*, 2 vol., Barcelona.

Nadal, Joaquim *et al.* (1986), *El memorial de grenges i el catalanisme polític*, Barcelona.

Nagel, Klaus Jürgen (1983), *El movimiento nacional y la clase obrera en Barcelona. 1898–1923*. Arbeitspapiere no. 30, Universitätsschwerpunkt Lateinamerika-Forschung, Universität Bielefeld.

Nagel, Klaus Jürgen (1988), 'Vasquismo y Catalanismo hasta 1923. El 'Catalanismo de izquierda y Euskadi', in Tuñón de Lara, Manuel (ed.), *Gernika: So años despues (1937–1987)*, San Sebastian.

Nagel, Klaus Jürgen (1989), 'Arbeiterschaft und nationale Frage in Katalonien zwischen 1898 und 1923', Ph.D. thesis, Bielefeld.

Pabón, Jesús (1952–1969), *Cambó (1876–1940)*, 3 vols, Barcelona.

Petschen, Santiago (1992), 'The Spanish royal privilege of Patronato. A political arm of control over the Catalan minority', in Donald Kerr (ed.), *Religion, State and Ethnic Groups*, Aldershot: Dartmouth.

Pi-Sunyer, Oriol (1984), 'The political economy of the Catalan nationalist movement', in Vermulen, Hans and Boussevain, Jeremy (eds), *Ethnic challenge. The politics of ethnicity in Europe*, Göttingen.

Pi-Sunyer, Oriol (1986), 'Catalan Nationalism. Some theoretical and historical considerations', in Tiryakian, Edward A. and Rogowski, Ronald (eds), *New Nationalisms of the developed West. Toward Explanation*, Boston, pp. 254–76.

Prat de la Riba, Enric (1906), *La Nacionalitat catalana*, Barcelona.

Ramisa, Maties (1985), *Els orígens del catalanisme conservador i 'La Veu-del-Montserrat' 1878–1900*, Vic.

Reglá, Juan (1974), *Historia de Cataluña*, Madrid.
Riquer, Borja de (1977), *Lliga Regionalista: la burgesia catalana i el nacionalisme (1898–1904)*, Barcelona.
Riquer, Borja de (1979), *Regionalistes i nacionalistes (1898–1937)*, Barcelona.
Riquer, Borja de (1987), 'La vida politica catalana (1856–1898)', *Catalunya i Espanya al segle XIX*, Barcelona.
Robledo Hernández, Ricardo (1975), 'L'actitud Castellana enfront del catalanisme, 1884–1918', in *Recerques* 5, pp. 228–34.
Rossinyol, J. (1974), *Le Problème national catalan*, Paris.
Rovira i Virgili, Antoni (1916), 'Els diaris de Barcelona', in *La Revista*, 2, no. 12, March.
Rovira i Virgili, Antoni (1970), *El nacionalismo catalán, su aspecto politico, los hechos, las ideas y los hombres*, Barcelona.
Simon i Tarrés, Antoni (1986), 'Fonts i arxius', in Sobrequés i Callicó, Jaume (ed.) *La història i els joves historiadors catalans. Ponències i comunicacions de les primeres jornades de joves historiadors catalans*, Barcelona, pp. 15–31.
Sobrequés i Callicó, Jaume (1982), *Els arxius per a la història del nacionalisme català*, Generalitat de Catalunya, Departament de Cultura, Barcelona.
Solà i Dachs, Lluis (1978), *Història dels diaris en Català, 1879–1976*, Barcelona.
Solé-Tura, Jordi (1967), *Catalanisme i revolució burgesa. La síntesi de Prat de la Riba*, Barcelona.
Solé-Tura, Jordi (1985), *Nacionalidades y nacionalismos en España*, Madrid.
Soler, Vidal Josep (1983), *Abdò Terrades. Primer apòstol de la democracia catalana (1812–1856)*, Barcelona.
Termes, Josep (1984), *La immigració a Catalunya i altres estudis d'història del nacionalisme català*, Barcelona.
Termes, Josep, *et al.* (1986), *Catalanisme, història, política i cultura*, Barcelona.
Termes, Josep (1987), 'Corrents del pensament i d'acció del moviment catalanista', in *Catalunya i Espanya al segle XIX*, Barcelona, pp. 177–87.
Termes, Josep (1987), 'De la revolució de setembre a la fi de la guerra civil (1868–1939)', in Vilar, Pierre (ed.) *Història de Catalunya*, vol. VI, Barcelona.
Torrents, Joan and Tasis, Rafael (1966), *Història de la premsa catalana*, Barcelona.
Torras i Bagès, Josep (1892), *La tradició catalana*, Barcelona.
Trias, Vejarano Juan (1975), *Almirall y los orígines del catalanismo*, Madrid.
Ucelay Da Cal, Enric (1986), 'L' "Esquerra Nacionalista" catalana, 1900–1931; unes reflexions', in *Catalanisme, història, política i cultura*, Barcelona.
Verdaguer i Callís, Narcís (1919), *La primera victòria del catalanisme*, Barcelona.
Vicens i Vives, Jaume and Llorens, Montserrat (1958), *Industrials i polítics (segle XIX)*, Barcelona.
Vilaclara, M. Josep (1983), 'Renaixença i particularisme català durant el Sexenni 1868–73', in *Recerques* 13.
Vilar, Pierre (1962), *La Catalogne dans L'Espagne moderne*, 3 vols, Paris.

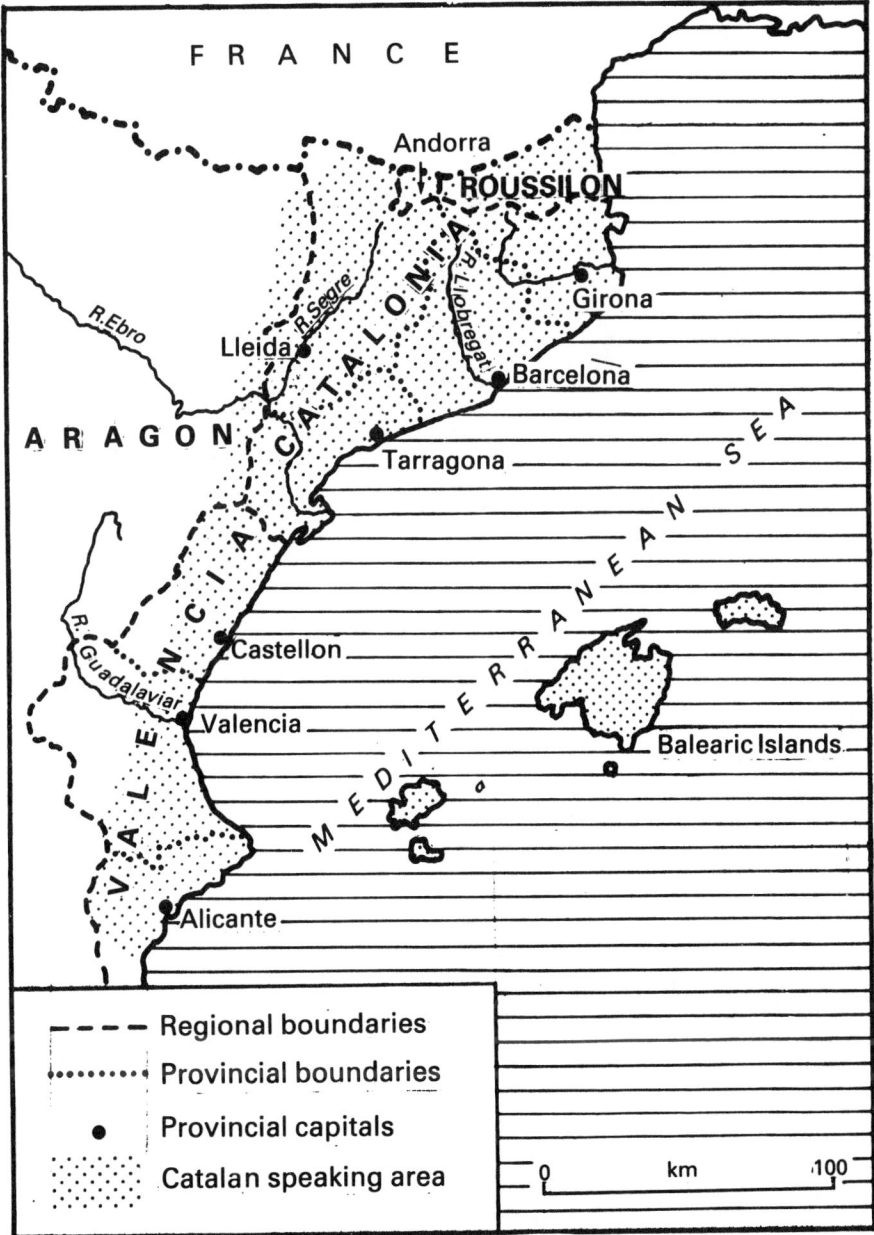

Map 6.1 'Països Catalans' and Catalan speaking area

7 The Macedonians in the Ottoman Empire, 1878–1912

FIKRET ADANIR

Introduction

Recognition of a Macedonian nationality is of relatively recent date, being connected with the formation of a Macedonian republic in the framework of the Yugoslav federation after the Second World War. Yet even today the existence of a Macedonian nationality is a controversial issue. Opposition to it is all the more vehement the earlier the beginning of the nation building process in Macedonia is set.

This study starts from the premise that the Macedonian nation today is a reality, although in the period under consideration many Macedonian Slavs referred to themselves as Bulgarians. In the case of the Macedonian Slavs such a designation had only incidental importance. Whether the struggle during the latter part of the nineteenth and at the beginning of the twentieth century was inspired by Bulgarian nationalism or by the ideal of a genuine Macedonian national autonomy, the goal remained in both cases the same: the political, cultural and economic emancipation of the Christian Slav population from foreign rule. It is inappropriate to speak of two separate rival national movements – the Bulgarian and the Macedonian – in the European provinces of the Ottoman empire. It was a matter of two wings within the same movement. For the activists it was perfectly normal to change sides, and it is no coincidence that both Bulgarian and Macedonian historiography today lay claim to the same tradition in the national liberation struggle. Both venerate the same heroes and legends.[1]

Considering these circumstances it becomes understandable that the Macedonian nation building process at the turn of the century was confronted with virtually insurmountable obstacles. Wherever Macedonian national consciousness was expressed, the accusation of 'separatism' or even 'betrayal' of the revolutionary cause was sure to come from the pro-Bulgarian majority within the liberation movement. In addition there were rival organisations which struggled for the union of Macedonia – or at least parts of it – with Greece or Serbia. When the Balkan war of 1912 finally freed Macedonia from Ottoman rule, the liberators hurried to suppress the idea of Macedonian national autonomy; the country was soon partitioned between the neighbouring Balkan states Greece, Serbia and Bulgaria.

General Conditions

Social and Economic Conditions

'Macedonia', a geographic term known since antiquity, describes a territory the extent of which varied through the ages. The kingdom of Philip II in the fourth century BC covered an area which was larger than that which is called Macedonia today, and the Byzantine province of the same name which was located in the eastern part of the Balkan peninsula had nothing to do with present day Macedonia. Neither the medieval kingdoms of the Bulgarians and the Serbs nor the Ottoman state, which ruled over the area from the second half of the fourteenth century until 1912, utilised the term (in Ottoman terminology it was common to refer to Macedonia as the 'three *vilayets*' – provinces – namely, Salonika, Monastir/Bitola and Kosovo/Skopje).

Cartographers of the nineteenth century, guided by ancient writers such as Ptolemy and Strabo, reintroduced Macedonia into European geographic terminology.[2] The limits of Macedonia are roughly defined in the map at the end of the chapter, with the northern border running from the Shar mountains over Skopska Crna Gora (Karadağ) to the Kosjak and the Osogov mountains; the Mesta (Nestos) river in the east separates Macedonia from Thrace, while in the south the border is thought to be marked by a line running from the Aegean along the river Aliakmon/Bistrica to the lakes Prespa and Ochrida; and in the west lies the Albanian mountain chain.

The region as defined above does not constitute a topographic unity. On the contrary mountains divide it into isolated basins with different climatic and soil characteristics which have influenced the historical pattern of settlement. The peoples who lived in or invaded this region – Thracians, Illyrians, Greeks, Romans, Slavs, the Turkic tribes such as the Cumans, Petchenegs, Oghuz and finally the Ottoman Turks – remained relatively isolated from one another, seeking protection from intruders in their respective zones of retreat. Except for the natural route to the north along the valley of the rivers

Vardar and Morava and the *via egnatia*, the ancient road from Italy through Albania and Macedonia to Istanbul/Constantinople, the region was marked by poor internal communications. These conditions produced over the centuries a remarkable mixture of ethnic groups in an area covering only 67 000 sq. km. As late as the beginning of the twentieth century the geographer Jovan Cvijić described the demographic situation in Macedonia as follows:

> The Slavs in the individual basins are often of different origin, having immigrated from different regions; in some basins they are mainly immigrants, in others primarily old-established groups. . . .Some basins are entirely Slavic; others are populated by the Turkish tribes of Yuruks and Koniars; in most cases the Slavs are mixed with Osmanlis, in the southern basins also with Greeks and Vlachs.[3]

No reliable figures are available on the numerical strength of the individual ethnic groups in Macedonia. In the multi-national Ottoman empire the ethnic origin of the subjects was of secondary importance. As is shown in Table 7.1 the official statistics stressed primarily confessional allegiance.

Table 7.1: Population of Macedonia 1906–7

Vilâyet	Muslim	Greek	Bulgar.	Vlach	Jewish	Others	Total
Selânik	419 604	263 881	155 710	20 486	52 395	9 283	921 359
Monastir*	204 587	203 976	185 566	2 356	4 583	1 315	602 383
Kosovo**	113 603	8 604	144 545		1 198	778	268 728
Total	737 794	476 461	485 821	22 842	58 176	11 376	1 792 470

* Only the data pertaining to the prefecture of Üsküb/Skopje have been considered.
** Exclusive of the districts of Görice/Korçë and Elbasan which are situated in Albania.
Source: Karpat, pp. 166–9.

However, European ethnographers as well as the protagonists of the national movements in the Balkans held language, not religion, to be the decisive criterion in determining national affiliation. They were therefore primarily interested in the ethnic–linguistic structure of the Macedonian population. A Bulgarian statistic that is representative is given in Table 7.2.

The population of Macedonia in the first decade of the twentieth century was somewhat over two million. With only 30 persons per square kilometre Macedonia was populated thinly by the norms of western and central Europe. This was not unusual when compared with its neighbouring countries however. This region was in the

Table 7.2: Ethnic and confessional composition of the population of Macedonia at the beginning of the twentieth century

Ethnic Group	Christians	Muslims	Jews	Total	in %
Bulgarians	1 032 533	148 803		1 181 336	52.31
Turks	4 240	494 964		499 204	22.11
Greeks	214 329	14 373		228 702	10.13
Albanians	9 510	119 201		128 711	5.70
Vlachs	77 267	3 500		80 767	3.58
Jews			67 840	67 840	3.00
Gypsies	19 500	35 057		54 557	2.42
Others	13 570	3 337		16 907	0.75
Total	1 370 949	819 235	67 840	2 258 024	100.00

Source: Kŭnchov (1900); reprinted in Kŭnchov (1970), vol. 2, p. 590.

forefront in the Balkans particularly with respect to the degree of urbanisation: the inhabitants of about 60 towns with municipal status comprised 30 per cent of the total population.[4] With over 120 000 inhabitants Salonika was the second largest city (after Istanbul) on the Balkan peninsula. A prominent port on the Aegean it was connected to Skopje in 1874 by a railway and from 1888 – via Belgrade – to central Europe. In the 1890s a branch line was completed to Monastir, and at the beginning of the twentieth century Salonika was connected by rail to Istanbul.[5]

Macedonian cities were distinctly Islamic in character as late as the first half of the nineteenth century. After that, however, the situation began to change with the Christian Slav urban element gradually attaining predominance. For example, around 1800 Skopje had about 10 000 inhabitants, virtually all being Muslims. By 1913 the population of the town had risen to 37 000, 40 per cent of whom spoke a Slavic tongue. Shtip experienced a similar development: it grew from a tiny Muslim market town of 5000 people at the beginning of the nineteenth century to an important provincial centre with more than 20 000 inhabitants at the beginning of the twentieth century, and here too the Slavs made up about half of the population. Towns such as Seres (35 000 inhabitants in 1906), Monastir (over 50 000 inhabitants in 1898), and Strumica (8900 inhabitants in 1894) experienced similar growth and change.[6]

Yet the population structures of the commercially important port towns such as Salonika and Kavala had peculiarities which, when seen from the perspective of Macedonian nation building, proved to be inhibiting factors. For example, the import–export business of the country lay in the hands of the Jewish and Greek merchants of Salonika. Through them European capital eventually gained control of the credit system in Macedonian domestic trade. The Jewish entrepreneurs of Salonika were at the same time the initiators of a modest industrialisation. In the first decade of the twentieth century some modern flour mills, breweries, textile factories, ship repair yards, tobacco processing plants and similar enterprises were operating in Macedonia.[7] The Jews of Salonika also were to play a decisive role in organising the trade union movement after 1908.[8]

The majority of the population lived in the countryside. The average peasant was an independent smallholder for whom the tithe of agricultural products delivered to the state represented the main tax burden. Furthermore non-Muslim adult males had to pay the military exemption tax, while Muslim peasants were subject to long and unpopular service in the army. Commercial agriculture on *chiftliks* (large estates) played only a secondary role in the economy, mainly because the wages were relatively high and modern technology was still unknown. But also the increasing cultivation of the cash crops tobacco and poppies, which were labour intensive, along with the profitable silkworm rearing in homes were factors favouring small peasant ownership. Nevertheless, there were regions where sharecropping was relatively widespread. The relationship between landowners and sharecroppers was of an economic nature and regulated on the basis of a contract. The state of research does not yet allow precision in calculating the extent of sharecropping during the last phase of Ottoman rule in Macedonia. It certainly played a more important role in the first half of the nineteenth century than in the second. Probably about ten per cent of the peasant households still lived as sharecroppers on *chiftliks* at the beginning of the twentieth century.[9]

The social phenomenon of *pechalbarstvo* (labour migration) also deserves attention. On the rise since the Crimean war it reached a peak at the beginning of the twentieth century. Migrant workers, particularly from the mountainous regions of western Macedonia, left every year for Istanbul, Asia Minor, Egypt and the neighbouring Balkan countries, Bulgaria and Romania, to return to their villages at the end of the season in late autumn. The number of adult males 'mobilised' annually in this manner reached tens of thousands. Emigration, primarily to North America, also played a role; between 1902 and 1906 about 25000 persons emigrated overseas.[10] Such migrant workers were unquestionably important agents of change in Macedonian society, not only because of the money remitted to their families but also with the wider political outlook they acquired abroad.

Political System

For the Ottoman empire the nineteenth century was a long period of crisis. Military defeats since the seventeenth century, frequent rebellions in the provinces, spectacular uprisings of the Christian Serbs and Greeks and the readiness of the European powers to intervene on behalf of the Christians, all seemed to confirm the impression that the final dissolution of this Muslim state was imminent.

The Ottoman ruling class was aware of the seriousness of the situation. In an effort to secure the survival of the empire they undertook a series of modernising reforms during the *Tanzimat* (Reorganisation) period (1839–76) – reforms that challenged traditional Ottoman society.[11] One result of this 'westernisation' was the introduction of free trade. The industrialised west was allowed to penetrate eastern markets, partly as a reward for support against rebellious pashas internally and against external threats as was the case during the Crimean war. This opening to external economic and cultural influences brought about profound structural changes. Domestic production dropped since it could not compete with the cheaper European manufactures, and modern industries could hardly be developed to employ the jobless craftsmen. While a *lumpenproletariat* was in the making, the Ottoman 'bourgeoisie', which consisted primarily of Christian and Jewish merchants in the cosmopolitan port cities such as Istanbul, Izmir/Smyrna, Salonika or Beirut, became dependent on the centres of the world economy. On the other hand the well-to-do peasants and commercial middle classes rising in the interior tended to become supporters of the national movements against Ottoman rule. Under these conditions Ottoman policy towards nationalities after the middle of the nineteenth century was determined by five factors: the *millet* (autonomous non-Muslim community) system, secularism, great power influence, Balkan irredentism and the Young Turk opposition to the Ottoman political establishment.

The Millet System

In the Ottoman empire the population was traditionally grouped into autonomous 'national' communities, the *millets*, under their respective religious leaders.[12] This system was based on the 'personality' principle which was common during medieval times. In contrast to the practice in a territorial state a person, regardless of locality, was subject to the jurisdiction of his own religious community. Although the 'personality' principle was confined essentially to civil matters, the *millets* enjoyed other far-reaching privileges. One such privilege was their jurisdiction in school matters and this at a time when public education was becoming a state task in most countries. This was to become a source of conflict between the *millet* hierarchies and the modernising centralist state.

The Secular Concept of Ottomanism

The bureaucratic elites of the *Tanzimat*, most of whom had received a European education, considered if not the abolishment, at least the limitation, of the old privileges of the *millets* one of the essential tasks of modernisation. The religious communities were to be given a new constitution which would permit laymen to have a voice in the elected councils. The distinctions in the legal status between the members of different *millets* were to be abolished. As citizens of a modern Ottoman state all subjects of the sultan should be equal before the law. Thus it was hoped that irrespective of religion the citizen would owe loyalty first and foremost to the common Ottoman fatherland. Ottomanism was therefore a concept of the political nation based on the territorial unity of the state. Within the egalitarian ideology of *Tanzimat* modernism, it was the keystone of the 1876 constitution.[13] Nevertheless the constitution recognised Islam as the state religion and the sultan remained the caliph of the Muslims – circumstances which reflect the contradictory tendencies in Ottoman secularism.

The Influence of the Great Powers

The rights and duties of the citizens of the late Ottoman empire were closely related to developments in the Eastern Question. Russia, France, the Habsburg monarchy and Great Britain claimed a right to protect the non-Muslim citizens of the Ottoman empire under the specific pretext that the traditional *millet* constitution discriminated against the non-Muslims. Viewed from this standpoint the European great powers had a rather ambivalent attitude towards the westernisation of the Ottoman empire. On the one hand they approved of the economic liberalisation and the development of the country's infrastructure; on the other hand, however, they did not welcome the creation of a truly secularised Ottoman state since that would have deprived them of the basis of their influence in the Eastern Question. A paradoxical situation emerged: together with the hierarchies of the Christian churches in the east, the European powers defended the old Ottoman legal system against the modernisation policy of the *Tanzimat* elite.

In the long run ottomanism was unable to compete with the national movements of the Christian peoples. The crisis of 1875–8 marked a turning point. The catastrophic defeat in the war against Russia, the large territorial losses and the imminent bankruptcy of the Ottoman state all discredited the entire western orientation of the *Tanzimat* period, including the idea of ottomanism, among the Muslim peoples in the empire. Also, after the war the Ottoman empire had to absorb hundreds of thousands of refugees from the territories lost in the Balkans and in the northern Caucasus. As a result the numerical preponderance of the Muslim population in the empire increased.

These changes were reflected in the nature of the regime of Sultan Abdulhamid II (1876–1909) who initiated a conciliatory policy towards Muslim provincial groups that had been estranged by the centralist administration as well as by the various secularising measures of the *Tanzimat*. The integrative power of the new policy was due to the ideological emphasis of Islamic values. As a counterweight to western culture medieval Islam was idealised as the source of civilisation. In the face of European imperialist expansion in Africa and Asia, often in regions populated by Muslims, the sultan succeeded in revitalising the office of the caliphate and in representing himself as the protector of the world's Muslims.[14] This Islamist emphasis also helped in regaining the loyalty of those Muslim peoples in the empire who, during the *Tanzimat* period, had rebelled repeatedly against state authority: along with the Arab notables and some Kurdish tribes in the east, the Albanians in the west were to play a key role in the new policy towards Christian nationalities. The interethnic and intercommunal conflicts in the last quarter of the nineteenth and the first decade of the twentieth century, in Macedonia as well as in other parts of the empire, should be seen in this context.[15]

Macedonia and the Neighbouring Nation–States

The policy towards national groups in the multi-national Ottoman state cannot be explained adequately without considering the irredentism of the neighbouring countries. None of the nation–states which had emerged between 1830 and 1878 on former Ottoman territory – Greece, Serbia, Montenegro, Bulgaria and Romania – were satisfied with the *status quo*. On the contrary they pursued an expansionist policy that had little to do with liberating their fellow nationals from foreign rule: the 'Great Idea' of the Greeks, for example, aimed at the reestablishment of the Byzantine empire.[16] In the tradition of Ilija Garashanin the Serbs strove to create a large south Slav state, a concept which was bound to collide with similar ambitious plans of neighbouring nations.[17] The Romanians laid claim to the heritage of ancient Rome in the Balkans and tried to mobilise the small ethnic group of Vlachs in European Turkey for the Romanian national cause.[18] Finally the Bulgarians saw themselves as victims of European diplomacy because the Congress of Berlin had halved the territory promised to them in the Treaty of San Stefano. Thus they demanded the return of the territories 'taken' from them.[19]

As a result the Balkans went through a series of national conflicts (the Cretan question, the Epirote question, the Serbo–Bulgarian War of 1885, the Greek–Ottoman War of 1897, the Albanian question, the Macedonian question, the Balkan Wars of 1912–3, the Aegean question, etc), some of which have remained potent into recent times.

The Young Turk Opposition

Opposition to the regime of Abdulhamid emerged first in clandestine student circles in Istanbul in the 1890s. Later it developed into a movement of liberals living in exile in Europe. The main goal of the opposition was the replacement of the autocratic rule of Abdulhamid by a constitutional monarchy. It was hoped that the old idea of ottomanism would be realised more easily under a constitutional form of government.[20]

The cadres of the Young Turk revolution of 1908 were not identical with the Young Turks living in exile. Young officers, civil servants and intellectuals in Macedonia who had been in contact with various ideologies of national liberation forced through a *coup d'état* the reinstatement of the 1876 constitution. However, the fraternisation among nationalities that this 'revolution' had ushered in lasted only briefly. The chief cause of discontent was the rigorous centralism of the Young Turk regime which infringed upon the old privileges of the *millets*. Under the influence of populist ideas the Young Turks also introduced comprehensive programmes of public education financed by the state. This not only interfered with the specific rights of the religious communities in school matters but also bestowed upon Turkish, the language of the majority, a new status. Once Turkish was the mandatory language of instruction in state schools, the ideology of ottomanism began to lose its cosmopolitan appeal.[21] Behind the educational policies of the government the non-Turkish ethnic groups saw the imposition of 'turkification.'

The National Movement and its Activists

History of the National Movement

The history of the Macedonian national movement, as indicated above, presents some difficulties for periodisation. Its Phases A and B in Hroch's scheme coincide largely with the respective stages of the Bulgarian national movement. For the latter the establishment of the exarchate in 1870 may be considered as marking the transition to Phase C which is characterised by mass-based support for the national cause.

It is justifiable of course to question the legitimacy of assuming such an early genealogy for the Macedonian national movement. As will be shown, only at the turn of the twentieth century did a distinct Macedonian consciousness begin to develop. It is, however, just as problematic to equate the proponents of 'Macedonianism' with those scholarly 'fathers' of the national idea whose activities constitute – in Hroch's concept – Phase A of national history. By the time that it was conceived as an idea, around the turn of the twentieth century, macedonianism was a viable political option with a fully developed national movement. Actually, in the Macedonian case as in the Irish one, characteristics of all three phases took place simultaneously. This suggests that Hroch's periodisation with its emphasis on developments in the social and economic spheres should be applied with caution when studying national history in the Ottoman Balkans. Apart from the multi-ethnic and multi-confessional structure of the society, political expediency in a given constellation of international power politics often proved to be of overriding importance.

The Church Question in Macedonia

The secularising reforms of the *Tanzimat* period created the conditions for a greater influence of the lay element in church and school affairs. The formation of Macedonian Slav school communities resulting from the reorganisation of the *millet* system in turn prepared the ground for the emergence of a specific Macedonian Slav consciousness. Old structures had favoured the hellenisation of the population, since Greek was used both in schools and churches. The population now demanded that a Slavic language, in this case Bulgarian, should take the place of Greek. The conflict over this issue eventually led to a confrontation with the Greek Orthodox patriarchate, ending in a schism and the establishment of the Bulgarian exarchate in 1870.[22]

However, the Macedonian dioceses were left outside the jurisdiction of the new autocephalous church. Their incorporation into the Bulgarian exarchate depended on the condition that at least two thirds of a given Christian community declared themselves for separation from the Greek Church in a plebiscite. Bulgarian, Greek and Serbian agents began now to agitate among the population for or against such a majority vote. Thus the establishment of the exarchate not only weakened the Greek Orthodox *millet*, it also resulted in splitting the Macedonian Slavs. The 'patriarchists' among them were henceforth considered Greeks, whereas the 'exarchists' were counted as Bulgarians.[23]

The church question in Macedonia acquired a new quality in the aftermath of the Russian–Turkish War of 1877–8. The Russian victory and the preliminary Treaty of San Stefano promised all of Macedonia to the future Bulgarian state. But the western powers, in order to counteract mounting Russian influence in the Balkans, imposed a considerable territorial reduction of the prospective Bulgarian state at the 1878 Congress of Berlin. As a consequence Macedonia was left under Ottoman sovereignty with the condition that comprehensive social and political reforms should be carried out. Yet the Slavic population believed that the annexation of Macedonia by Bulgaria was only a matter of time. When Bulgaria and Eastern Rumelia, in complete disregard of the Treaty of Berlin, declared their union in 1885, the Bulgarian 'party' in Macedonia seemed stronger than ever.

Internal Macedonian Revolutionary Organisation

The secret society that was founded in Salonika at the end of 1893 and that came to be known as the Internal Macedonian Revolutionary Organisation originally called itself the 'Bulgarian Macedono–Adrianopolitan Revolutionary Committees'. Its founders – four teachers, a physician and a bookseller – must have seen themselves at that time as the *avant garde* of the Bulgarian national movement. Their aim was to prepare for the union of the unredeemed territories with the Bulgarian fatherland. But being aware of the jealousies of the neighbouring states and of the need to take into consideration the interests of the great powers, they felt obliged to be discreet about their true objective.[24] In the earliest extant statute of the organisation, dating from 1896, article one states that 'the goal of the BMARC is the attainment of full political autonomy for Macedonia and the province of Adrianople'. It is worth noting that this document refers under article two only to the 'Bulgarian population' which was to be prepared for a general uprising, while in article three it is stated clearly that only a Bulgarian could become a member of the organisation.[25]

The difference between this early document and the 1902 statutes

of the organisation is striking. First there is the new name: the Secret
Macedono–Adrianopolitan Revolutionary Organisation testifies to a
significant change – the qualifier 'Bulgarian' is deleted. Secondly
article one of the new statute formulates the goal of the organisation
as being 'to unite in a whole all the dissatisfied elements in
Macedonia and the province of Adrianople, irrespective of nationality, in order to achieve full political autonomy through revolution'.
Further it is declared indispensable for the realisation of this objective
that the organisation should struggle 'to eliminate the chauvinistic
propaganda and national discordance which divide and weaken'
the population. Lastly, any Macedonian and any inhabitant of the
province of Adrianople now could become a member of the
organisation.[26]

With its stress on the solidarity of national groups and condem-
nation of outside interference, the Internal Macedonian Revolutionary Organisation of 1902 was far removed from the clandestine
committee of 1893 in terms of its programme. Cultural emancipation
accomplished under the leadership of the exarchist clergy and
supported chiefly by urban Slav occupational and commercial groups
seemed no longer sufficient. To achieve political liberation the
Organisation's activists now felt the need to appeal to the whole
population irrespective of religious and ethnic affiliation. To this end
they even risked a military confrontation with the Ottoman army.

Despite the democratic overtures to other national groups the
Organisation remained the political home of the exarchist population. It was generally assumed that the great powers would not
tolerate the bloody suppression of a Christian popular revolt in
European Turkey, and further hope centred on European intervention on behalf of the Christians which would pave the way, if not
for Macedonian statehood, then at least for the union of the country
with Bulgaria. At any rate the first task of the Internal Macedonian
Revolutionary Organisation was to prepare the population politically, economically and militarily for a general uprising in
Macedonia.[27]

The Ilinden Uprising of 1903

Ottoman officials became aware of the existence of the Internal
Macedonian Revolutionary Organisation in 1897. This forced the
revolutionary organisation to commence its activities prematurely
with a kind of guerilla warfare that was more in the tradition of
Balkan *hayduks* (bandits in the Slavic parts of Ottoman Balkans) and
klephts (bandits in Ottoman Greece). Each district committee of the
Organisation set up its own *cheta* (combat unit). It was hoped that low

morale and discipline would be improved by the carrying out of various actions against rival organisations, against state security forces and even against prominent local persons. Guerilla warfare was also seen as a very effective means of propagating the ideas and goals of the Internal Macedonian Revolutionary Organisation among larger sections of the rural population.[28]

However developments took a different turn in the spring of 1903. A small group of anarchists, known as the *gemidzhii* (lit. sailors), perpetrated a series of bombing attacks in Salonika. A French passenger liner was sunk, and the *Banque Ottomane Imperiale* (Imperial Ottoman Bank) – an Anglo–French institution – was blown up. The aim of these spectacular attacks was to induce the European powers to intervene directly in Macedonia. Such an intervention did not materialise however.[29] The importance of the Salonika bombings in the history of the Macedonian liberation movement must rather be seen in the fact that the Internal Macedonian Revolutionary Organisation was forced to act prematurely. It advanced the date for a general uprising to St Elias Day (*Ilinden*) on 2 August 1903, although the preparations were still incomplete.

The *Ilinden* uprising marks a climax and a turning point in the history of the Macedonian liberation movement. In their stronghold, the mountainous *vilayet* of Monastir, the insurgents gained impressive but ephemeral victories. They succeeded, for instance, in entering the small mountain town of Krushevo and in holding it for about a week.[30] The Ottoman army was taken by surprise and could not respond immediately. But the insurgents did not achieve the one essential goal: the unity of the popular masses against Ottoman rule. Not only Muslim Turks and Albanians resisted the insurgents, but also Greek Orthodox 'patriarchists' in southwestern Macedonia openly supported Ottoman troops against them. Of even greater importance, the expected intervention by the great powers – or at least by the principality of Bulgaria – failed to take place. The insurgents were already in a precarious situation by the second half of August 1903. At the end of August the *Ilinden* uprising had been virtually suppressed. Many Slavic villages were destroyed in the process and hundreds of insurgents sought refuge in Bulgaria.[31]

The period between 1904 and 1908 was difficult for the Macedonian liberation movement. The Internal Macedonian Revolutionary Organisation was clearly on the defensive with respect to the 'armed propaganda' of the rival Greek and Serbian organisations. Moreover, within the movement itself conflicts broke out between the right and left wings over matters of strategy and tactics.

The Young Turk Revolution of 1908

The Young Turk revolution of 1908 is inextricably linked to the further development of the Macedonian question. It was the work of young officers and intellectuals who had fought many years against the insurrectionary bands in Macedonia. They hoped that by reinstating the 1876 constitution they could check the dissolution of the empire. The Ottoman Society of Union and Progress, the secret organisation of the Young Turks, was radically opposed to great power interference in the internal affairs of the Ottoman state and believed that with the establishment of a parliamentary regime national differences could be reconciled peacefully.[32] Indeed the initial success of the Young Turks was remarkable. In Macedonia Muslims, Christians and Jews fraternised with each other. The guerillas came down from the mountains and walked arm-in-arm with Young Turk officers in the streets. An amnesty was granted to all political prisoners. Political activity of all kinds now was allowed and there was complete freedom of the press.[33]

The various factions of the Internal Macedonian Revolutionary Organisation had to adapt to the new situation. While the leftist Seres group under the leadership of Jane Sandanski organised themselves into the Federative People's Party and were ready to cooperate to a certain extent with the Young Turks, the rightists remained aloof. Their Union of Bulgarian Constitutional Clubs was not satisfied with the reinstatement of the 1876 Ottoman constitution. As earlier, they demanded European intervention on behalf of the Christian population of Macedonia.[34]

Events between 1908 and 1912 promoted the process of a political maturation of the peoples of European Turkey. Political participation on the basis of equal rights motivated Christian volunteers from Macedonia to fight side by side with the Young Turks to suppress the counterrevolution in Istanbul in April 1909.[35] Parliamentary elections from 1908 to 1912 were occasions to mobilise public opinion.[36] Furthermore the growing workers' movement in the Balkans, torn between nationalism and internationalism, had the opportunity of gathering experience by organising strikes and mass demonstrations in Macedonia.[37] To be sure international developments – the Bosnian crisis of 1908–9, the Italian invasion of Libya in 1911–2 and the Balkan Wars of 1912–3 – did not leave much time for the parliamentary regime of the Young Turk period to solve the Macedonian question.

The Balkan Wars of 1912–3 and the Partition of Macedonia

The expansionist tendencies of the Balkan national states came to a head in the wars of 1912–3, and Macedonia played a prominent role in the annexation plans of the allies. The principle of partition of Macedonia served as the basis of the alliance against the Ottoman empire.[38] The Internal Macedonian Revolutionary Organisation activists welcomed the outbreak of the war of 1912 as an opportunity to liberate Macedonia. Special units recruited from Macedonians and Thracians living in Bulgaria contributed to Bulgarian successes in the Rhodopes and in western Thrace.[39] However, on the issue of delimiting their respective zones of interest in Macedonia, the allies soon encountered problems. Whereas the Bulgarian military potential was chiefly spent in a spectacular drive through eastern Thrace in the direction of Istanbul, the Serbs and the Greeks could advance rapidly into Macedonia, the weak Ottoman defence system there having broken down quite early in the war. When the armistice was signed in December, 1912, the Serbian army controlled the north to northwestern part of Macedonia while the southern section, including Salonika, was under Greek occupation; the Bulgarian army managed to hold on to only a small district in the northeast.

This 'unjust' partition of Macedonian territory led to the second Balkan war in the summer of 1913. A Bulgarian threat to Serbia provoked the formation of a new Balkan alliance. Attacked from all sides (Serbia, Greece, Romania and the Ottoman empire) Bulgarian resistance broke down quickly. The 1913 Treaty of Bucharest sealed the partition of Macedonia.

Formation of the National Elite

The term elite is used here to denote the activists at the forefront of the Macedonian Slav national movement. Its formation took place under the powerful influence of social, economic and political forces in the country; and information about the social and geographic origins of the leaders, the education they received, the professions they pursued, the organisational structures they created and the channels of communication they utilised, all contribute to a better understanding of the forms as well as the outcome of the political struggle. Approximately 80 per cent of the leaders of the national movement were born in a Macedonian district, the rest originated either from Danubian Bulgaria or more frequently from Eastern Rumelia. More than 40 per cent came from southwestern Macedonia, a mountainous region of the country that became the centre of the 1903 *Ilinden* uprising. In the prefectures of Monastir and Skopje about two thirds of the activists had an urban background. By contrast in the eastern prefecture of Seres this proportion was almost inverted: 80 per cent of the leaders there came from villages.[40]

Given the structure and development of Macedonian Slav society as discussed in the section on social conditions, it is understandable that the activists of the national movement were recruited chiefly from 'middle class' elements from rural or small town *milieus*. The literacy rate of the activists' fathers was about 65 per cent, and merchants and priests made up the largest professional group among them.[41] A nobility did not exist and the few Christian landlords that had emerged during the nineteenth century tended in general to support the cause of hellenism.

The socio-political importance of *petit bourgeois* commercial groups in the Macedonian national movement was due mainly to the specific communalism developed in the framework of the *millet* system. Despite the dominating influence of neighbouring Balkan states the Macedonian communities retained considerable autonomy, not least because they had to finance their own schools and churches. It was incumbent upon the communal leaders in towns and villages to take the initiative in founding clubs and societies for cultural or religious purposes. This enabled them to exercise decisive influence in school and church matters such as the hiring of teachers and priests.[42]

Supported locally and supervised by the respective *millet* hierarchies, the national school systems in Macedonia showed a remarkable development during the last quarter of the nineteenth century. Table 7.3 gives an indication of their respective strengths.

Table 7.3: National schools in Macedonia in 1901

Vilayet	Bulg.	Serb.	Greek	Vlach	Ottom.	Uniate	Total
Salonika	319	21	525	12	462	10	1 349
Bitola*	227	35	305	33	391		991
Skopje**	136	65	2	2	253		458
Total	682	121	832	47	1 106	10	2 798

  * Excluding the 'Albanian' districts of Elbasan, Korçë, Kolonia, Starovo, Mat.
  ** Only the prefecture of Skopje is considered.

Source: Based on data in a report of the Austro–Hungarian consul in Skopje dated 16 September 1901, No. 212, and a table compiled by the Chief of the General Staff, Res. Nr. 1374, Vienna, 14 June 1903, both in *Haus–, Hof– und Staatsarchiv*, Politisches Archiv, Türkei, Liasse XXV, Karton 272 and 273.

Of special interest in this context are the exarchist schools. Table 7.4 reflects their rapid growth during the last decade of the nineteenth century.

The combined educational efforts of the various national movements helped raise the literacy rate in Macedonia considerably. In fact a contemporary diplomatic report claimed that illiteracy among

Table 7.4: Development of the Macedonian schools under the jurisdiction of the Bulgarian exarchate from 1893 to 1900

Vilayet	Salonika		Bitola		Skopje	
Year	1893	1900	1893	1900	1893	1900
Schools	256	318	204	273	86	190
Teachers	361	531	283	421	142	314
Pupils	11 718	14 838	10 603	15 161	4 476	9 455

Source: Bozhinov (1982), pp. 79, 133.

the Christians of Macedonia was practically unknown.[43] Recent research assumes a literacy rate of 80 to 90 per cent.[44]

However apart from some secondary schools and teachers' training establishments no universities or similar institutions of higher education existed in Macedonia. Moveover studying abroad was a luxury which only a few students from well-to-do families could afford. Table 7.5 clearly shows that Bulgaria ranked first among the destinations chosen for further study. Since Bulgaria attracted most of the Macedonian artisans and other seasonal labour, it is not surprising that almost half of the activists had resided there for some time, some even permanently.[45]

Table 7.5: Location of educational institutions attended by Internal Macedonian Revolutionary Organisation activists (in %)

Istanbul	Maced.	Bulg.	Serbia	Russia	Austria	Switz.	Other
8	12	42	4	16	2	8	8

Source: Data modified from de Jong (1982), p. 387.

Educational expansion brought the intelligentsia – non-clerical groups such as teachers, physicians and lawyers – to the forefront of the national movement. During the last quarter of the nineteenth and at the beginning of the twentieth century these professionals were reluctant to identify themselves with the ottomanism of the multi-national empire. Avenues of social advancement were limited. It was difficult for educated Christians to enter the Ottoman civil service. Whereas physicians and lawyers enjoyed a relatively high social status, teaching in village schools was the only prospective occupation for the majority of students. These conditions explain why teachers played such an important role in the Macedonian liberation movement. In the period of the 1903 *Ilinden* uprising about 60 per cent of the Internal Macedonian Revolutionary Organisation activists were teachers.[46] After the 1908 Young Turk revolution, when political parties were permitted, teachers were, as illustrated by Table 7.6, still the most conspicuous group in the Macedonian national movement.

Table 7.6: Professional origin of the delegates to the congresses of the Bulgarian Constitutional Clubs in Salonika in 1908 and 1909

Year	Priest	Teacher	Student	Free Prof.	Merchant	Farmer	Civil Serv.	Shopkeeper	Craftsman
1908	3	35	3	10	23	2	2	1	1
1909	1	43	1	17	20	13	1	3	1

Source: *Săyuz na Bălgarskite Konstitutsionni Klubove, Dnevnitsi na uchreditelniya i vtoriya kongresi* [Union of the Bulgarian Constitutional Clubs, Journals of the Constitutive and Second Congresses], Salonika 1910.

Whereas the teachers were prominent within the Internal Macedonian Revolutionary Organisation, in the case of the Supreme Macedonian Committee of Sofia persons with a military background were the most influential group. More than a third of the Supremist activists were members of the Bulgarian officers' corps.[47] Especially in periods when guerilla warfare was intensified with a view to instigating a mass uprising – this was the case in 1895, 1902 and 1903 – officers had the say even in the interior districts of Macedonia, no matter how much this might have been resented by the local leadership. Similarly the significance of the role played by priests in the Macedonian national movement hardly can be overrated, even though available data seems to suggest the contrary. A contemporary observer wrote: 'It is notorious, for example, that most if not all of the Bulgarian bishops and their lay secretaries are involved more or less directly, and more or less voluntarily, in the rebellious activities of the Macedonian Committee.'[48] On the local level it was generally expected that a prospective member of the revolutionary organisation would first join the Bulgarian exarchate.[49] Therefore as soon as the Internal Macedonian Revolutionary Organisation cast off the character of a clandestine subversive committee to become an organisation with mass public support, the exarchist priests in the countryside emerged as leaders, politically as important as the village teachers.

Organisational Structure, Channels of Communication and the National Elite

The tightness of the Internal Macedonian Revolutionary Organisation's internal structure resulted from the conspiratorial nature of its political programme. Although all major issues were discussed at the general congresses held in 1896, 1903 and 1905, the extant statutes and regulations reflect a rigidly centralised and hierarchic organisation. It was divided into committees on the regional, district and village levels, and the central committee in Salonika was the supreme authority. The committee had the right to delegate responsibilities on the regional and district levels to persons of its own choice. Even the heads of cells on the lowest level often were nominated from above.[50]

As a conspiratorial movement in Ottoman territory, the Organisation needed good relations with similar organisations abroad. In this respect Bulgaria, where so many people of Macedonian origin lived, played a decisive role. By the 1880s Macedonian Charitable Clubs were being founded in larger Bulgarian cities which tried to help the refugees and immigrants from the south and, at the same time, to draw the attention of world public opinion to the fate of the Macedonian Bulgarians. In 1894 a *bratski sŭyuz* (brotherhood) was founded in Sofia from which in the following year the Supreme Macedonian Committee emerged. Not only Macedonians but also officers of the Bulgarian army and high ranking Bulgarian politicians were members of this organisation which was responsible for coordinating the activities of the liberation movement inside and outside Macedonia.[51]

At first the Internal Macedonian Revolutionary Organisation was interested in close cooperation with the Supreme Macedonian Committee because Bulgaria was the only source for money and weapons. Through its external representation in Sofia, the former remained in regular contact with the leadership of the latter and with the Bulgarian government. Notwithstanding such a close relationship, conflicts were inevitable. The Supreme Macedonian Committee saw *de facto* in the Internal Macedonian Revolutionary Organisation an agency obliged to serve the interests of Bulgaria. Social democrats, like Dimitŭr Blagoev, Nikola Harlakov or Grigor Vasilev who had been active for the committee, were in particular not prepared to accept this. They resigned in protest in the 1890s.[52] Blagoev and with him most leftist intellectuals henceforth took the view that the autonomous Macedonia the Bulgarian bourgeoisie hoped to attain would be a bone of contention among Balkan nationalists. Since emancipation could not be expected from Russian or Austrian intervention either, it had to be achieved through the united struggle of the entire population.[53] Macedonians with leftist inclinations such as Gotse Delchev and Gyorche Petrov carried this strain of thought into the Internal Macedonian Revolutionary Organisation. In fact that organisation's 1902 statute was the work of these two men. Although the central committee in Salonika was quite submissive to the Supremists in Sofia, leftist circles in their stronghold of Seres remained demonstratively independent. Armed clashes between combat units of the two organisations revealed the extent to which 'independence' was translated into reality.[54]

The relationship of the Internal Macedonian Revolutionary Organisation to Macedonian student groups abroad developed on a different level. As early as 1891 some students in Bulgaria, later to become leaders of the Organisation, had helped found the Young Macedonian Literary Society which published its own periodical, *Loza*. Creation of a Macedonian literary language was the chief concern of the group. However such a development implied in the long run the emergence of a separate Macedonian nationality, and in Bulgaria all activities in that direction were bound to be interpreted as 'Macedonian separatism'. In 1892 the *Loza* movement was banned.[55]

The creation of a Macedonian literary language would have been welcomed in Serbia. The government in Belgrade took the view that only educated people in Macedonia spoke Bulgarian, whereas the vast majority of the population had their various dialects which had as much or as little in common with Serbian as with Bulgarian. It is therefore understandable that the ideas of *Loza* fell on fertile ground in Serbia. In 1894 a new periodical, *Vardar*, which demanded linguistic autonomy for Macedonia, began to appear in Belgrade.[56]

Folklore and a literary language were important aspects of the national question also for Macedonian students in Russia. Krste Misirkov and Dimitrija Chupovski in particular, who already had been active in this field in Sofia and Belgrade, were the propounders of a concept of national autonomy. They held the view that revolutionary methods in Macedonia served the nationalist interests of the neighbouring states. They advocated the idea of an autonomous Macedonia within the framework of the Ottoman empire to be achieved exclusively by evolutionary means. In addition to the development of a Macedonian literary language it was considered essential that the Ottoman government allow the foundation of an autocephalous Macedonian church. Only in this way could the Slavs of Macedonia hope to obtain recognition as a separate *millet* and Macedonian be established as an official language along with Turkish in an autonomous province. This concept was propagated in various memoranda of the Macedonian Scientific–Literary Society in St Petersburg and in the periodical *Vardar* published by Misirkov in Odessa.[57]

The Macedonian movement also had contacts with anarchism by

way of a group of Bulgarian and Macedonian students in Switzerland. These students moved largely in Russian *émigré* circles and came under the influence of Bakunin's ideas. In 1898 they founded the Macedonian Secret Revolutionary Committee and soon began to publish a periodical with the title *Otmŭshtenie* (Revenge). The anarchists demanded full political autonomy for Macedonia but rejected the idea of a peasant uprising. All peoples of Macedonia should join together in the struggle for freedom. In other words the passive Muslim population should be integrated into the liberation movement against the regime of the sultan. They declared war on Bulgarian, Greek and Serbian nationalism.[58]

The activities of the Macedonian socialists, who had found support in some regions affected by traditional labour migration, also deserve mention. As a social democratic group which sought to overcome national differences rather than to facilitate the success of one nationality, they devoted their attention at first to enlightening the population by founding local educational clubs and libraries. After the failure of the 1903 *Ilinden* uprising, however, at a time when the political course of the Internal Macedonian Revolutionary Organisation was being criticised strongly, Macedonian socialism experienced an upswing. Its moderate ideas on the solution of the national question now were adopted by the opponents of a general uprising inspired by Bulgarian nationalism. With the formation of the so-called Seres group, a leftist faction came into being within the Internal Macedonian Revolutionary Organisation which did not envisage liberation in union with Bulgaria nor in obtaining autonomy at Europe's hands but rather in a general democratisation process within the Ottoman empire.[59]

The Ottoman Government and the National Elite

Nationalist ideas in the multi-national empire of the Ottomans were always taboo. The emergence of national elites among the subject peoples in Macedonia, a strategically very sensitive region in the Balkans, was seen therefore as a serious challenge to Ottoman rule. During the early *Tanzimat* the government hoped to win the loyalty of the educated Christians by employing them in the expanding central bureaucracy. In the 1860s and 1870s new opportunities emerged, when the reform of the provincial administration was put on the agenda. The military defeat of 1877–8 however ushered in the oppressive regime of Sultan Abdulhamid II, which lasted until 1908. In Macedonia village teachers especially were under close scrutiny and all forms of revolutionary activity were regarded either as terrorism or outright banditry.

Yet the Ottoman state of the period could not be compared to a modern national state of the twentieth century. The means at its disposal were inadequate to implement its policies. For example, it was quite easy for national activists in Macedonia to evade police control or prison. Also the regime itself, often under the pressure of the great powers or European public opinion, frequently granted a general amnesty which served at the same time to palliate the intercommunal tension in the countryside. Furthermore the various reform programmes for Macedonia imposed by the great powers between 1903 and 1907 affected the relations of the Ottoman state with the activists of the national movement in a significant way. For example, Ottoman *gendarmerie* detachments operated against Christian guerillas under the supervision or even direct command of British, French, Italian or Russian officers. This was not only an effective check upon possible transgression on the part of the troops, but also provided the population the opportunity of airing their complaints more freely.[60]

After the 1908 Young Turk revolution the conditions for political activity in Macedonia improved in many respects. Impressed by the need for harmony between the various peoples of the empire, the Young Turks through their 'Ottoman Society for Union and Progress' invited all national organisations to participate in the political life of the country. The macedonianist faction of the Internal Macedonian Revolutionary Organisation responded favourably. Even the pro-Bulgarian wing of the Organisation showed some readiness to cooperate with the Young Turks. Distinguished activists like Jane Sandanski, the chief of the Seres region, the socialist Dimitar Vlahov, or the pro-Bulgarian Pancho Dorev represented Macedonia in the Ottoman parliament.

Nevertheless the Young Turk regime was not a 'democracy'. From the start it was obvious that the parliamentary elections would deliver results geared to minimise the strength of national or separatist tendencies. Moreover, out of fear of alienating Muslim landed interests, the Young Turks showed little inclination to tackle some pressing issues of the peasantry such as the question of uncultivated state lands, the *chiftliks* and agrarian credits.[61] The hard line the new regime took towards the working class movement that flourished after 1908 was especially disappointing for the left wing sympathisers of the Young Turks: a law passed in 1909 declared strikes practically illegal.[62]

Finally, the modernism of the Young Turks, inasmuch as it enhanced the authority of the central government, was a potential threat to vested political interests in every part of the empire. The attempt to 'disarm' the villagers, for example, though in normal circumstances a legitimate police measure, served only to estrange the Internal Macedonian Revolutionary Organisation partisans in Macedonia. Directors of exarchist schools were shocked when inspectors from the Ministry of Education wanted to supervise instruction. Teachers from Bulgaria – a country under the suzerainty of the sultan until 1908 – were offended at having to obtain, since they were now classified as foreigners, a special work permit.

Under these conditions even those groups which enthusiastically had welcomed the 1908 Young Turk revolution – and which had then engaged in a close political collaboration with the new regime – felt isolated when war broke out in the Balkans in 1912. Not only Macedonian peasant soldiers in the Ottoman army defected to the enemies of the empire, but also a well known national activist like Jane Sandanski, once an ardent supporter of the 1908 revolution, contributed to the defeat of the Ottomans with his celebrated guerillas.

State of Research

The Macedonian question began to occupy European diplomacy and public opinion after the 1878 Congress of Berlin. Apart from great power interests all three neighbouring Balkan countries – Bulgaria, Greece and Serbia – laid claim to Macedonian territory. Understandably therefore the literature on the subject has reached considerable dimensions.[63]

Contemporary western works generally belong to one of two categories: travel accounts and political journalism. They often contain useful information on the geography and ethnography of the country or about developments in political or religious spheres. Some publications even have the character of scholarly area studies.[64] Despite the ethnic or confessional biases of most authors such literature is valuable as source material and is utilised quite extensively.

Unfortunately, history writing in almost every Balkan country has been obliged to serve the needs of the respective national ideology. Historians have been expected to deliver the proof that Macedonia was populated, at least since the Middle Ages, even better since antiquity, by a people related to one's own nation. Greek authors had a relatively easy task in this contest. Two circumstances seemed to offer clear proof of the hellenic character of Macedonia: the term Macedonia itself which refers to the hellenistic empire of Alexander and the fact that the Macedonian Slavs were members of the Greek millet during Ottoman rule on account of their being Greek Orthodox Christians.[65] The Bulgarians on the other hand could emphasise the fact that in the ninth and tenth centuries Macedonia had belonged to the Bulgarian tsardom.[66] Finally, the Serbs could with some justification refer to the empire of Stephen Dushan (1331–55), the centre of which lay in modern Macedonia.[67]

The end of Ottoman rule during the Balkan wars of 1912–3 and the ensuing partition of Macedonia by Serbia, Bulgaria and Greece sharpened the rivalry among these countries. Political changes since 1945 have not brought about a reconciliation of rival historiographic positions.[68] The intention of many works published during the last decades, including those of a documentary nature, seems to be the justification of territorial acquisitions made or the support of claims calling for a future revision of the *status quo*. Even the old question of national minorities has not disappeared: for example, the Yugoslav Republic of Macedonia, which encompasses only part of the territory originally claimed, demands minority status for Macedonians in neighbouring states.[69]

In view of this situation international research gains special importance. However, access to primary sources is often difficult if not altogether impossible. Although the state archives of Austria, Great Britain, France, Germany, Italy and Russia accommodate rich stocks of documents related not only to the diplomatic history of the Macedonian question, but also to the history of Macedonian socio-economic structures and developments, the primary material preserved in the Balkan countries as well as in Turkey represents undoubtedly the main source for the researcher. However, for various reasons – incomplete cataloguing, linguistic and palaeographic difficulties, political or even professional considerations – the primary sources have not been evaluated adequately so far. More often than not the scholar has had to be content with a fleeting view of a selected set of documents kept at specialised institutes of national history in Skopje, Thessaloniki or Sofia.

For these reasons studies which have appeared to date either belong to the category of factualistic reconstruction of the diplomatic history of the Macedonian question or they dwell on criticising details in older works, perhaps emphasising more strongly the role of this or that party involved. Despite many deserving publications in the field, a theoretical clarification of the complex Macedonian national question remains a task for future research. This would require not only a broader basis of documentation, but also the treatment of the problem on a different conceptual level, namely in the context of comparative research on nationalism – an approach rarely attempted.

Notes

1   Goce Delchev for example is a national hero in both the Bulgarian and the Macedonian historiography, see Andonov-Polyanski (1972) and Panayotov (1978).
2   See Wilkinson, p. 1.
3   Cvijić, p. 248.
4   *Makedoniya kako prirodna*, pp. 283 ff.
5   Robeff; Vacalopoulos; Demetriades.
6   Adanır (1984–5), pp. 52 ff.
7   Milyovska, pp. 51–120; Zografski (1967), pp. 331–50, 413–45.
8   Dumont, pp. 76–88.
9   Boyanovski, p. 481. See also Adanır (1982), pp. 445–61.
10 Adanır (1979), p. 41.
11 On the Ottoman reform movement see Davison.
12 On the *millet* system see Braude and Lewis.
13 Petrosyan, pp. 13–24. General information in Devereux.
14 For a discussion of the characteristics of the Hamidian regime see Berkes, pp. 256–88.
15 Duguid, pp. 139–55; Samardžiev, pp. 57–79.
16 Poplazarov; Danova.
17 Jelavich, pp. 131–47; Hehn, pp. 153–71.
18 Peyfuss.
19 Bŭlgarski Patriarch Kiril (1955).
20 Hanioğlu.
21 On populist and nationalist influences see Toprak, pp. 69–81; Georgeon.
22 von Mach, pp. 13–15; Meininger, pp. 129–34, 180–90.
23 Bŭlgarski Patriarch Kiril (1969–70); Trayanovski.
24 See *Pŭrviyat centralen . . .*, p. 102. Tatarchev was the head of the Salonika committee of 1893–4.
25 Pandev (1970), p. 249.
26 *Ibid.*, p. 257.
27 Pandevski (1978); Pandev (1979b).
28 Pandev (1979a), pp. 72–94.
29 Adanır (1979), pp. 170–4; Troebst (1981).
30 See the proceedings of the symposia organised for the celebrations under the motto 'Ten Days of the Republic of Krushevo' in 1976, 1977 and 1978 which have been published in two volumes as *Prilozi za Ilinden*.
31 Panayotov (1983); Silyanov.
32 On Young Turk policies see Ahmad (1969).
33 Mokrov, pp. 228 ff; Pŭrvanov, pp. 67–79.
34 Pandevski (1965), pp. 204 ff.
35 Pandevski (1966), pp. 83–108.
36 Makedonski (1974), pp. 133–46; *idem* (1978), pp. 58–71.
37 Zografski (1950), pp. 207–45; Velikov, pp. 29–48.
38 Helmreich; Stoyanov.
39 Dŭrvingov, pp. 101–326.
40 de Jong, pp. 248–57.
41 *Ibid.*, pp. 268 f.
42 Dimevski (1970), pp. 35–54.
43 See the Annual Report for 1907 in Gooch and Temperley, p. 29.
44 de Jong, p. 257.
45 *Ibid.*, p. 271.
46 *Ibid.*, p. 388.

47 *Ibid.*, p. 388.
48 Brailsford, p. 18.
49 Matov, pp. 29–31.
50 Adanır (1979), pp. 111 f.
51 Bitoski, pp. 171–211.
52 Ivanoski, pp. 171–2.
53 See various articles of Blagoev, vol. 6, pp. 311–17, 592–94; vol. 7, pp. 71–6; vol. 8, pp. 563–83.
54 Katardzhiev, pp. 152–4.
55 Ristovski (1983), vol. 1, pp. 467–602.
56 de Jong, pp. 123 ff.
57 Misirkov; Ristovski (1966); *idem* (1978).
58 Adanır (1979), pp. 170 ff.
59 See Silyanov, vol. 2, pp. 369–73; Katardzhiev, pp. 300–19.
60 On *gendarmerie* reforms see Biagini, pp. 125–44.
61 See Ahmad (1983), pp. 275–88.
62 Ökçün.
63 For a recent annotated bibliography on Macedonia see Bernath and Nehring, pp. 301–424.
64 See, for example, Weigand; Schultze-Jena; Ancel.
65 Nicolaides; Colocotronis.
66 See the polemic on the origins of Tsar Samuil's state in Antoljak; Zaimov and Zaimova; Bozhilov, pp. 84–100.
67 Stanković; Slijepčević.
68 For an overview of the continuing polemic between Bulgarian and Yugoslav historians see Troebst (1983).
69 Popovski.

Select Bibliography

Adanır, F. (1979), *Die Makedonische Frage. Ihre Entstehung und Entwicklung bis 1908*, Wiesbaden.
Adanır, F. (1982), 'Zum Verhältnis von Agrarstruktur und nationaler Bewegung in Makedonien 1878–1908', in Melville, R. and Schröder, H.J. (eds), *Der Berliner Kongress von 1878*, Wiesbaden.
Adanır, F. (1984–5), 'The Macedonian Question: The Socio-Economic Reality and Problems of its Historiographic Interpretation', *International Journal of Turkish Studies* III/I.
Ahmad, F. (1969), *The Young Turks. The Committee of Union and Progress in Turkish Politics. 1908–1914*, Oxford.
Ahmad, F. (1983), 'The Agrarian Policy of the Young Turks 1908-1918', in Bacqué-Grammont, J.L. and Dumont, P. (eds), *Économie et sociétés dans l'Empire ottoman*, Paris.
Ancel, J. (1930), *La Macédoine. Son évolution contemporaine*, Paris.
Andonov-Polyanski, H. (ed.) (1972), *Gotse Delchev. Kon stogodishninata od radjanyeto na Gotse Delchev (1872–1972)* (Gotse Delchev. On the Occasion of His 100th Birthday, 1872–1972), vols 1–6, Skopje.
Anestopoulos, A.K. (1965–69), *O Makedonikos agon 1903–1908 kai e sumbole ton katoikon eis ten apeleutherosin tes Makedonias* (The Macedonian Struggle 1903–1908 and the Contribution of the Population to the Liberation of Macedonia), 2 vols, Athens.
Antoljak, S. (1969), *Samuilovata drzhava* (Samuil's State), Skopje.
Barker, E. (1950), *Macedonia. Its Place in Balkan Power Politics*, London.
Berkes, N. (1964), *The Development of Secularism in Turkey*, Montreal.

Bernath, M. and Nehring, K. (eds) (1988), *Historische Bücherkunde Südosteuropas*, vol. II, Part I. *Osmanisches Reich, Makedonien, Albanien*, Munich.

Biagini, A.F.M. (1981), 'La riorganizzazione della Gendarmeria turca in Macedonia', *Momenti di storia balcanica (1878–1914). Aspetti militari*, Rome.

Bitoski, K. (1977), *Makedoniya i Knezhevstvo Bugariya (1893–1903)* (Macedonia and the Principality of Bulgaria 1893–1903), Skopje.

Blagoev, D. (1957–60), *Sŭchineniya* (Works), vols 6, 7 and 8, Sofia.

Boyanovski, D. (1954), 'Chiflichkite odnosi vo Makedoniya okolu 1903 godina' (The Chiftlik Relations in Macedonia Around the Year 1903), *Godishnik na Pravno-ekonomskiot Fakultet vo Skopje* I.

Bozhilov, I.A. (1971), 'Bitolskiot nadpis na car Ivan Vladislav i niakoi vŭprosi ot srednovekovnata bŭlgarska istoriia' (The Bitola Epigraph of Tsar Ivan Vladislav and Some Questions Regarding Medieval Bulgarian History), *Istoricheski Pregled*, 27, 1.

Bozhinov, V. (1982), *Bŭlgarskata prosveta v Makedoniya i Odrinska Trakiya, 1878–1913* (Bulgarian Education in Macedonia and the Adrianopolitan Thrace, 1878–1913), Sofia.

Brailsford, H.N. (1906), *Macedonia. Its Races and Their Future*, London.

Braude, B. and Lewis, B. (eds) (1982), *Christians and Jews in the Ottoman Empire*, New York–London.

Bŭlgarski Patriarch Kiril (1955), *Sŭprotivata sreshtu Berlinskiya dogovor. Kresnenskoto vŭstanie* (The Resistance against the Berlin Treaty. The Kresna Uprising), Sofia.

Bŭlgarski Patriarch Kiril (1969–70), *Bŭlgarskata ekzarchiya v Odrinsko i Makedoniya* (1878–85), Parts 1–2, Sofia.

Colocotronis, V. (1919), *La Macédoine et l'Hellénisme*, Paris.

Cvijić, J. (1908), *Grundlinien der Geographie und Geologie von Mazedonien und Altserbien*, Gotha.

Dakin, D. (1966), *The Greek Struggle in Macedonia 1897–1913*, Thessaloniki.

Danova, N. (1980), *Natsionalniyat vŭpros v grŭchkite politicheski programi prez XIXvek* (The National Question in the Greek Political Programmes in the Nineteenth Century), Sofia.

Davison, R.H. (1973), *Reform in the Ottoman Empire 1856–1876*, 2nd edition, New York.

Demetriades, V. (1983), *Topografia tes Thessalonikes kata ten epoche tes Tourkokratias 1430–1912*, Thessaloniki.

Devereux, R. (1963), *The First Ottoman Constitutional Period*, Baltimore.

Dimevski, S. (1970), 'Sozdavanyeto, struktura i kompetentsiite na makedonskite tsrkovno-shkolski opshtini' (The Foundation, Structure and Jurisdiction of Macedonian Church and School Communities), *Glasnik na Institutot za Natsionalna Istoriya*, 14.

Dimevski, S. (1980), *Za razvoyot na makedonskata natsionalna misla do sozdavanyeto na TMORO* (On the Development of Macedonian National Thought until the Establishment of the Secret Macedono–Adrianopolitan Revolutionary Organisation), Skopje.

Duguid, S. (1973), 'The Politics of Unity: Hamidian Policy in Eastern Anatolia', *Middle Eastern Studies*, 9.

Dumont, P. (1975), 'Une organisation socialiste ottomane: la Fédération Ouvrière de Salonique (1908–1912)', *Études Balkaniques*, 1975, I.

Dŭrvingov, P. (1919), *Istoriya na Makedono–Odrinskata opŭlchenie* (History of the Macedono–Adrianopolitan Legion), vol. 1, Sofia.

Georgeon, F. (1980), *Aux origines du nationalisme turc: Yusuf Akçura (1876–1935)*, Paris.

Gooch, G.P. and Temperly (eds) (1928), *British Documents on the Origins of the War 1898–1914*, vol. 5: *The Near East, the Macedonian Problem and the Annexation of Bosnia 1903–9*, London.

Hanioğlu, M.S. (1986), *Osmanlı İttihad ve Terakki Cemiyeti ve Jön Türklük* (Ottoman Society of Union and Progress and the Young Turk Movement), vol. 1, 1889–1902.

Hehn, N. (1975), 'The Origins of Modern Pan-Serbism – The 1844 Nacertanije of Ilija Garasanin: An Analysis and Translation', *Eastern European Quarterly*, 9.

Helmreich, E.C. (1938), *The Diplomacy of the Balkan Wars, 1912-1913*, Cambridge, Massachussetts.

Ivanoski, O. (1970), *Balkanskite sotsialisti i makedonskoto prashanye*, Skopye.

Jelavich, Ch. (1968), 'Garashanins Nachertanije und das großserbische Programm', *Südost-Forschungen*, 27.

de Jong, J. (1982) *Der nationale Kern des makedonischen Problems. Ansätze und Grundlagen einer makedonischen Nationalbewegung (1890-1903). Ein Beitrag zur komparativen Nationalismusforschung*, Frankfurt.

Karpat, K.H. (1985), *Ottoman Population, 1830–1914. Demographic and Social Characteristics*, Madison, Wisc.

Katardzhiev, I. (1968), *Serskiot okrug od Kresnenskoto vostanie do Mladoturskata revolutsiya. Natsionalno-politischki borbi* (The District of Seres from the Kresna Uprising to the Young Turk Revolution. Struggles in National Politics), Skopje.

Kŭnchov, V. (1900), *Makedoniya. Etnografiya i Statistica*, Sofia.

Kŭnchov, V. (1970), *Izbrani proizvedeniya*, Sofia.

MacDermott, M. (1978), *Freedom or Death. The Life of Gotsé Delchev*, London.

Mach, R. von (1907), *The Bulgarian Exarchate: Its History and the Extent of Its Authority in Turkey*, London.

Makedoniya kako prirodna i ekonomska tselina (Macedonia as a Natural and Economic Unity), Skopje 1978.

Makedonski, S. (1974), 'La Révolution jeune-turc et les premières élections parlementaires de 1908 en Macédoine et en Thrace orientale', *Études balkaniques*, 10, 4.

Makedonski, S. (1978) 'La régime jeune-turc et les deuxième élections parlementaires de 1912 en Macédoine et Thrace orientale', *Études balkaniques*, 14, 2.

Matov, H. (1926), *Za upravlenieto na Vŭtreshna revolyutsionna organizatsiya* (On the Administration of the Internal Revolutionary Organisation), Sofia.

Meininger, T.A. (1970), *Ignatiev and the Establishment of the Bulgarian Exarchate 1864–1872*, Madison.

Milyovska, D. (1963), 'Ekonomski osnovi drushtvene strukture makedonskih gradova u drugoy polovini XIX veka' (Economic Bases of the Social Structure of Macedonian Cities in the Second Half of the Nineteenth Century), *Godishen Zbornik na Filozofskiot Fakultet na Universitetot Skopje*, 15.

Misirkov, K.P. (1903), *Za makedontskite raboti*.

Mitrev, D. (ed.) (1976), *Yane Sandanski i makedonskoto natsionalno osloboditelno dvizhenye. Materiyali* (Yane Sandanski and the Macedonian National Liberation Movement. Materials), Skopje.

Mokrov, B. (1980), *Razvoyot na Makedonskiot pechat i novinarstvo* (The Development of the Macedonian Press and Journalism), Skopje.

Nicolaides, Cl. (1899), *Macedonien. Die geschichtliche Entwicklung der macedonischen Frage im Altertum, im Mittelalter und in der Neuzeit*, Berlin.

Ökçün, A.G. (1982), *Ta'til-i eşgal kanunu, 1909. Belgeler – Yorumlar* (Law Concerning Stoppage of Work, 1909. Documents – Commentaries), Ankara.

Panayotov, L. (ed.) (1978), *Gotse Delchev. Spomeni, Dokumenti, Materiali* (Gotse Delchev. Memoires, Documents, Materials), Sofia.

Panayotov, L. (1983), *Ilindensko–Preobrazhensko vŭstanie 1903, Chronologiya*, Sofia.

Pandev, K. (1970), 'Ustavi i pravilnitsi na VMORO predi Ilindensko–Preobrazhenskoto vŭstanie' (Statutes and Regulations of IMRO before the Ilinden Uprising), *Izvestiya na Instituta za Isotoriya*, 21.

Pandev, K. (1979a), 'Chestnicheskiyat institut na VMRO' (The Guerilla Institute of IMRO), in *Problemi na politicheskata istoriya na Bŭlgariya 1878–1944*, Sofia.

Pandev, K. (1979b), *Natsionalnoosvoboditelnoto dvizhenie v Makedoniya i Odrinsko 1878–1903* (The National Liberation Movement in Macedonia and the Province of Adrianople 1878–1903), Sofia.

Pandev, K. and Noneva, Z. (eds) (1981), *Borbite v Makedonia i Odrinsko 1878–1912. Spomeni* (The Struggles in Macedonia and the Region of Adrianople 1878–1912. Memoires), Sofia.

Pandevski, M. (1965), *Politichkite partii i organizatsii vo Makedoniya (1908–1912)* (The Political Parties and Organisations in Macedonia 1908–1912), Skopje.

Pandevski, M. (1966), 'Kontrarevoluciyata vo Tsarigrad vo 1909 i Makedoniya' (The Counterrevolution in Istanbul in 1909 and Macedonia), *Glasnik na Institutot za Natsionalna Istoriya* 10, 2–3.

Pandevski, M. (1974) *Natsionalnoto prashanye vo makedonskoto osloboditelno dvizhenye (1893–1903)* (The National Question in the Macedonian Liberation Movement 1893–1903), Skopje.

Pandevski, M. (1978), *Ilindenskoto vostanie vo Makedoniya 1903*, Skopje.

Perry, D.M. (1988), *The Politics of Terror. The Macedonian Liberation Movements 1893–1903*, Durham, NC and London.

Petrosyan, E.I. (1903), 'On the Motive Forces of the Reformist and Constitutionalist Movement in the Ottoman Empire', in Bacqué-Grammont, J.L. and Dumont, P. (eds), *Économie et sociétés dans l'Empire ottoman*, Paris.

Peyfuss, M.D. (1974), *Die Aromunische Frage*, Vienna.

Poplazarov, R. (1973), *Grchkata politika sprema Makedoniya vo vtorata polovina na XIX u pochetokot na XX vek* (The Macedonian Policy of Greece in the Second Half of the Nineteenth and the Beginning of the Twentieth Century), Skopje.

Popovski, T. (1981), *Makedonskoto natsionalno maltsinstvo vo Bugariya, Grtsiya i Albaniya* (The Macedonian National Minority in Bulgaria, Greece and Albania), Skopje.

Prilozi za Ilinden, Krushevo (1978–79), 2 vols.

Pŭrvanov, G.S. (1984), 'Bŭlgarskiyat periodichen pechat v Makedoniya i Odrinsko (1908–1912 g)' (Bulgarian Periodical Press in Macedonia and the Province of Adrianople, 1908–1912), *Istoricheski Pregled*, 40, 3.

Pŭrviyat centralen komitet na VMRO. Someni na Dr. Hristo Tatarchev (The First Central Committee of IMRO. Memoirs of Dr. Hristo Tatarchev) (1928), Sofia.

Ristovski, B. (1966), *Krste Misirkov (1874–1926). Prilog kon prouchuvanyeto na makedonskata natsionalna misla* (Krste Misirkov (1874–1926). A Contribution to the Study of Macedonian National Thought), Skopje.

Ristovski, B. (1978), *Dimitriya Chupovski (1878–1940) i Makedonskoto nauchno–literaturno drugarstvo vo Petrograd. Prilozi kon prouchvanyeto na makedonsko–ruskite vrski i razvitokot na makedonskata natsionalna misla* (Dimitriya Chupovski (1878–1940) and the Macedonian Scientific–Literary Society in Petrograd. Contributions to the Study of Macedonian–Russian Relations and the Development of Macedonian National Thought), 2 vols, Skopje.

Ristovski, B. (1983), *Makedonskiot narod i makedonskata natsiya* (The Macedonian People and the Macedonian Nation), 2 vols, Skopje.

Robeff, T.A. (1926), *Die Verkehr- und Handelsbedeutung von Saloniki*, Lucka.

Samardžiev, B. (1972), 'Traits dominants de la politique d'Abdulhamid II relative au problème des nationalités (1876-1885)', *Études Balkaniques*, 1972, 4.

Schultze-Jena, L. (1927), *Makedonien. Landschafts- und Kulturbilder*, Jena.

Silyanov, H. (1933–43), *Osvoboditelnite borbi na Makedoniya* (The Liberation Struggles of Macedonia), 2 vols, Sofia.

Slijepčević, Dj. (1958), *The Macedonian Question. The Struggle for Southern Serbia*, Chicago.

Stanković, T. (1910), *Putne beleshke po Staroy Srbiyi* (Notes on Travels in Old Serbia). Belgrade.

Stoyanov, P. (1979), *Makedoniya vo politikata na golemite sili vo vremeto na Balkanskite voyni 1912–13*, Skopje.

Todorov, N. *et al.* (eds) (1978), *Osvoboditelnata borba na bŭlgarite v Makedoniya i Odrinsko 1902–1904. Diplomaticheski dokumenti* (The War of Liberation of the Bulgarians in Macedonia and Thrace 1902–1904. Diplomatic Documents), Sofia.

Toprak, Z. (1984), 'Osmanlı narodnikleri: "Halka doğru gidenler"' (Ottoman narodniks: those who went 'towards the people'), *Toplum ve Bilim*, 24.

Trayanovski, A. (1982), *Bugarskata egzarhiya i makedonskoto natsionalno-osloboditelno dvizhenye (1893–1908)* (The Bulgarian Exarchate and the Macedonian National Liberation Movement 1893–1908), Skopje.

Troebst, S. (1981), 'Anarchisten aus Bulgarien in der makedonischen national-revolutionären Bewegung (1896–1912)', *1300 Jahre Bulgarien*, ed. by Gesemann, W., vol. II/1, Neuried.

Troebst, S. (1983), *Die bulgarisch–jugoslawische Kontroverse um Makedonien 1767–1982*, Munich.

Vacalopoulos, A.P. (1963), *A History of Thessaloniki*, Thessaloniki.

Velikov, S. (1964), 'Sur le mouvement ouvrier et socialiste en Turquie après la révolution Jeune Turque de 1908', *Études Balkaniques*, 1.

Weigand, G. (1894–5), *Die Aromunen* 2 vols, Leipzig.

Wilkinson, H.R. (1951), *Maps and Politics. A Review of the Ethnographic Cartography of Macedonia*, Liverpool.

Zaimova, Y. and Zaimova, V. (1970), *Bitolski nadpis na Ivan Vladislav, samodŭrzhets bŭlgarski* (The Bitola Epigraph of Ivan Vladislav, a Bulgarian Autocrat), Sofia.

Zografski, D. (1950), *Za rabotnichkoto dvizhenye vo Makedoniya do Balkanskata voyna*, Skopje.

Zografski, D. (1967), *Razvitokot na kapitalisticheskite elementi vo Makedoniya za vreme na turskoto vladeenye* (The Development of Capitalistic Elements in Macedonia during the Ottoman Rule), Skopje.

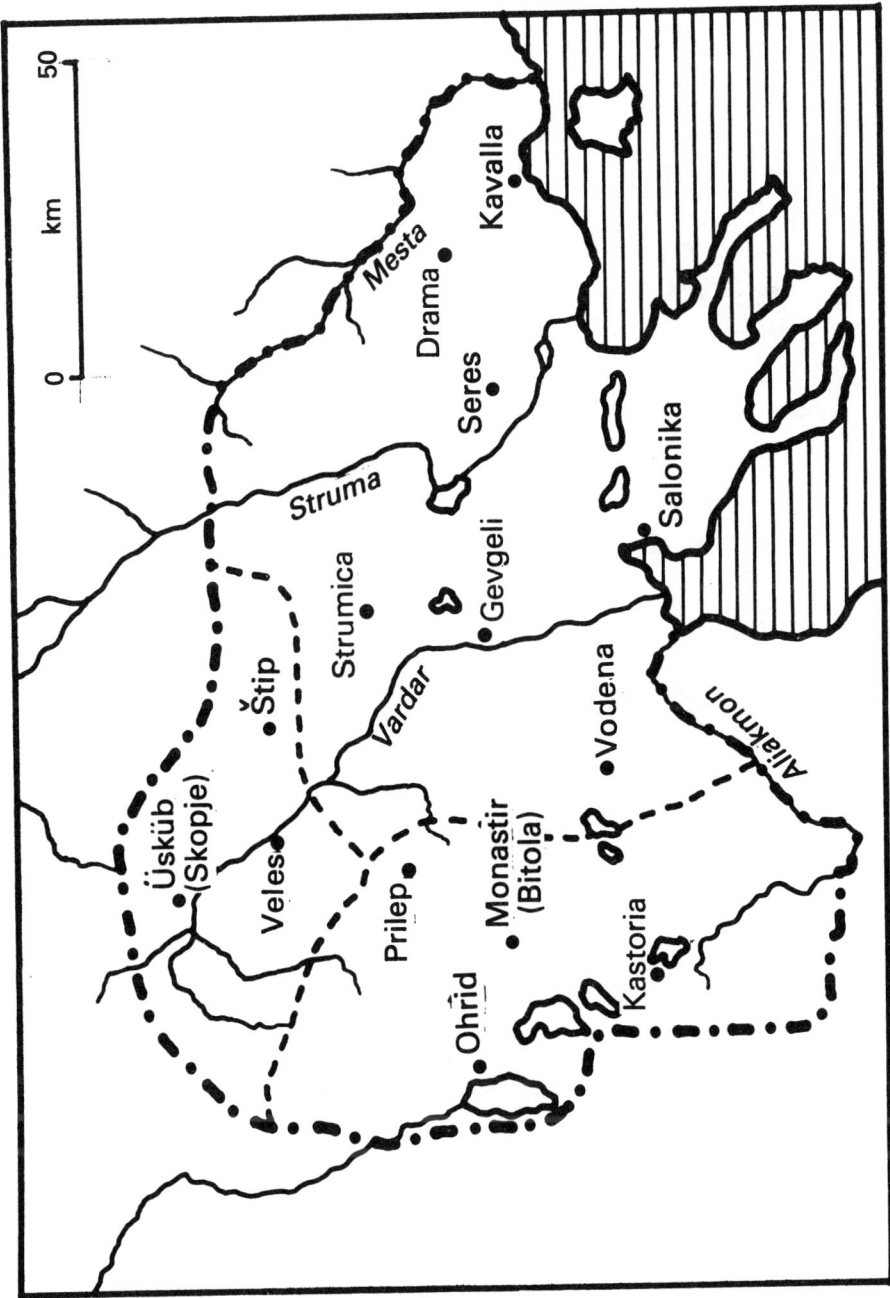

Map 7.1 Macedonia in the Ottoman empire (1878–1912)
Source: The Times Atlas of the World, Mid-Century Edition, vol. IV, plate 83.

8 The Germans in the Duchy of Schleswig before 1864: the German Minority in North Schleswig, 1920–33

ERICH HOFFMANN

The German Schleswigians in *Gesamtstaat* Denmark

The Duchy of Schleswig in Gesamtstaat *Denmark*

After the loss of Norway in 1814 *Gesamtstaat* Denmark[1] consisted of the Danish kingdom, the duchies of Schleswig and Holstein, which had close constitutional and administrative ties to each other, the duchy of Lauenburg from 1814, Iceland, the Faeroe Islands and Greenland as well as a few colonies in the West Indies, peninsular India and West Africa. Around 1840 (the following figures derive from the 1830s and the 1840s) the Danish kingdom covered 38 340 sq km and had a population of 12,8 million and Schleswig had an area of 9100 sq km and a population of 348 526. For Holstein the respective figures are 8500 sq km and 455 000 in population and for Lauenburg 1182 sq km and 45 342 people. The largest city was the capital Copenhagen with 115 000 inhabitants followed by five towns in the duchies including Altona (26 000), Flensburg (12 438 – and including the suburbs approximately 15 000), and Kiel (11 622). Several North Schleswig towns are important for the study: Haderslev/Hadersleben with a population of 6156, Aabenraa/Apenrade with 4021, Tønder/Tondern with 2792, and Sønderborg/Sonderburg with 3261 inhabitants – these were small towns in the kingdom although Haderslev had an economic importance at that time.

As far as the languages in Schleswig are concerned[2] historical developments up to 1840 created the following conditions: from the end of the Middle Ages the area between Eider and Schlei was predominantly German speaking. The western coast of Schleswig south of Højer was populated by North Frisians who used German in

193

official, Church and school matters. The cities of Husum, Eckern-förde and Schleswig were culturally and linguistically German. In central Schleswig German had been the predominant influence for centuries, being the language of literature and of official, trade and cultural affairs. Danish dialects were used for colloquial speech, in central Schleswig it was *Angeljysk* and in north Schleswig *Sønderjysk*. After the Reformation German was introduced as the language for Church services while Danish served this purpose in the rural areas of north Schleswig. When general compulsory education was introduced in 1814 the language of instruction was that used in the Church. In Angeln the peasants encouraged their children to adopt High German for business purposes and Low German for colloquial speech; by using the language of the educated they emphasised their social advancement. Thus the peasant population of Angeln voluntarily decided to change languages even before the national decision was made. This in only a few decades permitted German to spread up to the Flensburg fjord as the language for colloquial speech. The switch in languages was not made so quickly on the sparsely populated middle area between Angeln and north Frisia. (Today the change in languages has reached approximately the German–Danish border.)

In Flensburg German had been used in official, Church and school matters since the late Middle Ages. Most of the new citizens who had migrated to the city came from the surrounding countryside and from the Reformation about 30 per cent of these came from German speaking areas annually – a percentage which rose even higher after the language change in Angeln. Since the German speaking immi-grants usually belonged to the upper and middle classes which shaped bourgeois life Flensburg was a city in which the German vernacular was already dominant by the early modern period. On the other hand, continuous migration from the countryside insured the survival of Danish. In rural north Schleswig High Danish was used in Church; the Danish dialect *Sønderjysk* was the vernacular tongue; while German was the official language. In the cities of north Schleswig there were fewer German speaking newcomers than in Flensburg, nevertheless the official language and that of Church and school was German. The upper and middle classes of the cities usually used *Sønderjysk* as the vernacular, as did the rest of the city population, but they were also familiar with High Danish and High German. In Tønder Low German was spoken also.

In Schleswig, as was the case generally in *Gesamtstaat* Denmark, agrarian production was predominant during the first half of the nineteenth century.[3] At the end of the eighteenth century there was considerable economic activity resulting from neutral trade during the various English–French wars. Participation of *Gesamtstaat*

Denmark as an ally of France during the Napoleonic wars led to economic decline and state bankruptcy by 1813. The crisis was only overcome by the mid 1820s when England's demand for agrarian products increased noticeably as a result of her rapid industrialisation. Trade and manufacturing in Denmark were still relatively unimportant around 1840. In the kingdom of Denmark this kind of activity was clearly concentrated in the capital Copenhagen and its vicinity. In the duchies industrialisation advanced more quickly in several small centres. Those towns in Holstein (Altona, Kiel, Neumünster, Rendsburg) which oriented themselves towards Hamburg, experienced the first steps in industrialisation, for example textile manufacturing and metal working. Even in Flensburg and some North Schleswig towns small metal working factories developed. There was in addition in Flensburg the traditional processing of colonial goods (sugar and rum) and of agrarian produce. More rapid industrialisation in the duchies was due in part to the more extensive transport network. The Schleswig–Holstein canal, which connected the Kiel fjord via the Eider to the west coast, was opened in the eighteenth century and was being used intensively. The construction of main roads (for example that from Kiel to Altona in 1832) and the new railway lines (the first line in the *Gesamtstaat* being that running through Altona, Neumünster to Kiel opened in 1844; and then in 1846 branches opened to Rendsburg/Glückstadt) connected the duchies (especially Holstein) more firmly to Hamburg wholesalers. In the kingdom of Denmark the only railway line in existence at that time ran between Copenhagen and Roskilde. By using these new facilities the busy Hansa towns of Hamburg (a population of 161 390 in 1853) and Lübeck (a population of 25 360 in 1845) began to influence their northern hinterland toward a greater orientation towards Jutland. This was also due to the fact that many early factories were financed by credits from Hamburg.

Another factor aiding the industrial expansion in the duchies was the tariff law of 1838 which began to standardise tariffs while abolishing privileges and internal customs throughout the *Gesamtstaat*, although for several types of goods the customs boundary at the Königsau between the kingdom and the duchies continued to exist. In general however the economic ties of the duchies to the north declined while those to the south increased. In this process Flensburg managed to maintain an intermediary position as an independent wholesale centre between Hamburg and Copenhagen. In the long run the economic ties of the duchies to the south were bound to play an important role when the population had to reach a political decision regarding their future in an age of national awakening.

Agrarian reforms in *Gesamtstaat* Denmark at the turn of the eighteenth century (such as the reallocation of arable land and emancipation of the peasantry) considerably strengthened the social status of the peasantry.[4] In the duchy of Schleswig in 1840 792 out of 1000 inhabitants still lived in rural areas. Larger estates were concentrated in south eastern Schleswig, on Alsen and the opposite coastal region where however, the deconcentration of peasants, cottagers and agricultural labourers of the large estates was underway. Most farms were of medium size. With regard to income, property and education (compulsory since 1814), the 'farm owners' (Hofbesitzer) and the 'owners of a hide of land' (Hüfner) were quite well off. Over the centuries these owners of medium sized farms had formed a class of rural notables who generally occupied the various honorary positions in the rural administration which had continued to exist during the period of monarchical absolutism. Close family relations had existed for centuries between this rural upper class and the urban upper and middle class (merchants, intellectuals and craftsmen).

Since the late Middle Ages *Gesamtstaat* Denmark[5] was thus gradually united by way of dynastic policy. Around 1840 a king ruled as the absolute monarch over all parts of the *Gesamtstaat*. The duchies had their own superior authority in Copenhagen for administrative and legal matters – *die Schleswig–Holsteinisch–Lauenburgische Kanzlei* (the Schleswig–Holstein–Lauenburg Chancery). An administrative reform of 1834 created the *Schleswig–Holsteinische Regierung* (Schleswig–Holstein government) for both duchies as an intermediary between the Chancery and the lower administrative units. Other state functions were assigned to central authorities dealing with all of Denmark. The *Rentekammer* (taxation system) had a special department for the duchies. Holstein and Lauenburg, formerly part of the German *Reich*, had been members of the *Deutscher Bund* (German Federation) since 1815 and the former Danish fief of Schleswig had been a 'sovereign' duchy since 1658.

The goal of the last two absolute kings – Frederick VI (1784/1808–39) and Christian VIII (1839–48) – was to defend absolutist government and to unite more firmly the parts of *Gesamtstaat* Denmark. Thus Frederick VI between 1831/4 approved of advisory 'provincial estates' (for Holstein, Schleswig, Jutland with Fünen and Sealand) in order to prevent a common assembly for the duchies. During an age of national determination the centre, as the enemy of the 'national awakening', tried to achieve a balance between German and Danish interests. In 1848 under Frederick VII (1848–63) Denmark became a constitutional monarchy. At the same time politicians from the duchies sought to join the emergent German empire. The new *Landesversammlung* (parliament) of Schleswig–Holstein adopted a liberal constitution. After the failure of the Schleswig-Holstein

uprising of 1848–51 the European great powers forced the continuation of *Gesamtstaat* Denmark (albeit in a changed form) so that
Danish national wishes were unfulfilled also. The special ties
between Schleswig and Holstein were dissolved but Frederick VII
had to promise to Prussia and Austria that he would not bind
Schleswig closer to the kingdom of Denmark constitutionally than
the other two duchies. While the kingdom retained a constitutional
form of government the duchies were again subject to absolute rule.
This allowed high officials of the Ministry for Schleswig who were
supporters of Danish nationalism to initiate a danishisation policy for
the northern and central parts of the duchy. Influential members of
the central bureaucracy persuaded the rather untalented king (ruling
nominally as an absolute monarch) to support this policy.

*The Formation of a National Elite within the Schleswig–Holstein Movement
in the Duchy of Schleswig*

Christoph Friedrich Dahlmann (1785–1860), Professor of History
from 1812 to 1829 at the University of Kiel and simultaneously
secretary of the Schleswig–Holstein Knights, stands at the forefront
of the German Schleswig–Holstein movement.[6] He fought for a
common liberal constitution for the duchies as well as for the
awakening of a German national consciousness. Dahlmann argued
that since Schleswig had close ties to Holstein it should also become a
member of the *Deutscher Bund* and a member of a future German
Reich. He refused to recognise the affinity of northern Schleswig to
Denmark just as Danish national activists declined to recognise the
predominance of sympathies for Schleswig–Holstein in southern
Schleswig. Dahlmann was supported in his efforts by a circle of
friends including professors in Kiel (for example, Welcker and Pfaff)
who sympathised strongly with the German national movement.
Nikolaus Falck (1784–1850) a legal historian who came from northern
Schleswig, favoured the *Gesamtstaat* until 1846 but then referred to
the special constitutional status of the duchies which had strong ties
to each other and demanded, in accordance with the old land rights, a
common constitution and a state within the *Gesamtstaat*. Falck, like
Dahlmann, wished for the dominance of bourgeois and peasant
representatives over the nobles in a revived parliament in the future.
The students taught by this group of professors (in careers as
bureaucrats, physicians, lawyers and journalists) spread these ideas
through the duchies. Uwe Jens Lornsen thus could find support in
these circles for his constitutional movement centred on his draft of a
future constitution for the duchies. As a constitutional model for a
Gesamtstaat Denmark, which would answer to the needs of the
duchies, he propagated the idea of dual monarchy on the model of

the union of Sweden and Norway. To all appearances the Lornsen movement failed but in the long run it led to the recognition of provincial estates.

This assembly of estates, which met from 1835–6, had only an advisory function but contributed to the development of the political consciousness of the population. At first there was the contrast typical of the times – liberal versus conservative thinking. After 1840 however the language dispute in northern Schleswig provoked a national confrontation (see the contribution by L. Rerup). On both the Schleswig–Holstein–German and the Danish side, the liberals and the conservatives joined together under the national emblem. The clash which made the fissure unhealable occurred in the Schleswig assembly of estates of 1842. The national question was further complicated by the dispute regarding the succession to the throne. Since Frederick VII had no children the question of his successor became an issue.

Christian VIII wished to preserve the unity of the *Gesamtstaat* and thus aimed to have the descendants of his niece recognised as rightful heirs throughout the entire monarchy in accordance with the Danish law of succession. The politicians of Schleswig–Holstein however felt that the duke of Augustenburg had a superior claim to Holstein and hoped to withdraw the duchies from *Gesamtstaat* Denmark in an uncomplicated and peaceful manner. The monarch obtained legal opinions which supported his position and claimed – incorrectly – that the Danish law of succession (according to *lex regia*) applied to Schleswig and to parts of Holstein. In an open letter dated 8 August 1846 he stated that he wished to settle the matter of succession according to these legal principles. This and other measures designed to strengthen *Gesamtstaat* Denmark led the politicians of Schleswig–Holstein to the mistaken conviction that the king had moved closer to the Danish national movement.

National excitement in the duchies reached its first climax between 1842 and 1846. The first two stages of the new Schleswig–Holstein movement developed in the pattern of Hroch's[7] three phase scheme for 'small nations'. First, the national programme was formulated by individuals and 'political cells' were created by their students in various towns in the country. For several years the group of professors in Kiel issued a paper, the *Kieler Blätter* (Kiel Weekly) later *Kieler Beiträge* (Kiel Subscriber), until suppressed by the censor. The activists however continued to maintain personal contacts. In addition at the University of Kiel the forbidden *Burschenschaft* (student group) continued to exist, disguised as the *Germania*.

After the beginning of the national conflict political circles (in keeping with Hroch's Phase B) came into the open in order to win the support of large segments of the population for the national cause.

Their vehicle was the liberal *Wochenblätter* (Weekly Paper). In Schleswig the censors intervened with increasing severity however. Publications in Holstein did not have such difficulties due to membership in the German *Bund* (where the two major powers had to have regard for the national cause). In the cities the *Büger–Vereine* (citizens' associations) were engulfed by the wave of nationalism, taking sides or splitting into two rival camps. The agitators on both sides soon held large meetings in order to encourage support and to win over the undecided. On the Schleswig–Holstein side young, liberal, nationally conscious politicians took the initiative at such meetings. They found a receptive audience in the population in the southern part of Schleswig and to a lesser extent in northern Schleswig where German activists could exploit the desire for firmer government ties of the duchies as a bulwark against Danish nationalism.

Thus in the spring of 1843, almost simultaneously with the Danish folk festivals, similar Schleswig–Holstein gatherings[8] were held. They were not simply imitations of the Danish festivals. Despite some similarities their models were the festivals with a liberal and national tone in western Germany. Dahlmann and some of his colleagues at the University of Kiel were already sympathetic to the German movement for unification. Lornsen, as well as many of his younger followers including Wilhelm Hartwig Beseler, one of the most important politicians during the period of the uprising, were members of a *Burschenschaft*.

Festivities took the form of banquets attended by prominent politicians, of large folk festivals, where musical activity and social contacts were mixed with political speeches and declarations and of singing festivals. *Liedertafeln* (men's choirs) appeared at these festivals. They were modelled on similar clubs in the southern part of the Elbe river district where thousands gathered to listen to national songs and political speeches, thereby bringing about the feeling of solidarity desired by the organisers. Finally, when the confrontation became sharper public meetings with a purely political intention were held until the state took restrictive measures which brought about a superficial peace and quiet until March 1848.

Through these meetings between 1843–6 there was a remarkable increase in the active supporters of Schleswig–Holstein, political consciousness was strengthened and preparations were made to join the future German national movement of 1848. Of special importance for the mobilisation of supporters were the folk festivals on the Aunetzberg (near Aabenraa in 1843) and in Bredtstedt (North Frisia in 1844) where 8000 to 9000 participants from the area and outside guests supported the North Schleswig followers of the Schleswig–Holstein movement and integrated the North Frisians therein . The climax of these events was the singers' festival in Schleswig in 1844 (with 14 000 participants of whom 500 were singers). At this festival the future symbols of the national movement were presented for the first time – the 'Schleswig–Holstein song' and the country's colours: blue–white–red. Soon these symbols were joined by a phrase from the Ripener document of 1460 shortened to the slogan *Op ewig ungedeelt* (forever undivided).

The formation of a German Schleswig–Holstein consciousness can be identified in Schleswig during these years though it must be remembered that many people remained immune to its appeal. South of a line running north of Husum and Schleswig and along the west coast (North Frisia) Schleswig–Holstein sentiment prevailed among the politically active (Danish sympathies were practically non-existent). This applies likewise to the densely populated Angeln area whose peasant population had been germanised as a result of the language switch. Inhabitants of the sparsely populated middle part of central Schleswig were largely indifferent.

A majority of Flensburg citizens[9] favoured *Gesamtstaat* Denmark, were loyal to the king and indifferent to nationalist fervour. Their 'loyalty' to the central government arose from the economic interests of the city. However those with Schleswig–Holstein sympathies found support in several associations (*Casino* for merchants and entrepreneurs; *Gewerbeverein* for craftsmen; and *Turnverein* (gymnastic club), *Liedertafel* (song group) and *Germania* (for the strongly committed). The lawyer Bremer (deputy of the estate of the duchy Schleswig, spokesman of the duchies' delegation to the German Singers' Festival in Würzburg in 1845 and later a member of the provisional government) plus an entrepreneur and a physician (all native Schleswigians) as well as a director of a *gymnasium* (classical secondary school) were their political leaders. Although German immigration to the four North Schleswig cities[10] had been lower during the past centuries than to Flensburg nevertheless German cultural influence in the upper and middle classes was strong. This caused an important part of the population to opt for the south on the national level during the years of the national decision. This meant that the cities became very important centres for the future *Heimdeutschtum* (established residents of North Schleswig who felt German).

As is usually the case in times of upheaval early national spokes-men on both sides could change sympathies or become indifferent. Prior to the 1840s the representatives of the estates of the cities were loyal to the king or were liberal. This was true also of the prominent citizens except for the leftist liberal Peter Hjort Lorenzen. When the national conflict became more intense a shift took place. Then national liberals of the left and centre who were committed to the

Schleswig–Holstein side were elected – for example two lawyers, Gülich (who came from Flensburg and was elected by Aabenraa) and Wilhelm Hartwig Beseler (who came from north Frisia and later was a member of the provisional government, Vice President of the National Assembly in Frankfurt and then one of the two governors of Schleswig–Holstein 1849–51; elected by Tønder); in Haderslev another lawyer, then a court secretary; and in Sønderborg (after the death of P.H. Lorenzen) a judge. More comprehensive information about the political activists for the German side is available through studies of the managing committee of the respective associations (the *Bürgerverein* (Citizens' Association), *Union, Liedertafel* and *Schleswig– Holsteinischer Patriotischer Verein* (Schleswig–Holstein Patriotic Society)). In Haderslev the leading group consisted of 20 persons (two self-employed with an academic background; one high ranking civil servant, six master craftsmen, three merchants and one inn-keeper). In addition there were 20 to 30 upper and middle class citizens who were determined and committed. Fangel has given the following figures, which are probably roughly correct, for the percentage of pro-Germans in Haderslev within the social classes of the city:

- Upper class (self-employed professions with academic back-ground, clergy, civil servants, merchants, entrepreneurs, intel-lectuals, etc): 85 per cent
- Middle class (craftsmen, small businessmen and merchants): 40–50 per cent
- Lower class: 5–10 per cent

These estimates probably apply to Aabenraa and Sønderborg as well. In Aabenraa the group of Schleswig–Holstein spokesmen in the *Bürgerverein*, the *Liedertafel*, and the *Schleswig–Holsteinischer Patriot-ischer Verein*, consisted of six self-employed professionals (lawyers, physicians, apothecaries, journalists), three high ranking civil servants, one school head, two merchants and shipowners. The master craftsmen (who were continually augmented by German speaking migrants) were often committed to the German side.

Not much is known about the people with German sympathies in Sønderborg. There are indications (the political stand of the Sønder-borger Weekly, of the Deputy Esmarch and of the Mayor in March 1848) that the situation was similar to that in Aabenraa and Haderslev. National sympathies in Tønder have also not been researched thoroughly but both German and Danish historians testify to the clear predominance of German Schleswig–Holstein sympathies in this city. The migration of German speaking people to the city was not larger here than in other North Schleswig cities but the influence of the German language and culture was apparently much greater. In some families German was even the colloquial daily language and there are examples of a conscious effort on the part of parents to speak German with their children as it was the language of instruction in the schools. For the migrants to Tønder from North Frisia the literary, cultural and commercial language was German. Beseler's political influence (as estate deputy for the city – he visited Tønder often after 1842) certainly played an important role in influencing the majority of the population of Tønder as it reached a decision on its national loyalties. During the 1840s there were no national conflicts in Tønder 'for the simple reason that "Schleswig–Holsteinism" found no opponents here'.[11] The Tønder *Liedertafel* was invited to many festivals, the *Tondernsche Intelligenzblatt* supported Beseler's ideas, a festival in 1843 commemorating the six hundredth anniversary of Lubeck's city charter, all reinforced the national ties. The active persons in the Schleswig–Holstein movement here were apparently merchants and craftsmen. Professionals and civil servants were not in evidence. The merchant Johann Todsen (he was from a respected peasant family in the vicinity) was especially prominent.

In the rural north Schleswig regions mentioned above the foundations of a future *Heimdeutschtum* were laid in the 1840s. The estate deputies of the rural electoral districts were usually peasant proprietors and hide owners. Among the peasant deputies, some of whom were loyal to the *Gesamtstaat* and the king, there was at first support for the demand for Danish to be recognised as the official and legal language; later however they joined the pro-German National Liberals. They did not want Schleswig to have stronger links to the kingdom of Denmark and it was their intention to strengthen Schleswig's ties to Holstein. This last decision, taken during the sharp conflicts of the 1848–64 period, also led them to develop a German national feeling. In the end only two deputies, who originally supported the introduction of Danish as the official and legal language in North Schleswig, remained on the Danish side. These deputies Steenholdt, Posselt and Petersen-Dalby then favoured Schleswig–Holstein, where their colleague Todsen-Meierholm had stood from the beginning.[12]

Further peasant notables of north Schleswig, often *Kirchspielsvögte* (Parish overseer; an honorary position in peasant self-government), decided likewise. In March 1844 15 out of 70 *Kirchspielsvögte* of the rural district Hadersleben formed a *Kirchspielsvogt-Verein* (Parish Overseers' Union) in opposition to the Danish *Slesvigsk Forening* [The (Danish) Schleswigian Association]. By expanding membership to include more farmers and also urban dwellers the *Kirchspielsvogt-Verein* became the *Schleswig–Holsteinischer Patriotischer Verein*.[13] Economic motives favouring an orientation to the south, especially to

Hamburg, played a role in this political decision. Thus they supported the continuation of the Altona–Rendsburg railway to the north and were against the construction of the west–east Husum–Flensburg transit connection. Furthermore industrial exhibitions and livestock shows were organised at which favourable political speeches for Schleswig–Holstein were featured. The readiness of this large group of North Schleswig farmers to orient themselves in a different direction to the majority of the members of their class, that is to the south, can be explained by the centuries old family relationships[14] between rural and urban upper and middle classes (compare the Petersen-Dalby and Todsen[15] families) and by the similar national–political decisions based on family connections that were reached. Another type of peasant deputy was Thies Hansen Steenholdt[16] who came from a small farming family and advanced socially after performing military service to become part of the circle of rural politicians in Schleswig–Holstein. He succeeded in pressing his political convictions on people in several villages in the area east of Tønder, as was done elsewhere by the heads of old established peasant notable families. The political education of the elite of a future North Schleswig German national character took place in rural areas in a way comparable to the parallel Danish movement.

At the time that national decisions were being taken the areas of Angeln and North Frisia as well as Tønder and its eastern surroundings in the duchy Schleswig proved to be the main strongholds of Schleswig–Holstein commitment, even more than the areas and cities in the south which had been German speaking for a long time. Therefore it was not so much language as a mental attitude which was the product of intellectual and historical developments that was decisive in such decisions. Based on the sources and research available it is difficult to determine the percentages of the North Schleswigians committed to Schleswig–Holstein and to Germany in the middle of the nineteenth century. It is only possible to refer to the approximate evidence deduced from results of an election to the *Reichstag* (parliament) of the *Norddeutscher Bund* (North German Union) held on 12 February 1867, the first contest held under universal manhood suffrage.[17] There political events such as the unwanted incorporation into Prussia certainly affected the results. The votes for German parties predominated throughout Schleswig because of the virtual absence of pro-Danish voters in the southern parts. In the northern section the pro-Danish voters clearly predominated. Nevertheless the political stronghold provided by a pro-German mentality lay just north of today's border, in what is now Denmark. The highest percentage was in Tønder (82.8 per cent) but other cities also demonstrated strong pro-German feelings: such as Haderslev (41.3 per cent), Aabenraa (47.7 per cent) and Sønderborg

(34.1 per cent). Among the townlets and villages especially on the coast west of Tønder and in the southern part of the middle area of North Schleswig, some had German majorities and others strong minorities. The national orientation of these North Schleswigians towards 'germanness' took place simultaneously with the awakening of the North Schleswigians towards 'danishness'. This decision was not the result of linguistic, religious or 'biological' factors; but resulted from a 'conscientious decision' to attain a particular political identity.

The Government of Schleswig and the Pro-German Elite in the Duchy of Schleswig (1850–64)

In the Danish *Gesamtstaat* prior to 1864 the German population was a minority but in the duchies as a whole, however, they were clearly in the majority – in the duchy of Schleswig the majority was narrow; in north Schleswig they were in the minority. The national tensions in the *Gesamtstaat* came to a head in March 1848. After a bloodless revolution in the kingdom of Denmark a constitutional monarchy was established and the new government strove to bind Schleswig more closely to Denmark within the *Gesamtstaat*. Leading politicians in the Schleswig–Holstein uprising demanded a closely united Schleswig–Holstein and also the entrance of Schleswig into the *Deutscher Bund* while retaining only a personal union of the duchies with Denmark. The most important politicians among the Schleswig–Holstein national liberals had close contact in 1848–9 to the German national assembly in Frankfurt and in general to the German unification movement. Many of them were representatives in this parliament, Beseler was for a time even Vice President. Their political influence was substantial.

During the three year 'civil war' (1848–51) in *Gesamtstaat* Denmark Schleswig–Holstein initially received support from the German *Reichszentrale* (Central State) and then from Prussia, until efforts at German unification failed and Prussia had to withdraw under pressure from the European great powers. The military defeat of the Schleswig–Holsteinians in 1850 put an end to the uprising. The European great powers forced the preservation of the *Gesamtstaat*, if in a modified form. In the duchies the liberal constitution of 1848 was abolished and an absolutist government with advisory estates was reintroduced. However in 1855 the *Wahlzensus* (the men with a certain amount of property who were entitled to vote) was reduced and the right to legislate on specific matters for the respective duchies was permitted, though due to insurmountable differences a constitution for *Gesamtstaat* Denmark proved impossible. In the Schleswig estates the deputies committed to Schleswig–Holstein (conservatives as well as liberals) had a small majority over the pro-Danish or pro-*Gesamtstaat* deputies until 1864. After the elimination of the old activists of the Schleswig–Holstein movement the spokesmen were the gentry landlords and the new farming representatives.

Although both ethnic groups in Schleswig were supposed to be equal under the constitutional principles of the reorganised *Gesamtstaat* state authorities took a hard line attitude towards the politicians committed to Schleswig–Holstein while taking steps to make central Schleswig Danish and to suppress the German minority in North Schleswig. From 1850 to 1864 the statist thinking of high ranking Danish monarchist civil servants who wanted a uniform state (for example, the first Minister appointed for Schleswig since 1851, Kammerherr Tillisch) joined forces with the energetic nationalist younger, liberal and conservative civil servants.[18]

One of these civil servants was the North Schleswigian Th. A.J. Regenburg (1815–95)[19]. Initially he headed the department responsible for school and cultural questions before becoming the State Secretary in Schleswig. He was able to pursue a hard line against ministers who had been conciliatory as he had the confidence of that absolutist ruler Frederick VII who instructed the other ministers not to interfere with Regenburg's measures.

Before 1848 the enlightened absolutist central government had refrained from particularly harsh repressive measures against the activists in Schleswig–Holstein. It resorted to the measures usual at that time: censorship of the press, prohibition of the right to assembly and occasional petty harassments.[20] The events of 1848–50 hardened attitudes. Reaction starting in 1850–1 led to a settling of accounts with defeated opponents[21] though sentences of death were not carried out. Even during the war German activists in Schleswig–Holstein had been arrested by Denmark and imprisoned for months. The difficult circumstances that occurred during the complete occupation of Schleswig in 1850 (the southernmost areas near the front were under siege until the end of the war) were used to create a *fait accompli*. Supporters of the movement who were civil servants were removed without notice, other 'unbelievable' persons were suspended and carefully supervised. In 1850–1 290 administrative civil servants were dismissed and in 1852 20 more. In 1850 41 pastors were also removed.

Fewer primary or lower school teachers lost their jobs, apparently because they could not be replaced.[22] Many pastors and civil servants from the kingdom of Denmark were sent to Schleswig. This practice was implemented for teachers at the Latin schools where only eight out of 30 teachers at the Schleswig Latin schools survived into the new era. Instruction at the *Johanneum* in Haderslev was held in Danish; while the other Latin schools in Flensburg, Schleswig and Husum were largely staffed with teachers from the kingdom who sympathised with Danish views even though they generally taught in German. Of the lawyers who began to exercise their profession after 1848, only 18 out of 68 received permission to continue their practice and they were expected to disavow the Schleswig–Holstein cause. The 33 activists among the Schleswig–Holstein politicians who had left the duchy in 1850–51, were prohibited from returning unless they were prepared to stand trial. An amnesty on 15 May 1851 permitted others to return but they had to pledge their allegiance to the new *Gesamtstaat*, which most refused to do. During the period of siege supporters of Schleswig–Holstein had been punished for not greeting Danish officers, for singing prohibited songs (such as the Schleswig–Holstein anthem), for showing their symbols such as the blue–white–red colours and for the use of the forbidden name 'Schleswig–Holstein'. Their patriotic associations had been banned and a stricter censorship of the press had been introduced.

Antagonism between the government and the pro-German population was particularly apparent in school and religious affairs. In Regenburg's plans the *Heimdeutschtum* in North Schleswig was to be restricted permanently and the consequences of the language switch in Angeln would be made retroactive. During the last year of the war Danish already had been introduced as the language of instruction in all city schools in North Schleswig; though in urban centres religious services could still be held in either tongue. Then in February to March 1851 a 'mixed language zone' for schools and Churches was created in an area including a broad strip bordering on North Schleswig and the Angeln district in central Schleswig (including Tønder but excluding Flensburg and the areas speaking Frisian), covering communities where hitherto only German had been used. Thus Danish became the language of instruction in all schools in this area. Weekly Church services were to be held alternately in both languages. Vacancies for pastors and teachers were to be filled by applicants from the kingdom of Denmark. The colleges of education now used Danish instead of German in instruction. Teachers who retained their positions had to conform strictly to the regulations imposed by Regenburg's Department of Culture.

However this harsh policy in school affairs provoked the population to conscious passive resistance. Among the *Heimdeutschen* in North Schleswig and in the areas of northern and central Angeln which were subjected to language restrictions, the first national decision in favour of the union of the Schleswig–Holstein movement with the German nation was made. Acceptance of the new conditions, as intended by government policy, was seldom achieved. Demands by the pro-German estate deputies for a revision of the language policy reflected the views of the majority of the population in this part of central Schleswig. Petitions demanded the abolition of the language restrictions. In contrast to the years before 1848 the Schleswig government prosecuted the initiators of and collectors of signatures to such petitions. In several cases they were sentenced to prison. Critics of state policy among the circle of Schleswig–Holstein activists, such as the former Deputy Steenholdt, were also incarcerated . Only in 1861 did the situation ease up slightly so as to allow religious confirmations in German and private instruction in German (subject to extensive state controls). In Flensburg too leading 'loyal' and nationally indifferent politicians took a clear stand against restricting German in school. Similar to the germanisation attempts later in North Schleswig the policy of the Schleswig government between 1850–64 to enforce danishness in central Schleswig failed because of the people's passive resistance.

Liberal Schleswig–Holstein politicians living in exile in Germany maintained close contacts with the supporters of the movement for German unification, for example with the *Deutscher Nationalverein*. These politicans and the duke of Augustenburg insured that articles appeared in newspapers at home and abroad which reported the unfavourable conditions for the Germans in Schleswig. This prompted the English government to apply pressure in Copenhagen for an end to such conditions. In order to appease the German *Bund* and the German great powers (who lodged a complaint regarding the constitutional question of the *Gesamtstaat*) the government in Copenhagen agreed to the partial concessions mentioned above. But the events of 1864 soon led to the secession of the duchies from the *Gesamtstaat* and finally to the annexation by Prussia in 1866–7.

The German Minority in North Schleswig during its Incorporation into the Kingdom of Denmark (1920–33)

The German North Schleswigians as a National Minority in the Kingdom of Denmark after 1920

The Germans of north Schleswig, although it was now part of Germany, were already a numerical 'minority' in their local area during the period 1864–1920. After Germany's defeat in the First World War the Danish government, which had maintained neutrality during the conflict, revised its original plan of reaching a direct agreement with Germany by way of a plebiscite in favour of participation in the peace conference at Versailles.[23] Domestic public opinion and the insistence of the Danish North Schleswigians on quick action encouraged Denmark, which was also under strong pressure from the allies, to take this step.

Articles 190–114 of the Treaty of Versailles stipulated that in zone I (the southern line of which is today's German–Danish border) the decision would be made '*en bloc*' (that is according to the majority of all votes in this zone). In zone II (the city of Flensburg and parts of the Flensburg district plus Tønder and Husum) the decision should be reached individually in each community in order to permit border changes to the advantage of Denmark in localities with a Danish majority (this was the wish of French nationalists surrounding Clemenceau and of Danish activists in the border area). On 10 February 1920 in zone I, 75 431 votes against 25 329 were cast for union with Denmark. However there were German majorities in several rural communities in the immediate border area of the voting zone (such as in Tønder, 76 per cent; Højer, 73 per cent; and in a number of rural communities of the area east of Tønder; in Aabenraa, 54 per cent and Sønderborg, 55 per cent). The plebiscite in zone II on 14 February 1920 resulted in an overwhelming majority – 51 724 to 12 800 votes – for Germany. Thus the border between the two zones became the national boundary. The Germans of North Schleswig who had been part of the dominant group thus became a non-dominant ethnic minority.

The transition from Hroch's Phase B to Phase C was already under way in Schleswig around 1844–51. It was interrupted by the repressive policies of 1850–64 and during the period 1864-88, when the creation of the new German *Reich* in 1871 satisfied some of the aspirations of the Schleswig–Holstein movement. But when the Danes of North Schleswig began to strengthen and even expand as a result of the 'germanising policies' of Prussia, from approximately 1888, the Germans of North Schleswig had felt like a 'minority'. They too then began to found associations.[24] Particularly important were the local *Ringreitervereine* and *Schützenvereine* (Rifle Associations). Farmers, merchants and craftsmen were the most prominent figures in these associations.

The main association *Deutscher Verein für das nördliche Schleswig* (German Association for Northern Schleswig), founded in 1890, strove to be the spokesman for the Germans in this area. German mentality was strengthened and spread by means of national and cultural activity as well as by settling German farmers and tradesmen in the region. The annual meeting took place as a popular festival on the Knivsberg (north of Aabenraa), where a Bismarck tower was erected as a national monument. In 1907 this association had 47 branches in this region with 4825 members. In 1914 of the 11 000 members (as was customary at the time only adult men were in the association) 7000 must have lived in the region (5162 of whom were native north Schleswigians and of these 2444 were rural inhabitants). Not much research has been undertaken on the members of the managing committees of the local branches but it seems that most participants came from the local German population: in rural areas they were often farmers, in the cities members of the upper class (shipowners, rich merchants, factory owners) or were civil servants, pastors, teachers and jurists. The managing committee consisted of judges, secondary school teachers, a school head, a pastor, a shipowner and a book publisher. The earlier members of the managing committee were usually local Germans; after 1902 the newcomer Dr Hahn, a judge, was elected the first president and directed the course of the association. He was also a member of the *Alldeutscher Verein* (All-German Association) and supported the 'germanisation' policy of the government.

Various native German politicians, especially theologians, criticised this approach. In 1909 some of them founded the *Verein für deutsche Friedensarbeit in der Nordmark* (The Association for the Encouragement of German Peace Work in the North March), abbreviated the association was called *Friedensverein* (Peace Association)[25] with Pastor Schmidt-Wodder as chairman. The association's goal was to mitigate ethnic conflicts. The German and Danish cultures and languages were to be equally respected. The *Friedensverein* also wanted to win the Danish North Schleswigians for the German side but by 'honourable competition' in the cultural field. In 1914 the association had 405 members. Local people – pastors, physicians, jurists, farmers and – as a sign of the times to come – an unmarried woman – dominated the managing committee. But attempts to cooperate with the *Deutscher Verein* failed.

After the union with Denmark in 1920 the north Schleswigians were faced by several economic problems.[26] Until then the farmers had been able to sell their goods in Germany and had been protected by tariffs. Now they were part of an agrarian state and had to shift to exports. Considerable problems were encountered as a result of the switch in currency from the inflationary mark to the 'hard' Danish Crown. Later they were severely affected by the world depression.

The Formation of a National Elite in the German Minority after 1920

During the plebiscite most of the German associations and parties had worked together in the *Deutscher Ausschuss* (German committee).[27] The German *Reichskommissar* (State Commissioner) for the plebiscite, Dr Adolf Köster, led his Social Democratic party in working together with the associations united in the *Ausschuss*.[28] As a result of this cooperation in the *Deutscher Ausschuss* in North

Schleswig most of the politicians there continued to work together after its incorporation into Denmark in the German minority organisations. The old quarrel between the *Deutscher Verein* and the *Friedensverein* was healed. The members of the *Friedensverein*, of the *Ringreitervereine*, the *Schützenvereine* and other organisations dominated, especially when most of the members of the managing committees who sympathised with the *Alldeutscher Verein* left the country after 1920. The pro-German Social Democratic party members joined the Danish social democrats (as was typical of Social Democratic party followers when borders were altered). This initiated a slow absorption of these Germans by the Danish people which accelerated after the establishment of the National Socialist dictatorship in Germany in 1933 and the accompanying persecution of social democrats there. A special agreement between the German and Danish social democrats on 25 November 1923 for the mutual recognition of the new border did not have much effect in the border area itself.

Among the active politicians of the minority there were some who from 1920 adopted the thinking of the Schleswig–Holstein movement. Other groups (especially in Haderslev and Aabenraa) continued in the tradition of the German national liberals and free conservatives of the German *Reich*.[29] Most conspicuous was the stand taken by Schmidt-Wodder[30] who now devoted himself to minority politics and who was a representative for the German minority in the Danish *Folketing* (parliament) from 1920 to 1939. He was skeptical about the old state patriotism of the German *Reich* and favoured the ideas of the 1848 uprising though he added new ideals drawn from the youth movement before and following the First World War. The strengths of the culture with roots in the native land should be used to the advantage of the people and their fatherland. The influence of ideas of the 'trench generation' of the First World War, which aimed at natural community and common action, were evident.

As the main thrust of his political programme Schmidt-Wodder demanded a 'new decision' (that is, a new plebiscite) because the voting process in zone I had placed the Germans at an unfair disadvantage. This minority demand met with the approval of all the German parties of the Weimar Republic. A geographical definition of the area where such a plebiscite was to be held was, however, never made. A realistic chance of success of such a plebiscite could be envisaged only for the western border area (Tønder, Højer and Schiefes Viereck in the district east of Tønder). The realisation of such a demand would have brought about a rupture within the German minority since the Germans living to the north of this area would have felt abandoned. In Haderslev the *Königsaubund* group (The Königsau

Society) posited the unrealistic demand for a new plebiscite in all of North Schleswig. Thus for tactical reasons Schmidt-Wodder stuck to his basic demand to revise the border without becoming concrete. The minority also insistently demanded 'cultural autonomy'. Another important field for national conflict was the 'land struggle',[31] the maintenance and expansion of German rural property.

As a representative to the *Folketing* Schmidt-Wodder advocated a policy which had already been formulated in the first programme of the *Schleswigscher Wählerverein* (Schleswig Voters' Association) in 1920.[32] The goal should not be participation in the Danish state but rather the definition and delimitation of the minority as an independent group within Denmark that had the desire to return to the 'mother' country. By unconventional means and with the voluntary support of young people of both sexes who had usually belonged to different groups in the youth movement Schmidt-Wodder was able to build up an organisational network quickly. On 4 May 1920 the *Deutscher Schulverein* (German School Association for north Schleswig) was founded and before that probably, the *Deutscher Jugendbund* (German Youth Organisation); then came the political organisation, the *Schleswigscher Wählerverein* (Schleswig Voters' Association; in Danish the *Slesvigsk Parti*) in the period 20 July to 15 August 1920. The social demands which were originally planned for its programme were downgraded when the German social democrats joined the Danish 'sister' party. From then on middle class politics (the interests of farmers, traders, commerce and crafts) played the main role in the *Schleswigscher Wählerverein*. When a peasant protest movement[33] arose in the mid 1920s as a result of agricultural difficulties in North Schleswig the desire for regional autonomy was also propagated. This permitted the German minority to influence these movements and, after their failure, to recruit new supporters from the members of these older movements.

In 1921 an umbrella organisation encompassing the older *Wählerverein* (German Voters' Union), the *Schulverein* (German School Union) and the *Jugendbund* (German Youth Union) was founded. Further associations came into being: the *Wohlfahrtsdienst* (Social Service Association), the *Selbsthilfe* (Mutual Aid Association), for the 'Landstruggle' in 1926 the 'Kreditanstalt Vogelgesang' and in 1929 the *Höfeverwaltungsgesellschaft* (farm administration society) for new farms. Apart from the four German speaking communities of the Danish state Church, in the cities new German free communities were established such as the *Nordschleswigsche Gemeinde* (North Schleswig Community)[34] which had been connected institutionally since 1923 to the Schleswig–Holstein *Landeskirche* (Church of Schleswig–Holstein). In the elections to the Danish *Folketing* the *Scheswigscher Wählerverein* (German Voters' Union) usually received

14–16 per cent of the votes in north Schleswig. The decline compared to the German percentage during the plebiscite can be explained by emigration (usually to Germany) and the drift towards integration into Denmark by the workers' wing.

Table 8.1: German votes in the *Folketing* elections

1920	1924	1926	Year 1929	1932	1935	1939
7 505	7 715	10 422	9 787	9 867	12 615	15 016
14.4%	13.5%	15.6%	14.3%	14.3%	15.6%	15.9%

In absolute terms the number of German votes increased noticeably after 1926. This was due to the effects of the protest movement and the rise of Germany's prestige internationally after 1933. However, because of Danish migration to north Schleswig the percentage of German votes changed only negligibly. In order to facilitate the coordination of journalistic activity and to ensure finances the German newspapers in all four cities were merged in 1929 into the single press organ – the *Nordschleswigsche Zeitung* (North Schleswig Newspaper) – of the minority.[35] The *Wählerverein* had most of its members in and around Tønder as revealed in 1921, a statistic from the early years for the minority which has survived by chance (divided into the former Prussian *Landkreise*):

Table 8.2: Geographical   distribution   of   the   Wählerverein members, 1921 (incomplete)

Kreis Tønder	Kreis Sønderborg	Kreis Aabenraa	Kreis Haderslev
2002	251	718	789

An early source which cannot be exactly dated (probably the first half of the 1920s)[36] provides the following information about the members of the managing committee (see Table 8.3).

The leadership of the minority thus rested in the hands of the *Heimdeutschen* and the relationship between urban and rural areas was much more balanced than earlier in the *Deutscher Verein*. Urban academics, local notables and newspaper editors were joined by a large group of farmers who had considerable political influence. The percentage of craftsmen also increased. Information from the early

Table 8.3: Social structure of the managing committee (early 1920s, incomplete)

Place of Birth Origin		Profession of Father		Own Profession	
North Schleswig	15	Professionals	2	Professionals	4
Schleswig–Holstein	2	Craftsmen	4	Newspaper editors	4
Other parts of Germany	2	Peasants/farmers	5	Craftsmen	3
				Merchants	2
				Farmers	9
Total	19		11		22

1920s about other minority activists reveals a balanced representation between the cities and the countryside. The following statistics dating from the *Wählerverein* in the early 1920s gives information about the 'active politicians' (local chairmen, founding members,

Table 8.4: Active politicians

Place of Birth Origin		Profession of Father		Own Profession	
North Schleswig	24	Professionals	2	Professionals	8
Schleswig–Holstein	5	Teachers	2	Teachers	3
Other parts of Germany	3	White Collar employees	1	Trade Commerce	6
		Craftsmen	1	Employees	2
		Farm owners/ farmers	16	Craftsmen	2
		Workers	1	Farm owners/ farmers	28
				Others (retired)	2
Total	32		23		51

Table 8.5: Active members

Place of Birth Origin		Profession of Father		Own Profession	
North Schleswig	11	Lower level civil servants	1	Professionals	1
Schleswig–Holstein	2	Merchants	2	Teachers	1
		Farm owners/ farmers	3	Merchants/ self-employed	5
				Craftsmen	3
				Farm owners/ farmers	8
Total	13		6		18

candidates etc.) and the 'active members', who did not have special offices but were very committed to the *Wählerverein*.

Like their fathers, activists came from North Schleswig and belonged to the urban middle class and the rural farm owners though this pattern was less evident on the managing committee. The social breakdown of the minority and its deep root in the region and the increasing numerical balance between rural and urban supporters are reflected very clearly. The so-called 'free forces' (the young people who voluntarily supported Pastor Schmidt in building up organisations as mentioned above) were very important for the formation of a new elite generation.[37] This small but very idealistic group often came from the pre-1914 Boy Scout movement. Their parents were usually *Heimdeutsche* (indigenous Germans): often pastors, teachers and civil servants. Later almost all of them became teachers in the German minority schools and were active in the managing committees of the ethnic organisations. Those German students from north Schleswig who were studying in Copenhagen or at German universities were often members of the *Verband Schleswigscher Studenten* (Union of Schleswig Students).

The liberal Danish school laws permitted the free development of the German school system.[38] The law of 30 June 1920 stipulated that the communal schools were to be financed by the communities. The schools were supervised by an elected committee from which teachers were excluded. In the city communal schools, sections were created in which German was the language of instruction beginning with the third year but where Danish was taught four to six hours weekly. Parents could determine which section their children attended.

In the rural districts ten per cent of the voters in a school community had to express their wish for instruction in German. In order to establish German communal schools or school sections at least 20 per cent of the voters had to agree and ten children had to attend. After 1924 this rose to an attendance of 24 children. The minority was faced with the problem that the number of pro-German teachers who had attended German colleges of education decreased steadily. In the period cited the number of teachers who had received a German education decreased from 249 to 194. Instruction was still given as required but increasingly by pro-Danish teachers. In addition many pro-German teachers emigrated to Schleswig–Holstein in the first years, although most stayed in the country.

On the regional level there were some activities devoted to the Danish cause which tried to evade the legal requirements or which were not very generous to the minority. The hiring of teachers and the establishment of the curriculum are examples as these were in the hands of the communal school commissions which seldom had a German majority. As a result the German minority wanted their own private schools with pro-German teachers who had received a German education. Danish laws stipulated that a private school had to have at least ten children in attendance and that the curriculum should meet the requirements set for communal schools and also that the communal school commission should be able to inspect the school's finances.

If these conditions were fulfilled the private school would receive a certain subsidy per child as prescribed by law. German schools could be funded, however, only after inflation was overcome in the mid 1920s after which the Weimar Republic was able to assist financially. The German government granted funds, subject to parliamentary control, via the *Ossa GmbH* and the *Deutsche Stiftung* (German Foundation). Other German associations such as the *VDA* (Verein für das Deutschtum im Ausland – Association for the Germanhood in Foreign Countries) and the *Schleswig–Holsteiner–Bund* also furnished finance. Various German organisations in the border area created a joint *Nordausschuss* (North Committee) which set up a *Grenzmittelstelle Nord* (Border Funds Agency) in Flensburg (headed by the North Schleswigian Ernst Schröder). The private funds and the money granted by the German government to the *Deutsche Stiftung* were collected there and then channelled to North Schleswig where the private German schools were constructed in close cooperation with the *Nord Schleswig Deutscher Schulverein*. The cooperation between German School Inspector Dr Edert and Headmaster Koopmann, the President of the *Schulverein* was particularly effective.

Table 8.6: German communal and private schools

	German Communal Schools		German Private Schools	
Year	Schools	No of Students	Schools	No of Students
1921	23	2 830	6	311
1931	29	2 260	27	1 106
1935	34	2 361	52	1 948

The table above establishes that the German school system in North Schleswig developed with the start of financial help from the German *Reich*. It was now possible to compensate for the lack of German sections in communal schools. Families living in remote areas were visited by travelling teachers (40 per cent of whom were women).

The preference for private schools caused a drop in the number of German communal schools and school sections. Until 1933 the

German *Reich* did not influence the curriculum of the private schools; it remained a matter of the ethnic group. The teachers at the German private schools were members of the *Deutscher Lehrerverein für Nordschleswig* (Union of German Teachers of North Schleswig) which was also important for the education of the minority's elite. Teachers at communal schools could be politically indifferent or pro-Danish; they were hired if they were qualified with respect to language and professionally competent. The *Deutscher Lehrerverein* and the *Schulverein* worked closely with one another. Female members in both organisations were particularly committed and teachers in the private schools were often active in minority organisations, especially in the field of cultural activities and in communal politics. The teachers at the *Volksschulen* usually came from the lower middle class or from farming families and only rarely was the father a teacher. There was a school in Aabenraa after 1920 which strove to offer high quality instruction and to achieve the right to hold examinations in order to develop an 'academic elite' in a German private school. The Danish government granted the right to hold *gymnasium* examinations only in 1930. In 1931 the school had 313 and in 1935 268 students.[39]

From 1927 the *Schul- und Sprachverein* founded public libraries which were looked after by voluntary helpers (such as teachers) in rural areas. Funds from Germany were also channelled in them. Libraries were also supported by the *Wohlfahrts- und Schulverein für Nordschleswig* (Association for Welfare and Schools in North Schleswig) of the German *Reich*, founded in 1919, which created an excellent library system on both sides of the border.

Table 8.7: Number of German libraries in North Schleswig

Year	Cities	Villages	No of Books	No of Readers
1927	–	13	2 039	852
1931	6	35	28 661	5 583

Table 8.8: Number of books borrowed from the German libraries

1927	4 081
1931	85 908

Farmers also were prominent, occupying honorary offices in the *Schul- und Sprachverein* (41 per cent). This is not surprising since the establishment of private schools in rural areas had been their ambition. The following urban professions were active on the managing committees: craftsmen (approximately ten per cent); merchants and entrepreneurs (approximately 18 per cent); teachers (approximately ten per cent); independent professionals (around six per cent); with only one worker however.

Despite the economic difficulties the German minority had become stronger and had expanded their cultural activities considerably at the beginning of the 1930s. In the final analysis this was made possible by the support received during the Weimar Republic from the German government (both that of the *Reich* and that of Prussia) as well as private national associations. The period which followed – a turbulent time during which the National Socialists could not easily bring about the *Gleichschaltung* (regimentation) of the German ethnic group with the NSDAP-N (Nationalsozialistische Deutsche Arbeiter-partei – Nordschleswig, the local branch of the National Socialist Party) (1933–5/6) – undermined the internal structure of the associations and led to the subjection of minority leaders to the dictatorship in the German *Reich*.[40]

The Danish Government and the Elite of the German Minority (1920–33)

The members of the German minority in Denmark enjoyed the same constitutional rights as the other inhabitants (the period 1901–20 had seen Denmark develop as a parliamentary monarchy).[41] The central government in Copenhagen, in particular the Ministry of Cultural Affairs, was usually quite receptive to the wishes of the German minority. Nevertheless some things took time. On one occasion Schmidt-Wodder did not follow his own policy of not interfering in the domestic matters of the Danish state which had nothing to do with the German minority. He cooperated with the Danish social democrats during a *Landting* election by supporting their candidate. This persuaded the ruling party to be more favourable to the desires of Germans to have the right to hold examinations at the planned *gymnasium*.[42] In the eyes of the minority the difficulties in their relations with the state were matters of detail and were on the regional level.[43] The German minority was convinced that its members could enter the civil service but would never be assigned to positions in North Schleswig. In some cases communal school committees refused to set up German sections and made the foundation of private German schools more difficult by delaying the processing of such an application. As a result the German minority increasingly supported Schmidt-Wodder's demand for 'cultural autonomy'.[44]

State of research

There are many sources available pertaining to the national question in the duchy of Schleswig and the history of the minorities there.

Most of them are in good order and located in well kept archives. This applies particularly to the *Schleswig–Holsteinische Landesarchiv* in Schleswig, the municipal archives in the state of Schleswig, the *Landsarkiv for de sønderjyske landsdele* in Aabenraa and the *Rigsarkiv* in Copenhagen.

The crisis of the Danish *Gesamtstaat* and the rise of the German and Danish movements in the duchy of Schleswig have been studied extensively, especially from the perspectives of the history of ideas, politics and constitutional development. But a history of the Germans in Schleswig as part of a supra-national *Gesamtstaat* has not been written as yet. An account of the history of Schleswig–Holstein and studies of specific problems have all been written and these furnish important information (especially regarding the creation of national elites). Older studies on the subject dating from the nineteenth and early twentieth centuries were influenced by nationalism. In the last decades several studies have been published which treat the German–Danish border problem objectively.

On the nineteenth century see the *History of Schleswig–Holstein* edited by Klose; particularly volume 6 written by Degn, pp. 216 ff and volume 8 written by Scharff. Rohwedder gives a comprehensive description of the national awakening in northern Schleswig. The 're-Danishisation' period 1850–64 in Schleswig has been carefully studied by Bracker making extensive use of source material. Special articles on regional development and individual political problems are available also, particularly in the periodical published by the Gesellschaft für Schleswig–Holsteinsche Geschichte (The Society for the History of Schleswig–Holstein). Individual references to articles of interest are found in the following notes. While a satisfactory history of the German minority in North Schleswig 1920–33 has not yet appeared, preliminary studies have been made by Kardel and Salomon. There are, however, several useful, informative and detailed studies to which references are made in the notes following. Relevant biographies are to be found in Klose (1970 ff) and pertinent bibliographies are to be found in Brandt and Klüver pp. 131 ff. For an evaluation of the Danish studies see Rerup, Chapter 9 of this volume.

Notes

1 On Denmark and the *Gesamtstaat* see Skovgaard-Petersen, p. 20 ff.
2 Hoffmann (1981), p. 9 ff.
3 On the economic conditions see Skovgaard-Petersen, p. 59 ff.
4 Degn, p. 216 ff.
5 Hoffmann (1986), p. 23 ff and the bibliography. Around 1840 the king ruled as an absolute monarch in all parts of his kingdom. The duchies had their own superior authority – the 'Schleswig–Holstein–Lauenburg Chancery' in Copen-

hagen – in administrative and legal matters. Following an administrative reform in 1834 the 'Schleswig–Holstein government' was created as an intermediary between the Chancery and the lower levels of administration for both duchies. Other state matters were assigned to the central authorities of the monarchy. The *Rentekammer* (taxation system) had a special section responsible for the duchies. Holstein and Lauenburg, once part of the old (German) empire, were members of the German *Bund* from 1815, the former Danish fief of Schleswig was a 'sovereign' duchy from 1658.

6 Degn, p. 347 ff; Scharff (1975–80); Rohwedder; Rerup; Hagenah. Further bibliographic references are found in these books.

7 Hroch (1971), p. 121 ff.

8 Hansen.

9 Vaagt, p. 282 ff.

10 Especially important is Fangel, p. 320 ff; p. 395 ff. Also see Kragh, p. 218 ff, p. 64 (1936), p. 201 ff; Japsen (1961); *Sønderborg Bys Historie* (1960), p. 258 ff, p. 267 ff; *Tønder gennem Tiderne* (1938), p. 220 ff, p. 268 ff, p. 440 ff; Nyholm, p. 9 ff; Andresen, p. 4 ff; Gregersen p. 5 ff.

11 Fabricius, pp. 320, 323.

12 Rohwedder; Hagenah, (s.a.) *passim*; Fabricius, *passim*; Kragh *passim*. Literature about Petersen-Dalby is found in Rohwedder under 'Otto Scheel' in the bibliography, p. XX-XXI, no. 1–2; Rasch, p. 171 ff.

13 Kragh, p. 238 ff.

14 Hoffmann (1981); Hoffmann (1985), p. 5; p. 12 ff; Kraack, p. 125 ff; Hvidtfeldt, p. 70 ff; the contributions to the discussion by Fabricius, pp. 82 and 83, are very important.

15 On Petersen-Dalby see Rohwedder, reference to O. Scheel in note 12; Brenner p. 10 ff.

16 Rasch (1956).

17 *Sønderjyllands Historie* (1937), pp. 27 ff.

18 A similar reaction set in after 1888 when Prussia suppressed the Danish minority in north Schleswig

19 Hjelholt (1978). Compare also Bracker (1973).

20 On the following see Bracker (1972), pp. 127 ff; Bracker (1973), p. 87 ff; Scharff (1966), p. 193 ff; Hjelholt (1923); Hjelholt (1959f); Plesner, p. 225 ff.

21 An example is the court case against Beseler. Scharff (1959), p. 103 ff.

22 Ravn came across 37 dismissals during 1850, p. 45; the sources do not furnish clear information for the years after 1850.

23 Fink (1978f), Jørgensen; Lehmann; Köster; Alnor (1926f).

24 Japsen (1983); Hauser, p. 161 ff; Tiedje.

25 Alnor (1929); Schmidt-Wodder (1951); Hopp (1974), p. 243 ff; Molter, p. 5 ff.

26 Fink (1958), p. 209f; Rerup, p. 373 ff.

27 Lehmann.

28 On Social Democratic Party policy in 1920 see Callesen, *passim*.

29 For a summary of the various groups, political currents and the organisational forms of the minority, as well as their political, cultural, economic and social work, see note 24. Also see Kardel; Salomon; Tägil; Lenzing; Heuer.

30 See note 24.

31 Hopp (1975).

32 See note 35.

33 Schröder; Fink (1958), p. 212 ff, 244 ff.

34 Jessen.

35 Hopp (1979).

36 Most of the following statistics have been collected by J Zimmermann (Cand.

phil.) from material in several archives, especially in the Archiv der Deutschen Volksgruppe in Nordschleswig (in Aabenraa). Mr Zimmermann and I thank the European Science Foundation for having made it possible for Mr Zimmermann to work over a longer period of time in these archives.

37 Kardel, p. 64 ff; Christensen (1964).
38 On the school system see Kardel; Salomon; Tägil; Christensen (1964), p. 53 ff; Christensen (1971), p. 5 ff. On school laws see Kölln.
39 Doege, p. 106 ff.
40 Tägil; Kardel; Noack.
41 On the state and the minority see the literature cited in note 28.
42 Doege (see note 38), p. 143.
43 Kardel (1964); Christensen (1964); Christensen (1971).
44 In World War II, when Denmark was occupied by German troops, the Danish government made the concession that the regimented (that is, in line with the National Socialist party in Germany) German minority got its own committees and its own school councils for both communal and private schools. In school matters this was a kind of cultural autonomy. Obviously the concession was aimed at preventing more unpleasant measures by the occupying power.

Select Bibliography

Alnor, K. (1926), *Handbuch zur schleswigschen Frage*, vols I and III, Neumünster.
Alnor, K. (1929), *Johannes Schmidt-Wodder*, Neumünster.
Andresen. L. (1943), 'Siebenhundert Jahre Stadt- und Volkstumsgeschichte', in *Beiträge zur neueren Geschichte det Stadt Tondern*, Neumünster.
Beckes-Christensen, H. (1990), *Det tyske mindretal i Nordslesvig 1920–1932*, 2 vols.
Bracker, J. (1972), 'Die dänische Sprachpolitik 1850–1864 und die Bevölkerung Mittelschleswigs', *Zeitschrift der Gesellschaft für Schleswig–Holsteinische Geschichte 97.*
Bracker, J. (1973), 'Die dänische Sprachpolitik 1850–1864 und die Bevölkerung Mittelschleswigs', *Zeitschrift der Gesellschaft für Schleswig–Holsteinische Geschichte 98.*
Brandt, O. and Klüver, W. (1981), *Geschichte Schleswig–Holsteins*, Kiel.
Brenner, F. 'Ahnentafel Bendix Todsen', in *Die Sippe der Nordmark* (Nordschleswig-heft).
Callesen, G. (1970), *Die Schleswigfrage in den Beziehungen zwischen der deutschen und der dänischen Sozialdemokratie 1912–1924*, Aabenraa.
Christensen, F. (1964), 'Deutsche Aufbauarbeit in der Abstimmungszeit', *Schriften der Heimatkundlichen Arbeitsgemeinschaft für Nordschleswig 10.*
Christensen, F. (1971), 'Aufbau deutscher Schulen in Nordschleswig', *Schriften der Heimatkundlichen Arbeitsgemeinschaft für Nordschleswig 23.*
Degn, C. (1960) 'Die Herzogtümer im Gesamtstaat 1773–1830', *Geschichte Schleswig–Holsteins*, vol. 6, Klose, O. (ed.), Neumünster.
Doege, I. (1980), 'Das Deutsche Gymnasium in Apenrade von seinen Anfägen bis 1945', in *50 Jahre Deutsches Gymnasium in Nordschleswig (1930–1980)*, Apenrade.
Düding, D. (1984), *Organisierter gesellschaftlicher Nationalismus in Deutschland: 1809–1847*, Munich.
Fabricius, K. (1937), *1805–1864, Sønderjyllands Historie*, (History of Schleswig), vol. 4, Copenhagen.
Fangel, H. (1975), *Haderslev Bys Historie 1800–1945*, (Town History of Haderslev), Haderslev.
Fink, T. (1958), *Geschichte des schleswigschen Grenzlandes*, Copenhagen.
Fink, T. (1978), *Da Sønderjylland blev delt 1918–1920* (When Schleswig was divided), 3 vols., Aabenraa.
Gregersen, H. (1986), 'Nogle betragtninger over den historiske baggrund for

hjemmetyskheden i Nordslesvig – specielt med henblik pa Tønder og Højer' (Studies on the Historical Background of the Growth of Heimdeutschtum in Northern Schleswig, especially in Tønder and Hoyer), *Sønderjyske Aarboger*, Aabenraa.

Hagenah, H. (s.a.), 'Die Zeit des nationalen Kampfes', in Pauls, V. and Scheel, O. (eds), *Geschichte Schleswig–Holsteins* vol. 6, Neumünster.

Hagenah, H. (1916), *Revolution und Legitimität in der Geschichte der Erhebung Schleswig–Holsteins*, Neumünster.

Hansen, H. (1846), *Deutsche Volks- und Sängerfeste in Schleswig–Holstein*, Altona.

Hauser, O. (1960), *Preussische Staatsräson und nationaler Gedanke*, Neumünster.

Heuer, J. (1973), *Zur politischen, sozialen und ökonomischen Problematik der Volksabstimmungen in Schleswig 1920*, Kiel.

Hjelholt, H. (1923), *Den danske Sprogordning og det danske sprostyre i Slesvig mellem Krigene (1850–1864)* (The Danish Language Regulation and its Prosecution in Schleswig between the Wars (1850–1864), Copenhagen.

Hjelholt, H. (1959), *Sønderjylland under Treårskrigen* (Schleswig in the Three Years War), 2 vols.

Hjelholt, H. (ed.) (1960), *Sønderborg Bys Historie* (History of Sønderborg), vol. 1, Sønderborg.

Hjelhjolt, H. (1978), *A. Regenburg. 1815–1895*, Aabenraa.

Hoffmann, E. (1981), 'Historische Voraussetzungen für die Herausbildung der heutigen deutsch–dänischen Staatsgrenze', *Zeitschrift der Gesellschaft für Schleswig–Holsteinische Geschichte* 106.

Hoffmann, E. (1985), *Die Entstehung des nordschleswigschen Deutschtums*, Schriften der Heimatkundlichen Arbeitsgemeinschaft für Nordschleswig 51.

Hoffmann, E. (1986), 'Fürstlicher Absolutismus oder Mitbestimmung der Staatsbürger; Gesamtstaat oder Doppelmonarchie', President of the Schleswig–Holstein Landtag (ed.), *Zum 150. Jahrestag der schleswigschen Ständerversammlung*, Husum.

Hoffmann, E. (1990), *Grundlinien der Geschichte der deutschen Volksgruppe in Nordschleswig von 1920–1955*, Schriften der Heimatkundlichen Arbeitsgemeinschaft in Nordschleswig 61/62.

Hopp, P. (1974), Johannes Schmidt-Wodder, Schleswig-Holsteinisches Biographisches Lexikon 3, Neumünster.

Hopp, P. (1975), 'Bodenkampf und Bauernbewegung', *Zeitschrift der Gesellschaft für Schleswig–Holsteinische Geschichte* 100.

Hopp, P. (1979), 'Bemerkungen zur Zusammenlegung der deutsch–nordschleswigschen Zeitungen am 1.2. 1927', *Schriften der Heimatkundlichen Arbeitsgemeinschaft für Nordschleswig* 40.

Hroch, M. (1971), 'Das Erwachen kleiner Nationen als Problem der komparativen sozialgeschichtlichen Forschung', in Schieder, T. and Burian, P. (eds), *Sozialstruktur und Organisation europäischer Nationalbewegungen*, Munich.

Hroch, M. (1985), *Social Preconditions of National Revival in Europe*, Cambridge.

Hvidtfeldt, J. (1949), 'Hjemmetyskheden in Sønderjylland og dens Oprindelse', in *Det Nordiske Historikermøtet på Lillehammer*, Beretning (Edvard Bull); Oslo.

Japsen, G. (1961), *Den nationale udvikling i Aabenraa 1800–1850* (The national Development in Aabenraa 1800–1850), Tønder.

Japsen, G. (1983), *Den fejlslagne germanisering* (The missing Germanisation), Tønder.

Jessen, F. (1973), 'Kirche im Grenzland', *Schriften der Heimatkundlichen Arbeitsgemeinschaft für Nordschleswig* 27.

Jørgensen, H. (1970), *Genforeningens statspolitiske baggrund* (The Political Background to the Reunion), Tønder.

Kardel, H. (1964), 'Fünf Jahrzehnte in Nordschleswig', *Schriften der Heimatkundlichen Arbeitsgemeinschaft für Nordschleswig* 10.

Klose, Olaf (1970ff), *Schleswig–Holsteinisches Biographisches Lexikon*.

Kölln, H.J. (1932), *Minderheitenschulrecht in Nord- und Südschleswig.*
Köster, A. (1921), Der Kampf um Schleswig, Berlin.
Kraack, G. (1979), 'Die Beziehungen zwischen dem Patriziat der Stadt Flensburg and dem Patriziat der vier nordschleswigschen Städte vor 1750', in *Regionale Mobilität in Schleswig–Holstein 1600–1900* (Studien zur Wirtschafts- und Sozialgeschichte Schleswig–Holsteins, vol. I.
Kragh, P. (1933), 'Das Deutschtum in Hadersleben von 1840–1850', *Zeitschrift der Gesellschaft für Schleswig–Holsteinische Geschichte* 61.
Lehmann, H.D. (1969), *Der Deutsche Ausschuss und die Abstimmungen in Schleswig 1920*, Neumünster.
Lenzing, H. (1973), *Die deutsche Volksgruppe in Dänemark und das nationalsoziatlistische Deutschland 1933–1939.*
Mackeprang, M. (ed.) (1983), *Tønder gennem Tiderne* (Tønder between Time), vol. 2, Tønder.
Molter, B. (1969), 'Der Friedensverein', *Schriften der Heimatkundlichen Arbeitsgemeinschaft für Nordschleswig. 19.*
Noack, J.P. (1975), *Det tyske mindretal i Nordslesvig under Besaettelsen* (The German Minority during Wartime Occupation), Copenhagen.
Nyholm, A. (1958), *Nationale og religiøse brydninger i Tønder på Sprogreskripternes Tid* (National and Religious Conflicts in Tønder in the Time of Language Regulations), Tønder.
Plesner, J. (1925), *Partidannelsen i de slevigske Provinsialstaender i Tiden mellem de to danske–tyske Krige* (The Genesis of Parties in the Provincial Estates between the two Danish–German wars), Sønderjyske Aarboger.
Rasch, M. (1956), 'Thies Hansen Steenholdt 1784–1856', *Zeitschrift der Gesellschaft für Schleswig–Holsteinische Geschichte* 80.
Ravn, S. (1971), *Laererne under Sprogreskripterne 1851–1864* (Teachers in the Time of Language Regulations), Flensburg.
Rerup, L. (1982), *Slesvig og Holsten efter 1830* (Schleswig and Holstein after 1830), Copenhagen.
Rohwedder, J. (1973), *Sprache und Nationalität. Nordschleswig und die Anfänge der dänischen Sprachpolitik in der 1. Hälfte des 19. Jahrhunderts*, Glückstadt.
Salomon, K. (1980), *Konflict i Graenselandet 1920–1933* (Conflict in the Borderland), Copenhagen.
Scharff, A. (1965), 'Beselers politische Wirksamkeit vor 1848', in *Schleswig–Holstein in der deutschen und nordeuropäischen Geschichte*, Neumünster.
Scharff, A. (1966), 'Die dänische Sprachpolitik in Mittelschleswig 1851–1864', *Zeitschrift der Gesellschaft für Schleswig–Holsteinische Geschichte* 91.
Scharff, A. (1975/80), *Schleswig–Holstein und die Auflösung des dänischen Gesamtstaates 1830–1864/67)*, in Klose, O. (ed.), Geschichte Schleswig–Holsteins, vol. 7, instalments 1/2, Neumünster.
Schmidt-Wodder, J. (1951), *Von Wodder nach Kopenhagen, Von Deutschland nach Europa*, Flensburg.
Schröder, E. (1929), *Die nordschleswigsche Sammlungsbewegung*, Rendsburg.
Skovgaard-Petersen, V. (1985), 'Tiden 1814–1864' (Time 1814–1864), in Christensen, A.E. et al. (ed.), *Danmarks historie*, vol. 5, Copenhagen.
Sønderjyllands Historie (1937), vol. 4.
Tägil, S. (1970), *Deutschland und die deutsche Minderheit in Nordschleswig 1933–1939*, Stockholm.
Tiedje, J. (1909), *Die Zustände in Nordschleswig*, Marburg.
Vaagt, G. (1966), 'Kriegsjahre und liberale Strömungen. Die Jahre der nationalen Auseinandersetzung', in Gesellschaft für Flensburger Stadtgeschichte (eds), *Flensburg, Geschichte einer Grenzstadt*, Flensburg.

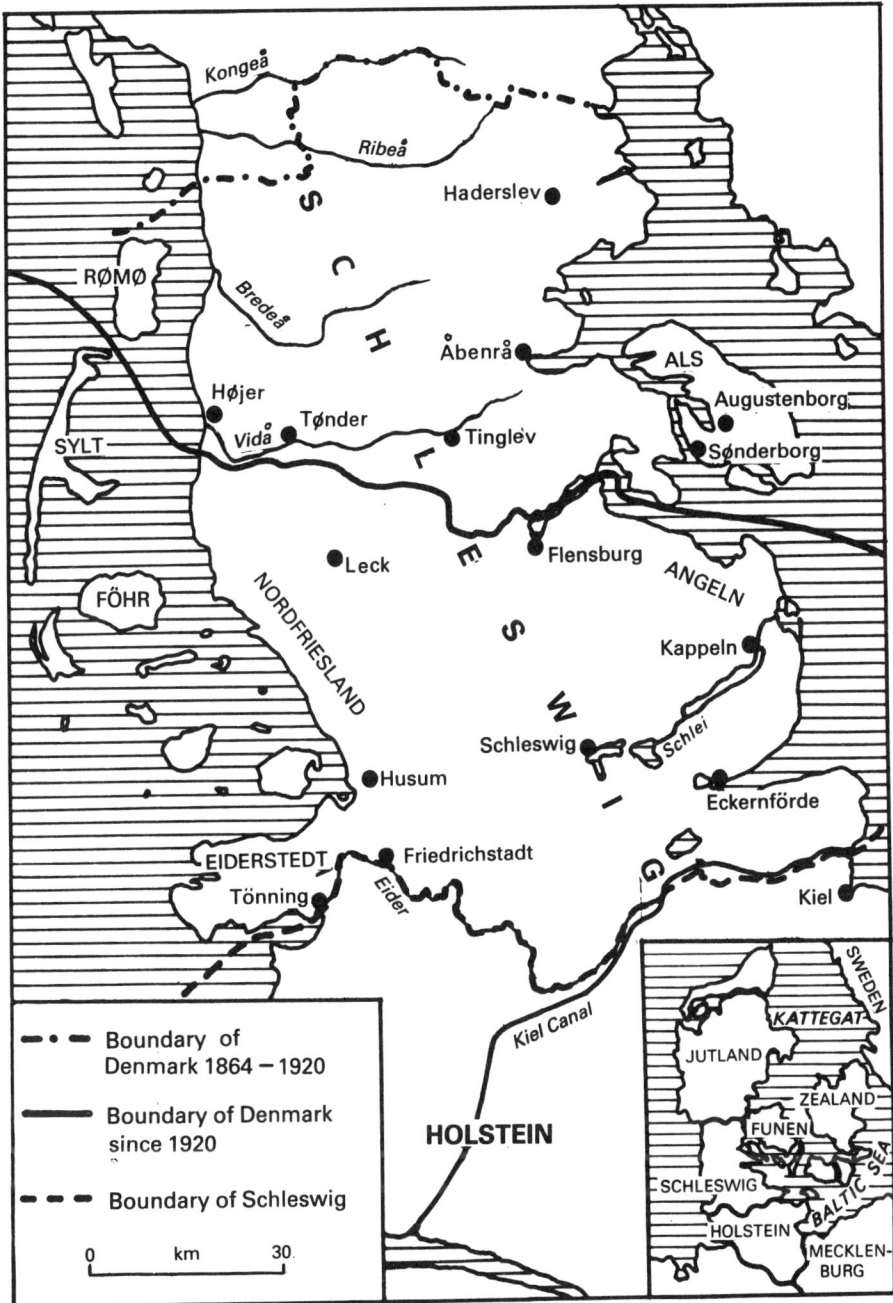

Map 8.1 Schleswig (1850–1939)
Source: Sarah Wambaugh, Plebiscites since the World War, vol. 1, Washington 1933, p. 47

9 The Danes in Schleswig from the National Awakening to 1933

LORENZ RERUP

Introduction

The duchy of Schleswig, called *Sønderjylland* in Danish, was part of the bi-national Danish *helstat*[1] but like the duchies of Holstein and Lauenburg it was subject to a special form of rule until 1864. A Danish speaking population existed only in the central and northern part of the duchy of Schleswig; in the other duchies the population spoke German exclusively. In 1840 Schleswig's population totalled 350 000, four fifths of whom lived in the countryside and half of whom spoke Danish in their daily life. It was there that a national Danish movement emerged towards the end of the 1830s.

Until 1864 the duchy of Schleswig was part of the Danish *helstat* which, apart from the old Atlantic dependencies and the overseas colonies, consisted of the kingdom of Denmark and the duchies of Schleswig, Holstein and Lauenburg. Lauenburg was only linked to Denmark from 1815 whereas the connection to Denmark of the other two duchies dated back to the Middle Ages and had become intricate due to a centuries old rivalry between branches of the royal dynasty. In 1773 the Danish king had managed to reassert a hold of all parts of the duchies although the formal status of Schleswig remained unclarified. Despite the fact that Danish kings were absolute rulers and the central administration of the duchies was in Copenhagen they retained a special status in the *helstat*. In some ways the duchies were governed jointly, in others separately. As parts of the old Holy Roman empire Holstein and Lauenburg were also after 1815 members of the new German Confederation though not Schleswig, however, which had been Danish from time immemorial.

As a member of the German Confederation Holstein had the right to constitutional provincial estates.[2] After considerable delay this constitutional system was granted in 1834. Simultaneously similar assemblies were called into being in Schleswig and in the kingdom of

Denmark in order to underline the unity of the state. These estates had only advisory functions but they intensified the process of formation of a public opinion. This could take place relatively freely although the publication of newspapers and periodicals was a special privilege requiring the submission of the individual editions as well as of smaller works and books to the police. The absolutist rule of the *helstat* was quite mild; nevertheless it remained suspicious of popular movements. In practice it was restricted by the legal system. Not until after 1846 when the Schleswig–Holstein movement called for the dissolution of the *helstat* when the male line of the Oldenburg dynasty had died out did the government tighten its rein.

The 1848 February revolution also shook up the *helstat* and led to a civil war from 1848 to 1850 resulting in a Prussian–German intervention which was halted by Russia and England in order to maintain the European balance of power. Both sides failed to achieve their war aims; neither the demand of Schleswig–Holstein for a separation of both duchies on the Kongeå/Königsau from Denmark nor the national liberal idea of dividing the *helstat* along the Eider and linking Schleswig closely to the kingdom materialised. In the reconstructed *helstat* the administrative and legal ties between Holstein and Schleswig were severed almost completely. As a result of foreign pressures and interests an open fusion between Denmark and Schleswig could not take place. In contrast to the liberal constitution in the kingdom from 1849 – a similar constitution also existed in Schleswig–Holstein between 1848 and 1851 – the estates in the duchies were reinstated. They acquired a certain limited right to make decisions. However in matters of common interest the absolute power of the Danish king was decisive since the elements of the *helstat* could not agree on a constitutional form for such matters. This being the case Schleswig was subject to rigid bureaucratic rule which in the so-called 'mixed language area' established Danish as the school and to a certain extent as the Church language. It was a policy which intended tying Schleswig as closely as possible to Denmark.

After the 1864 war the Danish king had to cede the duchies to Austria and Prussia, who initially administered them jointly and then, after 1866, separately. After the Austro–Prussian war Prussia annexed both Schleswig and Holstein and united them in one province. In the 1867 elections to the North German Confederation there was a Danish majority in the northern part of this province (that is, the area south of Flensburg/Flensborg but north of Tønder/Tondern and Højer/Hoyer). After the foundation of the German *Reich* the Danish Schleswigians were always able to send a representative to the German *Reichstag* (imperial parliament). Although the authorities exercised considerable pressure on them they managed to assert themselves as a minority in Prussia.

The Treaty of Versailles called for two votes in Schleswig in 1920, the first of which on 10 February led to a division of the province. The present border between Denmark and the Federal Republic of Germany was sanctioned by 74.2 per cent of the voters. The second vote on 14 March was a plebiscite restricted to the adjacent area directly south of the border. It was intended to give the individual communities – particularly the city of Flensburg – the opportunity to opt for union with Denmark. In this vote 80 per cent of the population decided to remain in Germany, in Flensburg it was 75.2 per cent. After this vote a Danish minority organised itself within the Weimar Republic. At its peak in 1923 it numbered 8000 members; in 1930 the figure was less than 4000. They could influence politics only on the local level.

The following article will deal with three different cases:

- the national movement of the Danish Schleswigians during the life of the *helstat*
- the Danish north Schleswigians as a minority in the German *Reich*
- the Danish south Schleswigians in the Weimar Republic.

General Conditions

Economically Schleswig was a predominantly agricultural area. Apart from numerous brickyards on the northern shore of the Flensburg fjord prior to 1933 only in Flensburg did independent industries develop. The kind of agriculture practised varied according to region. In the marshes on the west coast livestock was fattened, in the fertile hills on the east coast grain and fodder were cultivated – later sugar beet was also grown there – and in the northern part of the country in particular there was dairy farming. On the poor soil of the midlands grain and potatoes were grown and livestock was held before it was driven later into the marshes for fattening. Agriculture thrived between 1828 and the 1870s except for some bad harvests. Subsequently the results were inferior to earlier decades until the 1890s when there was a boom period which lasted until 1914 and led, especially in the western and eastern parts of the province, to prosperity. After the First World War agriculture in south Schleswig was destitute and except for a few years before 1927 Flensburg suffered from mass unemployment. Agriculture in the northern part of Schleswig also experienced difficult years after 1920 until it adapted to the Danish credit and market conditions. South of the new border south Schleswig and Flensburg (due to their remoteness) in particular were hit very hard by the economic problems of the Weimar Republic. This was the case also with the Danish minority who were primarily industrial workers.

Agriculture was carried on mostly on medium and large sized farms; substantial estates existed almost exclusively in south eastern Schleswig. In 1894 there were about 24 000 farms in north Schleswig, 47.5 per cent of which must be considered dependent, that is to say that they were smaller than five hectares and their owners could not subsist off them alone but had to work for others, at least in order to receive some help from the horses of the bigger farmers. Only 1.3 per cent of the farms were larger than 100 hectares, whereas 51.2 per cent ranged between five and 100 hectares and made up almost 83 per cent of the total agricultural acreage. It is necessary to distinguish between small farms (up to 20 hectares) and medium sized farms. The former represented 28 per cent of all farms and occupied 19.4 per cent of the land while the latter composed 23.2 per cent of holdings but covered 63.4 per cent of the land.[3] The relationship between these two categories of farms changed little before 1920. The farmers of northern and central Schleswig had been freed from villeinage as early as the turn of the sixteenth century. Originally they had the status of royal or ducal heritable long leaseholders or free peasants. Even before 1750 almost every north Schleswigian community had village schools. In rural areas general compulsory education was introduced in 1814.

Around 1830 there were three language groups in the Schleswig countryside: the German language group, originally located south of the Schleswig–Husum line but already crossing the Schlei/Slien by 1800; the Frisian language group on the islands in the tidal area and along the coast from Husum to Tønder; and the Danish language group which dominated the barren central area to the Schleswig–Husum line but which gave way to German in the course of only a few generations in the fertile Angeln. The language change in the southern part of Angeln was almost completed by 1850 though in the northern part it was still under way. These major language groups in the rural population spoke Low German and Danish dialects while the Frisians spoke various North Frisian vernaculars. In the cities of north Schleswig – apart from Flensburg and Tønder – the masses of the people spoke Danish while the upper classes in all cities spoke High German. Large sections of the population in Tønder and Flensburg spoke Low German as did the inhabitants of the other cities. The official use of the languages did not correspond to their geographic distribution. German was the legal and administrative language throughout the entire duchy. Not until 1840 was it replaced by Danish in those areas were it was the language of the Church and schools: in other words in the rural areas of today's north Schleswig. In the cities of north Schleswig German was generally used in the Church as well as in the municipal schools.

Demographic development in north Schleswig after 1864 was

characterised by mass emigration; at first in order to evade Prussian conscription and increasingly later because commercial life in the cities was stagnating and agriculture could not absorb the population surplus. From 1871 until 1910 the population of the cities of north Schleswig increased by only 44 per cent whereas that of Flensburg tripled and Kiel's increased tenfold. The population density throughout Schleswig–Holstein in 1914 was 90 inhabitants per square kilometre but in north Schleswig it was only 41. Between 1867 and 1910 60 000 north Schleswigians, mostly involved in agriculture, emigrated. The population of north Schleswig in 1871 totalled 154 256; but by 1910 it was only 166 603.

At the beginning of Prussian rule in 1867 the Danish north Schleswigians set their hopes on article 5 of the Peace of Prague of 1866. This article transferred the duchies from Austria to Prussia 'subject to the condition that if the population of the northern districts express their wish to be united with Denmark in a free vote, then they should be ceded to Denmark'. This clause in the peace treaty was included as a result of the interference of Napoleon III. Political support for it disappeared with the French defeat in 1870–1. Legally it was superceded in 1878 by an agreement between Austria and Prussia. Morally however article 5 continued to play an important role in Danish public opinion. The 1864 Peace of Vienna contained an option which gave the inhabitants of the ceded area the possibility over a period of six years to opt for Danish citizenship but on condition that the person concerned emigrated to Denmark. By 1868 those who opted for Denmark were permitted to return to reside in north Schleswig but as 'foreigners'. When war broke out again in 1870 there was a mass exodus of Schleswigians who were conscripted into the Prussian army. In 1872 a convention was agreed which also allowed these men to return to their home area. Since they were Danish citizens they could easily be deported and had no political rights. Children of Danish citizens born in Prussia were stateless until 1898 when a change in Denmark's law made those children born after that year citizens of the Danish kingdom.

After 1866 the old fashioned elements in the legal and administrative system of the duchies were adapted to the modern Prussian system. The new state was efficient and geared to acquiring the loyalty of the population in annexed territories. Compulsory schooling and military service as well as a strict application of the laws regarding the press and associations acted as effective means to this end. Later, in the 1890s, economic measures also were attempted. Compulsory military service was introduced immediately but prussianisation of the schools proceeded gradually. Private Danish schools could operate without interference until 1878 after which they disappeared. In the primary school six hours of German were compulsory weekly in 1871; from 1878 both languages were on equal footing and the language of instruction was emphatically Prussian. After 1888 Danish was restricted to six hours of religious instruction in the lower and four hours in the higher forms and teachers were urged to ensure that the children used German. These school decrees reflected, with some delay and in a somewhat milder version, Prussian school policy in the eastern provinces and have been interpreted as evidence of the gradual penetration of the Prussian administration by national ideas.[4] Danish associations and activities, including those of the Church, were deliberately harassed by local authorities; this applied to social democratic activity as well. The three class electoral system in the cities was devised in such a way as to limit the impact of Danish votes as far as possible.

It was a similar story in the *Kreistage* (district assemblies). The press often found itself faced with judicial proceedings. Economic measures implemented after 1891 included purchasing Danish farms and settling German farmers on them. This form of national struggle also was used from 1886 in Western Prussia and Poznań/Posen against the Poles.[5] Here it failed despite initial successes because Danish farmers refused to sell. As a result of German concerns about the foreign policy of Denmark between 1897–1901 harassment was intensified under Oberpräsident von Köller, the head of the provincial government, though it lessened again after 1902. As relations between Denmark and Germany improved there were some quiet years. The policy line hardened again in 1908–9 for local reasons. However it was possible to succeed in court against these encroachments or to have them evaluated by a higher authority. Danes won many such cases at High Court or at the *Reichsgericht* (Supreme Court) in Leipzig though that, of course, was expensive and time consuming.

During the Weimar Republic period – with the exception of the state of emergency 1923–24 – the laws usually granted the Danish minority virtually unlimited freedom. But the state of emergency was exploited to damage Danish newspapers written in German.[6] The activities of associations, clubs, libraries and churches did not meet with obstructions (except for the use of church buildings which was only organised in Flensburg). However until 1928 the Danish sections of the municipal schools had problems. These sections were important because the south Schleswig minority, which consisted largely of groups without any financial means, could not afford to construct private primary schools before 1926. Out of consideration for German minorities, especially in Poland, a 1928 Prussian school edict introduced the 'national consciousness' rule[7] which meant that children were admitted to Danish school sections if the parents wished so. During the first years after the vote many children were refused by the schools based on the results of language tests. After

1928 private schools also could be established outside of the voting area.

Formation of Elites in the Framework of the National Movement

The Period 1830–64

The Flensburger Christian Paulsen (1798–1854) came from a wealthy merchant family which was influenced profoundly by patriotism for the *helstat*.[8] During his studies at German universities he, like his fellow students, became enthusiastic about liberal and national ideas however he developed into a consciously Danish Schleswigian. He was professor of legal history at the University of Kiel from 1825. When in 1830 Uwe Jens Lornsen demanded the transformation of the *helstat* into a dual state in which the united duchies were to compose one half of the future union, Paulsen became angry over Lornsen's disregard of Schleswig's old legal status and the underestimation of Danish as the vernacular of the majority of the Schleswigians. In 1832 Paulsen presented his ideas in the booklet *Ueber Volksthümlichkeit und Staatsrecht des Herzogthums Schleswig* in which, among other things, he suggested reforms which would bring the status of Danish as a cultural language in line with its distribution as the vernacular. This increased status was necessary in order to enable higher education to have more influence on the people but also because language 'is a shrine of the peoples' and 'a people which totally forsakes the language of its forefathers for a strange language tears thereby its most inner thread of life'. Language – allegorised as a virgin enslaved in her own castle by foreigners – and the history of Schleswig soon became the ideological pillars of the Danish movement.

His booklet – as was typical of Phase A – was not even written in Danish and did not arouse much attention initially. However it led to cooperation with a colleague, the theologian Christian Flor (1792–1875) who was born in Copenhagen/København and who taught Danish at the University of Kiel. Flor was profoundly impressed by the thoughts of N.F.S. Grundtvig[9] and considered the language problem in Schleswig – that is the use of German as the legal and administrative language in Danish speaking north Schleswig – the suitable starting point for the 'awakening' of the people. The language dispute was intensified due to the strong tensions that existed between the farmers and the German speaking civil servants dating back to the pre-1828 agricultural crisis. In the 1835 elections to the Schleswig assembly the north Schleswig farmers voted only for their fellows and the election of the farmer Nis Lorenzen/Lilholt (1790–1860) was a clear demonstration of opposition to civil servants.

Paulsen sent this farmer his booklet, and a cooperation between them ensued.

In the first session of the assembly in 1836 Lorenzen demanded the introduction of Danish as the legal language in northern Schleswig, a plea which he supported with petitions carrying the signatures of many local people. Flor's ideas clearly influenced this motion. When the motion, again supported by numerous signatures, was once more presented during the second session of the assembly in 1838 and was passed by a narrow majority, the beginnings of a Danish movement in Schleswig could already be seen. Flor had succeeded in obtaining permission for a young north Schleswigian to publish a Danish weekly. Characteristically it was named *Dannevirke*.[10] Liberals in the kingdom also began to show interest in the language situation in Schleswig. Around 1840 the younger liberals became nationalistic and claimed the Eider as the border because Holstein's connection with the German Confederation may mean a delay in constitutional development as well as problems in foreign policy.[11]

In 1840 the king introduced the desired language reform and Danish became the legal and administrative language in the countryside in north Schleswig. At this point it met with the decided resistance from the Schleswig–Holstein party. For the king the reform was not a piece of national policy, it was the core of his *helstat* policy. By tying up Holstein with the half of Schleswig which was Danish speaking he hoped to link the former as tightly as possible to the kingdom. In the same year the Danish movement in Schleswig – which had grown in the meantime to include three small newspapers and many reading circles with books from Denmark – had gained a valuable supporter: Schleswig's leading liberal politician the merchant and Town Councillor P. Hiort Lorenzen (1791–1845) from Haderslev/Hadersleben. Frustrated by the increasing influence of conservative circles on the liberal movement in the duchies and a split in this movement he turned to the liberal movement in Denmark and, hesitatingly, also to the Danish movement though it was by no means liberal. For farmers liberalism was an urban elite movement. Their confidence in the king – who could help them if civil servants harassed them – was unswerving.[12]

In 1842 Flor persuaded Hiort Lorenzen to participate in the national demonstration in the estate assembly by speaking Danish although until then his political language had been German. When he started to speak in Danish he was forbidden to continue; the ensuing general commotion led to the first organisation of the Danish movement and thereby to Phase B. A group of parish leaders from the Haderslev area held a banquet for Hiort Lorenzen. At this banquet about 100 farmers agreed to meet again a few months later for a public festival at the Skamlingsbanke.[13] At the first Skamlingsbanke meeting on 18 May

1843 about 6000, mainly farmers, gathered. A few weeks later the farmers founded *Den slesvigske Forening* [The (Danish) Schleswigian Association]. This association was active until 1848 and then again after 1851 but only as a supporting organisation for the folk high school in Rødding (see below). The following table demonstrates the clear predominance of the farming element:

Table 9.1: New members of *Den slesvigske Forening*[14]

	1843	1844	1845	1846/7	TOTAL	%
Landowner	1	3	–	–	4	1.0
Traders	11	19	7	2	39	8.0
Craftsmen	4	24	12	2	42	9.0
Free professions	–	3	–	2	5	1.0
Officials	3	9	2	6	20	4.5
Clergy	2	3	–	2	7	1.5
Teachers	2	7	4	4	17	3.5
Students	–	17	2	1	20	4.0
Farmers	84	180	17	15	296	62.5
Poor peasants	1	13	6	5	25	5.0
Total	108	278	50	39	475	100.0

As the figures show membership of the association was modest, like the number of people who subscribed to Danish newspapers. The *Dannevirke* had a circulation of about 700, 200 of which were in the kingdom. Certainly these newspapers had more readers since they were circulated but the number of people in Schleswig speaking Danish was, after all, about 170 000.

With support from the kingdom the folk high school in Rødding was opened in 1844. It was the first folk high school of the Grundtvig type.[15] In the next year it became a boarding school with semi-annual instruction the aim of which – to put it in Flor's words – was to teach the student 'what was necessary to act as an independent and courageous man in a civic society'. Until 1847 87 per cent of the students were the sons of farmers. There were 522 students in the first 20 years. Of these 267 came from Schleswig, 118 from the neighbouring Jutlandic areas and the rest from other parts of Denmark. Of the Schleswigians 176 were the sons of farmers, with 25 being from larger farms. Smallholders' children were seldom involved. The age of the first students ranged from 16 to 27 years. Much larger sections of the population attended the Skamlingsbanke meetings, a mixture of speeches and popular festivities which were usually more plain than their German counterparts. In 1843 6000 people participated; in 1844 12 000; in 1845 9000; and in 1847 10 000.

The Danish movement was strongest in the coastal areas to the east and north of Haderslev and west north west of the city. Reading circles and libraries were numerous especially on the west coast between Tønder and Ribe/Ripen where lay movements were also active. A minor part of the Danish speaking population, particularly around Haderslev, decided in 1844 in favour of a development which ultimately gave them a German national consciousness. Although detailed studies do not exist it appears that the percentage of Danish speaking north Schleswigians who were not affected by the national movement but rather preferred to stick to their regional Schleswigism was quite high before the civil war. Even at the beginning of the war the essential question seems to have been loyalty to the king or to the 'rebels', a 'Schleswigian' or a 'Schleswig–Holsteiner'.[16]

The leadership of the Danish movement until 1848 – after it had been initiated by academics – was recruited almost entirely from common people. In the cities they were craftsmen, innkeepers and traders; in the countryside farmers. Flor, who had played a decisive role in initiating the movement, preferred to give advice and assistance discreetly. For example he wrote the speech of a young farmer at the first Skamlingsbanke meeting; though later this farmer was to compose his own addresses. A physician who edited a small Danish newspaper written in German in Flensburg and the well known local politician Hiort Lorenzen were rare exceptions. The managing committee which organised the first Skamlingsbanke meeting consisted of three farmers, a miller and a well-to-do farmer.[17] *Der Slesvigske Forening* was founded in 1843 by 25 farmers, all owners of sizeable holdings but not large farmers, and the first managing committee consisted of three farmers.[18] These farmers were often chairmen of their parish councils or had other important positions in a self-confident agrarian society which was thrusting towards prosperity. They had received their education from competent teachers (assisted by some clergymen) in the village schools and they were capable of participating in public life.

The changing fate of Schleswig during the war forced large sections of the population – including the city dwellers – to take a stand. National commitment could follow social lines – as for example in Haderslev and Aabenraa/Apenrade – or as in Flensburg could lead to a division into a Danish north and a German south of the city.[19] Generally the higher the social standing of a strata the greater the percentage of Schleswig–Holsteiner. Haderslev was however predominantly Danish and Tønder German. The war led undoubtedly to a clarification of the population's national commitment.

A new *Slesvigsk Forening* came into being in 1849 in Flensburg. Until 1851 it was led by Flensburg merchants who made up 80 per cent of the managing committee and – together with brokers and manufacturers – 23 per cent of the 392 Flensburg members. Craftsmen made up 47 per cent of the members and 13 per cent were shopkeepers. In the same year the *Forening* organised cooperation with social clubs in Aabenraa and Haderslev and also founded branches in rural areas. These branches had a total of 1414 members in 1851.[20] The *Slesvigsk Forening* considered itself the political organ of the loyal population of Schleswig, it used the dominant local language, it was anti-Schleswig–Holstein, strove for a customs border between Schleswig and Holstein and, in the longer term, wanted a free provincial constitution for Schleswig with strong links to Denmark.

The network began to disintegrate after the war and lost all importance upon the reestablishment of the *helstat*. Development of Danish initiative in the following years was left to the national liberal and conservative civil servants. The language dispute had lost its virulence for the time being. Meetings on the Skamlingsbanke were resumed in 1851 but there too civil servants and especially clergymen, dominated. Speakers at the 1851 meeting included one *Amtmand* (prefect), four clergymen, one parish clerk and one secondary school teacher. It was decided to hold meetings every three years and in 1859 they were discontinued altogether. Civil servants dominated even in the folk high school in Rødding. During the period 1850–2 14 per cent of the students were the sons of clergymen.[21] One of the prominent Danish leaders of the 1840s who had been a farmer became a civil servant and two of the most important editors moved to Denmark. The political life which could take place within the framework of the reinstated estate constitution was too meagre to inspire the population. It was only in western Schleswig[22] and around Rødding that there were local popular meetings and clubs, inspired by Grundtvig circles, which also criticised the Danish language policy in south Schleswig.[23]

Economic activity in this part of the country benefited the producers in these years. Livestock prices doubled between 1846 and 1866. During the years 1850–66 deposit holdings in north Schleswig savings banks quadrupled. After 1846 there were many agricultural associations and the seventh Danish Agricultural Meeting held in Haderslev in 1859 was attended by thousands of people, including many from the kingdom. From 1851/2–64 in the reestablished *helstat* the movement was stunted paradoxically by the Danish civil servants. Most likely the movement in the Danish speaking areas was consolidated and carried into others areas by the schools and the economic upswing but the state bureaucracy was by no means pleased with independent popular leaders.

The Period 1864–1920

The defeat of 1864, which led to the cession of Schleswig to Austria and Prussia and the withdrawal or expulsion of many civil servants numbed the people, who had had no need to develop political or national organisations in the preceding period. Furthermore dual Austro–Prussian rule was clearly provisional. Of particular importance in this respect was the *north Schleswig clause* in article 5 of the Peace of Prague which led people to expect an early end to Prussian rule. Immediately after the annexation clergymen, teachers and civil servants who remained in the country had to swear an oath of loyalty to the Prussian king, which many refused to do. At least 27 clergymen and approximately 100 teachers were dismissed without pensions and replaced by Germans. Those who swore the oath were avoided by the population and treated like traitors. Prussian military service met with the same reaction. Young people preferred to leave the country. When older age groups were called up to military exercises or merely were supposed to take an oath of loyalty in order to be registered as reserve soldiers they fled their homes and farms. In 1867 this number was between 5000 to 8000 men.[24]

As a result of this *protest policy* Danish politicians elected to the Prussian parliament refused until 1882 to take an oath to the constitution. New elections had to be held which led to the same form of protest. The protest was a reaction to the provisional nature of north Schleswig under the terms of article 5 and in such circumstances extensive organisational activity was limited. Nor was the population accustomed to elections. Only a little over two per cent had been entitled to vote for the provincial estates. For many years a loose network of men in the urban and rural areas would agree on the nomination of candidates – which was nearly always settled in advance because of re-election – and would pay their expenses. For the August 1867 elections 100 men from all parts of north Schleswig met to discuss participation in the election. Similar and even larger meetings were often convened but they were *ad hoc* gatherings in emergency situations. The short distances in the country facilitated this practice. It is also true that the protest policy made any discussion of tactics superfluous. All in all, the divisions were evident.[25] Attempts were made several times during the 1870s to found political organisations but they failed repeatedly. There also seemed to be no need to spread propaganda for the Danish cause. Three Danish newspapers had a total circulation in 1872 of approximately 3000.[26]

Not until the end of the 1880s was there a transition to Phase C. An imminent reunion with Denmark could not be expected after article 5 was nullified in 1878, and in Denmark as well as in the German *Reich* profound social changes were taking place. Emigration from Schleswig ensured that the population decreased. The number and percentage of Danish votes too was dwindling until 1887.[27] It became increasingly clear that a new generation in the political leadership would lead to a fresh policy which would take the long view, would gather the north Schleswigians in an organisation and would attempt to ease their lot, if necessary in an alliance with progressive German parties. Also the young north Schleswigians had to be persuaded to perform military service in the Prussian army in order to remain in the country. After the expiration of the 1864 option in 1870 the only alternative was emigration.

Initial Prussian intervention on the language of instruction in schools was followed by the foundation in 1880 of the *Association for the Preservation of the Danish Language in North Schleswig* which set up public libraries. By 1881 80 had been founded; in 1914 there were 172 plus 26 branch libraries. These distributed books, among others a history of Denmark, and a special song book. There was much singing at Danish social events – at the beginning and the end, before and following speeches. As in church music the national songs contained ideological elements; praise of the mother tongue and history, trust in justice, resistance to Prussia and similar emotions. Many of these songs became prohibited but the people already knew them by heart. The association functioned through members' subscriptions and won support from private persons in the kingdom such as the large brewer J.C. Jacobsen (1811–87) who helped to publish the history written by A.D. Jørgensen. This association had been founded and was led by the older elite, respected city people and their contacts in rural areas. The first managing committee consisted of a tobacco manufacturer, a teacher, a lawyer and a physician, all coming from various cities, as well as a landowner and two farmers; also from different areas. The association had 676 paying members in 1883; 1024 in 1893, 2532 in 1903 and 6173 in 1913.[28]

The *Voters' Union for North Schleswig* was founded in 1888 and quickly developed into the leading political organisation in Schleswig. Its originator, H.P. Hanssen (1862–1936), was the son of a large farmer. He studied in Leipzig, Copenhagen and Berlin after attending the folk high school in Askov in Denmark, all in order to prepare himself for political activity in his homeland. For instance in Leipzig he learned how the social democratic party there prepared for the 1887 election. In 1888 he returned to north Schleswig.

Every north Schleswigian entitled to vote could become a member of the Voters' Union on recommendation by a local agent. At first it was difficult for the Union to gain a foothold in western Schleswig where the impetus for organisation was lacking. The protest policy had lived on longest there. Membership figures for the Union were 1595 in 1888; 3034 in 1898; 5451 in 1908; and 8214 in 1913, which was 16.6 per cent of Danish voters in 1890. Not until after 1905, during the second large organisational wave, did this percentage increase decisively – in 1912 the Union contained 41.5 per cent of Danish voters.

The leadership of the Union had a management committee of 21 members who were elected to represent the various parts of north Schleswig. Eleven farmers and one landowner sat on the original committee, and of these 12 members five were also chairmen of savings banks, three of agricultural associations and seven were members of the *Kreistage*. Many were also active in church (including Free Church) affairs and at least seven had been students at the folk high school in Rødding before 1864. The chairman was a butcher, the treasurer an editor and the omnipresent secretary was H.P. Hanssen. By 1891 the Voters' Union had 494 agents all over north Schleswig who collected subscriptions and recruited new members. A closer study of a random sample of 102 agents during the years 1889 and 1903 shows the following occupational distribution: 79 farmers, four country dwellers and small farmers, three craftsmen, five retired farmers and rentiers while 11 had 'other' or unspecified employments.[29]

The *North Schleswig School Association*, founded in 1892, was a reaction to the Prussian school regulation of 1888. Its purpose was to enable young north Schleswigians to study at continuation schools, agricultural courses and folk high schools in the kingdom when they had passed the age when they had to attend the Prussian schools. This had been taking place even without an organised campaign. Before 1892 about 600 young people had attended continuation schools; 322 agricultural courses and 1400 folk high schools in Denmark. The School Association expanded these figures however and opened up opportunities to people of very modest means. It was supported by a gradual change in the political attitude of the farmers of north Schleswig who until then had been traditionally conservative whereas the respective schools were dominated by the liberal farmers in Denmark. The School Association accomplished its task with great skill. By 1910, 3707 (1921) north Schleswigians had attended continuation schools; 739 (209) agricultural courses; and 3322 (1981) folk high schools (the figures in parentheses are the number of students supported by the School Association). By 1914 the total number of students supported by the Association had risen to 6182.[30]

The School Association was funded by way of membership subscriptions and donations, particularly from the kingdom. In addition the students supported by the association paid only a reduced fee at these schools, which were always boarding schools. In 1894 the association had 4002 members; in 1901–6 a few hundred less which after 1907 increased again and in 1914 totalled 10 853. The association was strongest in western north Schleswig and members of the management committee also mainly came from western Schleswig farmers. The association worked with agents (371 in 1894) and a random sample shows that around 1895, 33 out of 45 agents were farmers, four were small farmers, only two craftsmen.[31]

All of the large organisations covering the whole of north Schleswig were founded after 1880 and smaller organisations also came into being then. The lecture clubs have been mentioned already. When Danish social events could no longer take place in public facilities, clubs and local groups constructed so-called *meeting houses*. The first one was completed in 1892 and there were 48 in 1914. After 1906–8 many local clubs, especially youth organisations (in 1913 there were 17 with 2700 members) and sport associations were founded – the latter created a federation in 1903. In 1913 it had 70 sections with 1200 athletes. Also between 1882 and 1912 the number of subscribers to Danish newspapers rose from 3500 to 19 278 (in 1902 there were 10 807).[32] Several agricultural associations belonged to this national network of organisations. For example after 1884 the specifically Danish system of dairy cooperatives spread throughout north Schleswig (in 1914 there were 126 such dairy cooperatives).

The random survey by Hans Schultz Hansen mentioned above offers interesting information about the social base of the large national organisations. Whereas 20 per cent of those with the vote were farmers in the area selected, 46 per cent of the members of the Voters' Union; 60 per cent of the Language Association; and 50 per cent of the School Association came from that group. Other independent agriculturalists made up a further 22 per cent of voters, and 23 per cent of the Voters' Union, 8 per cent of the Language Association; and 20 per cent of the School Association. Craftsmen, traders and innkeepers were present in numbers proportionate to their percentage among voters.[33] Schultz Hansen shows also that many of the agents, who were simultaneously farmers, were members of several organisations. Out of 109 of these agents 41 had managing positions in various associations: 17 in dairy cooperatives, 13 in savings banks and 15 in agricultural organisations. Eleven had such positions in two or three organisations.[34]

In a society where activists were denied state employment news-papers provided both a source of income and a platform. The press was privately owned. Jens Jessen (1854–1906) who was a member of the German *Reichstag* from 1902–6, and H.P. Hanssen, a member of the *Reichstag* from 1906–19, two rivals in the Danish movement, both owned and edited newspapers which acted as mouthpieces for their respective views. Jessen's predecessor in the *Reichstag* was also his predecessor as owner of the *Flensborg Avis*. The editor of the third largest newspaper was secretary to the first Danish member of the *Reichstag*. The editorial boards of these newspapers were not large but the few members often helped in other organisational fields. For instance one journalist was assistant secretary in the Voters' Union and later also treasurer and director in the School Association. Another abandoned journalism and went into the insurance business but at the same time became secretary and librarian in the Language Association. Some journalists had studied to become teachers – for example Jens Jessen, who was rejected by the school authorities – or had pursued general studies.

Apart from the journalists the farmers, after becoming thoroughly organised, were the key figures in the Danish movement. They were the group that took the initiative whereas during the first two decades of Prussian rule respected city people and their contacts in the countryside were usually the promoters. Only farmers had the necessary independence; within certain limits they could afford to participate in unpaid national activities without official reprisals. A highly developed agricultural system in north Schleswig had schooled them to recognise interrelationships and to plan for the long term. Apart from their practical experience they had opportunities for training in the kingdom. Many prominent figures were the leaders of the farmers in their area. The preponderance of medium sized farms gave them a firm base in a rural society which could certainly assert itself compared to the stagnating cities. Scarcely any professionals from north Schleswig were involved in national work.

The Period 1920–33

Most of the pro-Danish German speaking citizens of Flensburg who had made up the majority of the city in 1867 had either emigrated, died or been assimilated as a result of the strong economic upswing during the *Kaiserreich* (imperial Germany, 1871–1918). Until the mid 1880s the number of Danish votes remained constant, it then decreased swiftly and during the 1912 election to the *Reichstag* it made up only 3.9 per cent of the total, in absolute figures 455. By comparison the figure in 1871 was 48.4 per cent. In the countryside signs of the Danish way of life in central Schleswig virtually had disappeared although the Danish language was still prevalent in some places near the new border. South of today's border the older organisations had little support but there were a few Danish social clubs. Among the immigrants to Flensburg during the *Kaiserreich* there had been many Danish speaking north Schleswigians, who had joined the labour force especially at the flourishing shipyard. After 1886 these workers gave their allegiance to the German social democrats. Just before the First World War there were a few attempts at organisation. In 1908 the *Lecture Association* was founded which had 30 agents and approximately 1000 members by 1914, mostly ordinary folk.[35] In 1912 two journalists founded a Danish youth association. The most important Danish stronghold in Flensburg was the *Flensborg Avis*, founded in 1868, which Jens Jessen had developed into a newspaper with more subscribers than all other Danish newspapers in north Schleswig combined (9000 in 1906).[36] Its distribution area, however, lay in north and even more in west Schleswig and the conservative tone of the paper was uncongenial to Flensburger workers.

The plebiscites in 1920 resulted in a Danish minority south of the new border with its centre in Flensburg and its hinterland. Small groups were spread over the south Schleswig area. Nowhere did this minority have a local majority or a dominant position. The plebiscites had mobilised them and they were a minority which was different in many ways from the north Schleswigians of the previous era. They mainly were an urban minority usually residing in working class neighbourhoods, the majority being modest people, employees, shopkeepers, craftsmen and workers. Also they did not form a linguistic minority even if Danish was the language used in the clubs and many spoke Danish at home. Some people made a conscious decision to do so but in reality, however, there were no overt ethnic characteristics which distinguished the Danes from the Germans of Schleswig. What was different was an inner attitude, a mentality which manifested itself through participation in Danish activities, for example in the associations and the schools. The agents of this mentality defined minority who acted as its organisers on local level reflected its social composition. However the leadership of the minority lay almost entirely in the hands of independent business-men, liberal professionals, journalists, white collar employees (not uncommonly with Danish organisations) and – in the countryside – some farmers.[37] This group had a bourgeois background providing the leaders, who had adequate resources to assume leading functions, spoke both languages and were socially and ideologically close to the private groups in Denmark that were involved in national work south of the new border. The membership of the main organisation in 1921 totalled about 6000, in 1932 the figure was 4700 and the peak was reached in 1923 with nearly 8900. In elections several Danish candidates who had only local chances of being successful received about 4700 votes, for example for the Municipal Council of Flensburg where they generally cooperated with the social democrats. In the last extra-local election after 1930 the Flensburg branch of the *Slesvigsk Forening* did not participate because its working class members preferred to vote for social democrats.[38]

The *Slesvigsk Forening*, originally founded in June 1920 for Flens-burg and surroundings, had already arranged a section by September 1920 for the rural areas which later became more structured. In 1923 a special Frisian–Slesvigian Association was formed which en-compassed some of the north Frisians and which worked with

Danish associations during elections and for their newspapers published in German. The Flensburg branch remained the largest association with about 80 per cent of the members of the minority. It was divided into 22 districts to correspond with the voting constituencies of the city. The leading and deputy chairmen of these districts constituted the head committee of the larger association. This head committee in turn elected a managing body.

The association nominated the Danish candidates and prepared for the elections. It held a meeting annually for all pro-Danish south Schleswigians, organised cultural activities and cultivated contact with Denmark. Some other associations had special tasks: library work, care of the sick and aged, youth, women's and church organisations. The most important of these was the *Danish School Association* in Flensburg, which was founded prior to *Slesvigsk Forening* in order to organise the parents of Danish children and to negotiate with the authorities in education matters. With the help of private contributions and subsidies from the state of Denmark it first ran a secondary school and then – when the Prussian authorities allowed it in 1926 – five small private schools in the rural area around Flensburg. Similar to the North Schleswig School Association it too arranged for young south Schleswigians to visit industrial schools and folk high schools in Denmark (from 1920–33 it helped 1559 students).[39]

A granting of government funds for the cultural work of the Danish minority in south Schleswig was a new experience for the Denmark parliament and was approved only after difficult negotiations between the parties. It was assumed that the use of the funds would be supervised by a state committee which all parties could trust.[40] For instance the private Danish school established in the city of Schleswig/Slesvig in 1930 was supported by the *Grænseforeningen* (Danish Border Association) not by this committee. The same applied to the *Danish General Office* in Flensburg, an institution which was established in 1924 in order to coordinate the work of the many associations and institutions but did not apply to the activities of the School Association.

Danish minority organisations did not have irredentist goals although some of its leaders and also private groups in Denmark had the secret hope that one day Schleswig and Denmark would be unified. For such people the Schleswigians were basically Danes with an unfortunate fate. They were superficially germanised by centuries of German schemes helped by a thoughtless Danish policy. This process should be reversible. Such thoughts were neither official nor covertly practiced policy. The practical work of the organisations consisted of uniting the Danes of south Schleswig through schools, cultural activities and strong contacts to Denmark and strengthening their solidarity. Any other policy would have met with strong official disapproval from the Danish government.

The education question with its diverse obstacles to Danish children and private schools was partly resolved in 1926 and then completely solved with the Prussian regulation of 31 December 1928. Since the foreign policy of the *Reich* showed consideration for its own minorities in other countries it recognised through this regulation the principle of national consciousness in Schleswig. The declaration recognised that membership of a minority could no longer be contested or obstructed. Previously the children had been selected on the basis of language tests and after 1926 parents of children in private schools were supposed to come either from the second zone or from Denmark. German nationalist activists exercised some pressure on the members of the minority locally and privately but the Danish organisations and institutions could assert themselves and were not subject to legal restrictions. Towards the end of the 1920s conditions north of the border helped to stabilse the minority. On the one hand the German minority in Denmark was treated liberally, on the other north Schleswig itself was obviously undergoing economic and general development. The world depression did not hit Denmark until 1931 while Germany already was engulfed by the depression in the winter of 1929. In Flensburg the number of unemployed rose. This was a special burden for a minority whose members were highly dependent on industrial work. In the winter of 1932–3 80 per cent of the parents of Danish school children were without jobs.[41]

Danish minority organisations in south Schleswig neither wanted nor were able to alter the border and they refused to advocate a policy which would have meant a change in their social and political conditions. In principle the *Slesvigsk Forening* was apolitical. Its only task was a cultural one; it sought to strengthen the Danish language and culture in south Schleswig. This limitation facilitated division into an upper bourgeois national elite and a broad local leadership more attuned to the minority. Within the minority there was a kind of truce which disapproved of faction and the formation of wings. Under no circumstances should the public learn of dissension. At the same time this internal policy depended on a restricted programme: to live in as Danish a fashion as possible.

Members reconciled themselves to this situation with very little protest[42] although the election rules of the associations would have permitted a more aggressive stance. The national leadership was not closed, it recruited new members from – for instance – the teachers and officials of the minority who returned after receiving training in Denmark. The seizure of power by the National Socialists in 1933 entailed serious changes to the situation of the minority. It could continue to exist but individual members were subject to persecution and social pressure. Open membership shrank dramatically. Only after the collapse of the *Reich* in 1945 did the minority find itself as a core of a very strong regional movement which sought the reunion of south Schleswig and Denmark.[43]

Elite Formation in Different Periods

Looking back on a century of Danish movements or minorities it is plain that the formation of elites has taken place in different ways. In the *helstat* period two cases can be distinguished, the first one during the national awakening, the second in the repressive years after the civil war of 1848–50. Clearly the activists of the Danish movement before 1848 were groups of almost the same social composition as the middle class people who participated in the movement. Although two university men initiated it and played a part in bringing interested people together by supplying them with contacts, arguments and ideas, the farmers very soon took the movement in their own hands. Also in towns craftsmen, innkeepers and traders could alone promote the movement. In the population the level of education was high enough to make an elite of common people possible.

It was important that the movement was nourished by a widespread frustration resulting from the vernacular's position in relation to the administrative and judicial system. In a time of prosperity, especially in the agricultural sector, a growing middle class self-confidence sharpened this feeling. Before 1848 the highest authorities in the *helstat* did not counteract the movement. Its real antagonist was the Schleswig–Holstein movement competing with the Danes in attempts to mobilise the population.

After the civil war the government did not favour either the Schleswig–Holstein or the Danish movements but it had no reason to persecute Danish leaders. While Danish attitudes and linguistic positions were consolidated the national movement itself languished because public servants took the lead displacing the farmers and craftsmen of the earlier movement. In addition the original claims of the movement had been granted by the creation of a Danish civil service in the region.

As a result of this policy the Danes in north Schleswig had to rebuild a leadership after 1864. It had to consist of independent people who would not be affected by measures of the Prussian authorities. Again two cases can be selected. During the first two decades the protest policy prevailed. Waiting for a carrying out of the clause in article 5, the north Schleswig Danes were contented with a leadership by notables, a loose group of influential men in the cities and the country. Its chief goal was to maintain the protest against the Prussian annexation rather than to mobilise the Danish speaking population.

Mobilisation became the most important option, when emigration plus assimilation resulted in a loss of Danish votes and the Prussian authorities, especially the school authorities, tightened their hold on the remaining Danish north Schleswigians. The Danish leadership had to widen its functions and it became clear that the national struggle would run for a very long time. Leaders had to negotiate for improvement of the situation, while organising and mobilising the population to maintain its Danish culture. Agriculture was the leading – and most prospering – branch of the region's economy and farmers constituted the core of the Danish movement. They had a sophisticated agricultural organisational structure. It came naturally to these well qualified men to take on the leadership of the movement in conjunction with some journalists and editors who could articulate the Danish case in public. The new leaders were activists in many Danish organisations and often local leaders in the country too.

When the plebiscite border was drawn in 1920 the Danes of south Schleswig faced a quite new situation. Earlier they had been little organised but the agitation before the plebiscite created conditions for their mobilisation. The ordinary members were not as independent as the farmers of north Schleswig had been. Some even had difficulties in speaking Danish properly and many did not use it in everyday life. This minority developed a dual leadership, one corresponding to the social composition of the minority and in close contact with the members, the other – composed of upper middle class and professional men – who took the lead in organisations and represented the 'foreign policy' of the minority in the overwhelming German environment and in the vital relations with Denmark. In the new climate for national minorities after the First World War the private and official resources of Denmark were indispensable for the Danes of south Schleswig. In this respect the modest means of the members were crucial too. As in the previous cases the functions of the elite and the corresponding qualifications of the people chosen were an important precondition for its formation.

The Governments and the Danish National Minorities

The absolutist government of the bi-national *helstat* could not be cordial to national movements but it also was not hostile. Christian VIII liked to demonstrate paternal feelings for peasants, both German and Danish, in his realm. On the other side but only latterly the loyalty of the peasants to the king was shaken. The Schleswig–

Holstein movement was suppressed after it came out in strong opposition to the Open Letter of 8 July 1846 about succession to the throne which destroyed its hopes for a dynastic dissolution of the *helstat*. The Danish movement also angered the king when it took a stand against him in 1844. In that year, prompted by Hiort Lorenzen's verbal demonstration in 1842, Christian VIII decided that Danish could be spoken in the Schleswigian assembly only by those who did not have adequate command of German. Taking the king's decision as a pro-German step the movement responded by attacking the king openly. Christian VIII had the association suppressed and prosecuted the managing committee. After six months he decided to temper justice with mercy but added the threat that the slightest backsliding would cause the association to be closed permanently. In his dynastic way of thinking the national movements were useful. If a Danish movement in Schleswig made a separation of Denmark and Schleswig impossible then the Schleswig–Holstein movement, which demanded a stronger union of both duchies, would not be able to separate itself from Denmark.[44]

Both conservative and liberal governments in the reestablished *helstat* were guarded about the national movements which had shown their explosive potential in March 1848. The government policy until the 1860s consisted of holding the *helstat* together which meant not tolerating any such movement. Official language policy in central Schleswig was nationally motivated but this was to be accomplished by civil servants sent by the government not by a movement from below. The earlier elite became absorbed or passive and a few emigrated to Denmark.

For a surprisingly long time Prussian policy towards the Danes in north Schleswig was very hesitant on national questions. This can only be explained partly in view of the terms of article 5. After 1866 Bismarck envisaged at the most the loss of an area north of Aabenraa and after the foundation of the *Reich* the cession of territory ceased to be considered at all. Prussians were in no hurry since the Danes continued to weaken themselves numerically by their protest policy. The school regulations of 1871 already had been considered in 1867 and did not aim to displace the mother tongue of the population. First its extension in 1878 sought to encroach upon the Danish language and in 1888 the schools became a danger for the language of the people.[45] Other official measures consisted of banning assemblies, lectures and demonstrations, and of using judicial power against the press. The editor of *Flensborg Avis*, Jens Jessen, spent a total of 43 months in Prussian fortresses and prisons. Often he was convicted for *lèse majesté*. Suspect school teachers and minor officials risked transfer from the region. When von Köller was head of the provincial bureaucracy he tried to punish parishes collectively by deporting all

Danish subjects, for example because one inhabitant had sent his sons to school in Denmark and could not be reprimanded directly.[46] This period marked the climax of Prussian repression.

Danes were able to face these and other attacks on their nationality effectively by avoiding open confrontation and instead organised themselves, resorted to lawsuits and sometimes used humour to provoke the local police force. Of course the elite could not be joined by optants (those exercising their rights under the 1864 option) and people in professions who needed a license or authorisation to pursue their jobs. Journalists, speakers and committee members had to be very cautious. In the towns economic dependence probably had a limiting effect too. However it was only during von Köller's period of office that membership in the Danish associations declined, rising again quickly after the repression was relaxed. After 1891 Prussian authorities tried to buy Danish farms and to attract German settlers to the area. The latter attempt was successful only on domains, Danish north Schleswigians who owned farms would not sell to Germans once they realised that this was a new attack on the national movement.[47]

In the course of time the Danish movement lost ground in the cities, especially in Flensburg. Flensburg was the only industrialised city of the region and the workers became social democrats. In the north Schleswig towns on the Baltic Sea Danish votes did not decrease but unlike the German electorate they did not rise either.

The attitude of the Prussian authorities was influenced repeatedly by German foreign interests. This was particularly the case after 1890 when a realignment of the European powers began. The Kiel canal, opened in 1895, as well as the build up of a German fleet after 1898 heightened Denmark's strategic importance. Moreover Wilhelm II personally distrusted the Danish royal family because daughters of Christian IX were married to Alexander III of Russia and Edward VII of England. North Schleswigians could be used to put Denmark under pressure (as during von Köller's period of office) or to reward it (as with the 1907 treaty dealing with the children of optants).[48] In general it was Prussian policy to make loyal German speaking citizens of the Danes in north Schleswig.

During the Weimar Republic the status of the Danish south Schleswigians was not clarified until the mid 1920s. Both the after-effects of the embittered plebiscite in the second zone and the economic and political difficulties of the new republic delayed the process. Compared to pre-war conditions in imperial Germany the republic's official minority climate was quite different. Minorities had a right to exist and the republic did not intend to fight or absorb them. Locally the rights granted to the minority were less conspicuous. Social and economic pressure in particular was used to limit the minority. This did not affect the elite established in 1920 which consisted of well known people of independent standing and was not replaced in the short years of the republic. As in the previous period the young generation went to Denmark for supplementary education.

For the Weimar Republic the Danish minority was a very small issue but it had to be seen in context of the enormous problems of German minorities particularly in eastern Europe. Conditions in north Schleswig, where the German minority enjoyed a very generous treatment, also played a role. Prussia also had to keep in mind the great problems in its eastern territories. These consider-ations made possible the school decrees of 1926 and 1928 which brought about a substantial improvement in the status of the minority by recognising the principle of national consciousness.[49]

State of Research

The history of the southern Danish border since the days of the Vikings and the development of national conflicts in Schleswig which led to civil war (1848–50) and lastly to the dissolution of the Danish *helstat* have been a major theme of Danish historiography. Older works are marked by national feelings; their intention was not only to meet high scholarly standards, but also to influence the historical view of Danish public opinion. This holds true for many older studies as for example in the work of the Danish historian A.D. Jørgensen (1840–97) who wrote when Schleswig was a part of Prussia. But other times – as in the 1930s or as a consequence of the German occupation of Denmark 1940–5 – also induced historians to defend the Danish stand. Also the general Danish historiography had many reasons to deal with problems of Schleswig. Danish historians have invested a considerable amount of labour on legal and political topics and on themes related to language, folklore, education, church and foreign policy. In addition a comprehensive well researched local historical literature offers much valuable information about the Danish movement. The *Dansk Historisk Bibliografi* (Danish Historical Biblio-graphies) for the periods 1832–1912, 1913–42, 1943–7 contain sections on Schleswig's history which are comprehensive and classified by subject. Biographies of the leading Danes in Schleswig and many of their national opponents have appeared in the three editions of the *Dansk Biografisk Leksikon* (volumes 1–19 edited 1887–1905; volumes 1–27 edited 1933–44; and volumes 1–16 edited 1979–84).

In the many articles and books on the history of Schleswig, much knowledge about the elites of the national movements can be found. The formation and activities of these elites, however, has only recently been treated in more detail. G. Japsen, H. Fangel, A. Pontoppidan Thyssen, J. Wille and M. Hroch have studied social, economic and intellectual factors in the development of the Danish movement during the life of the *helstat*, that is the first of the three cases. Their works are mentioned in the notes and in the Select Bibliography at the end of this chapter. The book of H. Schultz Hansen about agriculture in north Schleswig and the Danish movement is particularly informative in this respect. It treats the second case the Danish north Schleswigians as a minority in the German *Reich*. The introductory chapter of Carsten R. Mogensen's book on the Danish minority in the Nazi *Reich* furnishes information about the conditions of the Danish minority in the Weimar Republic including information on the social composition of the minority and its leaders. J.P. Noack analyses this subject comprehensively in his dissertation on the Danish minority in south Schleswig 1920–45. Other research during the last 25 years makes it possible to catch a glimpse of the various Danish elites in the region of Schleswig, especially of their social composition and at the top level.

Much work still remains to be done. Material for the period considered is rich due partly to the authorities' keen interest in the national movements. The sources are concentrated in well organised archives in the towns of the region and especially in the *Schleswig–Holsteinisches Landesarchiv* in Schleswig, in the *Landsarkivet for de sønderjyske landsdele* in Aabenraa, and in the *Rigsarkivet* in Copenhagen. Many individual sources and editions of documents have been published and are available in the *Schleswig–Holsteinische Landesbibliothek* in Kiel, and in *Det kongelige bibliotek* in Copenhagen.

Notes

1 Name given to Denmark, the duchies and colonial possessions overseas; in German *Gesamtstaat*.
2 This problem did not exist in Lauenburg because it had an antiquated constitutional system of estates which remained in force.
3 Schultz Hansen, pp. 18 ff.
4 See Hauser.
5 Japsen (1980), pp. 57 ff.
6 Mogensen (1981a), pp. 125–60.
7 See Broszat.
8 See Runge.
9 Thaning.
10 Name of the old fortification line west of the town of Schleswig, established by Danish kings in the early Middle Ages, but still fit for use in 1864.
11 Rerup (1982), pp. 49–54 and 63–9.
12 See Rerup (1985), pp. 483–6.
13 Petersen, pp. 23–71.

14 Hroch, p. 119. The table is based on material published in: *Sønderjydske Aarbøger 1890*, p. 124 ff.
15 Rørdam (1966). For the students from 1844–64 see Lund (1960) pp. 152–62 and Hroch, p. 121.
16 Rerup (1982), pp. 123 ff.
17 Petersen, p. 52.
18 Lauridsen, V, p. 40.
19 Fangel I, pp. 399–404; Japsen (1961), pp. 260 ff; Hjelholt II, pp. 179 ff; Flensburg, pp. 349 ff.
20 Witte, pp. 180 ff. The governing board of the *Forening* during the war included several members who belonged to the leading economic and social class of Flensburg. After May 1851 it seems that the leadership passed into the hands of craftsmen.
21 Lund (1960), p. 158.
22 Especially in western north Schleswig there were many so-called enclaves, that is areas dating back to the Middle Ages, which belonged to the kingdom and in which Danish laws and the 1849 Danish constitution were valid.
23 Thyssen, pp. 338–45.
24 *Sønderjyllands Historie*, vol. V, pp. 44–50.
25 Lund (1932), pp. 301–17, especially p. 304.
26 Schultz Hansen, p. 167.
27 *Ibid.*, pp. 109 and 111.
28 *Ibid.*, pp. 146–50.
29 *Ibid.*, pp. 138–42, 145 and 184 ff.
30 *Sønderjydsk Skoleforening* (1942), pp. 268 ff.
31 Schultz Hansen, p. 185.
32 *Ibid.*, pp. 167 ff.
33 *Ibid.*, pp. 179–85.
34 *Ibid.*, pp. 189 ff.
35 Hjelholt, II, p. 280.
36 Rerup (1982), p. 272.
37 Mogensen (1981), p. 38.
38 *Ibid.*, pp. 28–32.
39 von Jessen (1938), pp. 486 ff, 502–9 and 526 ff.
40 *Sønderjydsk Skoleforening* (1942), pp. 204–18.
41 Mogensen (1981a), pp. 28–41; Hjelholt, II, pp. 361–67.
42 An exception is the decision of the Flensburg agents in August 1930 not to nominate any Danish candidates for the *Reichstag* election so that the members could vote according to their socio-political preferences. Consequently the entire managing committee resigned and a new one was elected – again with a member of the *Flensborg Avis* as chairman. See Jessen (1946–48), p. 521.
43 *Zur Geschichte und Problematik* (1984), pp. 29 ff and pp. 54 ff.
44 Rerup (1982), pp. 80 ff, 91 ff, 99 and 113.
45 Hauser, pp. 64–70, 77–80 and 80–108.
46 Sievers, pp. 90 ff.
47 Rerup (1982), pp. 292–5.
48 Fink (1961), pp. 123–31 and Fink (1959), pp. 38 ff.
49 Broszat.

Select Bibliography

Broszat, M. (1968), 'Aussen- und innenpolitische Aspekte in der preussisch-deutschen Minderheitenpolitik in der Ära Stresemann', in Kluxen, K. and

Mommsen, W.J. (eds), *Politische Ideologien und nationalstaaliche Ordnung. Festschrift für Theodor Schieder*, Munich.
Carr, W. (1963), *Schleswig–Holstein 1815–48. A Study in National Conflict*, Manchester.
Dansk Biografisk Leksikon (Danish National Biography), 1st edition, Bricka, C.F. (ed.), vols 1–19, Copenhagen 1887–1905; 2nd edition, Engelstoft, P. (ed.), vols 1–27, Copenhagen 1933–44; 3rd edition, Cedergreen Bech, S. (ed.), vols 1–16, Copenhagen, 1979–84.
Dansk Historisk Bibliografi (Danish Historical Bibliography) (1929), Erichsen, B. and Krarup, A. (eds) for 1831–1912, vol. II, Copenhagen; Bruun, H. (ed.) (1968), for 1913–42, vol. III, Copenhagen; Bruun, H. (ed.) (1956), for 1943–47, Copenhagen; Welling, A.R. and Kolding Nielsen, E. (eds) (1986), for 1974–76, Copenhagen.
Dansk historisk årsbibliografi 1967, 1968, 1969 (Danish Historical Bibliography for the Year . . .), Pedersen, B. (ed.) (1972–4), Copenhagen.
Fangel, Henrik (1975), *Haderslev bys historie 1800–1945* [The History of the Town of Haderslev] vol. I, Haderslev.
Fink, Troels (1958), *Geschichte des schleswigschen Grenzlandes*, Copenhagen.
Fink, Troels (1959) *Spillet om dansk neutralitet 1905–1909* [The Case for Danish Neutrality], Aarhus.
Fink, Troels (1961), *Ustabil balance 1894–1905* [Unstable Balance], Aarhus.
Flensburg – Geschichte einer Grenzstadt, 2nd edition (1966), Flensburg.
Hauser, Oswald (1960), *Preussische Staatsräson und nationaler Gedanke*, Neumünster.
Hjelholt, Holger, *et al.* (eds) (1955), *Flensborg bys historie* [History of Flensborg], vol. II, Copenhagen.
Hroch, M. (1985), *Social Preconditions of National Revival in Europe. A Comparative Analysis of the Social Composition of Patriotic Groups among the Smaller European Nations*, Cambridge.
Japsen, G. (1961), *Den nationale udvikling i Åbenrå* [The National Development in Aabenraa], Aabenraa.
Japsen, G. (1980), *Pastor Jacobsen fra Skærbæk og hans foretagender. Bidrag til det tyske mindretals historie efter 1864* [The Rev. C.J. Jacobsen from Skærbæk and His Enterprises. A Contribution to the History of the German Minority (that is in North Schleswig) after 1864], Aabenraa.
Jessen, Fr. von (ed.) (1938), *Haandbog i det slesvigske Spørgsmaals Historie 1900–1937* [Handbook of the History of the Schleswig Question], vol. III, Copenhagen.
Jessen, Tage (1946–48), 'Mellem to Verdenskrige' [Between two World Wars], in Kamphøvener, M. (ed.), *Sydslesvig gennem Tiderne* [South Schleswig in the Course of Time], Aarhus.
Jørgensen, A.D. (1882), *Fyrretyve Fortællinger af Fædrelandets Historie*, [Forty Tales of Our Country's History], Copenhagen.
Lauridsen, P. (1918), *Da Sønderjylland vaagnede* [When North Schleswig Awoke], vol. V, Copenhagen.
Lund, H. (1932), 'Fra 1864 til Vælgerforeningens Dannelse. Det politske Samarbejde og dets Former' [From 1864 to the Foundation of the Voters' Union. Political Cooperation and its Shapes], in *Festskrift for H.P. Hanssen*, Aabenraa.
Lund, H. (1960), 'De første Rødding–Elever 1844–64' [The First Rødding Students], in Lund, H., *Historiker i Højskolens Tjeneste* [A Historian in the Folk High School's Service], Copenhagen.
Mackeprang, M. (1909), *Nordslesvig 1864–1909*, Copenhagen.
Mackeprang, M. (1912), *Nord-Schleswig von 1864–1911*, Jena.
Mogensen, Carsten, R. (1981a), 'Forbudet mod den tysksprogede danske presse i Sydslesvig 1923–24' [The Ban on the German Written Danish Press in South Schleswig], in *Sønderjyske årboger 1981*.
Mogensen, Carsten R. (1981b), *Dansk i hagekorsets skygge. Det tredie rige og det danske mindretal i Sydslesvig* [Danish in the Shadow of the Swastika. The Third *Reich* and the Danish Minority], Flensborg.

Noack, Johan Peter (1989), *Det danske mindretal i Sydslesvig 1920–1945* [The Danish Minority in South Schleswig 1920–45], Aarhus.

Petersen, Jakob (1943), *Skamlingsbanken 1843–1943* [The Hill of Skamling], Copenhagen.

Rerup, Lorenz (1982), *Slesvig og Holsten efter 1830* [Schleswig and Holsten after 1830], Copenhagen.

Rerup, Lorenz (1985), 'Elitärer und emanzipatorischer Nationalismus', in: XVIe *Congrès International des Sciences Historiques*, Rapports II, Stuttgart.

Runge, Johan (1981), *Sønderjyden Christian Paulsen* [The Schleswigian Christian Paulsen], Flensburg.

Rørdam, Thomas (1966), *Folkehøjskolen* [The Folk High School], Copenhagen.

Schultz Hansen, H. (1985), *Det nordslesvigske landbrug og den danske bevægelse* [Agriculture in North Schleswig and the Danish Movement], Aabenraa.

Sievers, Kai D. (1964), *Die Köllerpolitik und ihr Echo in der deutschen Presse 1897–1901*, Neumüster.

Sønderjydsk Skoleforening 1892–1942 (1942), [The North Schleswig School Association], Kolding.

Sønderjyllands Historie, fremstillet for det danske Folk [The History of Southern Jutland, written for the Danish People] la Cour. Vilh. *et al.* (eds) (1937 & 1932/33), vols IV and V, Copenhagen.

Thaning, Kai (1972), *N.F.S. Grundtvig*, English edition (1972).

Thyssen, A. Pontoppidan (1977), *Vækkelse, kirkefornyelse og nationalitetskamp* [Revival, Church Renewal and National Struggle], Aabenraa.

Witte, Jørgen (1975b), 'Den Slesvigske Forening 1849–1892' [The Schleswig Association], in *Sønderjyske årbøger 1975.*

Zur Geschichte und Problematik der deutsch-dänischen Beziehungen von der Wikingerzeit bis zur Gegenwart. Empfehlungen zu ihrer Behandlung im Geschichtsunterricht/Det dansk-tyske forholds historie og problemer fra vikingetiden til nutiden. En vejledning til brug i historieundervisningen, Georg-Eckert-Institut (ed.) (1984), Braunschweig.

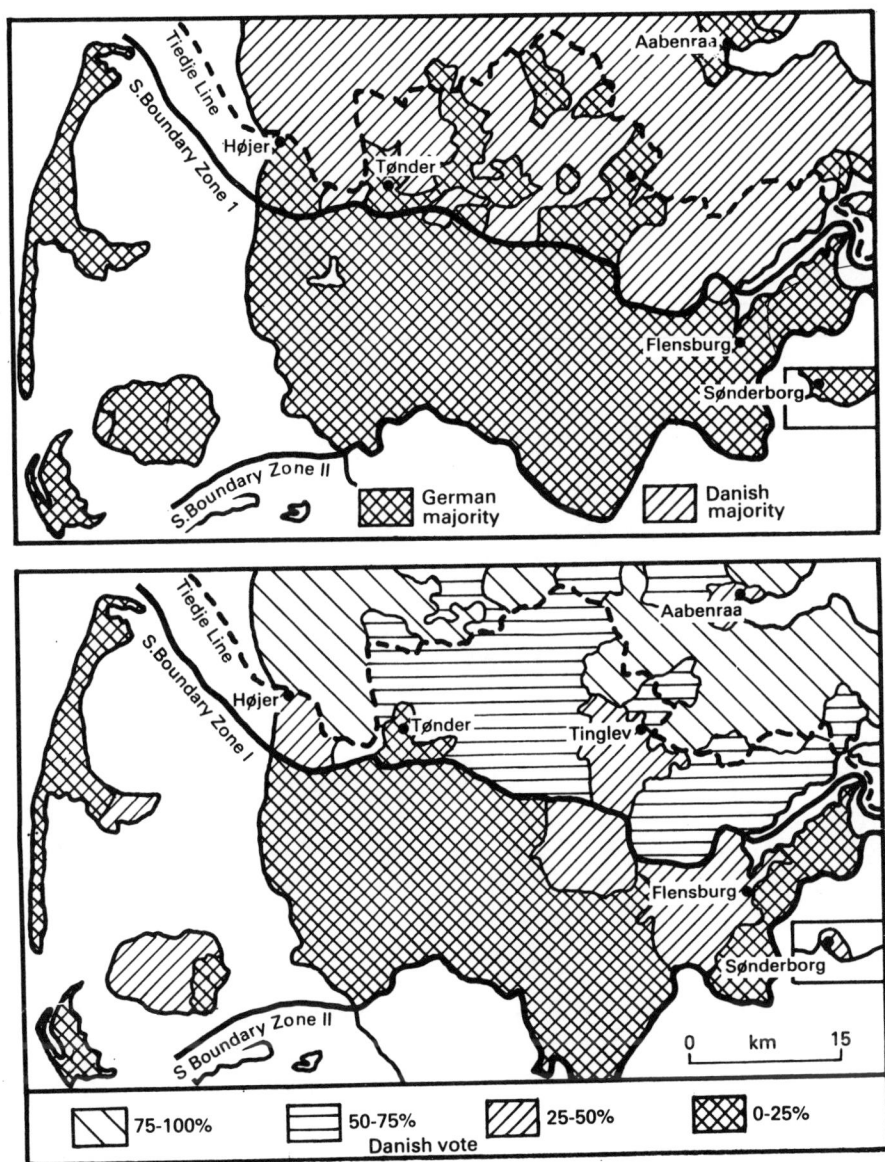

Map 9.1   Results of the Schleswig plebiscite in part of zone I and in zone II
Source: Sarah Wambaugh, Plebiscites Since The World War, vol. 1, Washington 1933, p. 87

Selected Problems in
Comparative Perspective

10 Social and Territorial Characteristics in the Composition of the Leading Groups of National Movements

MIROSLAV HROCH

Every national movement took place in real space and was supported and directed by actual persons. In evaluating the transformation of non-dominant ethnic groups into nations, territorial distribution of national activities and the association of their leaders with specific social forces cannot be ignored. This is one of the reasons why the social origins of the leaders and the territorial distribution of their activities is of historical interest. Far from being an end in itself the comparative study of both phenomena sheds light on basic causal relations.[1]

The social characteristics of the leaders of Phase A (according to the periodisation proposed in chapter 1) are predetermined by certain pecularities. They were predominantly scholars, earning their living as university professors, librarians, members of religious orders and others who were close to the ruling classes – the 'elites' of the ruling nation. During the period of national agitation – Phase B – a more complex situation developed. Two questions, above all, should be considered. First how to interpret the motivation underlying the patriotic activities of the leaders and second why the rates of success of their agitation differed. Motivation was not restricted solely to individual decisions, which might have happened fortuitously. Accident, it can be argued, ends where several hundreds – even thousands – of individuals strove at the same time for similar goals and responded to identical or analogous slogans. In this state influences, interests and contexts might be involved which were, perhaps, not fully or consciously reflected by those taking part.

Unreflected motivation is also important in the second question raised. Enthusiasm and readiness for sacrifice undoubtedly played an important part. They were supposed to be subjective pre-conditions for the success of a national movement. The actual success (or failure) of these endeavours, however, was not determined solely by the personal endeavours and good intentions of the leaders. Broader contexts determined success or failure. The transition from Phase B to Phase C (the mass movement) was neither a mechanical certainty nor the result of subjective decisions taken by a small group of leaders. A different goal needs to be set for enquiry into Phase C. At that point national consciousness already had spread among the broad masses of the population. It is still important to find out what animated the leaders but the topical question is now how this motivation was related to the social interpretation of the national programme.

It is not vulgar economic determinism to claim that value systems and behaviour norms have been formed differently in separate social conditions. An activist from the administrative class probably lived and reasoned differently from one with peasant origins. This also meant they held distinctive views on what were the crucial interests of the people of the emerging nation and about the methods of struggle which should be employed. Social diversity within the group of leaders who shared the same national ideas can be seen as showing several variants during Phase B. To a large extent these differences were, however, restrained by the common purpose of agitation. Their importance increased parallel to the advancing political differentiation which affected political goals and pro-grammes.

Comparative analysis will not only define those characteristics and contexts shared by all (or most) national movements but also their distinctive features, and permit interpretation of these using social criteria. Differing levels of development make it desirable to conduct separate analyses of the social origins of the leaders for Phases B and C. Absence of uniform data for all non-dominant ethnic groups, though, inhibits comprehensive comparative treatment. A further difficulty, particularly for quantifying comparisons, arises from the shifting boundaries of the activist groups in the various national movements. The problems make essential a broader definition of the term 'activists' (as already characterised in the introduction). A narrow definition including only the leading personalities within the movement would be too limiting.

The Representation of Specific Classes, Strata, and Professions

Involvement of certain social classes, strata and professional groups has been analysed across a range of different experiences. It is essential to stress that the social structure of Phase B activists differed in the various national movements. Though they came from a variety of strata and social groups they had one thing in common: in every case the intelligentsia was strongly represented. This fact however already has been recognised by numerous historians.

The Upper Classes

Apart from the Polish and Catalan movements, the number of noblemen and landed proprietors taking an active part was very small, sometimes nil, not only during the *ancien regime* but also after the capitalist upheaval. They were not a central feature of the movement. Some landed proprietors had a small share at the beginning of Phase B in the Ukrainian and Czech movements, for instance, or even in the initial stages of Phase C in Ireland. They did not however have a lasting influence on the course and the programmes of the national movement. In the Slovakian and the Croatian movements (not treated in this study) some landed proprietors of noble origin were present but also without marked importance. At the beginning of Phase C – if not earlier – activists of certain national movements tried to win over the local nobility. The Czechs and Irish in particular made this attempt but the results were disappointing. The Ukrainians in Russia, the Croats and the Slovaks did not have any greater success.

The nobility, or rather their mentality, played a certain part in the early stages of Phase B only in those regions where the non-dominant ethnic group, fully or partially, could claim a political identity (autonomy, existence as a state) dating from the feudal epoch. This does in fact denote a certain ambiguity on the part of these national movements. They were, as shown above, a component part of the anti-feudal bourgeois transformation (modernisation) but this did not preclude them from holding a jaundiced opinion of some results of the change. This was particularly true of those regions where modernisation first took place in the territory of the dominant nation, making the subject ethnic group feel threatened. The Polish movement in the Grand Duchy of Poznań, the Irish and Czech national movements fall into this category.

Activists coming from the new capitalist entrepreneural class (the bourgeoisie) were even more differentiated. It is generally supposed that the bourgeoisie, as a class engaged in capitalist enterprise, developed earlier and more strongly in the territories of the ruling nation. An implication of this might mean also that members of the non-dominant ethnic group rising as manufacturers or entrepreneurs found it convenient to change their ethnic affiliation (their national identity) in order to exploit fully new economic opportunities. Membership in the ruling nation through assimilation or integration proved a powerful attraction. Among movements considered in the case studies the bourgeoisie was probably represented most strongly in the Catalan instance, though only towards the end of Phase B. But in Catalonia the bourgeoisie as a class tended to support the idea of a unified Spanish nation. The bourgeoisie, of course, took a prominent part in the German national movement in Schleswig. It seems to be typical of most other national movements however that the first bourgeois activists appear during Phase C. This was true in the Czech and Polish cases though the occasional entrepreneur can be found among the activists of both movements, during Phase B. The Finnish movement (not treated here) showed a comparable development. As for the Estonians, the Ukrainians in Russia and Danes in Schleswig, their movements took place almost without bourgeois participation. A special feature of the latter movement was the numerous entrepreneurs domiciled in the kingdom of Denmark (important civil servants, large scale merchants, landed proprietors) taking part. It does not appear to be important for the course of Phase B whether the leaders could count few or any bourgeois members among their numbers.

Motivation for the participation of the noble landed proprietors was clear: they had been the ruling class of the previously autonomous state now under alien rule. In the case of the Czechs and, to a lesser degree, the Ukrainians of Russia, they were isolated relics from a late feudal, anti-absolutist territorial patriotism. Similar anti-centralist patterns were of some importance in Catalonia and Ireland, where in the latter case landowners though being frequently of dominant ethnic origins were alienated by treatment as colonial subjects. The question of bourgeois participation can be put in a negative manner. Why was their share in Phase B usually so negligible? Much is explained by the social structure of the non-dominant ethnic group and the desire to hasten economic success by identifying with the ruling nation. Sometimes this was even a precondition of social advancement. Only after the success of the national movement and the transition into Phase C did an alternative to assimilation (though this still remained a possibility) become feasible: in such a case a new enterprising bourgeoise confronted (as a weaker partner) the new dominating class of the ruling nation. In this situation national tensions became exacerbated; this only ceased when the bourgeoisie of the emergent (newly formed) nation also started to become internationalised.

Self-Employed Small Scale Producers in Town and Country: Artisans and Peasants

Urban or at least rural artisans and small scale merchants had been present in the social structure of most non-dominant ethnic groups even before the beginning of the national movements. During Phase B they can be found taking part in patriotic meetings, subscribing to patriotic periodicals and joining patriotic organisations and clubs. An exception to this rule were the Ukrainians in Russia (and to some extent the Lithuanians). In both cases the artisans and merchants predominantly were Jews. Estonians were an intermediate case because artisans, though not permitted to work in the towns, were present in the villages. The Macedonian rural merchants and artisans were of some importance. In the national activities of the Danes in Schleswig artisans participated less, being dependent on the German speaking citizens of their towns. Only among the Czechs during Phase B were artisans decisive activists, real leaders in the sense of being strongly represented and influential.

Where the national movement succeeded in attaining Phase C urban artisans and small scale merchants nearly always contributed to its success (though probably to a lesser degree in the Czech movement). But even after that time they did not necessarily attain leadership positions. This was particularly the case in the Czech movement; also at a later date in the Irish and Catalan examples. In the Irish movement artisans were very strongly represented in the Fenian movement which corresponds approximately to Phase B. In the mass movement they were no longer overrepresented. Small scale merchants, though, had considerable importance and some leadership functions as well.

Motivations for artisan activism could be ambiguous where the conditions of a feudal society still existed. Their participation enabled a political opposition to raise its voice against the surviving *ancien regime* and a feudal absolutism. Yet through them a strongly surviving guild mentality could be moblised as discontent with the beginnings of modernisation, industrialism and free competition. After all this modernisation came from the centre – the ruling nation. Ambiguity was less apparent in most cases were the old order was abolished and bourgeois reforms had been realised, though in Ireland such change further inflamed discontent. During Phase C the significance of the petit bourgeoisie rose as they became the most important exponents of national self-assertion, even of nationalism. They were responsible for spreading national consciousness among the working classes. The bourgeoisie of the newly forming nation was recruited mainly from their ranks. Myriad circumstances must be taken into account in analysing the programme of every national movement.

As already mentioned the participation of peasants was negligible during Phase B. Only in the Estonian national movement and in that of the Danish minority in Schleswig, and that of the Germans in northern Schleswig were there numerous peasant activists. In both instances they subscribed to periodicals, attended meetings and also took part in political decisions. For the rest the interest of peasants in the national movement only rose during Phase C, mostly in the Czech, Irish and Catalan movements. Even then generally there were no peasants among the higher echelon of the national leadership. Peasant participation in leadership only assumed importance during Phase C and largely in the Estonian and Irish movements from the 1880s. In Ireland they were prominent as local leaders. Contrary to hypothetical conjecture national activity of peasants during Phase B was very small even in those cases where they formed the overwhelming majority of the non-dominant ethnic group as they did in the Russian Ukraine and Ireland. But without the participation of peasant groups the national movement could not achieve the transition to Phase C – the mass movement.

In other cases, too, peasants were only converted to active national consciousness during Phase C with hesitation. Acceptance and involvement were stronger in those countries where the Church sided unmistakably with the non-dominant ethnic group or/and where the national programme was unequivocally in favour of the social demands made by the peasants. This was true for the Irish, the Estonians and the Lithuanians. This rather reluctant attitude of the peasantry towards the national agitation of Phase B and the nationalism of Phase C does not alter the fact that the rural population of all groups supplied an 'ethnic substratum' for the activists: the village was the guardian of folk culture, of the vernacular language and as such it was admired and celebrated as the healthy nucleus of the emergent nation. Peasants however did not accept this role with instant enthusiasm, sometimes they even refused cooperation.

The Secular Intelligentsia

Among the activists of Phase B the high percentage of members of the learned professions is apparent everywhere. The extent to which certain professional groups took part in the activist movement differed widely in the various national movements. To avoid misunderstanding, a definition of 'intelligentsia' in this context is vital. Included in this stratum are all those who attained a certain (not necessarily academic) advanced education and earned their living by intellectual activities. It is a definition which encompasses a broad spectrum of professional groups, from poor village teachers to wealthy lawyers. Thus different professional groups have to be examined separately.

The so-called liberal professions (above all lawyers and physicians) increased in number parallel to society's push towards capitalist development. As these were professions needing an academic education and resulting in great financial independence, their members played an important part in every reformist social activity. Among these the national movements are undoubtedly to be counted. At the top physicians, lawyers, independent scholars and, in some cases, university professors affiliated with the liberal professions are nearly always to be found. Journalists and (very few) writers, later evident among the leaders, had independence in common with the liberal professions but not always an academic education. Of all social groups actively taking part in the national movement, members of the liberal professions were the only ones more or less equal to the 'elites' of the dominant nation. Social proximity did not lead automatically to a readiness for compromise among the activists of the national movement. One thing is certain: if there were any direct social relations between the activists of Phase B and the 'elites' of the ruling nation these nearly always occurred in professional circles.

The proportion of professionals in the leading groups differed widely. During Phase B their share was tiny in Estonia where ethnic and social boundaries coincided even after the abolition of serfdom. There were also few of them in the Schleswig movement though Danes were free to engage in the liberal professions. The percentage of professionals in the Catalan, Polish and Irish agitation was very high – these were territories where the social structure of the non-dominant ethnic group was nearly complete or as in the instance of Ireland advancing swiftly towards that position. Between extremes are the instances of the Czech, Macedonian and Ukrainian national movements. Only in the Russian Ukraine did the proportion of professionals rise during Phase B; in other movements they declined. Members of these professions however played an important part in the movements, even during Phase C, though their percentage was small.

Whereas the role of the liberal professions within the national movements was determined by their comparative political and social independence, the opposite was true of the national activities of civil servants employed by public bodies or the state. It is not surprising that their numbers and influence among the activists in most of the national movements was minimal. During Phase C their numbers increased in places, but even then they rarely aspired to, or achieved, influential positions. In some national movements administrators were activists during Phase B; their material situation was similar to that of civil servants. These were particularly numerous in the Czech national movement: they were the so-called patrimonial (serving landed proprietors) and municipal civil servants. Moreover in the Estonian and Ukrainian movements also there were a number of clerks among the activists, such as scribes, and *Zemstvo* employees. After the abolition of the feudal system this group, naturally, diminished in number. The percentage of clerks in municipal and state employment, and in the emerging trade and industrial enterprises, rose proportionally. The high percentage of estate officials, except in Ireland, and clerks resulted because these employments were open to members of the non-dominant ethnic groups. On the other hand the professionalisation of civil servants could lead to a hardening of conflicts and linguistic barriers – as was, for instance, the case in Schleswig.

Two categories of activists among teachers have to be distinguished: those in institutions of secondary education, and primary school teachers. The former shared characteristics with the liberal professions: though few in number they were very influential among the activists. This pertained only in territories where the institutions of secondary education were open to members of the non-dominant ethnic group, which was not the case everywhere during Phase B. Teachers in secondary schools were, then, important among the leaders of the Czech, Polish, Ukrainian and Estonian movements though in the latter country their number was very small. In Ireland their participation was never extensive and their attitude usually tentative as education, even in national schools, was controlled by the clergy.

It is often stated that primary school teachers took an important part in all national movements. Among the cases examined teachers played an important, perhaps even the most crucial, part during Phase B in the Macedonian and the Estonian movements. They also had some importance in the Danish and German cases in Schleswig but in all other movements their participation was minimal and did not correspond to their numerical size. They were even rarely found among the more broadly defined sympathisers. However during Phase C the number of teachers taking an active part rose perceptably.

How can these impressive differences in the national activities of teachers be interpreted? Not by seeking contrasts in their status, incomes and educations. In these respects there were few differences between the Macedonian, Czech, Catalan and Estonian cases. They have played an important, even dominant, part among the leaders only in those territories where the teaching professions were a decisive, sometimes the only, means of social advance for members of the non-dominant ethnic group. For instance during Phase B becoming a teacher was the only way for an Estonian to achieve a higher education without shedding ethnic identity. It also is significant that teachers had always been very politically and materially dependent. In the various countries they depended on different institutions. Teachers had distinct experiences and opportunities depending on whether they were controlled by Church authorities, the state or the village community (for example Danes in Schleswig). A special position was occupied by the teachers of German and Danish minority groups after 1918 which were supported by state authorities of their respective mother countries.

Students from groups which had access to academic education were a driving force in most national movements though naturally they were rarely its actual leaders. Their percentage in patriotic activities and organisations rose significantly during Phase B but declined again with the emergence of the mass movements. Students from non-dominant ethnic groups who did not have a university in their native territory and therefore had to study abroad or at the universities of the ruling nation provide special cases. These students also sometimes formed patriotic groups but these were of differing importance. They were quite strong among the Poles in the Grand Duchy of Poznań, weaker in Estonia, and negligible among the Danes in Schleswig. Except in Ireland, where universities were situated in the ethnic territory, they were an important integrating factor for the intelligentsia and the whole national movement.

The Clergy

Differences in confession did not cause any fundamental distinctions of clerical participation in national movements. The Catholic clergy in the Czech and Irish Phase B, and partly in Phase C, took a leading role while priests hardly participated in the Catalan patriotic organisations. A high percentage of Protestant pastors were in the Finnish and Slovak movements though not conspicuous as activists among the Danes and Germans in Schleswig, nor in Estonia. Orthodox priests took a leading part in the Macedonian national movement and among the Ukrainians in Austria but were largely absent among the Ukrainian activists in Russia. These differences obviously were not determined automatically by the confession as such. They were, however, related to special conditions within specific national Churches, their organisation and the political position of the ecclesiastical hierarchy.

The small percentage of clergy taking part in the Catalan organisations is explained by the fact that the Catholic Church there was under the strict control of a unitary Spanish state and did not favour ethnic demands. The same applied in the Russian Ukraine, where the official position of the Church was 'all Russian', not Ukrainian. By contrast the Catholic Church in Bohemia was a territorial Church, identifying with the Bohemians, and had supported a territorial patriotism since the seventeenth century. The Bohemian Church did not prohibit national activism as long as such ambitions were formulated along linguistic and cultural lines. This accounts for the extraordinarily high percentage of priests in the Czech Phase B. It was only when the liberal political programme was formulated during Phase C that conflict arose. The Church was not prepared for such demands and developed over time a national–conservative clerical programme. Though this did not play an important part in Bohemia it had some significance in Moravia. It is easy to explain the higher percentage of priests in the Polish and Irish national movements where the ethnic and religious frontiers were identical. In many cases the seminary was for the sons of peasants the only way of rising socially. In Estonia and Lithuania conditions were entirely different. There a clerical career was a preserve of the ruling Germans and was for a long time closed to the Estonian speaking population.

Even where priests were numerous among the leaders of the movement they were unable to exercise a decisive influence in the formulation of national demands. Their influence on objectives were somewhat greater in those territories where the non-dominant ethnic group belonged to a different confession from that of the ruling nation – as in Prussian Poland, the Balkans and in Ireland. Where differences in confession coincided with the ethnic division it was of national relevance. Without this knowledge it would be hard to comprehend why the influence exercised by the numerous Czech priests active in the movement was much less than that of the (comparatively few) priests among the activists of the Polish movement in the Grand Duchy of Poznań. Priests, particularly in rural society, had a dual role. They exercised ecclesiastical and spiritual functions but were also often the most educated men in the region. Cultural functions, which might easily include national components, were in their hands. These two roles were combined or continued along parallel paths, depending on local circumstances.

Common and Specific Features in the Social Composition of Leading Groups

An attempt to formulate a generalising summary has to begin with a negative statement. Social (and even less, professional) groups were not represented equally in the leading circles of national movements. A group might be represented strongly in one movement and hardly visible in another. Even those national movements which took place contemporaneously differed markedly in the social origins of their leaders. Chronology, however, was crucial. National movements which started earlier (such as Czech, Irish, Polish) had a larger percentage of urban activists, while those movements entering Phase B later (about the second half of the nineteenth century) found more support in rural communities (such as Estonians, Macedonians, Ukrainians). The former experienced less difficulty in penetrating the rural population with the beginning of Phase C than the latter had in gaining a foothold in the towns. Nevertheless the leading groups of those national movements starting within the conditions of a bourgeois society already had an urban structure in spite of having begun later.

Despite enormous regional variations a further generalisation can be made. The national movements of Phase B were above all carried by members of those social groups and professions standing at the threshold of spontaneous linguistic assimilation. Social groups particularly were active which were on a level that could just be attained by a member of the non-dominant ethnic group which did not want to take the final step of assimilation. For the Poles in Poznań this might mean all strata; for the Czechs, the liberal professions and the lower administration; for the Estonians, the teaching professions. Another general conclusion appears to be that with the transition to Phase C members of the higher strata of the intelligentsia were represented more heavily than during Phase B.

The Social Origins of the Leaders

Social characterisation of the leading groups has to consider the environment from which the future activists sprang and how they were educated. The question of social origins is particularly important because of the extended drive towards nationhood. It took several generations for a non-dominant ethnic group to become a fully formed nation and some never reached that stage. Research into social origins is difficult because source material is incomplete. It is easier to reconstruct the social origins of the intelligentsia, the stratum from which the majority of the leaders was drawn. Marked differences can be seen in the social origins of the leaders.

The upper social strata, the ranks of the old dominant class of landed proprietors and leading civil servants, was well represented among the Catalan leaders. But this class provided only a small number of Polish activists in the Grand Duchy of Poznań during Phase B. In the Russian Ukraine there was a larger percentage of activists coming from noble landed proprietors while in Ireland their number was small. Activists of urban origin were represented strongly in several national movements. About half of all Czech leaders of Phase B were artisans or in trade. The percentage was somewhat lower among the Poles in the Grand Duchy of Poznań and in the Irish, Macedonian and Slovak national movements. In the German movement in Schleswig and in the Finnish movement (not treated in this study) fewer activists came from this strata, though the number was not negligible. Activists of urban origin were quite insignificant in the Ukrainian and Estonian movements.

Activists of peasant origin were less evident. It is obvious that they were most numerous in those movements having a low percentage of urban activists – mostly in Russian Ukraine, Estonia and Schleswig (Danish activists). In the case of Polish activists in the Grand Duchy of Poznań the peasant class was largely represented by Catholic priests. In the Finnish and, probably, the Catalan group of leaders in Phase B there were hardly any descendants from peasant families. In the case of the Irish, Czech, Ukrainian and Slovakian activists from peasant families made up about ten to 20 per cent, showing a tendency to rise during Phase C. This tendency does not however apply to all of the national movements treated.

Only in those national movements where the intelligentsia already had been represented among the members of the non-dominant ethnic group before or at the beginning of Phase B, can there be found a higher percentage of activists from this stratum. Above all the cases of the Polish, Irish, Catalan and Finnish movements illustrate the point. The percentage was somewhat lower among the Czechs (and Slovakians) at the end of Phase B. A significant number of Ukrainian activists in Russia came from the noble intelligentsia. But the largest leadership group in Estonia had its origins in the families of rural teachers and sextons.

Sons of pastors were represented very unequally. Their share was negligible in the Danish and wholly absent in the Estonian movements. Generalisation remains an elusive possibility however, as sons of pastors formed an important section of both Finnish and Slovakian activists. In both countries pastors were represented in the social structure of the non-dominant ethnic group. Among sons of the Orthodox clergy a difference is discernable between the Ukrainian national movement, where they were represented strongly, and Macedonia where only a small share was evident. The high percentage of the sons of clergy in the leading groups undoubtedly reflected the fact that most of the ministers lived in the countryside and were in close contact with the peasant people but also had sufficient means to send their sons to university.

A closed model showing the social origins of the leaders is impossible, but one fact is certain – that most of the leaders of Phase B came from the traditional middle classes and lower and middle strata of the intelligentsia. It may be taken for granted that most of these leaders occupied a higher position than their fathers, particularly in the Czech, Estonian and Irish movements, though in the Catalan,

Polish and Ukrainian groups, this is less apparent. Actual social recruitment of the leaders can be shown by defining three different categories: first national movements drawing leaders mostly from the towns, especially among the urban artisan and trade classes (such as Czechs); second those with most of their leaders coming from the countryside, from landlord or peasant families or from the petty village intelligentsia (such as Catalans, Russian Ukrainians, Danes in Schleswig or Estonians); third those with a majority of leaders from intelligentsia families (Poles of the Grand Duchy of Poznań, Catalans and Irish).

Comparison with the 'Elites' of the Dominant Nation

To date little attention has been given to the question of how the social composition and origin of the leaders differed from the 'elites' of the ruling nation. It raises the problem whether the national movement can be described as being a conflict between different ethnic groups (nationalities) representing the same social strata or a clash between distinct classes. It is therefore necessary to compare the social characteristics of ethnic leaders to those of the leading strata of those states against which the national movement was directed. Once again the results are not uniform.

In the Grand Duchy of Poznań members of the dominating Polish class confronted their Prussian social equivalents. Both consisted of landed proprietors belonging to the nobility, bourgeois entrepreneurs and industrialists (the latter being, of course, not as numerous as in the *Ruhrgebiet* (Ruhr region)). However the social structures of the two sides differed significantly in one point: civil servants, who played such an important part in the Prussian state, were not represented among the Polish leaders. Prussian civil servants were hostile to the Polish national movement. A similar feature can be detected in Spanish–Catalan relations. Members of the dominating class stood at the head of both camps, with the difference that the Catalan bourgeoisie joined the movement at a later date. Again it is possible to define the conflicts between different members of the same dominant classes and strata, but separated by ethnic loyalties. Though a large number of the activists were of noble birth in the Russian Ukraine they were drawn from the intelligentsia within the sector rather than from the landed proprietors. Nevertheless a certain analogy to the social characteristics of the Russian intelligentsia can be put forward. As in the Grand Duchy of Poznań there were no civil servants among the Ukrainian activists in Russia.

Fundamental differences existed in other cases between the social characteristics of patriotic activists and the 'elites' of the ruling nations. Generalisations are elusive. In Estonia peasants and petty intelligentsia challenged the German privileged class of landed proprietors and the academically educated. Macedonian activists were led by the middle class and the petty intelligentsia in opposition to the dominant privileged strata of civil servants and landlords. The German speaking 'elite' of landed proprietors, state officials, and bourgeois entrepreneurs were distinguishable from the Czech rural artisans and the middle and lower strata of the intelligentsia. Activists in the Danish movement in Schleswig belonged to a very different social stratum from the German 'elites' in Schleswig. But the Germans' resistance to Danish rule pitted two analogously structured dominating classes against each other.

Even when the differences during Phase C were no longer as significant as they had been earlier their results were of lasting importance. How did these distinctions influence the course and goals of different national movements? One way of interpreting these phenomena can be found by looking at the different conceptions concerning civil liberties and how these were applied. In territories where the leaders were associated with lower and middle classes having no political experience and sometimes lacking interest in politics, demands for civil liberties were represented weakly or, at the beginning, not at all in some programmes (such as Czech, Macedonian and Estonians). The greater the similarities between the social characteristics of the leaders of national movements and those of the 'elites' of the ruling nations, the more those leaders stressed political demands in their programmes (as in the case of Poles, Irish and Catalans). In the latter situation there was also an early differentiation of political ideas within the national movement. In both situations there was a conflict between moderate and radical activists. On the threshold of the mass movement or in its first decades the radicals represented, at the same time, the democratic wing whereas the moderates made up the rather conservative–liberal wing of the national movement.

Differences in social characteristics were of crucial importance in the formation of the national programme. When disparities between leaders of the movement and the ruling 'elites' were particularly great during Phase B, as in the case of the Czechs and, even more, the Estonians, social demands were more strongly represented in national programmes than, for instance, in those of the Polish and Catalan movements, where those differences were less strong. Social demands at the beginning were concerned with the liberation of peasants and sometimes also with obtaining better working conditions for artisans and craftsmen (or in Estonia with obtaining permission to join these trades at all). When these demands had been met, however, there survived in these national movements, even during Phase C, the stereotype of the national cause being a fight for social justice, for the rights of the weak and oppressed.

The Territorial Structure of National Activity

It is vital to examine where the agitation and organising activities of the leaders were located and the extent to which they succeeded in penetrating various sections of the ethnic territory. The results illuminate the deeply rooted causes leading to the success (or failure) of a national movement. Territorial characteristics of the activists – where they were born, educated, worked and secured followers – may be treated as symptoms or circumstantial evidence for the general receptiveness of all strata of non-dominant ethnic groups towards national agitation.

The Centres of National Movement

From the beginning of Phase B every national movement had a traditional stronghold or strove to establish a new territorial base. Leading personalities and the organisational headquarters were concentrated in the chief national centres. From such points patriotic intensity rose and pleas for action were directed towards the provinces. Such places were also crucial as collecting stations for information from the provinces. Because of their special situation the border minorities of Schleswig did not have a centre (or only an insignificant one) in their territories. They might have several provincial centres but the actual centre was situated in the 'mother country'. In most cases the national movement was located in the regional centre, the city within the territory of the non-dominant ethnic group where the administration of the ruling nation was domiciled. For Czechs Prague was the centre; Poznań for Poles in the Grand Duchy of Poznań; for the Catalans Barcelona; Kiev for Russian Ukrainians; Dublin for the Irish; and somewhat later Tallinn for the Estonians. Only the Macedonians had a certain provincial 'poly-centrism' rather analogous to the border minorities. There were rare, usually unsuccessful, attempts to create an alternative national centre which did not coincide with that of the ruling state adminis-tration. The concentration of the national life in Viljandi attempted by the Estonians was one such case. Other instances in areas not covered here can be cited. For example Slovakian patriots tried to establish an alternative centre to the Magyar–German administrative centre of Bratislava/Pressburg, first in Trnava and then in Martin.

Sometimes the non-dominant ethnic group was in fact a numerical minority in the chief city of the national movement as, for instance, the Ukrainians in Kiev and the Estonians in Tallinn. At times a number of leaders and their offices were located in the capital of the dominant state thus forming a 'supplementary centre'. A number of Macedonian leaders, for instance, were in Istanbul or Salonika; some Ukrainians in St Petersburg or Moscow; Slovaks in Budapest; and Irish in London. When the centre was situated within the territory of the non-dominant ethnic group, in a favourable position both for administration and communication, the influence of the leaders and the prospects of success rose. From the beginning of the respective national movements Prague, Barcelona, Kiev, Dublin and Poznań provided examples of this kind.

The Territorial Distribution of National Activity

Finally it is essential to reconstruct how the leaders and, above all, their activities were distributed within the territories of the non-dominant ethnic groups. Unfortunately the information available on this is neither comprehensive in scope nor complete. Though sources are often incomplete two factors stand out:

- National activity was distributed unevenly within the territory of the non-dominant ethnic group. Different regions did not contribute an equal number of leaders to the movement nor were activities distributed in equivalent density throughout the territory, and the results of these endeavours were not identical everywhere.
- This territorial inequality usually relates to whole regions rather than sub-regions. One or more compact territories usually stand out by being more active, others marked by a rather passive role.

Investigation of the characteristics of the active regions can provide evidence about social, economic and cultural factors leading to national integration. Regions with above average national activity, where a proportionally larger number of leaders were domiciled, sometimes formed the hinterland of the centres of the national movements, as for instance in Catalonia or the Grand Duchy of Poznań. More often, however, these regions were only a small section of the hinterland, such as in the environs of Prague, Kiev and Tallinn, where nationally passive regions can also be seen.

Did a relationship exist between industrialisation (as a dominant agent of economic prosperity and social mobilisation) and the distribution of national activities? The answer is in the negative. These regions were never congruent though sometimes their boundaries overlapped, and a certain correspondence existed in Catalonia. But it should not be concluded that the nationally active territories were economically backward. Industrialisation either took place in the territories occupied by members of the ruling nation (such as Bohemia, Ireland and Prussia) or by encouraging territorial mobility, it brought about a high degree of ethnic intermingling, allowing little scope for non-dominant ethnic groups. This was the case in the southern Ukraine, in Tallinn and Narva, Mährisch-Ostrau as well as in other instances.

Obviously in the determining characteristics of nationally active regions neither backwardness nor industrialisation predominated. Which, then, were the characteristics furthering national activity?

- They were regions having better than average school networks or conditions generally favouring education, so the number of illiterate people was comparatively low.
- They were market orientated regions; that is areas which regularly produced goods for the market and where urban and rural producers (artisans, craftsmen and peasants) took an active part in economic life. Sometimes the regular selling of a rather specific kind of wares – the export of labour into remote regions (such as seasonal workers from the Macedonian mountains) – played a part. The accompanying phenomena can only be touched upon briefly; an expanding monetary economy, horizontal social mobility and social communication extending beyond the traditional forms.
- They were regions of comparative ethnic purity, populated only or mostly by members of the non-dominant ethnic group. In these cases it was not only the compactness of the ethnic territory which was decisive but also the fact that in these regions the social structure of the non-dominant group was nearly complete, or that the incompleteness of the social structure had a less disintegrative effect than in places with an ethnically mixed population. The nearness of the ethnic boundary was not necessarily significant though it had importance in those regions where a political or social challenge radiated from the other side of the linguistic boundary.

Specific traditions could also be important. In the Russian Ukraine, for instance, the old tradition of the Cossack *Hetmanate* (autonomous area) proved to be vital. Later on growing railway construction and the resulting changes in population density and market structure formed an integrating (or, under certain circumstances, a disintegrating) factor. In regions having an extraordinarily low degree of social communication and mobility the activities of the national movements also were weak even if some of the leaders lived in this territory. Chance also played a part. A certain level of social communication and mobility was undoubtedly necessary for the advancement of national agitation but it was not the cause of success. Leaders were welcomed most warmly in those parts of the territory where education, social communication and mobility were high. This characteristic can be demonstrated from data on school provision and attendance, literacy, transport networks and market relations. There was however no compelling causation: there were regions where all these characteristics applied and which were, nevertheless, nationally passive.

A high level of social communication or of social mobility, however, was not decisive for the activism of the national movement and the success of agitation. More important were the matters of the nature of the message content transmitted and the conditions which existed within different social situations. The same is valid for social mobility. How often and under what circumstances members of the non-dominant ethnic group engaged members of the ruling nation was crucial. Empirical research has demonstrated that horizontal and vertical social mobility could facilitate assimilation but it also might provoke or deepen national tensions and conflicts. Which social groups and classes of the ruling nation and the non-dominant ethnic group met and how they reacted to the entire social context, was decisive.

Members of different or equal professions, social groups and classes whose interests partly coincide with, or contradict, each other are pertinent factors. Major antagonism could develop when rival individuals or social groups were reinforced in their hostility by ethnic differences. 'Antagonisms of interests with national relevance' could exist, as for example between the Ukrainian peasant and the Polish or Russian landlord, or as in the case of the Czech craftsmen and the German merchant or entrepreneur. Antagonisms of interests with national relevance could also rise among members of the same social group or class, as with competition for employment as officials, or between merchants. Unfortunately little is known about antagonisms of interests of national relevance within the 'old middle class' or among farmers or craftsmen who belonged to different ethnic groups. The antagonism of interests with social relevance thus made possible the national articulation of social and other matters. Such an antagonism in combination with nationalist agitation even could become an independent phenomenon. Fictitious, stereotyped antagonisms of interests were spread as national ones by social communication. As this is a field not yet examined thoroughly any suggestions must remain hypothetical.[2] Yet it is essential that the force animating non-dominant ethnic groups is analysed in the context of the social backgrounds of activists.

Notes

1 This comparative chapter is based primarily on the case studies. All the other material utilised is taken from the studies of the author cited in the introductory chapter.
2 In his classical work (1953), *Nationalism and Social Communication*, Cambridge, Mass., K.W. Deutsch, has underestimated this connection. It was only later that he considered the antagonism of interests at least partly as a driving force of nationalism.

11 The Role of Institutions of Higher and Secondary Learning

ERICH HOFFMANN

Dynamic teachers always have been able to inspire young people, winning them over to their ideas and spiritual goals. This leads to the obvious question whether teachers, as well as their pupils and students, have been of significant importance for the formation of the national political elites of the non-dominant ethnic groups. Some active members of these groups were convinced at the time that they could guide young people in the direction of nationalism thereby gaining influence over the coming generation of their own non-dominant ethnic group. The point was made by the director of a teachers' college in Catalonia: 'always remember: if a teacher is a good teacher he becomes master of his people. When we have won over the teachers, the trusting masses of the people and the leading elites will be ours tomorrow!'[1] Universities and schools, however, could become important for the national movements of the non-dominant ethnic groups only after the increasing literacy of the European population from the beginning of the nineteenth century made it possible to spread new political ideas and views among broad strata of the population. Then they began to take root together with a national consciousness which was assuming a definite shape.

Improvement and extension of primary education first took place in west, central and north Europe; the south as well as the east and south east followed somewhat later. In most countries the improvements were linked to the introduction of compulsory school attendance. There was, however, a not inconsiderable difference between the European north west and the middle of the continent on one side, and the east and south on the other side, both in the availability and the quality of the schools and in the introduction of compulsory education. Educational systems also differed widely from one European state to another. In order to find a terminology defining as closely as possible the various educational systems, the terms 'primary' and 'secondary' schools and 'higher education' are

277

employed. 'Higher education' describes universities and similar institutions with equivalent functions such as seminaries, colleges, and academies. 'Secondary education' pertains to grammar schools and various other higher schools but also to institutes (for the training of primary school teachers), trade and agricultural colleges and seminaries of the Greek Orthodox Church. The important role which universities in particular had in the early stages of the formation of national ideologies (Phase A) must not be underestimated. During this time new ideas formulated in the privacy of scholars' studies reached the students in the lecture rooms, effectively were imparted to young people destined to become the future intellectual leaders of their non-dominant ethnic group. It was however only with the beginning of the Phase B of national agitation that the full range of educational institutions became important for the national movement. For this reason attention has been focused on Phase B, referring to Phases A and C only when, in some special cases, they are necessary for understanding development as a whole.

The Importance of the Institutions of Higher Education for Emerging National Consciousness

For the non-dominant ethnic group, universities and similar institutions were places of importance sending out strong signals that helped in the arousal of national feeling. But universities were by no means all situated in the geographical territory occupied by the non-dominant ethnic group, though some of them of course were quite near to the region of national conflict. The University of Kiel was a case in point. For various reasons it had provided a starting point in promoting both the German (Dahlmann, Falck and Droysen) and the Danish (Poulsen and Flor) movements in the duchy of Schleswig from the beginning of Phase A. In a similar fashion Barcelona University became the spiritual capital for the Catalans, not surprising as this city was the administrative, economic and ecclesiastical centre of the province of Catalonia. Only sons of well-to-do parents attended universities in Rome or Paris. The University of Tartu, situated in northern Livonia (which had an Estonian population) but subject to the special laws for the Baltic provinces, was German in character. Later, when the tsarist empire sought to convert it into a Russian university, ethnic Estonian interests were equally ignored. Nevertheless most Estonian students naturally chose Tartu (Dorpat) because of its proximity and importance as a centre of Estonian culture. Other Estonians attended nearby colleges at Riga or St Petersburg. In 1863–4 about 75 per cent of Czech students went to university in Prague; and about 19 per cent to Vienna and to other institutions in the Austrian part of the Dual Monarchy. From 1882, when Prague University was divided into Czech and German language sections, the percentage of students attending the Czech part had risen by 1902–3 to 91 per cent; with only eight per cent of the students then going to Vienna. From 1889 there was also a Czech technical college in Prague. In the Ukraine the majority of nationally minded students also went to local universities. About two thirds chose Kiev while a significantly smaller number went to Charkov and Odessa.

During the period of the Danish *Gesamtstaat*[2] students from the duchies of Schleswig and Holstein mostly went to the University of Kiel, at least for the terms preceding their final qualifying examinations. From 1813 to 1851 this meant that they came under the influence of professors advocating the 'Germanness' of Schleswig–Holstein. Even after 1920 students from the German minority in north Schleswig went to Kiel, at least for some period, in order to learn about conditions in their mother country and to gain, at the same time, a clearer view of matters at home. Many students from non-dominant ethnic groups, however, had from necessity to study at a university outside their home territory. Polish students from the province of Poznań/Posen did not have a local university. In the beginning most went to Prussian universities east of the Elbe. Subsequently, after 1863-70, when tension increased due to a change in Prussian policy towards Poland, greater numbers studied at other German universities in and beyond Prussia such as those in Berlin, Breslau, Leipzig, Munich or Heidelberg. The universities in the Russian and Austrian partitions were not much frequented. Like the Poles in Poznań the Macedonians did not have a university or an academy of comparable standard in their territory. Higher education could, in the beginning, be pursued only at the University of Istanbul or at technical or general education colleges established by foreigners in that city. From 1878, when national opposition against the Turkish state became strong, Slav Macedonian students gave preference to colleges in Bulgaria, but they also went to Russia and Serbia for higher education.

During Phase A circles of scholars and students formed at many universities advocating national goals and demanding liberal constitutions. Patriotic ideals also grew within the non-dominant ethnic groups during Phases A and B. Did those universities situated near their core territory become spiritual centres of national movements, or were they made into bastions for the interests of the dominant nation? Neither case can be proved conclusively. Some universities gained special importance for the national movements during Phases A and B, such as Barcelona for the Catalans; Kiel for the Germans from Schleswig; Prague for the Czechs, increasingly so after the establishment of a Czech section in 1882; Kiev for the Ukrainians in Russia; the Bulgarian or foreign colleges in Istanbul for the Macedonians. None of the national circles formed at these universities, however, gained a decisive influence. State control might be too effective, as for instance in Russia; professors belonging to the non-dominant ethnic group might not be friendly enough towards national political activities; or, as in the seminaries in Ireland, professors considered subjection to church discipline to be paramount.

Governments ignored the interests of the non-dominant ethnic groups because they wished the universities to be used as centres of influence for the ascendant culture. Centralised states, inclined to assume an authoritarian or patronising attitude towards minority groups, often put pressure on them, as for instance in Catalonia or the Ukraine. Pressure also was exercised on universities where all student circles were regarded with suspicion whether their activities were constitutional–political or national, and where official concern was to assimilate the future elites, independent of their ethnic identity for the benefit of the central state. In the course of this assimilation adaptation to the dominant culture was a consequence of the uniformity which state functionaries, above all, thought essential for the country. Some members of the non-dominant ethnic group, professors as well as students, deliberately chose assimilation when it offered the opportunity for a successful professional career. Nevertheless, there were professors at the University of Kiel and at Kiev or Charkov who did put the underlying ideas of the national movements into concrete form and actively recruited support for their ethnic group, either through teaching, as for instance with Dahlmann in Kiel, or by private contracts with student circles.

Unions of Student Activists

Students from the non-dominant ethnic group who had been converted to the ethnic cause did not always content themselves with just absorbing what nationally minded professors taught in their lectures. During Phases B and C many of them became creative protagonists and activists, often showing great involvement with the goals of their group. Some of them came from families which had been engaged already in the cause. While at university they formed the corporations and unions which were a usual feature of university life. Their activities were rarely of an unequivocally revolutionary nature, though there are some instances to the contrary. German students from Schleswig joined the volunteer corps of the Schleswig–Holstein army at the outbreak of hostilities with Denmark in 1848 and some of them became officers during the war. Czech students actively and energetically took part in the fight for Prague during the 1848 revolution. Some small but determined groups of Macedonian students took part in armed combat, although they hoped to further their national political ideas less by open fighting than with assassinations.

As a rule, however, the activities of student groups with national motivations took the form of keen participation in the life of the student corporations. The readiness of the Poles from Poznań to devote all their leisure time to these corporations is a particular case in point. Nationally minded student corporations or circles also were formed by Estonians, Ukrainians, Czechs, Macedonians, Catalans and Irish, as well as by the Germans from Schleswig. The general purpose of these circles was to study the history and literature of their own community in order to deepen their conscious identification with it. Some organisations were concerned with general political questions as well, but they always came back to the spiritual, political and economic situation of their own group.

More than any of the others, however, the example of the Polish student associations in Germany shows how university attendance and active participation in national student affairs could become a *cadre* for the recruitment and training of an elite destined for leadership of the movement. Most of these student bodies came into being during or after the uprisings in 1848 and 1863. Identification with the national cause was furthered by frequent meetings, lectures, discussions, by Polish language courses, celebration of national commemoration days and the study of political problems. Student societies also concerned themselves with those Poles who lived in their university town, the diaspora so to speak, offering them lectures, general advice and instruction in the communal cause. They camouflaged their activities skillfully when the Prussian state became alarmed and prohibited their activities. In this way members of the student corporations already were being prepared for their future political career as Polish spokesmen or activists.

In a similar fashion German students from Schleswig–Holstein in Kiel organised in a *Burschenschaft* (union) during Phases A and B. When these organisations were banned by the Karlsbad resolutions, the union in Kiel was changed into a 'camouflage' society. From 1920, a 'Society of German North Schleswig Students' became active in the university cities of Kiel and Copenhagen. This society strove to strengthen their students' ties to their group and to become a gathering point for those Germans who lived in the North Zealand 'diaspora' – a parallel to the activities of the Polish students in Germany.

Under the guise of a 'compatriot society' activist Ukrainian students tried, during Phase B, to strengthen national consciousness and to plan political activities. Both the Czech and the Catalan student unions were also of some importance for the students from their regions; they were concerned with education and political enlightenment. The Irish and the Estonians, however, limited themselves in their national student circles to internal activities which had more restricted importance for the training of future political activists. The north Schleswig Danes did not form national student corporations during Phases B and C; their elite included few people with university educations.

Which social strata sent their sons to the universities? As could be expected Polish, Ukrainian, north Schleswig German and Catalan students mostly came from upper and upper middle classes, families with sufficient financial resources. In Poland and the Ukraine, where the middle strata were not developed strongly as yet, the percentage of students coming from the aristocracy and from large estates was rather high (27–45 per cent in Poland). To a lesser degree the same can be seen in Catalonia. In the Ukraine there were practically no urban middle classes; the sons of the Orthodox clergy were prominent as university students.

For the rest students mostly came from the upper and educated classes but also from the bourgeois middle class. Most Irish students belonged to the latter class. From the third decade of the twentieth century German north Schleswig students came increasingly from peasant families with no more than average sized farms. The highest percentage of students (59.8 per cent) at the University of Prague in 1860 (and also before 1848) came from the middle class (farmers, craftsmen, minor civil servants and traders) and no less than 14 per cent of these were the sons of peasants. By 1900 this percentage (now comprising all Czech universities) had fallen to 43.2 per cent including 20.6 per cent of students of peasant origins. The percentage of the students who came from the *Bildungsbürgertum* (intellectual middle class) rose from 17.2 per cent to 20.6 per cent. The University of Vienna had, in both of these years, a rather high percentage of students from the educated middle class (26 per cent in 1860, rising slightly to 31.2 per cent in 1900). The growing influx of sons from the Czech educated classes can be explained by the fact that these occupations had grown in size between the two dates. In Macedonia, where conditions were unlike those in any other region, most of the students were sons of primary school teachers but there were also some with trade or professional backgrounds. Teaching was the typical 'intelligentsia' occupation which could be taken up rather easily by the upwardly mobile in Macedonia.

The statistics on which this study is based, and from which our percentage figures referring to social origins have been taken, refer for the most part to all students from the respective ethnic group. Students rarely cited their fathers status as peasants, petit bourgeois or lower class occupations. This is not surprising considering the social conditions at the time. Rapid upward mobility out of the peasantry or lower orders was not normally achieved in a single generation but usually required an intermediate stage such as primary school teaching. Many activist students from the non-dominant ethnic groups chose the liberal professions, such as medicine or law. For a career in state service assimilation into the dominant culture was a prerequisite, a step many were unprepared to take. However, there was no uniformity for the areas studied. For the Poles medicine was consistently popular. Nearly as many of them studied agriculture (sons of landed proprietors, for instance) and theology. In contrast the proportions of Poles choosing law or secondary school teaching decreased sharply from 1863. After that date opportunities in these two fields and in secondary schools were restricted severely by the Prussian state.

For the Czechs during Phase C the study of law opened the path to politics. Of the nationally inclined Czech deputies active during the second half of the nineteenth century, no less than 57 per cent with a university education studied law, followed by engineering and agriculture including veterinary medicine with 15 per cent, theology and the philosophical faculty with 11 per cent respectively, and medicine with six per cent only. Around the end of the century an increasing tendency towards study in a philosophy faculty can be detected; the law lost some of its appeal. Ukrainian activists prior to 1900 had a preference for historical and philosophical subjects. Later, the law, medicine and attendance at technical colleges became more popular. The shift resulted in part from Russian policy but also as a consequence of the comparative freedom from state influence and freedom enjoyed by physicians, lawyers and engineers. A similar desire for an independent position made medicine and the law a frequent choice for the Irish and the Germans from Schleswig though both, at some periods, enjoyed access to the national and local civil service. For the Macedonians primary school teaching was the preferred choice in the beginning because there was no university or comparable institution in their region.

The Importance of Academic Education for the Political Elites of the Non-dominant Ethnic Groups

As a rule students who joined ethnic student societies improved their knowledge of the language and the culture of their group, and their 'sense of belonging' was strengthened. Nevertheless after their return home not all former student activists were motivated to engage in leadership functions in politics. Involvement in this respect was rather high in the case of Poles, Estonians, Catalans and Ukrainians. Polish and Ukrainian students often had the experience of prolonged periods in closely knit societies and the corresponding ethnic centred influence which heightened their group consciousness. Student societies proved to be veritable nurseries for future political leaders. Among the Czech leaders university graduates were important, particularly in the upper echelons where, near the end of the century, an influential circle of 'political professors' exerted compelling authority.

In the case of the Germans in Schleswig the proportion and the influence of university graduates were higher during Phases A and B than after 1920. By then members of the liberal professions, such as physicians and lawyers, were displaced by wealthy peasants, tradesmen and business men in local elective affairs, though they were not wholly eliminated. From 1920 Germans began to emigrate from north Schleswig. As their status had been reduced to a mere minority group, lawyers, especially those who were activists, no longer entered the state civil service. Other than at the time of the supranational *Gesamtstaat* they now had little prospect of being appointed to positions in their home region. Similar conditions existed for other minority groups. Macedonians had few university graduates in their elite, but the importance of these was considerable. In Ireland many parliamentarians had a higher education background. For the Danish in Schleswig the numbers of university educated activists among nationally committed politicians was quite small.

In all the cases investigated the percentage of national activists in the leading elites who had a higher education decreased between Phase A and B, and still further in Phase C, though precise documentation of the change is unavailable. By the end of the nineteenth century 90 per cent of the Irish parliamentarians had a secondary school education but only a quarter to one third had a university degree. The number of Danish activists with university degrees was consistently low; while as for the Germans their percentage of activists with a higher education also decreased significantly, particularly during the last phase, to about ten per cent. Among east European ethnic groups the percentage as well as the influence of political leaders having a university education was naturally very high because of the comparatively small number of political activists coming from the bourgeois and peasant middle classes.

Among the Poles of Poznań, priests and aristocrats had an important role, followed by students after they had entered employment. Similar conditions can be seen in the Ukraine, where more then 80 per cent of the national activists had a university education. In Macedonia about 36 per cent of the members of the militant organisation Internal Macedonian Revolutionary Organisation had attended a university for some period, though a considerable number of ex-students had left prior to taking a degree. The Catalan situation is comparable to that of eastern Europe. A majority of the leaders and activists were university educated. Like countries in eastern Europe, Catalonia, though situated in western Europe, had been rather late in educational development. Consequently the intellectual upward mobility of peasants and petit bourgeois tradesmen also came later than it did in west, central and north Europe.

The Importance of Teachers for the Formation of the Elites of the Non-dominant Ethnic Groups

The winning over of teachers in all schools in their territory had to be a particular concern of ethnic groups. Teachers at secondary schools educated the future academic generation of the region destined to become leaders and activists. Teachers, particularly if they taught classical subjects, could hold courses on the history, language and literature of the national group outside the schools, making a significant contribution to its consolidation. The influence of primary school teachers in west and central Europe was comparatively small but in the east, particularly in the Balkan countries, it was substantial. Instruction in reading and writing was still the most important concern during the second half of the nineteenth century in eastern Europe. As there were few university graduates (and consequently a scarcity of secondary teachers) primary school teachers and the Greek Orthodox clergy formed the educated classes of the non-dominant ethnic group. As a result of the introduction of compulsory education early in the nineteenth century the population of Schleswig, as well as the Czech population, and the Estonians, Irish and Poles had reached a high degree of literacy rather early. The Catalans followed later but they also acquired literacy during Phases A and B, as did the Macedonians. In the Ukraine literacy progressed – as in the whole Russian empire – during the second half of the nineteenth century, but as late as 1914 only about half of the children in the country attended primary school. As late as 1897 the percentage of Ukrainians having a secondary or higher education was only 0.28 per cent.

The training of teachers at universities or colleges respectively for both school teaching levels was much the same for the Irish, Schleswigians, Czechs and Poles, the secondary school training of Catalans was comparable as well but primary teachers there were less well educated. The secondary school system of Estonia was first germanised and later the Russian influence prevailed. Estonians committed to the national cause nearly always were restricted to primary school teaching. There were no primary teachers among the Czech activists of Phase B, but during Phase C they were more involved than their colleagues in secondary schools. In the Ukraine, Russian was the compulsory school language. Throughout the Russian empire, the training of primary teachers remained primitive; while that of higher schools conformed more nearly to general European norms. At the end of the nineteenth century there were only two colleges for the training of primary school teachers in Macedonia, apart from courses for this purpose held at the secondary school at Salonika. The demand for primary teachers had to be met, to a large extent, by graduates of seminaries, secondary schools and even through in-service training in the primary schools themselves where approximately 46 per cent had received their teaching instruction as late as 1906–7. Nevertheless Macedonian primary school teachers, due to the special conditions mentioned above, constituted an important part of the 'intelligentsia' there. This situation did not exist in the Ukraine, though there as well the middle classes were represented weakly. The percentage of activists and sympathisers among the university graduates (and, consequently, among the secondary school teachers) was rather high, but the educational level of primary teachers and their share in national leadership was comparatively low.

The social origins of secondary school teachers can be found in the educated middle class and in 'upwardly mobile families'. In quite a number of cases, the 'upwardly mobile' occupation was primary school teaching. Whether national movements had an impact on the school systems is a vital issue. In Ireland, at least, the influence was marginal. The curriculum hardly took notice of Irish history and culture. Yet the national school system was above all controlled by the local communities in which the clergy predominated. The clergy therefore discouraged national activities of teachers. Parents in Ireland were less interested in patriotic education than in training suitable for advancement in the civil service not only in Ireland but also in England and the colonies, and for emigration generally. For these reasons national involvement of Irish teachers came late and was most apparent in some Catholic and state secondary schools. This single instance may lead to the fundamental conclusion that the comparatively low percentage of teachers (at both school levels) in the elites of the non-dominant ethnic groups were more or less due to the fact that they were not 'dominant'. Moreover the governments of the dominant nations could exercise pressure or even repression, thus discouraging teachers from the non-dominant ethnic groups from open national activism.

For these reasons, secondary teachers who were also committed activists – though outside their schools – only can be found in numbers among the Catalans, the Czechs and the Ukrainians, and much less frequently among other groups. In Estonia primary teachers were to a large extent the 'intelligentsia' within the national elite, the secondary schools being more or less under German or Russian cultural domination. Czech activists also included a considerable number of primary teachers, more than the proportion of their secondary school colleagues. The most significant exception were the primary teachers in Macedonia. Within the Ottoman empire, up to the Young Turk revolution of 1908, Macedonians enjoyed a certain cultural autonomy. This enabled teachers to establish a prominent place as active members among the elite of the national independence movement – which initially was campaigning for a union with Bulgaria. Their importance as the intelligentsia within the national elite is demonstrated by the fact that about 43 per cent of the activists were teachers. Up to 1908 the weak Ottoman state did not exert strict school supervision, as was the usual practice of stronger states.

Apart from this unusual example the national activity of teachers in the privately owned schools of the German minority in Danish north Schleswig, from 1920 is of particular interest. The German primary schools and the numbers of teachers committed to the national cause decreased through emigration or retirement, with their replacements being Danish. To combat Danish influence the German minority was able to engage, for their private schools, their own teachers. These generally had been trained in Germany which made it natural for them to take over much of the cultural work serving the national interest. These teachers at all school levels made up a large percentage of the activists particularly as they quite often were natives of the region. Most education for the Danish minority in south Schleswig after the referendum of 1920 was in community schools. Like their colleagues at the German language community schools in north Schleswig, teachers rarely became activists and for the same reasons, whereas those at the few private schools more often engaged in national agitation. In these widely separated non-dominant ethnic groups, the Macedonians and the Germans in north Schleswig, the national leaders can be supposed to have taken an active part in the appointment of teachers (according to the *millet* (devolved local government) system or the minority school regulations respectively), making them prove their national commitment before they could be engaged.

Endeavours of the Governments to Eliminate the Influence of the Non-dominant Ethnic Group from the School System

As has been noted, teachers at both school levels sympathising with the non-dominant ethnic group were more often than not prevented from embracing its cause just because this group was not 'dominant'. After all the dominant state often used school supervision as an instrument for the attempt to enforce the national identity of state, population and nation, for assimilating those parts of the population which had a different nationality. Lessons and the compulsory use of a single language were means to this end. National conflicts in the schools therefore were provoked less by the activist teachers of the non-dominant ethnic group than by the dominant state. During the transition from Phase A to B efforts to control education almost inevitably led to a clash between the state and the non-dominant ethnic group. Ethnic groups nearly always found themselves on the defensive because the state, by means of imposing curriculum and a compulsory language, as well as by disciplining teachers, was in a strong position to enforce policy. Teachers who were committed to the cause of the non-dominant ethnic group had to resort to passive resistance. Use of state power in the drive for assimilation can be seen in the treatment of the Ukrainians by the Russian autocracy and of the Catalans by the Spanish central state. In these cases the state ignored unwelcome and hitherto unrecognised particularist characteristics, and teachers and pupils could not pursue ethnic aims openly.

Typical cases of the impacts of the assimilationist policies of European states on language and education can be seen in the following examples, the history of the two Schleswig groups, and the events in Estonia, the Russian Ukraine and Poznań. In all these illustrations the state endeavoured to extinguish competing identities. Moreover the state tried to restrict the number of teachers active in the cause of the non-dominant ethnic group. Teachers were obliged to adapt a non-political posture. Some teachers resigned because of their convictions; others were forced to vacate positions. The aim was to reduce the number of activist teachers. There were however some very committed teachers who found new occupations, stayed in the region and took over important functions as members of elective councils, cultural establishments, or became editors. For instance, among the Danes in North Schleswig after 1864–67 this pattern became entrenched.

The Formation of Elites at Vocational Schools

Danes in North Schleswig belonged for the most part to a rather homogeneous peasant population. The secondary schools in the region were conducted in German, and pupils were taught German subjects. After the Prussian decree of 1888 even primary education had to be in German. The few activist young intellectuals from this group had to be trained at German universities if they wished to seek teaching appointments in their native region. Some peasants' sons went to Denmark to attend *Heimvolkshochschulen*, in Danish *Folkehøjskoler* (popular boarding academies) – often with financial assistance from private sources. At these institutions they were familiarised with Danish culture and national history, their fluency in the standard Danish language was improved and they also were initiated into methods of organisation necessary for future political activism. So-called *Nachschulen*, in Danish *Efferskoler* (supplementary schools) also served to perfect North Schleswig Danes in the use of their own standard language. After 1920 this system of popular boarding academies and supplementary schools was adopted by the Germans in North Schleswig. For the most part these institutions thereafter were located within the region and no longer required residence elsewhere.

Conclusion

The optimism of the Catalan seminary director quoted at the beginning of this chapter was unwarranted. Schools did not have a decisive influence in winning pupils over to the political programme of their ethnic group. Because of restrictions teachers often failed to achieve much. Even outside the schools teachers were active as leaders and activists only in some groups. However where greater involvement was allowed teachers were more prominent. Primary teachers for instance stood out particularly in Estonia and Macedonia because there they were, in fact, the most important 'intelligentsia' of their non-dominant ethnic group. At the beginning of the Czech movement teachers at secondary schools were important even though they were few in number. During Phase C the percentage of primary teachers taking part in the movement grew but the secondary teachers, some of whom became politicians, played a more assertive role. This was all the more possible because in the Austrian part of the Dual Monarchy there was no dominating people although Germans, due to their high standard of education, took a prominent place. In the Czech territories of Bohemia, Moravia and Austrian Silesia however, educational provision increased at an early date and in these provinces the number of Czech secondary schools and teachers increased rapidly. Secondary teachers were also active in the national cause of the Russian Ukraine and Catalonia, though mostly outside the school system. From 1920 when conditions at the schools in north Schleswig became less repressive, German teachers at both primary and secondary private schools as well as private school teachers and migrant teachers of the Danish minority group in south Schleswig could become functionaries in the ethnic organisations without risks.

Compared to the influence of schools, universities, colleges and academies were more important for the formation of national elites. Little difference existed between institutions situated directly in or near the territory of the non-dominant ethnic groups and those located elsewhere, as was the case for the Poles from Poznań and the Macedonians. In many European nations universities were centres of national consciousness, for both dominant and non-dominant groups. Quite often the national feelings of students were kindled not by professors of their own ethnicity, but by scholars from the dominant group who revived the language and the history of the suppressed peoples. German scholars in Estonia and Bohemia, for instance, were active in this field.

University scholars who consciously engaged in the cause of their ethnic group were important for the formation of elites, particularly during Phase A, not only because their lectures were concerned with political problems but also as they gathered around themselves nationally minded circles. From these many national leaders and activists did emerge during Phases B and C. In the early stages of the movement direct political activity by these academics mostly took place outside the university. Additionally they acted as *diet* or parliamentary representatives or as publicists writing newspaper articles, fly-sheets and polemical pamphlets. Academics inspired students to become conscious of their own nationality and to participate in political action. It was, however, only seldom that they became active politicians, as in the case of several German professors at the University of Kiel, of some Czechs in the University of Prague after its division into ethnic sections, and also of certain historians in the Ukraine.

During Phase A in particular universities had been important for the development of consciousness through the presence of nationally committed scholars who revived the history, language and literature of these groups. Their crucial influence on the formation of societies and organisations of the non-dominant ethnic group was through student circles. There were often founded by pupils of nationally committed professors. Members of these circles were active in the cause of their ethnic group, both during and after their university education, though not always with equal intensity. These student circles were probably the most important contribution of the universities to the formation of the elites of the non-dominant ethnic groups. At first sight those students from Schleswig–Holstein who took part in the fighting during the uprising from 1848 to 1851 give the appearance of having been particularly active, as do the Macedonians. In fact, though, the national organisations profited more from the work of those student societies which prepared their members for their future leadership positions. The Polish, Czech and Ukrainian societies stand out as being veritable factories turning out leaders for national organisations. Though this was also the case in Estonia, Catalonia, Ireland and for the Germans in Schleswig it was to a much lesser degree. In these territories student organisations, though consolidating national consciousness, hardly thought of furthering their leadership qualities through activism.

Most student activists came from the upper and educated middle classes, or the upwardly mobile peasant and petit bourgeois families. The lower orders played little part. Among groups studied only the Czechs and Catalans had an industrial working class. In regions where the middle class was not very numerous as in the Ukraine and (at the beginning) in Poland, the percentage of aristocrats among the students was comparatively high. In Macedonia it was mostly the sons of professional men, primary teachers and merchants who went to the university. In choosing a career nationally active students had to consider the special conditions in their territory. The liberal professions, such as medicine or law, were often selected because unlike the civil service they were comparatively free from state interference. Ethnic groups whose activist students had lived in close-knit circles during their stay at the university, such as the Poles or the Ukrainians, had a comparatively large percentage of academically educated activists later. Their firm national convictions and capacity for political, even conspiratorial action, made them valuable leaders.

Nevertheless students from non-dominant ethnic groups were in danger of being caught up in the assimilation process during their stay at the university because this was the route to career advancement. Assimilation either could be achieved by adapting to the outlook of the majority population or, if there was no really dominant peoples – as in the Austrian Dual Monarchy – by professing national indifference and exhibiting both loyal state consciousness and an attachment to the dynasty. In spite of all these difficulties it was very often the time spent at the university and the active experience of a community committed to a common purpose which in the young students awakened a readiness for active political participation – a readiness which quite often led to a lifetime of patriotic involvement.

Notes

1 See Brunn, Gerhard (1978), 'Die Organisation der Katalanischen Bewegung 1859–1959', in *Nationale Bewegung und soziale Organisation I. Vergleichende Studien zur nationalen Vereinsbewegung des 19. Jahrhunderts in Europa. Hrsg. Theodor Schieder u.a.*, Munich
2 Name given to Denmark, the duchies of Schleswig, Holstein and Lauenburg and colonial possessions overseas; in Danish, *helstat*.

12 National Organisations

ANDREAS KAPPELER

Social organisations, new forms of free associations, have been an element of social change in the transition to a modern society since the eighteenth century. Included among such organisations are the most important manifestations of national movements. By studying these organisations the structure, development, broad effect and depth of penetration of the national movements can be understood and analysed. Thus for some time research on nationalism in the field of social history has concentrated on examining organisations. The research project in Cologne directed by Theodor Schieder[1] and Miroslav Hroch's comparative study introducing a new periodisation and typology based on the social groups supporting national movements[2] have been trailbreaking.

The formation of new, self-conscious and active elites takes place in national organisations. Activists examined in this volume are by definition members or leaders of national organisations and the institutions they dominated are the framework for their formation, for the development of their political consciousness and for their social integration. It is in these organisations that they acquire fundamental social and political experience and provide an apparatus for dealing with government officials. Simultaneously the national organisations are instruments of agitation and communication in which and with the help of which the activists mobilise larger segments of the population for their cause. A comparative study on the organisations of non-dominant ethnic groups should thus reveal insights into the process of formation of national leaders.

In the following attempt at such a comparison a limited number of questions have been selected. The criteria are partly determined by the availability of sufficient information for all cases covered and also by the possibilities for cross national comparisons. The heterogeneous social, political and legal conditions governing the rise of national organisations are described, followed by a short overview of the organisation building. Then the types of organisations, their structure and their interactions are analysed. The conclusions drawn here are not definitive. At the most they articulate some problems which deserve further research.

Social, Legal and Political Conditions

The rise of social organisations forms an integral part of the modernisation of society. The most important features of modern society – industrialisation, urbanisation and the development of literacy – are prerequisites for the rise of national organisations. Heterogeneous socio-economic and cultural conditions and the varying level of social mobility resulted however in considerable time or phase lags between individual national organisations, as is revealed in the eight case studies.

Social conditions alone do not, however, adequately explain the actual phase lag. Differing legal and political conditions must also be considered. Legal conditions were most favourable to the Irish where extensive rights of association already existed by the first half of the nineteenth century. The same is true though to a much lesser degree for the Germans in the Danish *Gesamtstaat* (greater Denmark), the Poles in Prussia, the Czechs in Austria and the Macedonians in the framework of the Ottoman *millet* (devolved local government) system. The revolutions of 1848 improved the situation in some countries, only to be followed by temporary setbacks. By the end of the 1870s a liberal legal order had been widely established: for the Czechs dating from the 1860s; also for the Poles and the Danes in the German *Reich*; and after 1876 for the Catalonians. This legal order permitted the foundation of the social organisations of importance. For the Estonians and the Ukrainians in Russia this situation only existed in 1906–7, and was thereafter restricted; and for the Macedonians civil rights and liberties were realised only in the twentieth century, after 1908. A constitutional state which guaranteed civil rights and liberties offered conditions which decisively facilitated the rise of national organisations. Nevertheless in many states the regulations and their application by the authorities resulted in restrictions on the right of association, as in the case of the Danes and the Poles in Prussia.

Whether activists could link up to an existing organisation or could remodel it in the national interest also related to social, political and legal conditions. A forum for national political activity existed, for example, in the assembly of estate representatives in the Danish *Gesamtstaat* and, in particular, in the constitutional democracies with elections and parliaments. This applied, despite the property qualification for voting, especially to the Irish, but also from 1861 to the Czechs; plus to the Danes and the Poles in Prussia and – of less importance and sometimes only temporarily – to the other groups. Those groups which did not belong to the dominant religion of the state, primarily the majority of Irish, the Macedonians and the Poles of the Grand Duchy of Poznań, found in their respective churches an ideal ally in the struggle with the dominant state.

Autonomous bodies also could contribute to national crystallisation, such as those of the Macedonians and, to a lesser extent, those of the Irish and the Ukrainians (*zemstvos*). Educational institutions on all levels, especially the universities (see chapter 3), were important. Pre-national organisations of estates or supra-national cultural associations were sometimes remodelled by the national activists – for example, the Bohemian Museum and the Art Societies of the Czechs, groups representing the interests of the Catalan bourgeoisie as well as *Bürgervereine* (citizens' associations) in Schleswig, which split in the 1840s into German and Danish branches. For the borderland minorities of Schleswig after 1920 there were organisations available in both 'mother' countries, as well as for the Macedonians in Bulgaria.

Overview of National Organisations

It is difficult to measure and compare the degree of organisation of the individual ethnic groups during Phase B (the phase of national agitation) and at the beginning of Phase C (the mass movement). The quality of organisations was determined by a complicated network of factors. There was undoubtedly a considerable phase lag. In the first half of the nineteenth century the Irish already had political organisations with a mass base; the Poles in the Grand Duchy of Poznań, the Czechs in Austria and the Germans and Danes of Schleswig were in the process of founding national organisations at that time, while it was to be much later that the Estonians, the Catalans, the Macedonians and the Ukrainians of Russia followed this pattern. Despite a setback in the 1850s and a partially accelerated development among the latecomers, this gap remained. In the relative chronology of Phases A through to C a few general tendencies of development of the national organisations can be discerned. These tendencies are mentioned here as hypotheses and will be examined and differentiated in the following sections. The number of national organisations, their differentiation, their regional and social spread increased. Their structure was formalised and streamlined, their goals became politicised. The degree of organisation of the ethnic group in general became greater.

Two different organisational models can be detected. One model is characterised by the fact that a single or a few organisations attained great influence and a broad coverage relatively quickly during Phase B. Only later, during Phase C, did a large network of organisations with different orientations come into existence (the Poles of Poznań, the Macedonians and the Ukrainians in Russia). The other model was characterised by a broad network of regional organisations with varying goals. These organisations usually united only during Phase C to form political organisations on the national level (Czechs, Catalans, Danes and Germans in Schleswig during the nineteenth century). Often both models are intertwined as in the case of the Irish and Ukrainians.

Types of Organisations

A typology of national organisations can be based on their fundamental goals. It is feasible to distinguish between cultural, recreational, economic and political organisations. This analytical classification of primary goals is not always precise, since some organisations pursued several goals simultaneously. Also, especially in the initial phase of the national movement and among small ethnic groups, individual goals defy separation. It should additionally be remembered that such organisations not only had national goals, but also had to perform many other functions.

A special type of organisation – the informal organisation – needs to be mentioned briefly. This form of organisation is more difficult to define than those with a definite structure and goals. Discussion and social circles which met regularly in coffee houses or inns, clubs, casinos, editorial offices of newspapers and periodicals or in private residences fall in this category. Even if their importance is difficult to quantify these informal organisations were important in most of the groups studied in terms of the leadership and the decision making of such organisations for the formation of activists and of national ideas during Phase B.

In Hroch's periodisation, organisations with cultural goals are typical for Phase A but less so during Phase B of the national movement. This is confirmed by several case studies of the so-called 'small peoples'. In other types of ethnic groups represented (the 'big' nation of the Poles, the 'national minorities' of the Danes in Schleswig) but also in the case of the Irish and Macedonians, the sequence of cultural and political goals was less clear, as mentioned in the introduction. Macedonian nationalism linked up directly with the Bulgarian cultural movement, which largely acted as a substitute for its Phase A. The most important factor in the position of the Irish lay in the democratic system of the United Kingdom which allowed considerable political activity and which channelled national demands through parliament. It is not surprising therefore that at the other end of the spectrum the Ukrainians in autocratic Russia had organisations which remained strongly culturally oriented until 1914.

The relative importance of cultural organisations was influenced also by the existence of other non-political associations, particularly the economic and recreational groups. Such organisations usually had a broader base, whereas politically moderate intellectuals were typically engaged in the culturally oriented associations which still searched for allies. But where literacy levels were quite high and where restrictive policies regarding language caused tension, cultural organisations such as schools, education and language clubs could mobilise many members during Phases B and C. This was true for the Danes and the Poles in the German *Reich* and for the Czechs and – though only in Phase C – for the Catalans and in some respects the Irish as well. Scientific and literary societies, historical associations, theatre groups and especially the organisations aiming at popular enlightenment were typical of Phases A and B and were important in forming and spreading a national ideology. Organisations which furthered education, such as those which existed among the Poles of Poznań, the Irish, the Macedonians, the Czechs, the Danes and Germans of Schleswig, contributed directly to the formation of national activists. In such a comparative, systematic evaluation, the special features of the cultural organisations of the individual ethnic groups diminish. Examples are the Czech *Matice*, which furthered book production and was typical for the Slavs of the Habsburg empire, the Catalan poetry competitions called *Jocs florals* (flower games) and the gatherings of the Danes in Schleswig during which they drank coffee and sang national songs.

Recreational organisations cannot be separated always from the cultural groups. This applies in particular to the choral societies which for some peoples such as the Estonians and Latvians were the most important focuses of the national movements. Choral societies were also important during Phase B of the German national movement, and in turn for the Germans in Schleswig. But the tradition of choral societies was not confined to Protestant groups. Choral societies among the (Catholic) Czechs and the Poles of Poznań were important. However they did not play so prominent a role among the Irish and the Christian Orthodox peoples.

In the realm of sport gymnastic clubs were integral to national movements. Here too the Germans led the way with *Turnvater Jahn*, but the German clubs in Schleswig never attained the importance of the Czech ones. The gymnastic club *Sokol* (Hawk) founded in 1862 was the first mass organisation of the Czechs on a truly national level. It influenced neighbouring Slav peoples, such as the Poles of Galicia.

In 1884 the Poles in the German *Reich* in turn adopted the *Sokol* from the Poles of Galicia and quickly developed it into an important national organisation. All the examples mentioned here were direct neighbours of the Germans but there were such nationally oriented clubs sponsoring games in other parts of Europe, as evidenced by the Gaelic Athletic Association in Ireland (1884). However, there and for the Danes of Schleswig athletics organisations came into being at a time when the importance of sports had generally increased in Europe. Other organisations such as riflemen's associations, fire brigades or the hiking and wrestling clubs never became as important as the two types of recreational societies considered already. A special feature of recreational organisations was that their general goals permitted them to mobilise a large number of socially hetero-geneous groups for the national cause to a certain extent already in Phase B, but primarily in the early part of Phase C. In the course of Phase C political organisations often took over the task of providing entertainment and social activities.

National organisations with principally economic goals did not exist in all the cases. This can be explained by the social structure of the national activists (see chapter 10). Organisations devoted to developing agriculture, which were founded first by nobles and then adopted by farmers, can be found among the Czechs, the Poles of Poznań and among the Danes of Schleswig (but without the participation of the nobles). Industrial societies supported by the middle classes existed among the Czechs, the Poles of Poznań and the Germans and Danes of Schleswig. The cooperative system, as developed by the Poles and the borderland minorities of Schleswig, generally belonged to Phase C. In Ireland the cooperative movement was founded by a Unionist and remained non-political though sometimes attracting nationalist hostility. One condition for an economic orientation of national organisations, as developed most clearly by the Poles of the Grand Duchy of Poznań, the Czechs and the Germans and Danes of Schleswig, was a capitalist type of society and the existence of nationally mobilised, economic middle classes in the cities and/or the countryside, who often were in competition with other ethnic groups or were engaged in the emancipatory struggle. That such a development was lacking among the Catalans was apparently due to the fact that their bourgeoisie attempted to realise its economic interests in non-national organisations.

In the course of Phases B and C of the national movement, the activists increasingly created political organisations. The timing of their appearance and their specific outlook depended on the nature of the political system and its changes (on constitution and civil rights) on the traditions of the political culture of the individual ethnic groups and on general political developments in Europe. As mentioned the Irish, the Macedonians and the Danes of Schleswig created political groups quite early, whereas among the other groups these were preceded by other types of organisations.

As a rule political organisations in constitutional states started as associations for political agitation. They were *Honoratiorenparteien* (parties comprising local notables) and later became mass political parties. Examples of such associations can be found among the Irish (the Catholic Association); the Czechs (with the Slovanská Lipa/ Slavic Lime of 1848–9); the national movements in Schleswig (patriotic clubs); the Catalans with the *Unió Catalanista* (Catalanist Union) and the Poles of Poznań with the *Liga Polska* (Polish League) and *Straża* (Sentry), as a reaction to the German *Ostmarkenverein* (Eastern Marches Association). In parliamentary states the voting committees (among the Germans and Danes of Schleswig, the Poles of Poznań, the Czechs, and the Macedonians after 1908) and the parliamentary clubs (among the Irish, the Poles of Poznań, the Czechs, and the Ukrainians 1906–7) merit attention. In non constitutional states secret societies and short term action groups were more typical.

Political parties, which were better organised and had greater continuity and whose members and supporters wanted to influence developments in the state, eventually pushed the agitation societies into the background. The transition was fluid. As could be expected, the Irish were the first to found national political parties (in the 1830s), later in the century the Irish parliamentary party became their most important national organisation. Among the Czechs the *Honoratiorenparteien* of 'old' and 'young' Czechs were being founded from the 1860s. Legal and illegal national parties were formed among the other groups studied here only after the 1880s when parties and mass organisations had already been founded in Europe. On the one hand, there are the Czech parties, Polish parties in the Grand Duchy of Poznań, the *Lliga Regionalista* (Regional League) of the Catalans and voting clubs of the Danes in Schleswig as well as small parties of the borderland minorities in Schleswig after 1920. On the other hand, there are the illegal parties, the Internal Macedonian Revolutionary Organisation and the Ukrainian Revolutionary party. Establishment of political parties had less of a phase lag than can be found in the formation of other national organisations. In those national movements developing late, a foreshortened phase lag was not only the result of developing political complexity and a sign of a certain degree of political maturity, but also reflected outside influences.

A differentiation among political organisations usually took place in Phase C. In some cases – the Irish, the Macedonians and the Ukrainians of Russia – this happened quite early. Often two groups – liberal-conservative and radical-democratic which were occasionally called the 'old' and the 'young' – opposed each other. Among the Poles, the Irish and the Macedonians the national revolutionary and the constitutional tendencies confronted each other over a long period. With the rise of socialist movements the contrast between liberal democratic and social revolutionary or social democratic tendencies became, especially for the latecomers, a matter of great tension within the national movement (notably among the Ukrainians of Russia, but also for the Macedonians and Catalans).

Despite this differentiation the comparison reveals a continuity of the basic political tendency. A moderate tendency is revealed by the political organisations operating in a constitutional framework (the Czechs, the Catalans, the Poles of Poznań (in Phase C) and the Irish). Among the Ukrainians of Russia and the Macedonians, whose political organisations arose in a non-constitutional system, the agrarian socialist, social democratic and anarchic tendencies were very important. Only among the Macedonians did revolutionary groups – sometimes using terrorist methods – take over the leadership of the national movement, in a way comparable to the Armenian movement. In the Ukraine the revolutionary movement of the Russians (in which a disproportionately high percentage of Ukrainians participated) developed such violent techniques while the Ukrainian national movement eschewed them almost entirely. Premature general conclusions which see a connection between the relative delay of the national movement in a non-constitutional political system and its political radicalism are invalidated by the revolutionary tendency among the Poles in the Grand Duchy of Poznań during Phase B and of the Irish. The Irish always had parallel constitutional and revolutionary organisations such as the Irish Republican Brotherhood founded in 1858. Apparently the existence of revolutionary organisations can be explained to a certain extent by a tradition of older, pre-modern protest movements – for example, the tradition of revolt among Polish nobles and of social banditry among the Irish, Macedonian and Ukrainian peasants. It would be useful to investigate the pre-modern organisational forms of the non-dominant or dominant ethnic group as a condition for national organisations. A simple conclusion follows: the national movement was relatively moderate if the activists were recruited primarily from an urban middle class (as was the case with the Czechs, the Irish, the Catalans, the Poles of Poznań – in Phase C – and the Germans of Schleswig) or from a rural middle class (as was the case with the Danes of Schleswig and the Irish again); if the national intelligentsia sprang from economically suppressed lower classes, such as the Macedonians and Ukrainians, then a radicalisation was more probable.

Mention must be made of two special types of national organisations which are relevant for a few of the groups studied. One was the organisation of particular social groups such as women, young people, students and representatives of various professions; the other was of those who had emigrated, in particular among the Irish and the Macedonians.

What conclusions by way of a typological comparison of the goals of national organisations can be drawn? First there are a great variety of organisations with different purposes. Occasionally one type is substituted by another, generally a non-political organisation replaces a political one. Second there are regularities, confirmed by exceptions, in the development of organisations towards functional differentiation and the greater importance given to political organisations. Several types of organisations, such as the associations for popular culture and education and the political parties, can be found in all case studies.

Apart from the general character of the political system it can be said that the legal and political conditions along with the specific policies of the government were very important for the orientation of national organisations. In addition to the internal factors there were external ones – cross currents of all European movements and ideologies and the examples set by other peoples. The effect of the highly organised German national movement on neighbours, of the Czech model on other Slavic peoples, of the Poles of Poznań on the other Poles, of the influence of the 'mother peoples' on the German and Danish borderland minorities, of the influence of the Ukrainians of Galicia on the Ukrainians of Russia, and finally the impact of the dominant nations (the British on the Irish, the Russians on the Ukrainians and the Germans on the Poles of Poznań) illustrate the point.

The formation and social composition of the activists also strongly influenced the orientation of national organisations. Equally the specific organisational forms in turn influenced the national elite coming into being during the various phases. Whether agitation took place in the framework of a parliamentary party or a gymnastic club, in an industrial society or in a revolutionary clandestine organisation affected the political experience and, in the medium range, the political culture of the new national elites. However this assertion needs to be properly verified in a more comprehensive comparative study. Individual organisations, for example the gymnastic clubs, their appearance and their importance for specific national movements in Europe, could be analysed. It could determine whether the types of organisations were all based on a common model, as for example the German gymnastic club, or whether they developed independently but under similar conditions. A comparison of their specific functions in the fields of agitation and communication in the various phases of the national movement would be feasible then.

Organisational Structure

National organisations were the framework for the activities of group leadership. It is therefore interesting to examine on a comparative basis their organisational structure, how they recruited their officials, the place and form of decision making, modes of finance, the extent of their social and regional influence and the intensity and management of conflicts with government authorities. Comparative study of such questions is particularly difficult due to the rich variety of organisations and legal conditions and also because of the constant changes these bodies underwent. Since the same kind of information is not available for each ethnic group it is only possible to focus on some common features. First there was a tendency to develop from a loose structure (in Phase A) to a formal, hierarchical, more centralised apparatus in Phase C in the majority of the cases studied. This holds true for the Irish, Czechs, Germans and the Danes of Schleswig and to a lesser extent for the Catalans and Russian Ukrainians. The Irish, the Poles of Poznań and the Macedonians attained a relatively advanced structure quite early.

Brief reference to the two organisational models described above is imperative: one had a structure developing from the bottom (from local and regional associations) to the top (to a national organisation) and the other from the top (a central organisation) to the bottom (with regional branches). In Phase B the organisations of the Czechs, Catalans, Ukrainians and the Danes of Schleswig were relatively loose in structure, whereas those of the Poles of Poznań and Macedonians were distinguished by a predominantly hierarchical, centralised structure. Different structures arose due to distinctions in historical development as was the case for the administrative traditions (the Poles) and the national revolutionary expressions (the Macedonians). Among the Macedonians, the Russian Ukrainians and the revolutionary branch of the Irish movement, secret organisations were prevalent. They had a structure which was adapted to their clandestine activities. There were no secret organisations among the bourgeois constitutional movements of the Catalans, Czechs (with the exception of the short lived 'Repeal' named after the Irish model) and the Danes and Germans of Schleswig. Among the Poles of Poznań they were important during Phase B but then diminished in significance. Ireland had both secret and legal organisations throughout the period.

The structure of legal constitutional organisations was defined by the regulations governing the right of association and assembly. Standing orders and statutes defined the basic structure. Nevertheless in addition to the formally elected bodies – the assembly of members and the executive board – informal bodies played an important role in decision making. The recruitment of the functionaries for the national organisations was crucial for the formation of a body of national activists. Regulations prescribed the election of the executive board by the assembly of members; but in reality the leading bodies often coopted new members, especially during Phase B. This was the rule for secret organisations; the most important functionaries of the Internal Macedonian Revolutionary Organisation were often appointed by the central committee.

It should be noted that in many national organisations informal internal circles or leading personalities played a decisive role. Some examples are provided by the Irish leaders Daniel O'Connell and Charles Stewart Parnell, the Pole Karol Marcinkowski, the 'Czech politicians' František Palacký and his son-in-law František Ladislav Rieger, the Ukrainian historians Antonovych, Drahomanov and Hrushevs'kyj, and H.P. Hanssen, the son of a rich Danish farmer from north Schleswig. Prominent among the Poles of Poznań were the so-called patrons who exercised great power by having important positions in several national organisations (such as Piotr Wawrzyniak, Maksymilian Jackowski). For the formation of the national activists, which took place largely during Phase B, informal contacts, friendships and clientele relationships were, as a rule, more important than democratic elections.

How were the national organisations and their leaders financed? Most organisations collected membership subscriptions, but apparently this source was more or less adequate only for the Poles of Poznań and the Czechs – and then only during Phase C. During Phases A and B donations from patrons, such as from the Poles Tytus and Jan Działyński and Seweryn Mielzyński, the Catalan industrialist Güell or the Ukrainian sugar manufacturer Semyrenko, a descendant of a serf family, were common. Until the First World War the Germans and Danes of Schleswig were financed by membership dues and donations, then during the 1920s they also received financial support from their respective mother country. The same applied to the Macedonians who received help from Bulgaria. The Irish received vital funds from the USA without which the movement could not thrive. Despite all these financial sources most of the national organisations suffered chronically from inadequate funds. The Internal Macedonian Revolutionary Organisation improved its financial situation temporarily by raids and the taking of hostages. Only a few leaders of the national organisations could be paid in such a way as to permit them to work as professional politicians and this only during Phase C. As a rule they worked on a voluntary basis. Some earned their living as editors and journalists. Thus activists coming from financially better situated groups had greater opportunities to advance.

The dominant society and the state strongly influenced the organisational structure of the non-dominant ethnic groups. A state's organisational structure served as a model while the policies and official measures towards national organisations forced the activists to react, whether this meant to adjust, to develop evasive strategies or to direct their energies into illegality. The history of most national organisations was replete with repeated encounters with the authorities. Repressive measures of the individual states varied from small fines and temporary prohibitions to prison sentences, banishment and even executions. Of course these measures depended also on how radical the organisation's goals became. The political stand of the activists was influenced decisively by the reciprocal relationship between the regime, whether constitutional or authoritarian, and the national movement, whether bourgeois or revolutionary.

Interaction between Organisations

Individual national organisations cannot be viewed in isolation. They were always interrelated to other national and supra-national groups. The functions of the individual national organisations of an ethnic group were largely complementary during Phase B and encompassed various regions and fields of activity. Thus it was common practice for many activists to be members of several organisations simultaneously, for example, in cultural, recreational and economic associations. Political conflicts usually took place in a particular organisation between different wings or between the 'older' and 'younger' generation. There were more conflicts between the different associations of an ethnic group during Phase C and the rise of national political parties as a result of the increasing complexity of the organisational structures.

Relations of organisations in one country to bodies of the same ethnic group in another presented a special problem. An obvious instance was the close relationship the Russian Ukrainians had with those in the Austro–Hungarian empire and the connections of the Macedonian organisations with Bulgaria and those of the borderland minorities with the organisations in the respective 'mother' country. By contrast the contacts of the Polish organisations in the Grand Duchy of Poznań to those in other parts of partitioned Poland were limited. For the organisations and their leaders, who were constantly threatened by the changes in policy particularly of the authoritarian governments, support from national organisations in more liberal countries abroad was extremely important.

Cooperation within 'pan' movements such as between the Czechs and other Slavs of the Habsburg empire or between the Irish and other Celts of the United Kingdom was not significant. The same applies to the occasional contacts of the Catalans with the Basques, or the Macedonians with the Albanians and Armenians. In the Prussian Chamber of Deputies and in the German *Reichstag* (imperial parliament) representatives of the national minorities (Poles, Alsatians and Danes) did manage to cooperate.

More complicated but vastly important were the interrelationships of the national organisations with non-national groups of the same ethnic community or of the dominant nation itself. During Phase B national activists tried, as mentioned above, to bring about a reorientation of the supra-national organisations. One of the main problems was the supra-nationally orientated church, which the activists tried to mobilise for their cause, an effort in which they were not always successful (as in the case of the Czechs, the Ukrainians of Russia and the Catalans). In parliamentary systems non-dominant ethnic groups often had to cooperate with the organisations and parties of the dominant nation in order to realise their own goals. Thus the Irish cooperated for a long time in parliament with the British Whigs and later with the liberals, Czechs often worked with the Austrian conservatives prior to 1890, and Catalans with the Conservative party in Madrid. Furthermore the moderate Ukrainians entered a coalition with the Russian Cadets in the first and second *duma* (parliament) (1906–7), and the Macedonians cooperated with the Young Turks after 1908.

Organisations of the earlier national movements of the Irish, Poles and Czechs, but also of the Catalans coincided with liberal democratic currents, whereas the latecomers had to face the challenge posed by the socialist movement. This can be said for the Macedonians and Ukrainians, who at the end of the nineteenth century were still in Phase B, at a time when the majority of the population had not yet been mobilised for the national cause. In the Russian Ukraine the social revolutionary and social democratic parties were more successful in mobilising Ukrainian intellectuals, dissatisfied peasants and workers than the young national parties. Many Ukrainians considered the abolition of tsarism the primary goal and they pursued this aim through a revolutionary movement dominated by the Russians. Macedonian activists were strongly influenced by social revolutionary ideas and wavered later between national and international revolutionary organisations. For the older national movements, the workers' organisations could be a serious competitor during Phase C (this applied to the case of the Czechs, the

Germans and Danes of Schleswig and the Catalans). It gave cause for concern to orthodox nationalists in Ireland. But generally the goals and the existence of the national organisations were not seriously questioned. For ethnic groups whose movements were delayed and who had to live in authoritarian systems, the challenge of socialism was of great importance, both with respect to the orientation of the national organisations as well as to the political culture of the elite. A comparative study of the interrelationship between national and socialist ideas, between national movements and the working class movement would be another area for future research.

Conclusion

- National organisations were the most important framework for the formation of national elites. In them the activists met one another, leaders emerged, political experience was gained and groups were created with a specific identity and goals. The formation of national organisations and evolution of activists during Phase B of the movement had an effect on the political culture of the individual ethnic groups extending beyond the period dealt with here. This applies to the groups which remained non-dominant, as well as to those which later became dominant nations and were thereby in turn confronted with non-dominant ethnic groups within their borders. A comparative study of continuities of this kind would make a rewarding research project.
- The importance of the dominant 'government' for the formation of national organisations and elites has become clear. The role of the nature of the political system, the legal conditions (particularly the guarantee of the right of association and assembly) and the respective 'policy towards nationalities' can hardly be over-estimated. An absence of political and legal status could not prevent the formation of national organisations and elites but could delay it considerably. Different legal and political conditions undoubtedly influenced to a great extent the character of the national organisations and their programmes and thereby the activists.
- The socio-economic and socio-cultural conditions were as import-ant as the political ones. Close connections between the structure and the programme of the national organisations and the social composition of the national activists, the degree of social and economic differentiation as well as the social and economic problems of broader strata of the population are readily apparent.
- Specific development patterns in the formation of national organisations from Phases A to C can be observed – from a loose to

a formal centralised structure, towards a greater differentiation of the organisation and its goals, thereby resulting in more conflicts within the national movement. Finally political programmes gained priority over cultural, recreational and economic goals.

• In addition to the relative chronology, the absolute chronology also must be considered. The general political and intellectual situation in Europe confronted the older national movements, such as that of the Irish and the Poles, which had virtually completed Phase B by the middle of the nineteenth century, with other problems than those faced by the latecomers, such as the Macedonians and Ukrainians, who were still in Phase B at the end of the nineteenth century and who encountered new challenges – political parties, the working class movement, socialist ideas. General European developments such as the national movements (of the Germans, Italians, Irish, Greeks, Poles and Czechs), revolutions (especially the revolutions of 1848), political currents such as liberalism, socialism and populism exercised an influence on the individual national movements and their organisations at different times. The effect of such external factors varied greatly depending on the phase of development of the national movement, whether it had just entered Phase B (national agitation) or had already become a mass movement. It is not possible to present definitive conclusions here, more detailed comparative studies are still necessary.

This brief comparison has shown that organisation was a key problem of the national movements in general and the formation of national elites in particular and deserves study in a comparative perspective. Further case studies are essential to a more balanced picture.

Notes

1 The most important results have appeared in *Studien zur Geschichte des neunzehnten Jahrhunderts*, in particular vol. 3: Theodor Schieder and Peter Burlan (eds) (1971), *Sozialstruktur und Organisation europäischer Nationalbewegungen*, Munich-Vienna; vol. 9.1: Theodor Schieder and Otto Dann (eds) (1978), *Nationale Bewegung und soziale Organisation I. Vergleichende Studien zur nationalen Vereinsbewegung des 19. Jahrhunderts in Europa*, Munich-Vienna, compare in particular the Introduction by Dann, pp. XIII–IXX; vol. 13: Dieter Düding (1984), *Organisierter gesellschaftlicher Nationalismus in Deutschland (1808–1847). Bedeutung und Funktion der Turner- und Sängervereine für die deutsche Nationalbewegung*, Munich. See also Otto Dann (ed.) (1984), Vereinswesen und bürgerliche *Gesellschaft in Deutschland*, Historische Zeitschrift Beihefte N.F.9, Munich.
2 For a discussion of Hroch's concept see chapter 1 pp. 1–8.

13 Channels of Communication

LORENZ RERUP

Introduction

Since publication of Otto Bauer's pioneering *Die Nationalitätenfrage und die Sozialdemokratie*[1] intensive social communication has been seen as the central element in the formation of nations; a view conclusively reaffirmed in the works of Karl W. Deutsch.[2] Bauer's focal point is the interacting transport and cultural community; Deutsch puts complementary social communication at the centre of his theory. A close network of communication is crucial to a national movement; simultaneously communication within an ethnic group is greatly intensified by it and the activities of patriotic leaders.

Deutsch uses the term 'social communication' in a rather broader sense than merely the 'exchange of information'. To simplify case study comparisons in this volume a modified version of the customary meaning of the term is employed. Account has been taken of channels which were used for the exchange of information and also those which served to disseminate ideas, political or cultural views, attitudes and historical conceptions, aimed at influencing or shaping public opinion – in short, intended to mobilise broad strata of the population. Certain general conditions essential to facilitating or hindering communication, such as the level of education (literacy) and legal conditions (freedom of the press, of association and assembly), are treated. However comparisons can be no more than tentative. Diversity of cases along with differences in available research which exists for the various groups renders precision impossible. Two forms of communication – oral and literary – are assessed. Communication has a wider ambit. Dancing, drama, dress, diet and popular culture express distinctive values or national *mores*. Similarly symbols and emblems have a vital function.

Oral Communication

Because of the problems of survival and accumulation of evidence
oral forms of communication are sometimes neglected. Yet oral
communication was the chief channel of ideas in the less complex
societies of the last century when broad strata of the population were
scarcely literate and remained parochial in outlook.

In Phase C, when mass mobilisation had taken place, organised
oral communication occurred in a large number of societies, associations and clubs. The broad strata of the population resorted to these
groups for political, cultural, vocational and leisure pursuits: the
enclosed atmosphere enabled the masses to ferment ideas and
reinforce loyalties while resisting assimilative pressure from the
surrounding society which threatened to erode the national movement. It was an important function of these bodies to be instruments
of agitation and communication. Moreover a distinctive 'community
culture' developed in some, as in the numerous Danish clubs in north
Schleswig after 1864. Singing national songs – as far as these were
permitted – and the common coffee table strengthened ethnic
solidarity.

Schools were a major vehicle of organised oral communication. In
the cases examined they were nearly always government institutions
and the dominant state generally tried to use them as instruments for
furthering assimilation of minority groups. Nevertheless schools
often had a profound mobilising influence. For both Danes and
Germans in north Schleswig minority schools, both private and
public, were becoming the norm after the First World War. These
played a crucial part particularly if they were financed by the mother
country, making them independent of the local dominant state.
Compulsory state schools before the war proved unsuccessful agents
for assimilation when the parents of the threatened ethnic group
actively thwarted the proselytisation.

For Macedonians schools were exceptionally vital, the Ottoman
millet (devolved local government) constitution having left communities with sufficient autonomy for dealing with their own
religious and educational affairs. Such independence was contingent
upon two thirds of the inhabitants of the community choosing to
leave the jurisdiction of the Greek Orthodox patriarchate in Istanbul
and for acceptance of the Bulgarian exarchate. It nevertheless
ensured the development of an extensive school system from about
1880.

The case of Macedonia, though distinguished by two churches of
the same creed, nevertheless demonstrates the important role
of confessional allegiance. Churches always had a close network of
communication which was tightened during the second half of the

nineteenth century by the founding of youth and social clubs and similar communal activities. Even through their language Churches have a national impact. As with the schools this can be negated when the population remains resistant. But the national impact is greatly enhanced where, as in the case of the Irish and the Poles, the religion of the ethnic group differs from that of the dominant people. The long pattern of religious grievance in Ireland underscored the ethnic conflict. Quite naturally the churchyard of an Irish village became a regular meeting place after Sunday mass and priests often took the leadership of political meetings.

Nearly all the Poles in the Grand Duchy of Poznań were Catholics, pious in their observance of confessional rites. The attempts to germanise the Catholic clergy failed. No more than approximately 15 per cent of the priests were of German stock. Often national celebrations were held in churches with the priests giving patriotic addresses. In church buildings and later in the Catholic houses established in many villages, meetings of diverse political organisations were held, amateur performances and similar events took place and Polish newspapers were available. Moreover important information was disseminated from the pulpit; this might include the elections for the Prussian *diet*, diverse public events and meetings. The 'brothers in the faith' were encouraged to take part in the activities of the Polish national movement. Burial rites for key figures and intellectuals also played an important part in Poznań and other towns. The frequently well attended funeral orations were delivered by eminent priests who praised the virtues and merits of the deceased. These eulogies were not limited to the memory of the deceased but were also meant to extol Polish virtues in the population as part of the struggle against germanisation. Many of these funeral orations were published subsequently.

In the early stages of the national movements, during Phases A and B, less formalised channels of communication were vital as well. During Phase A when circles were necessarily still small communication was transmitted through the social life of intellectuals or at regular meetings of local peasant leaders at markets or trade centres. With the beginning of Phase B wider communication began. Though the activists often used handbills, newspapers and books, these reached rather small numbers. This was not due to an inability to read – only the Ukrainians among groups investigated were late in achieving literacy. However most people were not accustomed to having their opinions and attitudes shaped by newspapers and also the circulations for periodicals were small. The spoken word and personal contacts were much more effective and the impact longer lasting. Activists always engaged in patriotic work in populous places. In Schleswig, for instance, two rival movements competed for control of the social and shooting clubs in the towns as early as about 1840.

The rather strong involvement of publicans in the early Danish movement indicates that inns played a part during this phase. In the Prussian period that influence was curtailed because licensees were dependent on the goodwill of the administration. University teachers had their lecture rooms, the duke of Augustenborg his hunting parties. Of prime importance were political bodies, such as the *stænderforsamling* (assembly of the estates) in Schleswig from 1836 or the communal self-government in Bohemia. After 1861 the Czechs needed no more than a few years to gain firm control over these institutions. Banquets were popular occasions which gave activists opportunities to speak, thereby increasing popular recognition of individuals. From 1842 there was a *Kasino* in Poznań, a social club which put more than 30 Polish and foreign periodicals at the disposal of its members. The *Beseda* founded in 1845 in Prague by the Czech citizens as a counterpart of the German *Casino* initially had 500 members. Soon almost every town had a circle of this kind. Amateur theatres and choral societies were founded everywhere in quick succession. Balls also played a role during the initial stage of the Czech movement; at such functions the mother tongue was spoken, patriotic music was featured, and poems recited. In a number of cases during the 1860s political decisions were even initiated in Czech drawing rooms. In the Ukraine clubs became meeting places for the intelligentsia in spite of the legal restrictions imposed by the Russian empire. The club in Kiev was, from 1905, particularly active in the cultural field; and 40 out of the 63 Ukrainian *duma* representatives belonged to a political club in St Petersburg.

These informal places of communication were, however, completely outdone by the Catalans' coffee houses. Acquaintances and friends met regularly in them to exchange ideas and news. At the beginning of the century Catalan politicians met every night at the Café Continental in Barcelona for discussions. These occasions enabled exchanges of information with members of other circles. In coffee houses candidates for elections were often selected in advance of the official procedure and political arrangements were settled. Similar or somewhat different discussion circles existed everywhere in Catalonia. In the small town of Granollers for instance a circle met for years following the local market in the printing works. Editors' rooms were also meeting places for leaders in Poland (for example, those of the *Posener Tageszeitung* (Poznań Daily Journal) and the *Posener Kurier* (Poznań Courier)). Similar informal collectives existed for most national movements, particularly in places where, as in Granollers, channels of communication (market and newspaper) crossed.

Apart from these social clubs and societies which were as yet the meeting places of rather narrowly defined groups, popular meetings were extremely important for nearly all national movements, both in the early stages and in the later phases. The special atmosphere created by crowds could make the listeners more receptive for the messages of the speakers and increased their effect – always supposing that the speaker had a voice that could make itself heard. When the meeting was coupled with a celebration the mass impact could be even greater.

Following an indigenous tradition the Irish began to hold mass meetings as early as 1830 and the 'monster meetings' of Daniel O'Connell in aid of the repeal campaign made a great stir. These meetings were held not only to underline the demand for a repeal of the Union but also to mobilise the masses. They were often held in places which had been important earlier in Irish history. Mass 'meetings', nearly all devoid of rioting or violence, were a feature of the Irish movement until 1920. They constituted an essential aspect of Ireland's political culture and became a direct model for the numerous Czech popular meetings held from 1868 to 1871 in protest against the 1868 settlement between Germans and the Hungarians which excluded their aspirations. At first these events were called meetings but soon they were rechristened *tabors* (open air mass meetings) in memory of the Hussite movement. More than 100 of these were held in Bohemia plus another 40 in Moravia and Silesia. Tens of thousands participated; being drawn from among the peasantry and workers as well as the urban petit bourgeoisie.

In the Schleswig region popular meetings with several thousand participants were held for the purpose of national mobilisation from the spring of 1843 onwards. The Danes were the first to meet in this way but Germans followed the example almost immediately. Apart from the speeches there were musical performances and a multitude of entertainments such as dancing, shooting competitions, fireworks and dinners for special guests. Because they appealed to a rather different social milieu from the German counterpart Danish meetings were generally more simple in character. Musical entertainment at the Schleswig–Holstein meetings was often provided by *Liedertafeln* (glee clubs). These had started in Germany but soon became a popular feature in the duchies from 1839, keeping up an effective network of communication by mutual visits and through organising both regional and interregional events. Originally the *Liedertafeln* were founded in Germany under the Napoleonic occupation for the purpose of cautiously expressing a hope for liberation. Later in the duchies they proved to be an effective instrument for awakening national feelings in the people. Through the medium of popular songs politics could be brought closer to the people, gripping and enkindling their hearts 'where words could not and would not do so'.[3]

In Schleswig popular meetings with up to 12 000 participants were held, mostly in the initial stages of the movement. After a lively beginning they were usually held annually and were meant to demonstrate the strength of the movement, both to the government and to the rival ethnic community. However they also provided opportunities for recruitment. Some were used – as for instance the Schleswig *Sängerfest* (popular music meeting) given by *Liedertafeln* (glee clubs) in 1844 – to launch the new Schleswig–Holstein flag and the new anthem of the movement. After 1851 Schleswig–Holstein meetings were suppressed and the Danish ones became less important. Much later the popular meetings in Schleswig were replaced by festivals whose purpose was consolidation rather than mobilisation but they naturally also served to demonstrate the strength of the movement. Choral festivals assumed prominence for the Estonian and Lithuanian national movements somewhat later.

Popular meetings gained added importance for Poles from the 1850s. They grew out of electioneering meetings and by 1870 had developed into a Polish form of protest. The interference of the German government in the established rights of the Catholic Church during the *Kulturkampf* (cultural struggle) after 1870 inspired Church meetings which attracted thousands. Such meetings were frequent, a dozen sometimes being held within the space of a few weeks. They were occasions for speeches, discussions and resolutions. By the turn of the century these popular protests had reached the mass of the people. Now the fury was directed against the intensifying germanisation policy of the administration but meetings also were organised mainly for women because of their special responsibility for keeping the mother tongue alive by teaching it to the children. The *Reichsvereinsgesetz* (Association Act) banned Polish language meetings in territories with less than 60 per cent Poles in the total population. Meetings continued to be held in regions where they were permitted officially. Danes in Schleswig were bound by the same legislation but had been granted a transitional relief period of 20 years.

Public meetings held for a municipal borough, a region, or the whole country, were among the most important means for exerting political influence in Catalonia. They could be organised at a maximum number of places simultaneously in order to increase their impact. As a rule there were numerous orators and an impact on the surrounding region was intended. One central rally in May 1906 was attended by approximately 200 000 people – about one tenth of the entire Catalan population.

Popular meetings worked in inverse directions: inward to increase mobilisation and outward to demonstrate the existence and the nature of the movement. In the national festivals the accent was on the latter function. National feeling and the strength of the movement were displayed; they were attended only by those who already had been politicised and joined the movement, though the common experience might strengthen their convictions.

The Irish had St Patrick's Day and also Lady Day. Poles commemorated the death of eminent national figures (in the beginning with memorial masses only) or held celebrations on anniversaries of past uprisings. From 1870 an imposing repertory can be seen. In many places in Poznań there were celebrations on the four hundredth anniversary of the birthday of Kopernikus in 1873; in 1880 on the fiftieth anniversary of the November uprising; in 1883 for the two hundredth anniversary of the battle of Vienna; in 1898 on the centenary of A. Mickiewicz; that of J. Słowacki in 1909 and Chopin in 1910 as well as of the Kościuszko uprising in 1894. There was also the half millennium of the battle of Grunwald (Tannenberg) in 1910 and a commemoration of the half century of the January uprising in 1913. The majority of the population joined in these festivities, concerts and amateur performances: 6000 have been recorded as partaking in celebrations in Poznań in 1884, while in small towns and villages between 100 and 200 participants were counted. For many Poles these celebrations, which frequently faced petty obstructions from the authorities, provided the main channel through which to obtain knowledge of their culture and history. A contemporary periodical praised such occasions as 'the best school in which patriotism, respect for the traditions, as well as Polish manners and customs are implanted in the Polish people; by them the love of the mother tongue is disseminated and strengthened and youth is protected from denationalisation.'

Germans in Schleswig celebrated the *Sedanstag* (in memory of the battle of Sedan in 1870) and the emperor's birthday. From 1894 they held a Knivsberg festival which began with speeches and sporting events; later on a religious service, festival plays and similar activities were added. In 1901 a Bismarck monument was inaugurated. The Danes celebrated the anniversaries of the battle of Idstedt/Isted in 1850 and the fall of the Dybbøl/Düppel Redoubts in 1864. The 1920 referendum afterwards was remembered annually by many small and large celebrations, generally with speeches, communal singing and the serving of coffee. The reunion of north Schleswig was celebrated on the battlefield of Dybbøl in a giant festival in which more than 50 000 people took part. From 1933 popular meetings took on a new meaning: to mobilise the population, and the youth in particular, against the pressure of National Socialist Germany.

Ukrainians did not hold popular festivals and meetings. The

movement was promoted predominantly by urban intellectuals, the distance between town and country was still very great and the communication network quite sparse. No genuine mass movement was possible under the circumstances. Moreover, as in the Ottoman empire the rigid Russian laws prevented the movement from coming into the open except in the years between 1905 and 1907. The elite however could gather to unveil monuments of writers and poets. The centenary of the poet Shevchenko in particular gave occasion for a veritable flood of activities. The theatre also offered opportunities to the Ukrainian intelligentsia. At the beginning of the 1870s performances of the Ukrainian operas by M. Lysenko were festive occasions for the local intelligentsia. During the 1880s and 1890s over 30 theatre companies were founded, quite a number being amateur groups. They did not stay in the towns but also toured in the country. They performed popular 'ethnographical' plays, taking their subjects from the life of the people and the history of the Cossacks. After 1905 literary drama became more frequent.

From about 1890 11 September was celebrated in Catalonia. Between 1900 to 1920 public demonstrations marked the day, after which mass rallies were held. On that day in 1714 the then Spanish king had repealed most of the liberties and special privileges which the Catalans had enjoyed. Later on there was also a Catalan national festival, a Catalan language day and a Sardana assembly. The latter was in honour of the ancient folk dance of the country; 50 000 people attended it in 1922 according to contemporary accounts.

Popular meetings are a very conspicuous example of oral communication. The role of mass meetings was not identical in all movements and it could change within each and over time. In spite of their diverse functions (mobilisation of the population, demonstration of strength and consolidation of attitudes) they had a common characteristic: they were a platform for the activists who organised them. It should come as no surprise that the methods of oral communication are quite diverse in nature. Some played a decisive part in mobilising broad strata of the population during the early stages when they could not be reached in any other way but others were created because the national movements, in order to make their goals known, had to invent forms of publicity where none had existed before. Those parts of the network of oral communication which can still be seen today are surviving fragments of this publicity. Contrary to the one way direction of communication at mass rallies, the societies and clubs in particular, though their many social contacts also, could give the leaders a direct insight into the many shades of the aspirations and ideas of their followers.

Written Communication

Of all forms of written communication, newspapers and periodicals are by far the most important. Jens Jessen, the editor of the *Flensborg Avis*, once noted of a Danish paper in Flensburg 'it is like a lone railway station on the heath around which a whole town may spring up, like a flood which may bring fertility even to the desert'. Newspapers and periodicals convey the opinions and attitudes of the activists, but this process also works in the obverse direction. If a newspaper does not meet the mood and the taste of readers it usually loses subscriptions. In most national movements the newspaper also had another essential function: it used the native language in daily affairs. This was of special importance during the early phases when a written standardised language was not fully established and people did not use it regularly for written communication. Through their linguistic role newspapers were able to counteract assimilation by the dominant society. Moreover newspapers select the material which they regard as suitable for their readers from a multitude of information. They have the power to raise issues, to bring conditions or practices to public attention; determining in fact what information receives prominence. It goes without saying that the scope allowed to the press by the dominant society is decisive.

In view of the influential position of the press its operational scope often was very restricted before the First World War. In the Danish Monarchy prior to 1864 – particularly between 1851 and 1864 – freedom of the press was narrowly defined; in the Habsburg Monarchy and in Prussia it had not even been introduced before the 1848 revolutions. In the Russian empire only the 1905 revolution pushed the state towards even what proved short lived liberalisation. Only the Irish newspapers and the Czech press after 1860 had a wider ranging freedom. The Catalans, Poles and the Danes in Prussia had to tread warily in spite of a freedom of the press guaranteed by law or heavy punishment for so-called libels, *lèse-majesté* or similar offenses could be incurred. The editor Jens Jessen altogether spent over 43 months in Prussian prisons because he wielded a formidable pen. Fines and imprisonment also handicapped Polish journalism. Nearly all Macedonian papers were published abroad before 1908 and the Ukrainian language press first developed in Austrian Galicia because literature in the vernacular was banned in Russia until 1905. But those national minorities in Schleswig who owed their status to the border adjustments of 1920 enjoyed much better conditions.

Some newspapers' origins pre-date 1840. The Poles, Irish, Czechs and Germans in Schleswig already had low circulation newspapers by 1830. When the national movements began to emerge a press soon complemented them. This press activity was hedged by restrictions except in Ireland but the rather primitive printing equipment required made publications feasible with a minimum of capital. A great variety of publications developed in regions where the legal situation permitted them. They were generally printed in the language of the national group. The Irish, who had a flourishing English language press, are an exception as are the Catalans to a certain extent. The Czechs, the Poles and the Danes also had German language organs aimed at the parts of the population who had been victims of linguistic 'germanisation' beside the press in their own language.

In the eastern parts of Ireland and among the younger generation, literacy was general by 1880 and the national press was not obstructed as a rule. As early as about 1840 a number of newspapers taking the national line existed, including from 1842 the influential weekly *The Nation*, founded by the Young Irelanders for disseminating their Mazzini inspired ideas. During the following decades it became a publication advocating a moderate and clerical outlook on national questions. The Fenians founded the *Irish People* in Dublin in 1863, later banned in 1865 shortly before the outbreak of a rebellion. During the 1870s one of the most prominent papers in Dublin, *The Freeman's Journal*, advocated the national cause. It had a large readership in the eastern part of the country. A widespread provincial press also developed at the time, as for instance *The Cork Examiner*, *The Ulster Examiner*, and *The Connaught Telegraph*. During the 1890s more militant papers began to appear which supported the Irish-Ireland movement and from 1905 *Sinn Fein* (Ourselves).

The Spanish constitution of 1876 guaranteed the classic civil liberties including freedom of the press and of publication. State security however could impinge on these rights – and this happened with some regularity. Yet by 1883 only criminal offences could be prosecuted. Alarmed by anarchist and Catalinist tendencies an act reducing these liberties was passed in 1900. From that time those who attacked the 'integrity of the Spanish nation' or advocated separatist goals were threatened with penal servitude. From 1906 'insult to the nation' by words, writing or pictures was also punishable. Offences of this kind could lead to temporary bans which forced Catalanist newspapers to change their location or name rather frequently until they were allowed to resume publication.

Illiteracy was a thing of the past even at the start of the Catalan movement but the population was not accustomed to reading Catalan texts. An overwhelming majority of the newspapers available to the Catalans continued to use Spanish. The Catalan language could only assert itself through weekly and monthly periodicals, most having brief and financially precarious existences. Newspapers in Catalan began to appear in 1880 but their circulation was small.

Their number increased around the turn of the century, when a party press came into being, but even in Barcelona they made up no more than 20 per cent of all newspapers sold there. From 1910 circulation of these papers fluctuated between 5000 and 15 000 copies. It was not usual to employ the Catalan language in print; even the national movement used the leading Spanish newspaper of the city. According to a leading publicist 'The spiritual food which the newspapers represents, the only spiritual food which reaches the great mass of the people in our day, is delivered to Catalonia in the Castilian language, in a foreign language.' However this foreign language did not hamper the movement. The biggest newspaper in Catalonia, the Castilian *La Vanguardia*, devoted quite extensive space to the spiritual life of the country and the paper *Diario de Barcelona* gave firm support to the movement. One exception that broke through the language barrier was the children's paper *En Patufet* (Tom Thumb) which started in 1904. By about 1920 it had a circulation of 65 000, a surprising figure considering general Catalan conditions.

In the Grand Duchy of Poznań, Prussian compulsory education had put an end to illiteracy at an early date but the schools had not succeeded in displacing the Polish language. Printed literature was censored prior to publication. This censorship intensified in 1819 under the Karlsbad resolutions which imposed strict control over all printed matter and prevented polemical writing on political and religious subjects. These rigid rules were relaxed somewhat in 1841. The 1850 Prussian constitution embraced a degree of press freedom but within a year this was considerably restricted. In 1874 a *Reichsgesetz* (act of the *Reich*) finally guaranteed the freedom of the press. Nevertheless newspaper editors could be made to appear before a court of law for a multitude of offences and be sentenced to long imprisonment or heavy fines. Sentences of this kind were often inflicted on Polish newspapers but were not able seriously to check the development of the press. The fines were paid by private benefactors and the prison sentences could often be served by proxy, at least in the beginning.

In the Grand Duchy 21 Polish language newspapers appeared as early as 1846–50. They had been preceded by non-political papers and periodicals, written in German or in both languages, such as *Der Volksfreund* (The Peoples' Friend), *Das Literarische Wochenblatt* (The Literary Weekly), *Die Hauszeitung* (The Home Newspaper) or *Das Jahr* (The Year), all founded in the 1830s. When the laws governing the press became more restrictive the number of newspapers initially declined but soon recovered and in 1885 as many as 28 newspapers were available in Poznań. Shortly before the First World War there were 70 papers with a circulation of about 350–400 000 (65 000 in 1898, 180 000 in 1906). Most of them were general information papers aimed at the educational level and the interests of their readers. In particular there was an increase in those papers designed to appeal to a broad urban and rural strata, and so published local reports as well as carrying news about the kingdom of Poland, Galicia and Germany. They also covered religious affairs and gave practical and educational advice, for instance on how to teach the Polish language at home.

Literacy was widespread in Schleswig. The practice of censorship was generally rather mild before 1848. Publishing a newspaper depended on a licence, a privilege which the government could grant at its own discretion though this usually was given. Only with the *stænderforfatning* (estates constitution) did political publicity become more widespread. From 1842 national tension led to repression of such severity that open ethnic agitation (by both sides) became nearly impossible. Early newspapers had appeared in German but it was only from 1838 that the mostly small weekly and 'correspondence' papers began to show tentative 'German Schleswig–Holstein' tendencies. Some Danish newspapers continued to appear in German. The duke of Augustenborg financed a small newspaper in Danish. The most important paper in the duchies was the *Itzehoer Wochenblatt* (The Itzehoer Weekly) which was even read by the rural population; it had a circulation of about 7000 during the 1840s. In 1838 the first Danish language newspaper appeared in Haderslev bearing the significant title *Dannvirke*. Other papers followed, gaining from 200 to 700 subscribers.

People were not accustomed to Danish as a written language. After the civil war of 1848–50 the national press experienced a difficult phase, particularly Schleswig–Holstein periodicals. Following the Prussian annexation of the duchies the Danes in north Schleswig, like the Poles, had to conform to the Prussian Press Act but even this could not prevent periodicals from developing quickly from the later 1880s. Their editors, particularly those of the leading national conservative paper *Flensborg Avis*, were hit hard by fines and imprisonments however. The total circulation of the Danish press in north Schleswig at the outbreak of the First World War is estimated at 27 000 copies, clearly reaching a high percentage of the population. *Flensborg Avis* remained in Flensborg after the referendum and retained its position as a Danish newspaper although it had been read mainly in north and western north Schleswig which became a part of Denmark in 1920. Later the *Flensborg Avis* had to be subsidised by private groups in the kingdom. One German language Danish newspaper in south Schleswig survived until 1924. The four German newspapers existing in north Schleswig were amalgamated for financial reasons in 1929, creating the *Nordschleswigsche Zeitung* (North Schleswig Newspaper) which was subsidised by the Weimar Republic.

For Czechs newspapers began to thrive obviously at the very time when the national movement was gaining in strength – during the transition from Phase B to Phase C. This was not an isolated phenomenon however. In central and north European societies the press had been developing as mass media during the 1870s and 1880s. New technology for printing and typesetting allowed publication of more expanded and varied editions without adding to the cost of production. The telegraph had made it possible to transmit news swiftly. Illiteracy had ceased to hinder the spread of the national movement.

Except during the revolution years of 1848–9 only a few low circulation newspapers and periodicals were published by the Czech press before 1860 owing to the Austrian press laws. Up to 1848 only a single official paper, the *Prager Zeitung*, was licensed along with two patriotically inclined cultural periodicals and one scientific magazine which had been founded in the 1830s. Not until 1846 could the *Prager Zeitung* be transformed into a national newspaper. Of the six papers and periodicals of the revolutionary years, which had a circulation of about 5000, some were directed at the urban and rural masses. After the liberalisation of 1860 there were between ten and 19 political papers in the 1860s; a decade later, 20 to 32; from 39 to 90 in the 1880s, and more than 100 after 1890. From the middle of the 1890s the number of political newspapers and periodicals as well as that of trade journals for artisans and workers grew much faster than did non-political periodicals. Circulation also went up steeply during the 1880s. The leading Czech newspaper *Národní listy* (National Papers) had, from the early 1860s up to the early 1880s, a circulation of about 4000, growing to 10 000 by the end of the 1880s. In 1895 the morning edition alone printed more than 14 000 copies. The popular *Národní politika* (National Politics) had a circulation of 8000 in 1883; 17 399 in 1890; and 32 000 in 1895.

In the Russian Ukraine written communication was greatly restricted. Fewer than 20 per cent of the Russian Ukrainians over ten years of age could read, only 0.33 per cent of them had a secondary or higher education. Ukrainian schools and publications, even the singing of Ukrainian songs, were prohibited from the 1860s. Necessarily the Ukrainian activists, like the Catalans, used the language of the dominant nation and right up to 1914 repeatedly founded Russian language periodicals. After the restrictions had been relaxed in 1905 written communication in Ukrainian became at least possible within the Russian empire – in spite of subsequent fresh restrictions. Nevertheless communication could not flourish because the overwhelming majority of the 25 million Ukrainians were peasants who had not been politicised. When state repression was moderated Ukrainians lacked journalists, typographers, printers, readers and a standard written language. Such deficits made it almost impossible to motivate the broader public to take part in the cause.

Between 1860 and 1904 Ukrainian language periodicals could be published only in Austria–Hungary, most originating from L'viv/Lemberg. Post–1905 only three Ukrainian daily papers in Russia survived for some years; other publications appeared weekly or bi-weekly, or monthly. Most were published in Kiev. These faced repeated bans and some of the small papers and magazines collapsed. In 1912 the 19 Ukrainian language periodicals in the Russian empire had a total circulation of only a few thousand copies. In Austrian Galicia however 78 Ukrainian publications appeared in 1912, though only 12–15 per cent of the ethnic group lived under Austrian rule. The most important daily paper available in the Russian Ukraine was the moderately liberal–radical *Rada* (Council) published between 1905 and 1914. It had a circulation of no more than 4000 and required its three patrons to meet a deficit of 30–40 000 rubles a year. The weekly *Ridnyj kraj* (Homeland) was published in different places from 1906 to 1916, addressing itself not only to the urban but also to the rural population. In addition to this there were scientific monthlies for the small Ukrainian intelligentsia. This meagre and cautious publishing activity nevertheless enabled activists to keep contact with each other and to consolidate the position of a standardised written language.

The Macedonian press also had to appear abroad almost exclusively (in Bulgaria) from 1880 to 1908; not until after the Young Turk Revolution could it be published at home. Literacy was almost universal. In several Bulgarian towns so-called 'Macedonian Welfare Organisations' were founded in the 1880s; they devoted themselves to the refugees and the numerous seasonal workers from Macedonia. These associations created their own organs, the newspaper *Makedonec* (The Macedonian) in 1880 and the weekly *Makedonskij glas* (Voice of Macedonia) in 1885 which brought the Macedonian question to the attention of the public. The periodical *Loza* (The Vine) in 1891, however, brought out by Macedonian students in Sofia, was banned after no more than six issues; it had tried to increase national consciousness by creating a Macedonian literary language. Revolutionary, socialist or even anarchist papers, some of them very small, were founded but none survived for long.

When the Young Turk revolution made journalism and the publication of newspapers possible in the Ottoman empire the factions of the Internal Macedonian Revolutionary Organisation founded a number of newspapers and periodicals in all larger towns, particularly in Salonika. The 'left wing', which collaborated with the Young Turks, edited the paper *Konstitutionna zarja* (Dawn of the Constitution) from 1908 which appeared twice a week and following that *Edinstvo* (Unity) also from 1908. In the following year these merged to form the paper *Narodnaja volja* (Will of the People) which became the organ of the Federative People's Party. The Bulgarian national 'right wing' founded *Otečestvo* (Fatherland) in 1910 which was followed by the weekly *Rodina* (Homeland) again in 1910 and *Pravo* (Law) from 1910–3, the first daily newspaper to appear regularly in Macedonia. A social democratic press also developed. General conditions were rather similar to those in the Ukraine which made the development of newspapers rather late, but in other respects the situation was quite different. A strong urban representation and the high degree of mobilisation in the Macedonian population made it possible to profit from the new developments even though the circulation of the new periodicals remained low.

Compared to the importance of newspapers which were able to influence their readers continuously and in many fields of interest, the impact of other printed media was certainly much weaker. However there were three kinds of printed matter which also had a mass circulation and could be distributed to the people at very short notice when the situation demanded: fly-sheets, pamphlets and posters. Little is known at present about the last but they certainly played a part in Catalonia, not only in announcing mass meetings but also in urging peaceful and disciplined participation at them. In Schleswig posters were used, for instance, to influence the two referendums of 1920. A number of Danish artists had designed the posters for the first referendum on north Schleswig whereas the German posters were simple letter press productions. For the second referendum, held in Flensburg and south of the present border, well-known graphic artists from Germany were called in who also designed impressive posters.[4]

Fly-sheets also were used by the Catalans: 100 000 copies of the 'Compendium of Catalanist Doctrine' were distributed among the people. They were indispensable for calling people to the big popular meetings. In Schleswig–Holstein the liberal Uwe Jens Lornsen and his friends succeeded in distributing 5000 copies of a fly-sheet in 1830 before the authorities could seize the remaining 4000. This leaflet called forth over 40 replies which, even if slight in number, served to spur political discussion in the duchies. Macedonians and Ukrainians used fly-sheets and leaflets and in Poland an extensive advice literature developed, in other words instructional pamphlets for peasants, artisans, priests, landowners, women and young people. From 1870 such pamphlets also explained the 'election laws' or concentrated themselves on the 'duties of a priest in our present sorry time'. There was also a *Handbook of the Polish People* published in 1907. Fly-sheets contained, for instance, 'Ten Polish National Commandments' or 'Ten Polish Cardinal Sins'.

In all movements books played an essential part which, however, is difficult to define. They could not convey topical information but they did encourage the use of the native language, disseminate national ideologies and attitudes. Books on national history, both of a literary and a scientific nature, also could implant certain historical perceptions. The Poles and Czechs developed a flourishing literature; Germans and the Danes in Schleswig could fall back on their respective national literature or even enrich it. For the Ukrainians, fiction and poetry also played an important part and the Ukrainian publishing trade in the Russian empire saw a growth from 1905 to 1914. Numerous private publishing firms mostly brought out fiction and poetry in sizeable editions. The leading Kiev publishing house Vik, for instance, sponsored more than 140 titles before 1914 comprising more than half a million copies. The Macedonians, whose activists rarely were literary figures or intellectuals, could nevertheless publish many books on the history of their movement and its goals after 1908.

Concluding remarks

Lack of appropriate information has limited comparison in this chapter to the most general forms of oral and literary communication. Churches and schools were institutionalised channels of oral communication. The Church and religious allegiance had an overwhelming influence when – as in the Irish, Polish and the Macedonian cases – the faith of the ethnic group differed from that of the state, but the local community also offered a bulwark against assimilation in cases where the differences were small or nonexistent. The importance of the Church was emphasised during the later half of the century by the founding of youth and social clubs.

Before the First World War compulsory primary school education clearly was dominated by governments and used as a tool for the assimilation of disparate ethnic groups. An exception to this was the Macedonian case where the Ottoman *millet* constitution gave local communities sufficient autonomy for managing their own school affairs. The general assimilation policy conducted by nation–states was however almost ineffectual when the parents counterbalanced it. They could undermine the school's impact on the minds of the children and – as in the Danish case – provide alternative schooling in the mother country when compulsory education was ended. Only after the First World War were schools, especially private schools, more or less independent of the dominating state, becoming important centres of communication for those non-dominant ethnic groups which could afford an independent education system.

Leaders were often recruited from among teachers or prior to the war from groups of discharged teachers.

In the early stages of national movements less formalised means of communication also played a vital rôle. The spoken word and personal contact often had a decisive impact. Various forms of clubs, lecture rooms, banquets and most importantly the first political bodies had a momentous impact. The Catalans developed informal coffee house meetings with a view to exchange ideals and news. As in the numerous organisations founded in the later half of the century these informal channels of communication not only offered the leaders opportunities to influence the population but gave them a direct insight into the aspirations and ideas of their followers. Mass meetings, however, were rather dominated by a one way communication. They were utilised to mobilize a population or later on they might be employed to demonstrate the strength of a movement or even to stabilise it. Festivities might be arranged to celebrate eminent national figures as well as past uprisings (as for example in Poznań). Of course they were a platform belonging to the activists who organised them and like broadcast and television communication they demanded special skills of the actors. Oral channels of communication sometimes have been neglected by historians. Surviving evidence for such channels is usually found in written form and may not convey the strong impression made by the original medium.

By far the most important forms of written communication were newspapers and periodicals. In most national movements newspapers had at least two crucial functions: they conveyed the opinions and attitudes of the activists and they used the native language in daily affairs. As a rule at least the last function could be fulfilled. In addition they often provided leaders with a livelihood. The influential position of the press was well known and for this reason the dominant governments in the nineteenth century restricted its operations. Restrictions varied from total banning of the native language – as in Russia in the case of the Ukrainians – to a fair degree of freedom of the press combined with fines and imprisonment of editors who overstepped the limits. A national Irish press, however, developed early without overrigid legal hindrances. In most countries the years shortly before the First World War brought some relief. After 1918 the problems of a minority press were mainly financial rather than legal. Technical development had made each newspaper larger and cheaper but the capital and equipment needed to edit and print them had grown even faster.

Illiteracy might hamper the dissemination of information through newspapers and periodicals but only in the very early stages. The one exception examined was the Ukrainian case where illiteracy remained high. In the early phase – though in Catalonia and Ireland over the whole era – people were commonly not accustomed to reading newspapers in their own language and they therefore had to be published in the dominant nation's tongue. Compared with newspapers the impact of other printed media was much weaker. Books were certainly important, often distributed by small libraries, but they hardly touched the masses. Mass circulation fly-sheets, pamphlets and posters, especially the last, were better able to catch the attention of people who did not read very much. Posters played a role in Catalonia and during the plebiscites of the Schleswig region. Poles used numerous instructional pamphlets.

Written forms appear to have depended much more than oral communication on the general conditions existing during the formation of the national movement. They were as accessible to suspicious authorities as to historians. The intensity of communication shows a distinct parallel development to the phases of the movement – though there is no lack of exceptions. As a rule the transition to Phase C was also a time when mass communication were developed fully. There must have been a continuous interaction between mass mobilisation and extension of communication. Central for all cases is the factor that every ethnic group touched by nationalism wished to create a communication of its own – a national dialogue. This had to be done even if the language of the dominant nation had to be used. Activists of course were forerunners in this process. They created a communication which enabled members of an ethnic group to make common cause.[5]

Notes

1 Otto Bauer (1907), *Die Nationalitätenfrage und die Sozialdemokratie*, Vienna, 2nd edn, 1924.
2 Karl W. Deutsch (1969), *Nationalism and Social Communication. An Inquiry into the Foundations of Nationality*, Cambridge, Mass., 2nd edn 1966 – with a special introduction on some changes in nationalism and its study 1953–1965; Karl W. Deutsch (1969), *Nationalism and Its Alternatives*, New York.
3 W. Carr (1963), *Schleswig-Holstein 1815–48. A Study in National Conflict*, Manchester, p. 187. The statement was made by a leading figure of the 'Landespartei'.
4 Troels Fink (1979), *Da Sønderjylland blev delt* (When Schleswig was divided), vol. III Aabenraa, p. 33 ff, and Fritz Fuglsang 'Das Plakat im Kampf um die Nordmark', in: *Das Plakat*, 11.Jahrgang, Heft 5, p. 241 ff.
5 See Deutsch (1953) 'Peoples, Nations and Communication', *Nationalism and Social Communication*, chapter 4.

14 Historical Consciousness and Historical Myths

GERHARD BRUNN

I

The historical consciousness of rising elites in non-dominant ethnic communities commands special interest for two significant reasons. First because it was one of the chief elements of emerging ethnic consciousness. Also it was the basis of the ideology which initially was to integrate the elites and then, under their leadership, the whole group. This historical consciousness reflects the social composition of both the elites and the ethnic group. Furthermore it developed in confrontation with the historical consciousness of the dominant culture and the government. Thus history became a central matter of dispute between the new ethnic elites and the ruling nation.

Ethnicity as an active force may be in abeyance for a long time and then gain a new lease of life. Under what conditions does it surface? It was for all ethnic groups an indispensable prerequisite that their members were conscious of a common bond that distinguished them from others. The point at which an ethnic group considered itself, by positive or negative connotations, to be unique marked the beginning of its group consciousness. Cultural consciousness stands at the apex of ethnic identity above political conflicts or competing material interests. Ernest Gellner has made the pertinent point that nationalism becomes a political factor only when cultural homogeneity and continuity are demanded from within the ethnic group.[1] In the development of this cultural homogeneity and continuity, historical awareness, ideas and conceptions have played a central role. Most non-dominant ethnic groups were obsessed with their own history. Both dominant nations, and subordinate ethnic groups have made history the ideological nucleus of their existence.

Where the dominant nations defined and created their relevant histories the very power structure worked, as it was once said, as a great recording machine, shaping the past in its own image; making the non-dominant ethnic groups within it 'history-less', in important senses, thus threatening, or rendering elusive, their ethnic identity.

327

Therefore a non-dominant ethnic group needed its own history, preferably a long past with brilliant epochs, as a means of creating and asserting pride and establishing group legitimacy. In these conflicts of interest and cultural encounters the rising elites, especially the intellectuals, played the key part.

The 'ethnic memory' which served to define the community during the initial phases was the product of a small cultural elite which drew upon existing histories and myths. Their innovative matrices of collective identity were a central community forming element. For the leading personalities of the non-dominant ethnic groups controversies concerning the past and historical conceptions were among the most important issues in conflicts with the dominating nations and governments. One ethnic leader succinctly summed up the role of history as follows:

> In their decline, nations also forget their own existence. The mighty invent for themselves, if necessary, a glorious past, they construct political theories and use them to glorify the misdeeds which made their triumph possible. The losers have been vanquished not only in their future but also in their past; the glory of the victorious ennobles not only their sons but also their parents and grandparents.
>
> In remembering the history which was taught in our schools we think in shame of the methodical oppression of our souls; and sometimes this happens to the children of Catalonia even nowadays.
>
> When a nation has an inherent consciousness of itself it begins to regain its personality. There is an interaction between the strength of nations and their consciousness both of present worth and of ancient glory. The reborn history of Catalonia has been a blazing and stirring fire, a beacon leading to the ideal. . . . It has been proved anew: the study of the past has opened a great future to Catalonia. Brought up knowing its mother country, the present generation will triumph in the future.[2]

This declaration, stressing the crucial function of history for ethnic identity provides an exemplary text. History is credited with distinctive qualities, and has critical tasks. To begin with, it is an analytical tool. With the aid of history, nations discover their existence, their innate personalities or souls – which had been obscured earlier. Moreover, history is a creative force. It knits a nation together and creates solidarity. History also points to the future, inspiring a resurrected people who have discovered their identity with a glorious epoch.

II

The quotation is also significant in that it reveals the path by which emergent ethnic groups come into possession of their history or, rather, of a particular version of the story: by a struggle against the ideas of the dominant group. The Catalans, the Germans in Schleswig up to 1864 and the Poles in the province of Poznań were engaged in controversies with the respective dominant groups which were shaping or had already created a historical conception of the inevitable development of an all-embracing united national state where there was no room for separate autonomous ethnic groups. The Germans – and after 1864 the Danes in Schleswig, the Poles in Poznań, the Catalans and in some measure, the Irish, had to develop their historical conceptions in opposition to interpretations which allowed them little distinct identity. A separate existence was denied to them in the past as well as for the future.

In central and eastern Europe, with the rich diversity of ethnic groups living at least partly in the same territories, different and conflicting conceptions of history resulted in even more complicated relations and tensions. Non-dominant ethnic groups had to formulate individual pasts in opposition to the counterclaims of either those who were dominant or had hopes of achieving hegemony and wanted to incorporate peoples living in the territory into their own history. Ukrainians, an object of the integrationist ideology of the Russian empire, were coopted in an official Russian conception of history which was pre-national, dynastic and in which the estates had a major role. During the nineteenth centuries further elements of a new nationalism with strong linguistic and cultural orientations were included in the Russian imperial version of history. The (west) Ukrainians also were claimed by Polish historical consciousness because large parts of the western Ukraine had been dominated by a Polish aristocracy. Macedonians were subject not only to the integrationist outlook of ottomanism which strove for a political nation based on territorial unity, but also to the historical vision of Greeks, Bulgarians and Serbs, all wanting to claim Macedonia for their own pasts.

The Czechs were caught in a web of conflicting historical rivalries of a different sort. The existence of an independent medieval Czech kingdom was not questioned, but the notion of ethnic and political continuity up to the eighteenth and nineteenth century was challenged. Czechs were confronted by the Habsburg idea of the *Gesamt-Monarchie* (Austrian–Hungarian Monarchy) which stressed the legitimacy of the supra-national empire and also with the historical or state consciousness of Bohemians or Moravians. Initially the Czech cause was taken up by a section of the aristocracy and subsequently by the German bourgeoisie. This was often combined with a provincial patriotism which was not, however, congruent with Czech national consciousness. In fact the relationship was extremely complicated. In a later phase, when contradictions intensified, a third rival historical consciousness – that of the German nationalists who treated Czech and Bohemian history as part of the German national, or *Reich*, past – added to the difficulties.

III

Historical consciousness is nourished by diverse sources. There is the interaction of generations, the collective, unreflective memory of individuals and groups. Furthermore, there is the deliberate or intellectual reconstruction of the past which, from the beginning of the nineteenth century, relied upon the techniques of contemporary science. In almost all ethnic groups this second variety became a major factor in the building of group consciousness. Writing history on this level demands a standard of education and a pre-existing consciousness of the past that is usually the preserve of intellectuals. During an initial phase history generally was an antiquarian amateur pursuit, indulged in by members of the dominant classes who arbitrarily mixed myths, fiction and reality. Self-trained intellectuals, for instance from the knighthood in Schleswig, the nobility in the Russian part of the Ukraine and also in Bohemia and Moravia, plus, increasingly, members of the upwardly mobile middle classes (lawyers, clergymen and writers) were the men who laid the foundation on which, a few decades later, professional historians began to build.

In Ireland a small group of Church of Ireland clergymen, lawyers and landed gentlemen pioneered exploration of the Gaelic past in the middle of the eighteenth century. Later during several phases of cultural revivalism in the nineteenth and twentieth centuries this interest was forged into a political instrument. Parallels can be seen in other countries. Nikolai Grundtvig, a leading figure in the creation of a Danish historical consciousness in the nineteenth century, was a theologian and a poet. Victor Balaguer, author of the first popular history of Catalonia, had a legal education, wrote poems and plays and became, though self-educated, a professor of history.

The increasing number of historians who employed scientific and critical methods became the leading practitioners. Scientific truth became the new ethic, giving influence and authority to the findings of historical research. The use of such methods by academics at the University of Kiel assumed immense importance for German national consciousness in Schleswig and Holstein. For Czechs the influence of Franz Palacký was equally significant, as was that of Hrushevs'kyj for the Ukrainians or Bofarull for the Catalans. Many of these historians were in the vanguard of the activists of their respective ethnic groups.

Where circumstances made an indigenous historical school impossible the works of foreign historians or of patriotic authors residing outside the national frontiers became substitutes. In Macedonia teachers resorted to foreign historians. In Poznań, which did not have an intellectual centre, works of historians in the other Polish partitioned territories, or the writing of exiles, were used. But it was only in isolated instances that historians achieved a direct impact outside the educated classes. For a wider impact their views had to be popularised, a task left in the hands of journalists, writers, poets, painters, musicians and sculptors as well as those of politicians. They utilised and transmuted the writings of historians and thereby transformed elitist cultural forms into popular movements and beliefs having a wide appeal.

In this way the types of publicists mentioned above gained an importance in the consolidation of historical conceptions comparable to that of the historians themselves. In Bohemia, for example, historical novels were read by a large percentage of the Czech speaking population; much more, relatively speaking, than analogous German fiction was consumed by people in the German federation. The Danes devoured the historical novels of Bernhard Severin Ingermann. Though there has been no systematic research into the subject of Poznań it seems certain that the historical novels of Josef I. Kraszewski – who wrote no less than 323 such tomes – and Henryk Sienkiewicz as well as the popular historical novels of Józef Chociszewski were standard literature among the educated classes. For the Ukraine, the impact of the works of Taras Shevchenko can scarcely be overrated.

All the other elements of the cultural media were also steeped in history and used by artists to impart a specific historical consciousness. Poets, writers of historical plays (important for instance in Bohemia and Catalonia), painters, sculptors or musicians conveyed images of the past in their works. Painters of historical subjects were highly popular in Bohemia, Denmark and Poznań. From about 1820 innumerable prints brought historical pictures into the family circles of the Grand Duchy of Poznań. In Bohemia artists took an active part in popularising historical ideals, particularly during Phase C. Sculptors, with their creation of historical monuments, must not be ignored; they were important for instance in Catalonia and in Bohemia. During Phase C even opera and symphonic music were used for inculcating history. For the Danes and Poles music had been an important way of spreading significant historical ideas from the very beginnings of the new ethnic awareness. Ballads with a historical theme were sung widely, both in public and at home, and had a national–didactic function.

In all ethnic groups, culture was interwoven with history, and the educated elites used the entire cultural palette to make historical ideas come alive. If in the beginning history had been a subject for educated amateurs, historical research and writing soon made their triumphant way into the wider consciousness of all ethnic groups, though not at the same pace everywhere. History based on scientific methods supplied interpretations which gained credence because of the authority given to science. The interpretations were then drawn on by journalists, literary men, artists and the political activists (who included some historians) for the creation of political, economic, social and artistic programmes. Historic law gained similar importance for justifying political demands. It was employed by the Catalans, the Czechs and the Irish for example and proved crucial for the Croats, though they are not treated in this volume.

If historical consciousness was produced by an elite there were still important differentiations. For groups with little historical tradition of autonomy or national existence, popular myths and oral traditions were of paramount importance. A populist Ukrainian historiography went back to the so-called *Dumy*, to heroic ballads glorifying the times of the Cossacks, which were sung to the accompaniment of the *bandura* (musical instrument). Similar heroic ballads, the *Hajduk* songs, kept the collective memory alive in Macedonia. They were part of a Christian anti-Turkish literature and are to be seen in the context of the liberation movement. Written by monks in the eighteenth century they became folk ballads, sung epics, in which political heroes were raised to the status of saints.

IV

For ethnic groups history was the ideological nucleus of their endeavours to hold their own against the dominant societies. This permanent confrontation determined their historical outlook, their conception of the past. There were, of course, great variations between groups. Historical conceptions always reflected the social character of the classes who formulated them; moreover they were frequently adapted during the course of a struggle to reflect new historical findings or to respond to changing political developments, as may be seen in the Czech and Irish cases. Up to 1848 the Czech heroes were kings and aristocrats; then the Hussite period was discovered and from the third quarter of the nineteenth century the popular democratic ideas of the middle classes were emphasised. Equally significant alterations of historical interpretations of Irish nationhood also evolved between the eighteenth and early twentieth centuries.

History served to confirm the existence of the ethnic group and its legitimation was then built on evidence of an unbroken history. The annihilating designation 'unhistorical people' had to be disproved by the evidence of an organic continuous past. At an early date histories of the group experiencing as a quasi-natural process birth, adolescence, flowering and decline – and subsequent rebirth – were published. National histories provided testimony of the continuous existence of the national group.

It was particularly tempting to 'discover' and then expand upon a golden or heroic era in the remote past. In this context ethnic groups frequently have different golden eras in their specific historical conceptions. For the Poles the golden era was the time of the last Jagiellones; for the Czechs it was that of the autonomous state of the Premyslides; for the Ukrainians, the Cossack era between the sixteenth and the eighteenth centuries; for the Macedonians, that of the Bulgarian tsars in the ninth and tenth centuries. In Denmark the four great novels of Ingermann on the age of the Waldemars (twelfth to fourteenth centuries) with the motto 'What Denmark Was, It Can Become Again' were a strong influence on historical consciousness. In Ireland the early Celtic kingdoms were used to establish the existence of an old nation, one diametrically different from England and superior to it. In Catalonia the flourishing Mediterranean trade empire of the high Middle Ages was seen as a golden age. Depictions of the 'golden age' revealed it as a time of heroism, prosperity, blossoming culture and power but also as an era of liberty, self-determination and an absence of alien rule. The political appeal to the present was obvious.

Starting from such a point of national glory historiography outlined other epochs and rediscovered further proud episodes. Czech historians first studied the rule of Karl IV and the cultural flowering of the sixteenth century as high points of their national story. In the post-revolutionary atmosphere after 1848 the Hussite period was treated as the great moment in the Czech ethnic past. Poles experienced a similar expansion of historical consciousness by including the seventeenth century wars with the Ottomans and the Swedes in their catalogue of national achievements.

Golden eras were contrasted with those marking declines. These could be described as self-induced – as in the case of the aristocratic Polish republic – but were as a rule attributed to oppression and exploitation by alien powers or rulers in a way which could be identified with contemporary governments, as for instance in Catalonia where decline coincided with the rise of alien rulers. Ireland's demise, it was alleged, had a similar cause and the same pattern occurred, Czechs argued, in the countries of the Bohemian crown after the defeat of the uprising of the estates at the hands of the Habsburgs in 1620.

By using history to convey a particular message national or ethnic identities were created or reinforced. Political disputes with the present regimes were projected into the past. History was depicted as a permanent struggle against a 'hereditary enemy'. This particular outlook is paradigmatically represented by Palacký who saw Czech history as a centuries long conflict with the Germans. Territorial disputes in the past and controversies between rulers and social groups were treated therefore as part of national conflicts, forerunners of the contemporary clash between the ethnic group and the government of the dominant nation. Rival groups were seen as members of different nations and their conflict as a national confrontation. Czech historiography, for instance, saw the relationship of Bohemia with the *Reich* from the Middle Ages to the present in the national categories of the nineteenth century. This was, however, a response to the 'nationalisation' of Bohemian history by German historians who described Bohemia as being a historic part of the old *Reich* and consequently also as a part of the emerging German nation–state of the nineteenth century. Countering a historical conception which claimed Bohemia and Moravia for Germany, Czech writers even portrayed quarrels of the estates with the Habsburgs as national insurrections, though they had been quite different in character and had united Czechs and Germans against their rulers. A similar course applied to the Poles in Poznań. Polish publications first quoted German historiography, particularly with respect to its justification of the German 'urge towards the east', then they vehemently criticised the German conception and countered with their own contrary version of events.

In the German–Danish controversy the pattern was also broadly the same. Class or dynastic politics in the past were regarded as national politics. Success or failure of rulers in achieving their aims were uncritically utilised to glorify a 'national' past. What was white in the historical conception of one nation was black in that of the other. In German eyes King Waldemar fought against the politics of his German opponents by perfidy. In Danish historiography he appeared as a heroic national figure leading the disintegrated Danish nation to new greatness.

In these conflicting conceptions history was employed to highlight 'exemplary enemies'. Present conflicts were given historical depth as a continuation of a centuries long conflict of opposing principles. For Bohemia/Moravia, Palacký created a theory in which Czech history was a constant struggle of Slav democratic principles against German authoritarianism. A comparable interpretation had been propagated by the Poles, while the Ukrainians in Russia contrasted their own democratic tradition with the aristocratic principles of the Poles and the autocratic–tyrannic practices of the Russians. In western Europe the Catalans constructed a contrast between the 'democratic' tradition of Catalonia and the authoritarian attitudes of Castile. When intensified such a conflict of principles then became a fight between culture and barbarianism.

Historical conceptions were not allowed to remain abstractions. Opposing principles were moulded into the concrete forms of good and bad national characteristics. Members of the opposing ethnic groups were viewed negatively from contrary perspectives. They were the villains, crafty and perfidious, whereas one's own ethnic group was depicted as incapable of insincerity, deceit or plotting treason. The members of the dominant nation, their rulers and governments, were the threatening enemies appearing time and again in history with expansionist, aggressive and oppressive intentions. In contrast one's own ethnic group was portrayed as full of steadfastness, seeking liberation from oppression, and in the vanguard of the realisation of humanitarian principles.

It is worthy of notice that in the historical conceptions of non-dominant ethnic groups specific social classes, such as peasants, citizens, Cossacks, Hajduks – the people in fact – had a prominent place, especially in a later phase, and even when princes and monarchs were glorified as national heroes. The fight of the group for emancipation, liberty, liberal or democratic tradition was more important than dynastic memories. This becomes particularly apparent in the myth of the free community of Cossacks in the Ukrainian historical vision. In Bohemia the Czechs used the glori-fication of their Hussite period to present liberal–democratic elements – the equality of the bourgeois, the noble classes, and the broad masses – as historic images. Slav democracy and German authoritarianism run through the Polish conception of history as the eternal contrasts. In the remote period of the original Slavs Polish historians such as Jędrzej Moraczewski and Karl Libelt thought they could see contemporary ideals of liberty, equality and fraternity, the original forms of democracy. The idea of a continuous liberal–democratic strain running through the history of an ethnic group can also be found in Catalonia. Here the right of codetermination in the affairs of the principality of Catalonia, granted in the Middle Ages and lasting until the eighteenth century as well as the institution for exercising these rights, the legislative body of the *corts* (legislative body related to the estates), were compared to the basically monarchic authoritarian character of Castile–Spanish history.

Generally the conception of history reflected the social origin of the leaders or/and the social affiliation of the people addressed by respective movements. The social stratum from which they came or to which they assigned a leading function in the present was also given a prominent role in history. Accentuation of the role of the bourgeois and peasant classes by the Czech authors was due in no small degree to the lower middle class origins of the activists of their movement. In Catalonia historians sang the praise of the merchants of the Middle Ages not least because they thus could endow that class in the present and the economic structure of Catalonia – markedly different that of from Castile – with historical meaning and legitimisation.

Assignment of special historical importance to different social groups according to the origins of the activists was also evident in the Ukraine: an aristocratic wing emphasised the role of the leaders of the Dnepr Cossacks whereas the leading populist tendency accepted only the simple Cossacks as fighters for the freedom of the Ukraine. Two successive interpretations of history were propagated in Poland: those of the early period which were written and popularised by aristocrats; and those of the second half of the nineteenth century when a bourgeois–national historical vision developed, even though some underlying aristocratic ideas were never quite made redundant.

There were, however, more reasons for the special consideration given to certain social groups in historical visions. In the beginning the members of the cultural elite were, so to speak, generals without an army. Through their historiography, they created their own soldiers. The Danish national liberals, for instance (through their publications), more or less invented the formation of the free peasantry which they needed as allies. History also supplied suitable justifications for the different political programmes and helped to gloss over setbacks in contemporary political developments. This was particularly important for the Poles whose historical outlook had to be adjusted after each unsuccessful uprising. Something of that nature can also be seen in Ireland where ideas fluctuated between a deliberately romantic view of far away Gaelic times and the idealisation of a new Irish society created by amalgamation of the native Irish and the colonists. From about 1840 the Danes vigorously channelled historical ideas into a national and liberal direction, as the by-product of conflicts with German ambitions. History now served to legitimate a nationalism encompassing the Germans; it also had to prepare the ground for the inevitable assumption of power by the bourgeois intelligentsia, who were aided by the peasants after these had been liberated through the agrarian reforms.

But there is still the problem of 'national history' for those non-dominant ethnic groups, which never actually possessed political independence, illustrated in this study by the Macedonians. Among such groups – also including for example the Finns, Estonians,

Slovaks and Slovenians – there were very earnest discussions about the question 'what is national history?' and the meaning of 'national history' for them.

V

According to Ernst Renan it is part of the consciousness of a nation to misunderstand its own history.[3] Does this mean that the historical consciousness of the emerging ethnic groups was founded on myths far removed from reality? In the beginning when history was being discovered mythical elements, fictions, deliberate forgeries or crass misinterpretations of so-called original texts certainly contributed significantly to the development of a 'false' historical consciousness. This was particularly apparent in Denmark, Ireland and Bohemia. However historiography working according to scientific standards, with a critical assessment of sources, has – with the exception of the Macedonians who had no historiography of their own – very gradually led to a separation of myths from history. Nevertheless this historiography had a definite bias, being apt to construct beginnings and continuities, particularly when coming into conflict with rival views of the same episodes. This could go even to the length of creating a new myth serving the purposes of the movement and its activists.

VI

What was the reception, the broad appeal, of historical ideas? There can be no doubt that the impact particularly was impressive in Poland. By all accounts the Poles have been addicted to history. The means of spreading it were so numerous and diverse, so omnipresent, accessible to and understood, even by stratums having no formal education, that it is accurate to speak of a firmly anchored and comparatively uniform conception of history. Ireland shared these traits. To a lesser degree this also applied to the Danes in Schleswig and the Czechs as well as to the Catalan educated classes. From the beginning of the nineteenth century there had been special ways of popularising history in Denmark. General publication figures for historical poetry and fiction also gave an indication of their reception. In the Russian Ukraine, for instance, more than two million copies of an anthology of poems by Shevchenko had been printed by 1914 in spite of attempts at suppression. Epics and folk songs kept alive in popular memory can be supposed also to constitute a pre-national consciousness which could be activated for the political movement by means of historical works of fiction. It is however, not easy to discern the ways in which a conception of history produced by an educated middle class could be conveyed to and received by ordinary people such as the Catalan masses, more than 50 per cent of whom could neither read nor write and whose formal education, though advancing, was achieved within a system of schools controlled by the government and not allowed to include Catalan elements. But that was not a Catalan problem alone. School attendence in most cases had no relevance for the formation of the historical ideas of non-dominant ethnic groups, because the curriculum was dictated by the ruling state.

VII

It is one of the special features of the political movements in the nineteenth century that they produced historical myths internally. This was also true for all non-dominant ethnic groups. Their political and cultural leaders became heroes and cult figures immediately after death. Historical consciousness was conveyed to a large extent by personality cults. This consciousness had very little historical dimension but it was all the same very potent because it was based on living memories of a not very remote personality, on direct experience or that of parents and other narrators. The cult surrounding the Ukrainian national poet Shevchenko, the Polish national poet Mickiewicz, the Catalan poet Frederic Soler provide cases in point. Funerals, commemorations, or the unveiling of monuments were attended by thousands of people.

Notes

1 Ernest Gellner (1983), *Nations and nationalism*, Oxford, pp. 18, 35ss., 45ss., 55ss., etc. Surprisingly there are very few general studies about the topic of historical consciousness. The following works may serve as an example of different approaches: Ernst Birke and Eugen Lemberg (eds) (1961), 'Geschichtsbewußtsein', in *Ostmitteleuropa*, Marburg/Lahn; Oswald Hauser (ed.) (1981), *Geschichte und Geschichtsbewußtsein*, Göttingen/Zürich; Eric Hobsbawn and Terence Ranger (eds) (1983), *The Invention of tradition*, Cambridge; Peter Boerner (ed.) (1986), *Concepts of national identity. An interdisciplinary dialogue. Interdisziplinäre Betrachtungen zur Frage der nationalen Identität*, Baden-Baden; Anthony D. Smith (1986), *The ethnic origins of nations*, Oxford; Elisabeth Tonkin e.a. (eds) (1989), *History and ethnicity*, London and New York. One instructive case study is John Hutchinson (1987), *The dynamics of cultural nationalism. The Gaelic Revival and the creation of the Irish nation State*, London, etc.
2 J. Puig i Cadafalch (1922), 'Pòrtic', in Antoni Rovira i Virgili (ed.), *Historia nacional de Catalunya*, vol. I, Barcelona.
3 Ernest Renan (1947), 'Qu'est-ce q'une nation?', in *Oeuvres complètes*, tome I, Paris, p. 891.

15   Conclusion

GERHARD BRUNN, MIROSLAV HROCH and ANDREAS KAPPELER

The formation of 'national elites', of the activists of the national movement, is – as has been shown in the eight case studies and the five comparative chapters – a crucial problem in the history of the non-dominant ethnic groups and their interaction with governments. The social origin and the structure of the activists, their specific development, the organisations, channels of communication, and the historical myths they created have been of decisive importance for the political culture of the non-dominant ethnic groups. Also of importance were the respective political systems and specific government policies. Though their activities were generally directed against governments and dominant ethnic groups the leaders of the national movements were influenced in the majority of cases by the dominant political culture. This can be demonstrated not only in the case of the Irish and the Czechs but also in that of the Ukrainians in the Russian empire (compared to the Ukrainians in Austria) and by the 'Prussian' Poles of the Grand Duchy of Poznań as contrasted to the Poles in the Russian or Austrian partitions.

A fundamental question in analysing the formation of political activists is that of the relative weight to be attached to social and political factors. Social, economic and educational pre-conditions presented in the case studies and the comparative chapter on the social origins and the structure of the activists clearly show how crucial such factors were for recruitment of leaders, for the formulation of their goals and for the communication of their programmes to the broader population. Recent research on nationalism has given attention to these issues.

At the same time sections in the case studies on the role of the governments show that neither different political systems nor government policy can be neglected. A policy of consistent repression and assimilation, as practised by the tsarist government in dealing with the Ukrainians after 1863, effectively hindered the formation of national activism and its freedom of operation. A constitutional law respecting system such as that of the United

Kingdom or of Austria after 1860 facilitated the activity of nationalist leaders and gave them an opportunity to direct their demands into parliamentary channels. As non-dominant groups were usually in a numerical minority they generally could not achieve their aims through central parliaments. Thus even in constitutional states there were recurring tendencies among national activists to resort to extra-parliamentary methods. Not all ethnic groups reacted against constitutional methods to the same extent. Differing and frequently changing government policy towards the non-dominant ethnic group had moreover a general influence on the formation and the work of national activists. Nationality policy in separate states was not necessarily dictated by the political system. Sometimes there are surprising parallels between centralist techniques of constitutional (Spain) and absolutist (Russia) forms of government.

To what extent have the questions outlined in the introduction proved effective in exploring the history of national elites? The phase model of M. Hroch has been confirmed as a frame of reference for studying the analogous historical stages in the development of the national movements. For the evaluation of some cases, though, it must be modified. In Ireland the phases overlapped and took place simultaneously. For Macedonians Phase A did not properly exist for the group itself but it had a substitute in the cultural revival movement of the Bulgars. Qualification is also necessary in those instances which fall outside Hroch's definition of a small nation, such as the Poles who, being an 'old nation' with political deficits alone, did not need Phase A and for the national minorities in Schleswig whose movements were influenced by events in both Denmark and Germany.

The typology outlined in the introduction also has proved to be a useful instrument in the study of national activists. It has been shown that the small national minorities in Schleswig do indeed constitute special cases, as do the Poles on the other side of the spectrum because they had a complete social structure with a native aristocracy and an unbroken linguistic, cultural and political tradition. In the case of Hroch's 'small nations' the sub-categories of the 'integrated type' (the Czechs), 'belated type' (the Ukrainians in Russia), 'disintegrated type' (the Catalans) and 'insurrectional type' (the Macedonians) can also be applied. It becomes obvious however that some cases do not appear in a pure typical form but constitute a mixed type. The Catalans for instance show elements of the 'belated type' as well as the 'disintegrated type'; the Macedonians, strongly orientated towards the Bulgarians, show traits of the so-called national minorities. The Irish appear to be a mixed type defying simple classification. Ireland can be described either as a type of its own (with two instead of three deficits) or as a mixture between 'integrated' and 'insurrectional' type. If other criteria are employed groupings which differ from these types may result. For instance the common tradition of pre-modern risings unites the Irish, the Poles and the Macedonians; the importance of falling back on the tradition of a long lost state of their own the Czechs and the Catalans; the comparatively great importance of clerics among the activists the Czechs, Poles, Irish and Catalans; the importance of universities as nurseries for national activists the Czechs, Catalans, Russian Ukrainians and the Germans in Schleswig.

It is useful to apply different typologies according to the questions posed. These do not necessarily meet the requirement of giving an all encompassing explanation but can be used as heuristic tools. The typological mode of enquiry has however proved successful. Though the traditional juxtaposition of west European on the one side and middle and east European national movements on the other (according to Hans Kohn) has its merits, a more detailed interregional comparison is necessary to reveal those common characteristics of west and east European movements which do however emerge from the present enquiry. This is why the European wide scheme has proved to be a fertile field of experiment for new attempts at formulating a typology.

Although the case studies and the comparative chapters have advanced understanding in several ways, the results concerning the formation of national activists cannot automatically be applied to all non-dominant ethnic groups in Europe after 1850. The range of the cases studied is not sufficiently wide and the present state of research too uneven. It is therefore an important concern of this volume to suggest further research perspectives and articulate questions deserving further study. Apart from the problems highlighted in the preceding chapters, the following suggestions can be offered as requiring investigation:

- The comparative study of acculturation and assimilation processes (upward mobility assimilation) and the counter-strategies of national activists. This also includes questions of dual loyalty, the relative importance of different identities among the activists and their development during the course of the national movement.
- The comparative study of success or failure of national movements viewed from the aspect of the formation of their activists. For the late-comers in the formation of nations, this would have to include the counter-attractions exercised by the dominating nation and of alternative political movements such as socialism.
- Extensive comparative analyses should consider the different types and the different regions of Europe to a larger extent. In such a way regional differentiations could be better assessed.

- Based on specific cases of European national movements and their activists comparisons with the non-European experience can be attempted. The example of the Macedonians for instance has relevance to national development in the Third World.
- It has emerged that national activists were not an unvariable quantity but, both in internal structure and mentality and also in relation to governments, subject to constant change. This can be seen most clearly in a question which goes beyond the focus of this volume: what part was played by the activists when their ethnic group had become a nation with a complete social structure and political independence or autonomy, after they had grown from being activists of a non-dominant ethnic group, from 'national elites' of the ethnic sub-society into general dominant elites? How under these new conditions did they treat the minority groups in the territories controlled by themselves? This problem would also merit a comparative study.

Index